Called Out of Darkness
into Marvelous Light

Called Out of Darkness into Marvelous Light

A History of the Episcopal Diocese of Pittsburgh, 1750–2006

Jeremy Bonner

WIPF & STOCK · Eugene, Oregon

CALLED OUT OF DARKNESS INTO MARVELOUS LIGHT
A History of the Episcopal Diocese of Pittsburgh, 1750–2006

Copyright © 2009 Jeremy Bonner. All rights reserved. Except for brief quotations in critical publications or reviews, no part of this book may be reproduced in any manner without prior written permission from the publisher. Write: Permissions, Wipf and Stock, 199 W. 8th Ave., Suite 3, Eugene, OR 97401.

Wipf and Stock Publishers
199 West 8th Ave., Suite 3
Eugene, OR 97401

www.wipfandstock.com

ISBN 13: 978-1-60608-163-1

Manufactured in the U.S.A.

To Jennifer

For the years shared and all the years to come.

Ask them concerning the religion of their forefathers. They all answer, they were Church people. Many of these people still retain an old Prayer Book as a venerable relic of antiquity. They still have a reverence for Baptism and the Lord's Day. The Church, they say, was once pure and good, but it is now fallen, and, they fear, will never be revived again . . . Had we imitated at an early period the example of other societies; employed the same means for collecting our people into societies, and building churches, and with the same zeal, we should have had by this time, four or five Bishops, surrounded by a numerous and respectable body of Clergy, instead of having our very names connected with a fallen Church.

—The Reverend Joseph Doddridge to Bishop John Hobart, 1816

I maintain most strenuously—and the future will vindicate the position— that what is needed in Western Pennsylvania, as elsewhere, is . . . a Churchmanship broad enough to recognize all that is good in scholarship and criticism, and that fears no onslaught of unbelief from whatever quarter, because firmly planted on the ancient Creeds and denying not one word of them; a Churchmanship that meets social questions with a brave front, and will gladly use every method, whether it supposedly bears the label of Rome or Geneva, whereby spiritual truth may be taught and spiritual power exerted . . . a Churchmanship which knows itself, and therefore is not *afraid of itself,* which clearly perceives the difference between the Churchly and the sectarian spirit; a Churchmanship which is ready to make *ventures,* because it seeks first the Kingdom of God and His righteousness; which holds as its center the Divine Manhood of the Lord Jesus Christ, and is based upon the Incarnation, not as a past fact but as an abiding and eternal reality; a Churchmanship which is not stupid or cramped, or fearful or ignorant, but tolerant, hospitable, bright, courageous, and "up to the times" in the truest sense.

—Bishop Cortlandt Whitehead, Address to Convention, 1898

The frontier is post-modern America: where political candidates no longer explain themselves by identification with a party heritage or tradition, where truth is relative and subjective and experiential, where conflicts are settled by guns and arguments by excommunication (whether of distance or divorce), where plenty and pain abound, and where everyone secretly yearns for some relationship or meaning that might hold beyond tomorrow.

—Bishop Robert Duncan, Address to Convention, 2000

Contents

Acknowledgments • xi

Introduction: The End of the Beginning • 1

PART ONE: Mission to the Frontier, 1750–1881

1 Frontier Days: Pittsburgh's First Anglicans, 1750–1832 • 19

2 Ritual, Righteousness, and Rebellion: The Establishment of the Diocese of Pittsburgh, 1833–1881 • 42

PART TWO: Mission to America, 1882–1943

3 Proclaiming the "National Church Idea": Cortlandt Whitehead and Industrial America, 1882–1909 • 75

4 Division, War, and Depression: The New Face of the Diocese of Pittsburgh, 1910–1943 • 114

PART THREE: Mission to the World, 1944–2006

5 New Men and New Methods: Austin Pardue, Sam Shoemaker, and the Civil Rights Debate, 1944–1969 • 187

6 The Center Cannot Hold: The Neo-Evangelical Challenge to Modernity, 1970–1987 • 235

7 The City on a Hill: Confessional Anglicanism, the Episcopal Church, and the Anglican Communion, 1988–2006 • 295

Conclusion: *Lex Credendi, Lex Orandi* • 349

Bibliography • 357

Photographs appear following page 164

Acknowledgments

AT THIS CRITICAL JUNCTURE in the life of the Anglican Communion, it is helpful to look back to our roots and understand what has shaped the process that led a majority of the Episcopal Diocese of Pittsburgh into the newly formed Anglican Church in North America in 2008. Nevertheless, this is a history both for those who have departed the Episcopal Church *and* for those who remain, an exercise in self-knowledge that will, God willing, stand all in good stead in the years ahead.

Thanks are due to the people of the Diocese of Pittsburgh, who provided a stipend to the author while working on the project. To archivist Lynne Wohleber should go the credit for bringing the diocesan archives—from which most of the primary source material for this study was drawn—into sufficiently good order that it was possible for a researcher to find what was needed. Working alone and with extremely limited resources, Lynne has done more than most to preserve a historical record of the Anglican presence in southwestern Pennsylvania. To Bishop Robert Duncan—who first conceived the idea of a written diocesan history—and to all other diocesan personalities who contributed memories or advice, similar thanks is offered.

Finally, and on a personal note, I wish to commend the congregation of Trinity Cathedral, to which I have belonged for most of my sojourn in Pittsburgh. In their statement of July 24, 2008, the cathedral chapter proclaimed its intention to remain part of both the Episcopal Church and of the realigned Diocese of Pittsburgh, in the spirit of a Christian community "in which the love of God may be evidenced in our practices of self-restraint, mutual accountability, and extending respect and forbearance to those with whom we differ; and in which the fellowship of the Holy Spirit may be exemplified in our choosing to forgive rather than retaliate, to heal hurts rather than nurse grudges, and to remain together when it would be easier and less costly to go our separate ways." In the years ahead, may our resolve continue to be lived out, both in Pittsburgh and in the wider Christian community!

Introduction

The End of the Beginning

In the spring of 2007, as the fate of the Episcopal Church (TEC) in the United States hung in the balance, the lives of three men resident in southwestern Pennsylvania spoke to the history both of the local diocese with which all had been associated at some point in their lives, and to the unfolding drama of North American Anglicanism over the past half century. Walter Righter—though a product of the Episcopal Diocese of Pittsburgh—had spent much of his life far removed from the mill town of Aliquippa where he first exercised priestly ministry. In 1996, Righter, by then an Episcopal bishop, was on trial for ordaining a noncelibate homosexual in the Diocese of Newark. This event provided one of the defining moments for conservatives within TEC. Righter returned to Pittsburgh in the immediate aftermath of the fateful decision of the 2003 General Convention to confirm the election of Gene Robinson as bishop of New Hampshire and the church's first openly gay bishop. To this day, he serves as an enduring reminder of Pittsburgh's Broad Church contribution to the development of the Episcopal Church in the late twentieth century.

Far removed from Righter—geographically and otherwise—is the pastor of Christ Church, Grove Farm. Although ordained in the Church of England (and still canonically resident in the Diocese of Pittsburgh), John Guest oversees a nondenominational evangelical church near Sewickley, Pennsylvania. Yet it is Guest who must be credited with—or criticized for—helping to jump-start the Evangelical renewal movement within TEC at roughly the same time that Righter was elected bishop of Iowa. If Righter reflects the Broad Church desire to engage actively with secular modernity, Guest personifies the Evangelical determination to resist it. St. Stephen's, Sewickley—which he oversaw for almost twenty years—has become a model Evangelical parish dedicated to evangelizing the unchurched. Guest was also one of the founders of Trinity Episcopal

School for Ministry (TESM) in Ambridge, one of only two conservative Episcopal seminaries left in the nation and the only Episcopal seminary established since the Second World War. The reputation of the Diocese of Pittsburgh as a conservative Evangelical bastion, then, owes much to the work of the "long-haired Englishman" who first arrived in southwestern Pennsylvania in the late 1960s.

The third member of this clerical triumvirate, Robert Duncan, is the present bishop of Pittsburgh. Since his arrival in Pittsburgh in 1992 and his election as bishop in 1995, Duncan has been increasingly identified as the leading American voice in opposition to theological modernism. Uniting a Catholic liturgical style (he is, after all, a product of New York's General Theological Seminary) to an Evangelical commitment to mission, both in Pittsburgh and in the wider world, Duncan has become de facto leader of conservative Episcopalians throughout the United States. From the Plano Conference of 2003 and the establishment in 2004 of the Anglican Communion Network (for which he serves as moderator) to the Episcopal Church's General Convention of 2006 and the Dar-es-Salaam meeting of the primates of the Anglican Communion in 2007, all eyes have been on Robert Duncan and the Diocese of Pittsburgh. As the process of Anglican realignment rolls inexorably on, even Pittsburgh Episcopalians who share their bishop's vision both lament and rejoice that their diocese has achieved such public notoriety.

GLOBAL ANGLICANISM: THE INTERNATIONAL CONTEXT

Across more than two centuries, it has been a commonly accepted axiom that most members of the Episcopal Church have a limited sense of what it means to be part of a global communion. Ecclesiastical identity in the United States, deprived of the imperial mandate embraced by the Church of England, tended to be defined more by those denominational markers common to the great majority of American churches. While many first-generation Episcopalians of British extraction continued to maintain an interest in the affairs of the mother church, expression of a formal inter-relationship between their new and former jurisdictions was rare. By the early twentieth century, the Episcopal commitment to globalism was most readily embodied in the person of Charles Brent, bishop of Western New York from 1918 to his death in 1929. Brent developed a profound concern with the cause of visible Christian unity while serving as missionary bishop of the Philippines (1902–18) and, as a leading American voice in the worldwide ecumenical movement, he helped organize the first World Conference on Faith and Order at Lausanne in 1927.[1]

The transformation of the Faith and Order movement into the World Council of Churches in 1948—and its implications for the ecumenical movement—was accompanied by a growing interest in the worldwide Anglican family among Episcopalians that paralleled the greater involvement of the United States in the Cold War world. Attending the Lambeth Conference of the Anglican Communion in 1948, Stephen Bayne, bishop of Olympia, was struck by the diversity of the bishops present. Anglican Congresses in 1954 and 1963, which brought together clergy and lay delegates (unlike the decennial Lambeth Conferences, which were attended only by bishops) only heightened interest in the global nature of the Anglican Communion, even as most of the former British colonies moved toward independence and the African and Asian ecclesiastical provinces began to elect indigenous bishops. In 1959, Bishop Bayne became the first Anglican executive officer. For five years he traveled the world, encouraging the formation of autonomous national churches throughout the Anglican Communion. Though critical of the confessional formulae popular in ecumenical circles, Bayne began in 1963 to promote the notion of a "new confessionalism" capable of challenging militant secularism and the irrational use of power. His solution was Mutual Responsibility and Interdependence in the Body of Christ (MRI), adopted by the Anglican Congress of 1963, which sought to replace historic notions of mission based on "giving" and "receiving" churches with mutual relationships in which both parties cooperated in determining needs and how to address them and in which the materially poor party was provided with opportunities to contribute. Though MRI was overshadowed in the United States by the domestic conflict over civil rights, it could be considered another step away from the Episcopal parochialism of the nineteenth century.[2]

A growing awareness of the outside world proved no guarantee of a common worldview, however. For members of the Protestant mainline churches—including many Episcopalians—African religiosity (steeped as it was in the imagery of the East African Revival that began during

---

1. On Brent, see Zabriskie, *Bishop Brent*.
2. Booty, *American Apostle*, 62–67, 92–136.

the 1930s) was not within the frame of their cultural experience.[3] Third World Anglicans could speak without reserve only to the minority of active Evangelicals who had assumed a higher profile within the Episcopal Church during the cultural conflicts of the 1960s and 1970s. Represented by the American branch of the Evangelical Fellowship in the Anglican Communion, which had been established in the early 1960s, they reorganized as the Fellowship of Witness in 1968 to offer Evangelicalism to the wider church as a model for conversion and renewal.[4]

The effectual marriage of MRI principles with the missionary zeal of the Fellowship of Witness cemented ties between the majority in the Third World provinces of the Global South (as it came to be known) and a vocal minority within the Episcopal Church. Southwestern Pennsylvania, where the strength of the Evangelical party only deepened during the 1980s, proved a popular location for parachurch ministries devoted to international outreach, most notably Trinity Episcopal School for Ministry, with its deep ties to Africa.

On the diocesan level, theological affinities between Pittsburgh leaders and bishops of the Global South helped foster strong and abiding connections with Anglican communities in Chile, Rwanda, and Uganda, to name but three. As the growing intensity of the culture wars within the Episcopal Church increasingly shut Pittsburgh Episcopalians out of the national debate, so the diocese cultivated its links to the Global South. The consecration of John Rodgers, a former dean of TESM, as a bishop in the Anglican Mission in America in 2000, only confirmed the trajectory on which his former diocese was already headed.

Since the 2003 General Convention of TEC, which approved the election of a man in a homosexual relationship as bishop of New Hampshire, there has been a massive upsurge in American Anglicans debating their denominational future, not only in parish meetings and diocesan conventions but—this being an age of electronic media—on the web pages of the blogosphere. As these discussions have progressed, new understandings of ecclesiology and church authority have come to the fore and new

---

3. On the East African Revival, see Church, *Quest for the Highest*; MacMaster and Jacobs, *Gentle Wind of God*.

4. 1991 interview with Pr. Bill Lovell of the Fellowship of Witness, a group organized to bring biblical renewal to Episcopal theology and piety. Lovell was at the time the rector of Christ Church in South Hamilton, Massachusetts. See http://members.aol.com/rlongman1/EFAC.html (accessed February 29, 2008). The link appears to be dead.

Introduction: The End of the Beginning   5

relationships spanning continents have been brought into being. In her timely study of global trends, anthropologist Miranda Hassett notes:

> Many [North American conservatives] have lost patience and faith in the possibilities of remaking the Anglican Communion through its existing structures into a more unified and doctrinally controlled body. These developing networks of affinity, which are particular connections between individuals, parishes, diocese and provinces, instead bypass and even subvert the centralized, nested geographical authority structure of the Communion . . . Today many believe that such networks will become, functionally if not officially, the new organizing structure of the whole Anglican Communion.[5]

As the majority within the Diocese of Pittsburgh increasingly sees itself as a beleaguered remnant within the once-orthodox Episcopal Church, so it appeals to the demographic shift in global Christianity to the Global South, so eloquently described by historian Philip Jenkins in his *The Next Christendom*, as evidence of the inevitable triumph of its point of view on a global scale. The political implications of the rise of evangelical Christianity in the Global South, to which Jenkins drew attention in 2002, were rudely brought home to Anglicans in the Global North as early as 1998, when Third World bishops provided an overwhelming vote in favor of a resolution (1:10) of the Lambeth Conference of the Anglican Communion expressing a traditional and conservative view of homosexuality and the Christian response to it.[6]

Pittsburgh Evangelicals like Stephen Noll have welcomed such African allies to a cause that seemed lost in the Episcopal Church at large, yet their cause has proved larger than a simple debate over sexual morality. In 2000, Noll left TESM for Uganda, where he now serves as vice-chancellor of Uganda Christian University, a move that complemented the training that his former seminary had provided to many African clergy (including several future bishops) over a fifteen-year period. In 2005, when Pittsburgh hosted the Hope and a Future Conference for conservative Anglican groups throughout the United States, pride of place was given to a panel discussion led by several of the more outspoken Global South primates.

---

5. Hassett, *Anglican Communion in Crisis*, 165.
6. Hassett, *Anglican Communion in Crisis*, 71–101; Solheim, *Diversity or Disunity?*

The globalization of the Diocese of Pittsburgh reflects the culmination of half a century of self-differentiation from the prevailing culture of TEC. Prior to the Second World War, there was little in the story of the diocese that suggested a unique religious culture, and Episcopalians in southwestern Pennsylvania were not radically different from their counterparts in New York or Chicago. The cultural conflicts of the 1960s and 1970s, most notably the fateful decision of TEC to ordain women to the priesthood in 1976, marked a sea change in outlook. Though female ordination was accepted by the rest of the Anglican Communion as a legitimate exploration of the principle of women's ministry (and embraced by the Diocese of Pittsburgh, which today boasts many female presbyters), the accompanying debate crystallized the concerns of many in the diocese about the theological trajectory of the national church. By the early 1990s, Pittsburgh enjoyed a reputation for cultural and theological (though not necessarily political or social) conservatism that distinguished it from most other dioceses in the Northeast.

Today, across the United States and Canada, the debate over Anglican identity has finally come down to one question: When it becomes impossible to be both Anglican and Episcopalian, which identity will triumph? The emergence of the Global South is reshaping the diverse forms of Anglican witness in the United States. In the face of what they view as rampant heresy, whole congregations have steadily been removing themselves from the jurisdiction of TEC and have placed themselves under the jurisdiction of Global South bishops, thus breaching the tradition of inviolable diocesan boundaries. New international partnerships have been formed that unite communities in the Global North with those in the Global South, a dynamic with consequences for all involved.[7] In the Diocese of Pittsburgh, the Anglican Communion Network (ACN), which unites conservative dioceses opposed to the present course of the national church, includes those parishes under "foreign" oversight. In 2007, the diocese took steps toward a severing of the relationship between the diocese and the national church in favor of oversight by a foreign primate. The incursion of Global South bishops as overseers for dissenting Episcopalians represents a departure from the prevailing American Protestant model of dissent, conflict, schism, and new denomination. Whether or not it reflects a long-term commitment to a more catholic vision of the church remains

---

7. Hassett discusses some of these consequences in *Anglican Communion in Crisis*, 130–66.

to be seen, but for many Pittsburgh Episcopalians the acceptance of such oversight seems unlikely to produce a severe crisis of confidence.

CONFESSIONAL ANGLICANISM: THE NATIONAL CONTEXT

While global developments have unquestionably shaped the orientation of the Diocese of Pittsburgh, it is equally important to address the local cultural context. By international standards, U.S. Episcopal dioceses are numerically small in membership, and Pittsburgh is no exception. Although most Global South Anglicans represent a minority faith within their national culture, they are numerically far stronger than their Global North counterparts. Pittsburgh Episcopalians constitute a tiny fragment of the Christian population of southwestern Pennsylvania. The diocesan endowment is small (at least compared with those of its neighbors to the east) and the diocese has few major financial assets. For at least the past one hundred years, the region's dominant culture has been Roman Catholic and working class. Ethnic enclaves—foreign territory to the Episcopal Church for much of its existence—have long permeated the region, while the economic recession of the 1980s has left lasting scars on the local economy.[8] Though Pittsburgh now boasts something of a postindustrial economy, growth remains uneven.

The story of southwestern Pennsylvania is the story of a region contested. For many Americans, steeped in a Hollywood-inspired vision of a frontier set on the High Plains, it is a salutary reminder that the first great American frontier lay along the Appalachian mountain range. Here the French and British empires in North America strove for mastery of the Mississippi Valley and the trade routes that it commanded. Here the Native Americans of the Midwest sought to preserve their hunting grounds from the waves of immigrants who passed over those mountains, first to trade and then to settle. The notion of contested ground would remain part of the folklore of western Pennsylvania long after the expulsion of the Native American population from the region and the removal of the French threat from Canada. The long dominance of the Presbyterian Church in religious affairs ended with the advent of industrialization in the 1840s. Heavy immigration from central and southeastern Europe led to the supersession of a historically English and German Protestant as-

---

8. On the construction of Pittsburgh's enclave communities, see Bodnar, *Lives of Their Own*; and Kleinberg, *Shadow of the Mills*.

cendancy by Roman Catholics of Irish, Polish, and Italian ancestry (as well as African Americans from the southern United States). This demographic shift further strengthened industrial unionism in the region and ultimately led to political realignment during the 1930s. Since the 1960s, struggles on the postindustrial frontier have shaped the region's identity. Western Pennsylvania has been economically bled white as much of the historic industrial base has crumbled, but it remains a culturally conservative region more sympathetic to religious renewal movements than the Philadelphia metropolitan area.

Until recently, regional historians have given surprisingly little attention to the impact of religion. In an article written almost twenty years ago, historian Linda Pritchard lamented the persisting piecemeal approach to the study of religion in the Pittsburgh area. "In order to enhance Pittsburgh as an important case study of religion from frontier settlement to post-industrialism," she wrote, "religious historians with a social history outlook must put religion at the center, not at the periphery, of new studies."[9] In the past ten years there have been a number of useful corrective studies. In 1999, Kenneth Heineman produced a fascinating study of how the Roman Catholic cultures of southwestern Pennsylvania informed the rise of industrial unionism during the 1930s, a healthy corrective to accounts of the New Deal that assume the labor movement to be broadly secular in outlook.[10] From the Protestant side of the divide, Michael Sider-Rose has explored Pittsburgh's evangelical subculture in the late twentieth century, demonstrating the ways in which its representatives have sought to bring a Christocentric ethos to the life and work of Pittsburgh's professional and business classes.[11] Most recently, Keith Zahniser produced a study of Pittsburgh's Protestant response to the industrial crisis of the early twentieth century and the evolving model of Christian social witness.[12] This present volume shares with these other scholars an interest in the wider influence of religious culture, even while it acknowledges that despite Episcopal influence in civic life, most notably the first decade of the twentieth century and the 1950s, Anglican ability to shape local culture has been restricted in this enclave society.

9. Pritchard, "Soul of the City," 352.
10. Heineman, *Catholic New Deal*.
11. Sider-Rose, *Taking the Gospel to the Point*.
12. Zahniser, *Steel City Gospel*.

Pittsburgh's Anglican and Episcopal witness owes much to such environmental factors, and is embodied in the colorful cast of personalities whose deeds come down to us through 250 years. Men like the inimitable Dr. Joseph Doddridge, the Methodist preacher turned Episcopal priest, whose pleas for a western bishop went unheard for so many years; and John Henry Hopkins, second rector of Trinity Church, Pittsburgh, who helped plant many of the region's earliest Episcopal parishes and laid the foundation for the diocese erected in 1865. During the nineteenth century, Joseph Wilson, rector of Calvary Church, Pittsburgh, briefly drew national attention with his attempt to lead that parish into the Reformed Episcopal Church, while George Hodges, a later rector of Calvary, served as Pittsburgh's first Episcopal exponent of the Social Gospel. A more active proponent of Hodges's views, Alfred Arundel, later stunned the comfortable congregation of Trinity Church, Pittsburgh, with his belief in Christian Socialism and even defied his bishop on this issue, while the legendary Sam Shoemaker, the postwar pioneer of experiential religion and the father of the Pittsburgh Experiment, took Calvary Church in a new direction with a stress on personal renewal that was to have lasting consequences for many throughout the diocese.

While Pittsburgh's pre-1960 roll call of Episcopalian servant leaders laid the foundation upon which the present generation is now building, it is important to recognize that postwar Pittsburgh has undergone a shift toward what might today be termed confessional Anglicanism. The role played by the Fellowship of Witness has been noted above, but it is significant that two of its founders—Peter Moore and John Guest—were products of the region.[13] After Guest became rector of St. Stephen's, Sewickley, in 1971, the parish became known as a center of the renewal movement, together with, among others, St. Paul's, Darien, Connecticut, and the northern Virginia parishes of The Falls Church and Truro Church.[14] The Neo-Evangelicals of this period represented a new strain in the American Anglican family, eager to define themselves in terms of their opposition to the creeping modernism that they felt had undermined the very bases of Anglican faith and practice. Conscious of how nineteenth-century Evangelicalism had been subverted by Broad Churchmanship, they en-

13. Moore served his first parish in North Versailles, Pennsylvania, in the early 1960s, while Guest first came to southwestern Pennsylvania later in the decade to work for the Pittsburgh Experiment.

14. On St. Paul's, Darien, see Slosser, *Miracle at Darien*.

deavored to erect a panoply of parachurch institutions capable of sustaining the movement culture that they were endeavoring to propagate. During the 1990s, many of these institutions relocated to Ambridge, Pennsylvania, home of Trinity Episcopal School for Ministry, where they could easily network with each other. Representative organizations include the South American Missionary Society—one of the oldest—Anglicans for Life (formerly National Organization of Episcopalians for Life), Rock the World Youth Alliance, and New Wineskins (formerly the Episcopal Church Missionary Community).

This parachurch strategy has been accompanied by a growing emphasis on the need for a confessional understanding of Anglicanism. In some respects, this represents a marked departure from the practice that hitherto prevailed, yet it also reflects the increasing unwillingness of certain provinces to seek Communion authority for doctrinal changes with potentially church-wide consequences. While critics insist that there is no precedent for such authorization and no body vested with the authority to give it in the Anglican polity, it has become axiomatic to most Evangelicals that national church autonomy in all matters can no longer be tolerated. Appeals to the authority of resolutions of the Lambeth Conference—about which nineteenth-century Evangelicals had considerable reservations—have become commonplace in the last few years, even as the ties with the Global South have strengthened. What is true on a national level is equally true in Pittsburgh. The vision of those who make diocesan policy *and* of those who oppose it is now refracted through the lens of Evangelical Anglicanism. While those of a more liberal disposition continue to hold to a vision of *ecclesial autonomy* and the belief that, in the final analysis, there is no entity with greater authority than the national church, many conservatives are now preoccupied with *conciliarity* and the singular role of bishops in defining fundamental doctrines.[15]

---

15. "The complaint by American autonomists," writes Ephraim Radner, "that the Lambeth Conference (from which came the 1998 teaching on gay inclusion's 'incompatibility' with Scripture) is not really a 'council' because it did not set out, in 1867, to be such a gathering is beside the point: Lambeth's 'representative' character (given Anglicanism's catholic episcopal polity) and its recognition as speaking consensually on behalf of a range of more local provincial voices, grant it a conciliar status *de facto*." Radner and Turner, *Fate of Communion*, 238.

PITTSBURGH ANGLICANISM: THE DIOCESAN CONTEXT

Periodization of Episcopal history is always a problematic exercise. For the purposes of this study, I will suggest a threefold approach, characterized by separatism (1780–1880), institutionalism (1880–1950), and postinstitutionalism (1950–present). During the first period, the Episcopal Church was largely focused on internal questions of theology and polity and only peripherally engaged with the wider issues in society at large. Beginning in 1880, first at the parish level and later at the diocesan and national levels, Episcopalians turned their attention to filling a niche in the denominational landscape, joining the wider Protestant crusade on behalf of the Social Gospel and offering their church body as a rallying point for organic church unity. After 1900, the development of a regional and national administrative apparatus for the church took on a new priority, which was not completely fulfilled until the close of the Second World War.

The immediate postwar years were characterized by a sense of Episcopal triumphalism and growth, which saw the church reach the pinnacle of national influence, but this did not survive the social turmoil of the 1960s and the theological shift becoming evident in many of the nation's Episcopal seminaries. A new generation of clergy informed by social action theology was buttressed by a House of Bishops unwilling to take disciplinary action against those of its members whose doctrinal writings seemed to challenge classical Christian teaching. The basic theological consensus that had underpinned previous disputes within Anglicanism had been broken.

As noted above, the Diocese of Pittsburgh did not greatly deviate from the national pattern during the separatist and institutionalist eras. Beginning in the late 1960s, however, evidence of a widening gulf between those in authority in diocesan affairs and the national church leadership began to make itself evident. While some progressive commentators might be tempted to blame the shift on "outside" influences (the English-born John Guest, Trinity Episcopal School for Ministry, and Alden Hathaway, bishop of Pittsburgh from 1980 to 1995), the notion of an Evangelical coup seems unduly dismissive of the agency of many Pittsburgh Episcopalians who embraced the cause of conservative renewal long before the election of Robert Duncan and the Lambeth Conference of 1998.

Episcopal identity may be said to be defined by whether a diocese is global or national in its orientation; whether it is confessional or nonconfessional in its theology; and whether it is countercultural or embraces the surrounding culture in its efforts to evangelize. During the separatist era, the diocese was national in its orientation, confessional in its theology (in the sense of asserting an explicitly Anglican identity), and countercultural in its relations with the surrounding culture. During the institutional era, by contrast, Pittsburgh remained national in orientation, but became less confessional in its theology and more inclined to engage with the surrounding culture. Only in the postinstitutionalist era has the diocese adopted a stance that runs directly counter to that of the national church. For the first time in its history, the diocese has become as much global as national in its orientation, while its theology has become markedly confessional (though in a rather different form from that espoused during the nineteenth century), and its evangelism is decidedly countercultural.

It is revealing, in light of TEC's historic commitment to the episcopate, that studies of the Episcopal Church at the diocesan level are comparatively thin on the ground.[16] While many such studies appeared during the nineteenth and early twentieth centuries, since 1950 the focus has been much more upon personalities and movements within the church. Directed as this scholarship is toward those most engaged in religious life, it inevitably gives less attention to local ministry. The typical Episcopal worldview is arguably best witnessed at the grassroots level and in the context of diocesan life and practice. Naturally, it can be debated whether what is typical in Pittsburgh holds for most jurisdictions. Pittsburgh Episcopalians, progressive and conservative alike, can agree that the diocese has become one of the focal points—indeed, the principal focal point—of the current conflict, with all the pain and anguish that entails. Parishes have been divided, friends estranged, and parish outreach impaired. Terse exchanges have taken place at diocesan conventions, district meetings, and in the press, and Calvary Church is presently engaged in a lawsuit with the diocesan leadership with the aim

---

16. Post-1960 studies include Burr, *Story of the Diocese of Connecticut*; Brown, *Episcopal Church in Texas*; McDonald, *White Already to Harvest*; Brown, *Hills of the Lord*; Duffy, *Episcopal Diocese of Massachusetts*; Lindsley, *This Planted Vine*; London and Lemmon, *Episcopal Church in North Carolina*. A more recent example is Bond and Gundersen, "Episcopal Church in Virginia, 1607–2007."

of preventing conservatives who wish to leave TEC from taking diocesan or parish property with them. This study endeavors to delineate how Anglicans in southwestern Pennsylvania have transformed both their region and their denomination. Chapter 1 outlines the course of Anglican witness in the region prior to the rise of the Tractarian party within the Church of England. Then a scattered frontier church, dependent on the efforts of roving clergy, the local church benefited from the work of John Henry Hopkins, a future presiding bishop of the Episcopal Church. Chapter 2 discusses the emergence of Anglo Catholicism, during which period western Pennsylvania became a battleground between the dominant Evangelicals of eastern Pennsylvania and High Church clergy, many of them trained in the Diocese of Maryland. Pressure for a new diocese ultimately led to the creation of the Diocese of Pittsburgh under a High Church bishop, John Kerfoot.

The shift toward the institutional church is addressed in chapter 3, in which the diocese began to develop its own institutional structure under the leadership of Cortlandt Whitehead, who would serve in that capacity for forty years. Whitehead vastly expanded the network of Episcopal parishes and missions and oversaw the establishment of such entities as St. Margaret's Memorial Hospital and the Guild of St. Barnabas. In 1910, the Diocese of Pittsburgh subdivided, surrendering its northern counties to create the new Diocese of Erie. The history of the southwestern diocese from 1910 until the close of the Second World War is the subject of chapter 4, in which the last ten years of Whitehead's episcopate and the episcopate of his successor, Alexander Mann, are reviewed. During the interwar period, the diocese entered upon a period of stasis, which the exigencies imposed by the Great Depression did nothing to relieve.

The final three chapters explore the moment at which the Diocese of Pittsburgh began to define itself in terms different from those of the national church, a process that I explain in terms of the growing influence of three processes: deinstitutionalization, self-definition, and globalization. Chapter 5—focused on the 1950s and 1960s—is concerned with deinstitutionalization. While all parts of the American church experienced a retreat from institutional structures, in only a few dioceses was there interest in developing parachurch structures that existed apart from the national church.

The key figures in this shift did not set out with the deliberate intention of establishing such structures, however. Bishop Austin Pardue, an eloquent writer and charismatic speaker, proved an active proponent of prayer ministries and championed innovative outreach efforts to the working classes. He was joined in this endeavor by Episcopal legend Sam Shoemaker, whose work at Calvary Church would culminate in the Pittsburgh Experiment. Though neither was formally identified with the renewal movement, they nevertheless laid the basis on which Evangelicals would later build.

Chapter 6—focused on the 1970s and 1980s—explores the Diocese of Pittsburgh's self-definition as a Neo-Evangelical stronghold, a process that owed much to the work of John Guest, rector of St. Stephen's Church, Sewickley; the establishment of Trinity Episcopal School for Ministry; and the election of Alden Hathaway as bishop of Pittsburgh, a decided coup for the national renewal movement. The chapter also explores the administrative reorganization of the diocese in the 1970s, the impact of female ordination, and the diverse efforts of individual parishes to ameliorate the regional suffering caused by the economic recession of the early 1980s.

The final phase of Pittsburgh's story—globalization—is addressed in chapter 7, which explores the shift promoted by Bishop Hathaway's successor Robert Duncan and exacerbated by growing theological tension with the outlook of the national church. The close ties cultivated by Duncan with church leaders throughout the Anglican Communion at the 1998 Lambeth Conference have served only to enhance Pittsburgh's reputation as a bastion of conservative theology. The Anglican vision, as refracted through the Diocese of Pittsburgh, is now conceived as much in terms of relationships with Uganda and Rwanda as with New York and Philadelphia.

In acting as he has done, Duncan draws comparison with Charles Brent, not least as one of the few American bishops whose name is well known outside the United States. The comparison may only go so far, however, for where Brent devoted his labors to the cause of church unity and the discernment of theological commonalities between diverse Christian bodies, Duncan strives for the assertion of theological essentials that must, he believes, underpin a renewed Anglican Communion. Whether he will ultimately prove more successful than Brent is unclear.[17] Just three months before the 2006 General Convention, at which TEC was expected to respond to demands of leaders from elsewhere in the

---

17. The ongoing discussions over the Anglican Covenant and the general rejection of such a concept by the churches in the United States and Canada foreshadow the likely outcome of such debates as far as the Episcopal Church is concerned.

Anglican Communion to clarify what it was prepared to do to answer criticisms raised since 2003, the bishop of Pittsburgh explained to me why he had been inspired to commission a historical account of Pittsburgh's travails for the proposed 2008 celebration of 250 years of Anglican presence in the region since the expulsion of French military presence in 1758. "When I came here," he said, "I couldn't believe that the diocese didn't have a history. One of the reasons I'm so committed to telling the story, warts and all, is that when a family can tell its story, it both knows what its dangers are and what its strengths are, and you keep paying attention to the dangers and you keep building the strengths."[18]

The story of the Diocese of Pittsburgh has more than been fulfilled the famous utterance of Sam Shoemaker when he encouraged his followers to make Pittsburgh "as famous for God as for Steel."[19] From a simple Prayer Book service led by a Presbyterian clergyman on the banks of the Allegheny River in 1758 has grown up one of the most culturally significant dioceses in the history of the Episcopal Church. Contested ground at the beginning of our tale, Pittsburgh remains contested ground at its close: a costly witness for all concerned, but a witness to the world nonetheless.

---

18. Duncan interview.

19. Despite the fame of this quote—and its frequent employment by Pittsburghers—it has proved impossible to find a printed source that documents it.

Part One

Mission to the Frontier, 1750–1881

1

Frontier Days

Pittsburgh's First Anglicans, 1750–1832

UNTIL THE CLOSE OF the American Revolution in 1780, individuals rather than congregations constituted the Anglican presence in western Pennsylvania. Though William Penn's "holy experiment" came into being with the signing of the Pennsylvania colony's royal charter on March 4, 1681, almost a century would pass before the lands west of the Alleghenies were open to white settlement. In the interim, the region's original inhabitants had first to be dispossessed (through either voluntary land sales or involuntary expulsion) and two great empires had to be driven from the North American continent. These early struggles were far from purely economic in nature, pitting as they did a Protestant maritime empire against the leading Catholic power of the era. With the French trader and soldier came the Catholic missionary, dedicated to the conversion of the native Indian population. Such enthusiasm prompted an analogous Protestant religious response. In 1701, Henry Compton, bishop of London, had founded the Society for the Propagation of the Gospel (SPG) to provide clergy for the underserved colonies of the British Empire. As British expansion pushed the line of colonial settlement further westward, SPG missionaries found themselves not only concerned with service to lapsed Anglicans, but also engaged in the conversion of the indigenous population to Christianity. By the mid-1750s, men like Thomas Barton of the SPG were striving to bring to the Native American population of the Pennsylvania frontier a vision of Christianity very different from that of their French Catholic rivals.[1]

---

1. On the work of the SPG, see O'Connor, *Three Centuries of Mission*. On Barton, see Rhoden, *Revolutionary Anglicanism*, 20, 109, 112, 120.

This marriage of secular and religious interests (the conversion of Native Americans to Anglicanism had geopolitical as well as religious significance) illustrates the ambiguous relationship that North American Anglicans enjoyed with the nation-state before and after the Revolution of 1776.[2] The prevailing interest of the Church of England in the preservation of the social order increasingly placed it at odds with a majority of Americans—inside and outside Pennsylvania—who had come to see the wisdom of Penn's commitment to religious pluralism. Between 1780 and the War of 1812, Anglicanism in western Pennsylvania gave every evidence of being a spent force, outclassed by the greater energy and enthusiasm of its Presbyterian and Methodist rivals. "I then lost all hope of witnessing any prosperity in our Church in this part of the country," lamented local priest Joseph Doddridge, as conditions reached their nadir in 1816. "Everything fell into a state of languor. The Vestries were not re-elected; our young people joined other societies."[3]

THE EARLIEST PRESENCE, 1750–1780

Prior to the fall of Fort Duquesne to the British in 1758—and the establishment of a permanent military presence in the region—there were only scattered settlements in the region. While the central Pennsylvania frontier witnessed dramatic advances in settlement between 1720 and 1740, the Cumberland Valley proved less a gateway to the west than a conduit for immigrants to Virginia and the Carolinas.[4] Consequently, the region's first white residents were those whose livelihood depended upon trade with the indigenous population. Preeminent among them was George Croghan, a Dublin-born Anglican and a skilled negotiator with an eye to the main chance. It was Croghan who negotiated the Treaty of Logstown (now Ambridge) in 1748, which strengthened the ties between local Indian tribes and the English traders.[5] Not all traders were nominal in their religious convictions. In 1750, Christopher Gist was sent as an agent of the Ohio Company (formed in 1747 by a group of Virginia

---

2. For a discussion of this relationship, with particular reference to British policies in Canada, see Doll, *Revolution, Religion and National Identity*.

3. Rev. Joseph Doddridge to Bp. John H. Hobart, December 1816, in Doddridge, *Memoirs*. This bound volume lacks pagination.

4. Florin, *Advance of Frontier Settlement*, 52–58.

5. Buck and Buck, *Planting of Civilization*, 54–55. See also Wainwright, *George Croghan*.

gentleman to acquire land west of the Alleghenies) to conduct a survey of the region. Lodged in an Ohio Indian village on Christmas Day, Gist felt it necessary to offer some form of religious devotion and provided his hosts with a discourse on salvation, faith, and works drawn from his *Homilies of the Church of England*. That his good intentions had been misinterpreted became clear when several Indians begged him to baptize their children, under the belief that he was in Holy Orders.[6]

In 1752, the Marquis Duquesne, governor of New France, launched a series of military incursions intended to exert French control over the Ohio River and its tributaries. French troops drove a small garrison of Virginia militia from the future site of Pittsburgh in 1754 and began the erection of a military installation to control the river forks (Fort Duquesne arguably represents the first instance of an established religious presence in the area, for there was a chaplain attached to the fort from 1754 to 1756).[7] Military expeditions against Fort Duquesne led by George Washington in 1754 and Edward Braddock in 1755 both ended in failure.[8] Not until the outbreak of the Seven Years' War in 1756, when the removal of the French presence in the Ohio Valley acquired a strategic significance, was the British government prepared to commit resources to such an undertaking. An expedition under the command of Brigadier General John Forbes in 1758 prepared the way for invasion of the Pennsylvania backcountry by building new lines of communication. Not only did this central trade route ease future migration from eastern Pennsylvania, it also ensured better lines of supply for the British forces. On November 24, the French commandant, viewing his position as untenable, burned Fort Duquesne and withdrew his troops. Two days later, army chaplain Charles Beatty led a service of thanksgiving for Forbes's victory.[9]

Chaplain Beatty, a member of the Presbyterian Church, represented southwestern Pennsylvania's dominant religious culture until at least the 1860s. The soldiers to whom he ministered, however, had taken oaths of

---

6. Walkinshaw, *Southwestern Pennsylvania*, 1:48. For more on the Gist expedition, see Buck and Buck, *Planting of Civilization*, 63–66.

7. Buck and Buck, *Planting of Civilization*, 68–71, 74–75, 83–84.

8. Ibid., 73–74, 75–77, 79–82.

9. Ibid., 86–95; Ward, *Breaking the Backcountry*. Although the fall of Fort Duquesne concluded the French and Indian War in western Pennsylvania, the conflict in North America was only ended by the Treaty of Paris in 1763, when France surrendered its claims to New France.

loyalty to a nation that repudiated the theology of the Presbyterian divines. Cortlandt Whitehead, Pittsburgh's second Episcopal bishop, spoke to this Anglican worldview at the 1898 ceremony of commemoration of John Forbes's life. "We hail him as the leader by whom God established for this country and for our Anglo-Saxon race so very much of good which only later years have made manifest," Whitehead explained. "We revere his name as forever associated by God's providence with the onward march of liberty and civilization in this western land. We honor him for his loyalty to his flag, for his endurance of pain and hardship, for his bravery in the face of obstacles natural, barbarous and inimical, all of which qualities we are the better able to understand and commend because of what our eyes have seen and all the American people have learned to value, in the conduct of our own soldiers and sailors during the exciting month of our recent war with Spain."[10]

By linking Britain's imperial past with the new "imperial" destiny of President William McKinley's United States, Bishop Whitehead once again demonstrated the bifurcated identity that the Episcopal Church inherited from its colonial parent. Though obliged to live down the imperial connection during the early nineteenth century, Episcopal self-understanding continued to be informed by an enduring bond with the Church of England. For decades, its missionary efforts would be shaped, first and foremost, by its desire to draw British immigrants into its ranks. Where other Protestant denominations with British roots—Methodist, Presbyterian, and even Congregationalist—quickly shed their ancestral ties, the "British" ethos of the Episcopal Church endured.

There are no definitive records concerning the religious identity of the settlers who began to arrive in western Pennsylvania in the 1750s, but something can be said of the diverse influences that shaped those Anglicans who were numbered among them. For the sizable body who hailed from Maryland and Virginia—particularly the latter—Anglicanism constituted one of the bedrocks of the social order. The commonwealth had instituted a religious establishment in the mid-seventeenth century that gave to the elected vestries the power to collect church levies and—after 1642—to elect the parish minister. Virginia vestries were civil as well as ecclesiastical bodies whose members exercised roles in local government and the colonial assembly, while churchwardens were officers of the

---

10. Whitehead, *Capture of Fort Duquesne*.

county court who administered relief and supervised road maintenance. The power of the increasingly oligarchic vestries was only furthered by the activities of the bishop of London's commissary, James Blair, who believed in the notion of a "moderate" episcopacy on the Scottish Episcopal model and sought to superimpose the latter's quasi-presbyteral system of church government on the Church of England in Virginia.[11]

During the 1740s, the Virginia establishment suffered a significant reverse, as the "enthusiasm" of the First Great Awakening openly challenged the authority of the clergy to control religious practice. Moved by the sermons of the English-born Anglican evangelist George Whitefield, increasingly large numbers of Virginians turned to religious tracts and prayer meetings, neglecting the Sunday worship that had hitherto characterized church life in the colony. As the progress of dissent spread from the poorer classes to the gentry, clergy resentment at their exclusion from oversight of religious governance was fanned into open flame by attempts of the assembly to limit their state-assured stipends. Clergy appeals to the British government in 1753 to preserve their privileges only intensified anticlerical sentiment and set the stage for church disestablishment thirty years later.[12]

Many of those who moved into the western regions in the late eighteenth century were almost certainly products of Maryland and Virginia Anglicanism. In the years preceding the Revolution, when title to western Pennsylvania was contested by the two colonies of Virginia and Pennsylvania, a few clergy from Virginia's westernmost parish ministered to communities in and around Pittsburgh. Augusta Parish—covering the western counties of Virginia—was constituted in 1746, and while little is recorded of its early history, Alexander Balmaine (elected rector in 1773), appears to have taken his extra-parochial duties seriously. He served as chairman of the committee that instructed the delegates sent by Augusta County to the Virginia convention debating whether or not to support the American Revolution. He subsequently left the area to become a chaplain in the Continental Army, and during the Revolution the Anglican presence in western Pennsylvania experienced a severe decline.[13]

---

11. Mills, *Bishops by Ballot*, 87–88, 92–94; Woolverton, *Colonial Anglicanism*, 141–43, 146–48. See also Gundersen, *Anglican Ministry in Virginia*.

12. Mills, *Bishops by Ballot*, 95–97, 104–6; Woolverton, *Colonial Anglicanism*, 203–5. See also Goodwin, "Anglican Reaction."

13. See Meade, *Old Churches*, 317–21.

In Pennsylvania, Anglicans represented a much smaller proportion of the total population than in Virginia and enjoyed none of the establishment privileges accorded their coreligionists to the south. Nevertheless, they shared the Virginian distrust of excessive ecclesiastical centralization. Moreover, while they lacked formal control of the political process, Pennsylvania Anglicans—especially after 1700—enjoyed the grace and favor of the proprietary party of William Penn. One of the founder's successors, one Thomas Penn, who became sole proprietor in 1746, even acted as an agent to the bishop of London on behalf of the Philadelphia clergy. Philadelphia's Anglican community included some of the more powerful members of the merchant elite, and by the 1750s almost two-thirds of the provincial council were members of Christ Church, Philadelphia. The vestry and clergy of that parish were intermittently involved in the political struggles of the early eighteenth century, generally siding with the strongest force opposed to the Quaker-dominated assembly.[14]

Pennsylvania Anglicans remained a socially diverse body during the colonial era, if the experience of Christ Church, Philadelphia, can be considered typical. Unlike Virginia churches, where pews were allocated according to social status, assignments at Christ Church—assuming that a family had bought or rented that pew—depended upon how long that family had been a part of the congregation. The congregation also made some halting (though ultimately unsuccessful) attempts to challenge the authority of the bishop of London to approve its choice of rector in the early eighteenth century. The advent of the Great Awakening ruffled some clerical feathers in the city, but Pennsylvania Anglicans largely resisted the blandishments of Whitefield. In 1760, however, the refusal to accept the evangelical clergyman William Macclenachan as an assistant minister at Christ Church (the bishop of London having denied him a license) led to the secession of a significant proportion of the congregation and the establishment of St. Paul's Church, an evangelical congregation that rejected episcopal oversight but continued to use the liturgy of the Book of Common Prayer.[15]

Such competing visions of religious involvement in the secular world had implications for western Pennsylvania Anglicans as the colo-

14. Schwartz, "Mixed Multitude," 40–41, 44, 49–51, 53, 57–61; Mills, *Bishops by Ballot*, 63–66, 69–72, 76–79; Gough, *Christ Church*, 12–18, 47, 68, 70–71.

15. Gough, *Christ Church*, 23–24, 30–38, 53–55, 78–82; Woolverton, *Colonial Anglicanism*, 196–97, 198–99, 200; Schwartz, "A Mixed Multitude," 121–24.

nies lurched toward revolution. With the negotiation of the Treaty of Fort Stanwix in 1768, government efforts to limit settlement in the Indian country came to an end. A steady stream of immigrants poured into western Pennsylvania between 1769 and 1774, and although that early stream receded during the Revolution because of renewed Indian raids, it resumed after 1780, boosting the local population to 75,000 by 1790.[16] Despite this slow increase, organized religion continued to fare poorly. "Pittsburg [sic]," reported a Virginian visiting the settlement in 1784, "is inhabited almost entirely by Scots and Irish, who live in paltry log houses, and are as dirty as in the north of Ireland, or even Scotland ... There are in the town four attorneys, two doctors, and not a priest of any persuasion, so that they are likely to be damned, *without the benefit of clergy.*"[17]

Compounding the region's problems was a conflict over land titles that raged between the colonies of Virginia and Pennsylvania for much of the period. In 1772, following the withdrawal of the British garrison from Fort Pitt, the Earl of Dunmore—then governor of Virginia—encouraged George Croghan and his nephew John Connolly to establish a local administration in the region loyal to Virginia. For the next few years the civil jurisdiction was highly contested, although the Virginians enjoyed control of the local militia and Fort Pitt. In 1775, a county court was established for the district of "West Augusta," with George Croghan as presiding judge. Sympathy for Virginia was strong in the Monongahela Valley, but the contest of jurisdictions diminished in 1775, when Dunmore was forced to flee Virginia in the wake of the Revolution and Fort Pitt was surrendered to troops of the Continental Army. Only in 1780 did the two states finally agree upon the present boundary.[18]

While the American Revolution was kindled in New England, it had advocates on the Pennsylvania frontier, many of whom resented British efforts to curtail settlement and defend Indian rights. Nicholas Cresswell, a Tory merchant trading at Jacobs Creek in Fayette County in 1775, disapprovingly reported the visit of Virginia clergyman Alexander

---

16. Florin, *Advance of Frontier Settlement*, 62–74; Buck and Buck, *Planting of Civilization*, 143–46, 152–54. After the Revolution, western Pennsylvania appears to have been a popular place of relocation for former Tories, who viewed the frontier as less hostile than their former places of residence. Such persons, it seems reasonable to assume, were likely to be disproportionately Anglican.

17. Journal of Arthur Lee, December 17, 1784, in Harpster, *Crossroads*, 157.

18. Buck and Buck, *Planting of Civilization*, 159–69.

Balmaine to deliver a "Political discourse." "The people here are Liberty mad," he concluded. "Nothing but War is thought of."[19] Although some Loyalist sentiment was reported in the Monongahela Valley, outright opposition was soon put down, and several local Tories then fled the region for Detroit in 1778. Henceforth, the English cause would never again be openly proclaimed in southwestern Pennsylvania, but a series of increasingly brutal Indian raids and American reprisals would take place along the western Pennsylvania frontier, perhaps the most notorious being the invasion of eastern Ohio that ended with the massacre of Indian converts to Moravian Christianity at Gnadenhütten in 1782.[20]

For American Anglicans—particularly the clergy—the American Revolution represented a profound challenge to what they had always been taught to understand as the foundation of civil authority. One historian has calculated that while 38 percent of colonial clergy were Loyalists and 28 percent were Patriots, over one-third adopted a neutral stance. A clear majority of Pennsylvania's (comparatively small) body of clergy was neutral, with fewer than 10 percent espousing the Patriot cause. On the other hand, while 45 percent of Virginia's clergy supported the Revolution, more than one-fifth inclined to Loyalism.[21] In Philadelphia, most members of the congregation of Christ Church initially rejected the cause of independence, and Anglicans from Philadelphia represented a variety of perspectives in the First Continental Congress.[22]

---

19. Journal of Nicholas Cresswell, July 29–31, 1775, in Harpster, *Crossroads*, 126.

20. Buck and Buck, *Planting of Civilization*, 179–83, 189–90, 193–98.

21. Rhoden, *Revolutionary Anglicanism*, 89. The neutrality adopted by many Pennsylvania clergy may well have reflected their knowledge of the sanctions that might be imposed. A notorious general order was issued by the state legislature in 1777—on the advice of the Continental Congress—for the detention of forty-one persons in Philadelphia, including a number of Anglican priests, for seditious activities. It was subsequently recognized that these warrants had been issued illegally. See Schwartz, "A Mixed Multitude," 284–85.

22. Gough, *Christ Church*, 128–40. While the Anglican laity in Pennsylvania generally supported the Revolution, almost a quarter of the members of Christ Church displayed Loyalist inclinations. It was the latter that pressed for cooperation with the military authorities during the British occupation of Philadelphia, a circumstance that led to a Whig takeover of the vestry in 1779 after the British abandoned the city. The parish then elected as its rector William White, who had embraced the cause of the Revolution. Unlike many of his New England counterparts (including Samuel Seabury), who had served as chaplains to the British forces, White was a former chaplain to the Continental Congress. Ibid., 141–45.

War decimated the body of Anglican clergy in North America, reducing their numbers from 286 in 1774 to 155 in 1785. Though the losses were heaviest in New England and New York, a particular blow to Anglican fortunes came with the disestablishment of the church in Virginia.[23] A new approach to American Anglican identity was becoming necessary, and Pennsylvania's tradition of religious pluralism seemed to offer the best way forward. Indeed, a predilection for church order in an environment shaped by the principle of religious pluralism had some appeal to those in religious denominations that were accustomed to an excess of religious freedom. It is no accident that two of the earliest Anglican presbyters in southwestern Pennsylvania—Robert Ayres and Joseph Doddridge—had previously been Methodist circuit riders.

FROM DISESTABLISHMENT TO DENOMINATION, 1781–1818

In 1784, the Pennsylvania legislature distributed land warrants to former veterans of the Continental Army and then made the remaining lands available to the general public. While intensive settlement did not take place until the War of 1812, when the New York frontier lost much of its appeal,[24] Pittsburgh continued to grow and steadily acquired a more sophisticated cultural veneer. Western Pennsylvania also experienced a steady increase in the number of schools and colleges, most of them underwritten by the various church bodies in the region, including the Presbyterian academies at Canonsburg and Washington. By 1816, there were around twenty incorporated academies and in 1819, the state legislature made provision for the Western University of Pennsylvania, located in Pittsburgh.[25]

This increasingly cosmopolitan orientation of Pittsburgh did not undermine the influence of the Presbyterians and Methodists in the region. The frontier offered scope to men like John Wrenshall, driven from England by family disapproval of his abandonment of the Church of England for Methodism, but it was the Presbyterians who generally held the upper hand in western Pennsylvania. While their missionary efforts began as

23. Mills, *Bishops by Ballot*, 158–59, 163, 172–74.

24. Buck and Buck, *Planting of Civilization*, 205–13. Western Pennsylvania (especially Washington County) also helped "colonize" Ohio. Many of the clergy and local schoolmasters hailed from western Pennsylvania, as did twelve of the state's governors and a majority of the state house of representatives in 1817 (227).

25. Ibid., 375–78, 389–98.

early as 1772, it was not until 1776 that the legendary John McMillan accepted a call to Chartiers, Pennsylvania, in central Washington County. Five years later, the Presbytery of Redstone was erected. By 1801, it had seeded the Presbytery of Erie, whose first five ministers were trained at the Canonsburg Academy. American Methodists, though less influential than their Scottish brethren, established a Redstone circuit south of Pittsburgh in 1784 (a Pittsburgh circuit was created in 1788), and Methodist founder Bishop Francis Asbury recruited Joseph Doddridge—whose father, a "Wesleyan" farmer in western Washington County, had erected a building for public worship on his land—as an itinerant preacher for the region.[26]

The prospects for the scattered Anglican families of western Pennsylvania initially seemed far less propitious than for their Presbyterian and Methodist neighbors. Desperate to shed their image as a shelter for former Tories, American Anglicans now faced the dilemma of being a church with episcopally conferred orders yet without a native bishop to ordain new aspirants to the priesthood. It was a Pennsylvania presbyter, William White, who first sought to address the problem in his *The Case of the Episcopal Churches in the United States Considered*. Published in 1782, White's proposal outlined a horizontal basis for church authority inhering more in the laity and the congregation than in bishops, whose powers were to be distinctly limited.[27]

To White fell responsibility for organizing the first statewide convention for Pennsylvania, which took the unprecedented step of including laymen in an authorized Anglican ecclesiastical body. Over the next few years, a series of regional meetings coalesced into a single structure—the General Convention—which met for the first time in Philadelphia in 1785. The following year, Samuel Provoost and William White were elected bishops of New York and Pennsylvania respectively and sailed for England, where a revision of the oath of allegiance now made it possible for them to accept consecration by the archbishop of Canterbury. Reconciliation was still required with the High Church Anglicans of New England, led by the former Tory Samuel Seabury, who had been consecrated bishop of Connecticut by the Scottish Nonjurors in 1784. Only after southern and mid-Atlantic churchmen accepted the necessity of veto powers for the House of Bishops and the adoption of the Scottish

26. Rishel, *Founding Families*, 41, 62; Buck and Buck, *Planting of Civilization*, 404–6, 410–11; Doddridge, *Memoirs*.

27. Mills, *Bishops by Ballot*, 183–89.

Prayer of Consecration in the American Communion rite could the national church be formally constituted. In 1789, the same year that the federal Constitution was promulgated, the Episcopal Church took form as an ecclesiastical body that was politically independent of the Church of England, yet closely associated with it. The association of the new national church with the establishment of the new nation would have profound consequences in later years.[28]

These national debates had limited impact on Episcopalians in western Pennsylvania, who now belonged to the Diocese of Pennsylvania under the authority of Bishop White. Their first step toward organization on congregational lines occurred in 1780 when General John Neville, his son, Presley, and a number of local notables accepted a gift of land from William Lea at Woodville in Chartiers Township. Worshippers continued to meet in each other's homes until 1790, however, when a permanent structure (later known as Old St. Luke's) was erected. The Neville family also provided the means for a young man named Francis Reno to study for the ministry (Reno subsequently left the Chartiers area to serve as an itinerant minister in what is now Beaver County).[29] During the early 1780s, the congregation of the future Trinity Church gathered to worship in a variety of locations in Pittsburgh (though it lacked a building until 1805), after 1795 under the leadership of John Taylor (see below). In 1788, St. Peter's Church was organized on Little Redstone Creek near the Monongahela River in northern Fayette County. Several southwestern Pennsylvania congregations thus preceded the establishment of the Episcopal Church as a national body. With a very remote system of episcopal oversight in place, a number of new congregations emerged in 1789, including Christ Church in Brownsville (Fayette County), Carmichael's Church in Carmichael (Greene County), and Immanuel Church at West Pike Run (Washington County)—to be followed by St. Luke's, Georgetown (Beaver County) a year later.

To serve such congregations, Pennsylvania Episcopalians were frequently obliged to rely upon dedicated men who had emerged from a Methodist milieu. The first of these was Robert Ayres, born in York County in 1761, who had served as a western Pennsylvania Methodist circuit rider from 1785 to 1789, including a year on the Redstone circuit

---

28. Gough, *Christ Church*, 153–61; Mills, *Bishops by Ballot*, 196–98, 237–42, 273–87.
29. Byllesby, "History of the Protestant Episcopal Church."

(1786-87). Increasingly dissatisfied with the outlook of his denomination, Ayres approached Bishop White, who agreed to ordain him into the Episcopal Church. Returning to western Pennsylvania as an Episcopal priest in 1789, Ayres adopted a mode of operation not far removed from that which he had pursued as a Methodist preacher, visiting scattered families in widely dispersed communities. At West Pike Run, worshippers included members of the Gregg, West, and Dowler families, while at Gillespie (north of Brownsville), he ministered to the Nobles and Goes. He also visited that area of Greene County where Carmichael's Church would later be erected, preaching to members of the Boreman, Hook, and Swan clans. Interestingly, the presence of an ordained priest did not elicit a universally positive reception, for the Episcopal residents of Brownsville made it clear that they did not want Ayres as their preacher. By 1795, he was largely responsible for the congregations at Immanuel and St. Peters, but also began traveling further afield to minister to Episcopalians in Greensburg and Ligonier. Surprisingly, given his Methodist background, he appears to have done little to promote Bible classes and prayer fellowships; such work would have to await the rise of the Evangelical party in the early nineteenth century.[30]

Another key figure in the expansion of the Episcopal Church was Joseph Doddridge, who had abandoned the Methodist ministry upon the death of his father in 1791. After study at Canonsburg Academy, Doddridge refused to return to Methodism, which he viewed as having spurned Prayer Book worship. Advanced to the diaconate by Bishop White in 1792, he was soon ordained a priest but also adopted the itinerant model, visiting families and gathering small congregations in both western Virginia and eastern Ohio.[31] In this undertaking, he became acutely aware of the sense of religious deprivation felt by those in the rural backcountry. "The very idea of a Bishop several hundreds of miles from his flock is discouraging in the extreme," he complained in 1816. "The Methodist bishops have been frequently through this country, and even the Catholics, though few in number, have been comforted by the presence and services of their Episcopal pastor. No such event has hap-

---

30. Leggett, "200th Anniversary."
31. Doddridge, *Memoirs*.

pened to us."³² The persisting sense of isolation and neglect would bedevil western Pennsylvania Episcopalians for the next fifty years.

Another clerical force in the region was John Taylor, who enjoys the distinction of being the first resident clergyman in Pittsburgh. A native of Armagh in Northern Ireland and a convert from Presbyterianism, Taylor was ordained a deacon in 1794. In 1797, he became a teacher in Hanover Township (later a part of Beaver County), serving a school jointly funded by Presbyterians and Episcopalians. Though well respected, Taylor found the uncertainty of life as a teacher (he was paid largely in kind and never received more the $40 a year) too much to bear, and in 1799 he left to pursue his vocation in Pittsburgh. (After his departure from Beaver County, most of the Episcopalians in the community joined the local Presbyterian congregation). For his first three years in Pittsburgh (then boasting a population of only 1,565), Taylor focused on education, preparing a generation of men and women who would go on to important roles in the life of the city. These included the daughter of Samuel Ewalt—a key figure in the Whiskey Rebellion—the son of one of Pittsburgh's first doctors, and (as an adult pupil) Peter Eltonhead, who later organized Pittsburgh's first cotton factory. When Trinity Church began work on its first building in 1805, Taylor was the natural choice to serve as its minister, filling that capacity until 1818. Greatly loved for his humble bearing and effective teaching, he was a keen amateur astronomer and vocalist.³³

Despite the hard labors of these all-too-few clergymen, Anglicanism in southwestern Pennsylvania fared poorly over the next two decades.³⁴ Only three new congregations were formed during the 1790s, after which there would be no new congregations until 1817, when St. Paul's, Kittanning, came into being. One cause was the infectious enthusiasm of the Second Great Awakening as manifested in the Cane Ridge Revival, which began in Kentucky in 1797 and reached western Pennsylvania

---

32. Rev. Joseph Doddridge to Bp. John H. Hobart, December 1816, in Doddridge, *Memoirs*.

33. Dahlinger, "Rev. John Taylor."

34. Rishel's verdict on Pittsburgh is more positive: "Although the Episcopalians were plagued by financial woes and an inability to keep a pastor, they claimed a large portion of the city's most respected citizens and most of the old military elite." He calculates that they represented about 18 percent of the city's founding family members. Rishel, *Founding Families*, 63 (quotation), 65.

five years later.³⁵ The advent of this new brand of enthusiastic religion spurred Presbyterian and Baptist growth, but was generally repudiated by Episcopalians, who valued sacramental order. "To a great extent," Joseph Doddridge disapprovingly told Bishop White in 1818, "a profession of supernatural feelings and those too of a particular stamp and configuration, in conformity to the respective models, furnished by different societies, constitute the larger amount of the claim of the applicant to Church membership and ministry [of revivalist churches]."³⁶ Seven years later, Bishop White would issue an official warning against the fruits of the Second Great Awakening, repudiating prayer meetings "wherein others [*sic*] than an authorized ministry, are set to exercise themselves in public instruction and in prayer of their own suggestion or devising."³⁷

That Anglicanism defied prevailing trends in popular religious culture was not its only handicap. Potentially far more damaging was its association with social elitism, in a frontier society that generally favored a more democratic and egalitarian style of politics. The backcountry had long-standing cause to resent the dominance of eastern interests in the affairs of the commonwealth, and delegates from western Pennsylvania had been vocal supporters of the state constitution of 1776, which was designed to maximize citizen participation. Within a decade, however, a conservative opposition had emerged in the west, led by Hugh Henry Brackenridge. Western radicals opposed ratification of the proposed federal Constitution in 1788 and defeated Brackenridge when he stood as a candidate to the national convention. Two other proponents of ratification—one of them John Neville—were elected, however, and they joined the large Federalist majority in Philadelphia. After 1790, a growing conservative clique could be discerned in western Pennsylvania, many of whose members belonged to the "Neville Connection," led by John Neville, his son, Presley, and his son-in-law, Isaac Craig.³⁸

John Neville did much to further compromise the reputation of the Episcopal Church by the part he played in the Whiskey Rebellion—western

---

35. Buck and Buck, *Planting of Civilization*, 425–27. On the Cane Ridge Revival, see Conkin, *Cane Ridge*.

36. Rev. Joseph Doddridge to Bp. White, December 14, 1818, in Doddridge, *Memoirs*.

37. *Convention Journal of the Diocese of Pennsylvania*, May 10–13, 1825, 17.

38. Buck and Buck, *Planting of Civilization*, 455–64; Main, *Anti-Federalists*, 41–47, 187–94; Shankman, *Crucible of American Democracy*.

Pennsylvania's first test of federal authority—in 1794. Resenting the imposition of a federal excise on the only product that they could profitably export to the East, western Pennsylvania farmers responded with mass meetings and petitions of grievance and refused to register their stills. Active resistance increased after warrants were served on certain producers who had not complied with the law. When John Neville, in his capacity as excise inspector, served a warrant on a farmer in Mingo Creek, his home was attacked by men demanding his resignation. Although the local militia was mustered in support of the insurgents, President Washington responded by dispatching a militia army to the West, and resistance soon collapsed. Such associations, however, did nothing for the reputation of the Episcopal Church in western Pennsylvania.[39]

From 1800 to 1818, the Diocese of Pennsylvania displayed little interest in the rural West, although such neglect was by no means confined to Pennsylvania. The fervor of prerevolutionary days had given way to a period of religious quietism, in which the role of the episcopate was confined to confirmations, ordinations, and consecrations. Visitations were infrequent, church building intermittent, and clergy disinclined to disturb the prevailing order. "They abhorred enthusiasm," wrote a later church historian. "Correctness was more important than conversion." In 1808, Bishop White was the only U.S. bishop in attendance at the General Convention.[40] East of the mountains many congregations did enjoy the attention of bishops, however sparing, but in the interior the absence of direct episcopal oversight concerned men like Joseph Doddridge. In 1811, White responded to Doddridge's fervent pleas for a bishop for the west by agreeing in principle that western Pennsylvania might come under the authority of a western bishop, as soon as one was created for the western territories, but he saw this as a merely temporary solution until a second diocese could be erected for Pennsylvania.[41]

That White was aware of some of the problems faced by western Pennsylvanians is evident from his decision, on April 18, 1812, to char-

---

39. Baldwin, *Whiskey Rebels;* Buck and Buck, *Planting of Civilization,* 466–73. Joseph Rishel notes the wisdom of members of the elite in supporting the winning side in the Whiskey Rebellion, just as they had during the Revolution. Neville, after all, had been a general in the Continental Army. See Rishel, *Founding Families,* 36–37.

40. Chorley, *Men and Movements,* 27–31 (quotation on 30).

41. Bp. William White to Rev. Joseph Doddridge, October 10, 1811, in Doddridge, *Memoirs.*

ter the Society for the Advancement of Christianity in Pennsylvania (SACP), which dispatched the youthful deacon Jackson Kemper to make a western tour the same year. Kemper's visit brought hope to many rural Episcopalians as yet unconnected with the parent body.[42] "Let the church be but fairly established at the conflux of the Monongahela and the Allegheny," Kemper reported back to the SACP's board of trustees, "and there is no fear but that many of its professing members who are scattered through Ohio, Kentucky and Tennessee, will yet be firmly settled in the faith of their fathers."[43] The following year, Deacon Jehu Clay made a similar tour, stopping at Uniontown in August 1813, at a time when that community had no church building except one erected by the Methodists. "The few Episcopalians with whom I conversed here," he concluded, "are extremely desirous of having something done in the way of obtaining a place of worship and an officiating clergyman."[44]

For all the enthusiasm of Clay and Kemper, suitable clergymen were in short supply. During his 1812 visit, Kemper consulted with the venerable Joseph Doddridge, now residing across the state line in Virginia, but that conversation evidently did not satisfy the latter.[45] Encouraged by the Episcopal revival begun under Bishop John Henry Hobart of New York, Doddridge now embarked upon a new campaign for a western diocese, this time centered on Ohio. When a convention of clergy and lay delegates met at St. John's, Worthington, in October 1816, "for the purpose of erecting and constituting a regular Diocese in the Western Country," the three Pennsylvania presbyters (Ayres, Reno, and Taylor) all proved too frail to attend.[46] To Ohio Episcopalians would come the prize of a bishop of their own, while western Pennsylvania would continue to languish in its splendid isolation. It is revealing that until the Reverend Abiel Carter and

42. *Convention Journal of the Diocese of Pennsylvania*, May 26–27, 1812, 8; Gardner, "Society for the Advancement of Christianity."

43. First Annual Report of the Trustees of the Society for the Advancement of Christianity in Pennsylvania, 1813, 10, quoted in Gardner, "Society for the Advancement of Christianity," 330.

44. Second Annual Report of the Trustees of the Society for the Advancement of Christianity in Pennsylvania, 1814, 10–11, quoted in Gardner, "Society for the Advancement of Christianity," 333.

45. This meeting is reported in Gardner, "Society for the Advancement of Christianity," 327–28.

46. Rev. Joseph Doddridge to Bp. John H. Hobart, December 1816, in Doddridge, *Memoirs*.

Henry Baldwin, both representing Trinity Church, Pittsburgh, attended the Pennsylvania diocesan convention in 1818, no western delegate had ever put in an appearance.[47]

TRINITY CHURCH AND PARISH GROWTH, 1819–1832

If the emergence of the Diocese of Ohio temporarily eclipsed hopes for a bishop for western Pennsylvania, a new dynamism had nevertheless been imparted to Anglican missionary efforts in the region, with approximately one new congregation being organized each year over the next fifteen years. From St. Paul's, Kittanning, in 1817 to Christ Church, Indiana, in 1831, new Episcopal congregations blossomed. Although two—Christ Church, Allegheny, and St. Paul's, Erie—served a largely urban population, most were still located in more rural settings, seven in the southern part of the diocese and six in the north, including parishes in Greensburg, Butler, Blairsville, and Indiana.

Nationally, the Episcopal Church had received a considerable boost with the 1811 consecrations of John Henry Hobart as bishop of New York and Alexander Viets Griswold as bishop of the Eastern Diocese (embracing the New England states). For Pennsylvanians, Griswold was arguably the more important figure, since he championed the cause of a resurgent Anglican Evangelicalism that would soon find a home in the Diocese of Pennsylvania. Soon added to this Evangelical company were Richard Moore, elected bishop of Virginia in 1814, and Philander Chase, elected bishop of Ohio in 1818. In such fashion did western Pennsylvania's nearest neighbors come under the oversight of Evangelical spokesmen.[48] In Philadelphia, meanwhile, the Evangelical tradition begun at St. Paul's, Philadelphia, in the colonial period endured into the early Republic. Representative figures included Stephen Tyng, rector of St. Paul's after 1829, and Geoffrey Bedell, rector of St. Andrew's.[49]

With their emphatic theology of sin, atonement, and justification by faith, these Evangelicals represented a conscious shift of American Anglicanism toward a more Protestant perspective. Though most Evangelicals continued to express respect for both episcopacy and the

---

47. *Convention Journal of the Diocese of Pennsylvania*, May 5–6, 1818, 3–4.

48. Chorley, *Men and Movements*, 36–42; Butler, *Standing against the Whirlwind*, 10–16.

49. Chorley, *Men and Movements*, 51–54.

sacraments, they emphatically denied the notion of baptismal regeneration.[50] Worship occupied much of their Sundays, with morning and evening services and as many as two Sunday school sessions involving frequent use of the parish library, supplemented by weekday services, prayer meetings, and Bible classes.[51] The Evangelical party also sought to create educational institutions to reinforce its position. In 1823, the Diocese of Virginia established a seminary in Alexandria, and Bishop Chase of Ohio soon followed suit with Kenyon College (incorporating Gambier Seminary).[52]

While Evangelicalism would shape many of the region's early missionary priests, John Henry Hopkins, the driving force behind the revival of the Episcopal Church in western Pennsylvania in the 1820s, could not strictly be counted in the Evangelical camp. Born in Dublin in 1792, Hopkins attended St. Peter's, Philadelphia, while teaching at a school run by his mother. While there, he met the minister James Abercrombie, who oversaw the Philadelphia Academy, a boys' school that stressed personal spiritual development. Abercrombie was a vocal Federalist who made very clear his opposition to the War of 1812, but if Hopkins did not share Abercrombie's politics, he would come to emulate him in his approach to teaching after he entered the ministry.[53] Hopkins began his professional life as the supervisor of iron furnaces in western Pennsylvania. However, during this time he underwent a conversion experience[54] that inspired him to hold services at his home, using a combination of the Book of Common Prayer, the Bible, and Scott's Commentaries. "His notions at the time touching the sacraments were very nearly those of the

---

50. Ibid., 61–76. Joseph Doddridge, by this time residing in Ohio, had this to say regarding apostolic succession: "I respect the claim and feel satisfied that my Priesthood descended to me through so respectable and valid a channel. From this claim, however, I will not conclude against the efficacy of the ministry in other hands; 'tis enough for me that I *know* and *feel* that other societies are Church too." Joseph Doddridge to Rev. J. Waterman, September 6, 1822, in Doddridge, *Memoirs*.

51. Chorley, *Men and Movements*, 89–96; Butler, *Standing against the Whirlwind*, 32–38.

52. Butler, *Standing against the Whirlwind*, 111–15, 129–30.

53. On Abercrombie, see Gough, *Christ Church*, 174–77, 202.

54. "The habit of private prayer had never been interrupted ... [but] it was not until the hour of this great change that the full consciousness of deep repentance, sincere humility and loving faith, wrought in him maturity of Christian manhood." Hopkins, *Life of Hopkins*, 44.

Quakers;" his son later wrote, "for some time he inclined not a little towards Swedenborgianism; it was apparently a mere accident that decided his attaching himself to the Church rather than the Presbyterians."[55]

This "accident" stemmed, in part at least, from Hopkins's decision to enter the practice of law. Admitted to the Pittsburgh bar in 1818, he was fifth-ranked of twenty-four attorneys within a year and by 1820 enjoyed an annual income of $5,000.[56] He and his wife initially worshipped at a Presbyterian church, for it would hardly have boosted his legal career to "join the Episcopals," but an invitation to play the new organ of Trinity Church led him to become a communicant member within three months and to be elected to the vestry in 1822 and 1823. That year, the vestry approved a resolution to elect Hopkins as rector of Trinity provided he sold his practice and sought Holy Orders as soon as practicable. Despite the dramatic reduction in salary (to $800) Hopkins agreed to this proposition and was subsequently ordained to the diaconate in December 1823 and to the priesthood in May 1824.[57]

The world of church politics upon which Hopkins now entered was one torn between the old-fashioned Low Churchmanship of William White and the younger breed of Evangelicals who took their cue from bishops like Moore and Chase. In 1826, the latter attempted to elect an assistant bishop who would share their convictions. They sought to pack the lay order with sympathetic delegates and to import Evangelical clergy trained at Virginia Theological Seminary. By a single vote in the clergy order, the Evangelical candidate failed of election, forcing a second election in which Henry Onderdonk of New York carried the High Church banner. While Hopkins had always been counted as a supporter of the High Church party, he refused to pledge to vote for himself in the event of a tie and so was passed over in favor of Onderdonk. Ironically, his expressed sympathy for the moral crusades of Low Churchmen and his willingness to exchange pulpits with them ensured that a majority of the Evangelicals at that convention voted for Hopkins rather than Onderdonk.[58]

In Pittsburgh, Hopkins put his liturgical talents to good use. He personally designed the new Trinity Church in the Gothic style, an un-

55. Ibid., 33–36, 43–44 (quotation on 44).
56. Ibid., 53–54, 57–59.
57. Ibid., 61–68.
58. Ibid., 84–111; Holmes, "Making of the Bishop—Part I"; Holmes, "Making of the Bishop—Part II."

dertaking that brought expressions of interest from many other Episcopal churches. Revealing an interest in patristic studies that predated the English Tractarians (see chapter 2), Hopkins restored certain ancient liturgical practices. He adopted a mixed Eucharistic cup—citing St. Cyprian as his authority—and had the Communion bread baked at his home in unleavened cakes that could easily be broken by the celebrant. He also began to move toward the active use of vestments and liturgical lights, radical changes for their time.[59] In 1826, Hopkins instituted junior and senior Bible classes, for those aged twelve to eighteen and for adults respectively, to complement the juvenile instruction classes. Two years later, he modified his approach to confirmation instruction by dividing his class of eighty-one into small groups that met in people's homes on a weekly basis for a discussion of baptism, the catechism, and confirmation "in a free and conversational manner, questions being put to and from the class at pleasure." At the final class, the rector would inquire of his candidates if they believed that, with the assistance of the Holy Spirit, they could keep the promises they were called upon to make. Those who hesitated were asked to delay their formal profession of faith.[60]

The stability of Trinity Church was not necessarily reproduced in the rural hinterland. In 1825, when Bishop White finally signified his intention to visit western Pennsylvania, Hopkins took on the role of unofficial planter of churches in the region. In 1824, he visited Meadville, where he baptized seventy-five and administered Communion to twenty-four. For the occasion, the Presbyterians loaned him their meetinghouse, and many Presbyterians attended the Episcopal services. The following year, Hopkins preached twelve times at Greensburg, four times at Meadville, twice at Lawrenceville, and once at Erie.[61] When Bishop White arrived in June 1825, he found 135 people to be confirmed in Pittsburgh and a further 60 at Greensburg. Trinity Church, White declared, was "a work

---

59. Hopkins, *Life of Hopkins*, 71–73, 113–15. He also earned the wrath of Bishop Hobart at the General Convention of 1826 for opposing his compromise proposal, which would have declared baptismal regeneration to be a purely titular regeneration. Ibid., 77–81.

60. *Convention Journal of the Diocese of Pennsylvania*, May 9–11, 1826, 38; *Convention Journal of the Diocese of Pennsylvania*, May 20–23, 1828, 47.

61. *Convention Journal of the Diocese of Pennsylvania*, May 10–13, 1825, 30; *Convention Journal of the Diocese of Pennsylvania*, May 9–11, 1826, 38. He also preached eleven times at Youngstown.

of correct taste, and an ornament to the state."⁶² The benefits of White's visit proved fleeting, however. Within a year, Charles Smith of the SACP reported the morale of the Meadville congregation to be at low ebb: "I discovered . . . a congregation had been organized but a year previous, but in consequence of their limited numbers and means, they entertained not the least idea of soon being supplied any portion of the time with the regular services of our church. So disheartened were they that a portion had already engaged their assistance to another denomination, and the remainder were generally on the eve of following their example."⁶³

John Henry Hopkins not only helped form congregations but also sought to ameliorate the problem of a persisting shortage of clergy. Already engaged in schooling boys and girls in his own home to supplement his income, he now took on the task of preparing a number of young men for admission to Holy Orders. In so doing, he became aware of the disadvantages that stood in the way of a postulant traveling to Philadelphia or New York to attend seminary. In 1829, therefore, he presented a memorial signed by sixty-eight members and friends of the Episcopal Church in Pittsburgh calling for a seminary to be based in that city. Eastern members of both church parties, however, favored their existing seminaries in New York and Virginia, and Hopkins, the only westerner on the committee appointed to investigate the issue, refused to sign its final report. In 1831, he vented his frustration by accepting the rectorship of Trinity, Boston, fully aware that the Eastern Diocese was keen to establish a seminary of its own, but within a year he had been elevated to the episcopate as the first bishop of Vermont.⁶⁴

Some of those whom Hopkins trained would outlast him and leave their own mark upon the region. Perhaps the best known was Sanson Brunot, who studied with Hopkins from 1828 to 1830 and subsequently served St. Peter's, Blairsville. Brunot proved a candid observer of the religious landscape, as fragments of his journal demonstrate. In a visit to Ohio Township (Beaver County) in June of 1830, he confessed himself impressed by the extent of rural Episcopalian devotion. "There was much rusticity about the people, building and arrangement," he wrote, "but then the sincerity, the attention, the feeling, the simplicity visible among the

---

62. *Convention Journal of the Diocese of Pennsylvania*, May 9–11, 1826, 13–15.
63. Ibid., 42–43.
64. Hopkins, *Life of Hopkins*, 116–27.

communicants and people made ample amends for the little inconveniences and want of refinement in small matters."⁶⁵

Some of Brunot's problems were distinctly pastoral in nature. Visiting a dying member of his congregation who was a vestryman but not a communicant, he learned that the latter had become so disgusted with the denominational chaos around him that he now resorted solely to the Scriptures as his guide to salvation: "I feared that he might be resting on his good, moral life, but he assured me that he understood the system of faith laid down in the Bible, and he said many other things which convinced me still more that we should be slow to judge our brother but that we should remember that the Lord sees not as man sees."⁶⁶

Brunot was also forced to grapple with the equally weighty question of how Episcopalians should relate to their Protestant neighbors. "The church was full at night," he wrote of a visit to Greensburg in August 1830, "many of the Presbyterians being there."⁶⁷ Even so, as early as 1822, Bishop White, in calling for respect for other denominations, had warned against "intermixture of administrations in what concerns the faith, or the worship or the discipline of the church."⁶⁸ This was advice more easily followed in Philadelphia than further west, where many communities might have only a single house of worship and any minister might attract a crowd of diverse denominational allegiance. The self-deprecating Brunot described his edification at the sermon of the Presbyterian divine Obadiah Jennings, then preaching in Brownsville. When Jennings returned the compliment by attending the Episcopal service in the afternoon, along with many of his flock, Brunot worried that "my poor sermon must have been tiresome indeed after such a one as Mr. J. gave us."⁶⁹ A further source of anxiety came when he attended a Methodist Meeting, at which the minister invited Brunot to join him in the pulpit. With some sadness, Brunot declined. "It seems hard," he later wrote, "that we should not mingle together, we who profess to preach the same Gospel and adore the same Savior, but

---

65. Brunot, Journal, June 9, 1830.
66. Ibid., October 1, 1830.
67. Ibid., August 10, 1830.
68. *Convention Journal of the Diocese of Pennsylvania,* May 7–9, 1822, 13.
69. Brunot, Journal, July 1, 1830.

no good has ever been found to result from too much intermingling and interchange among ministers of different denominations."[70]

The struggles of men like Hopkins and Brunot demonstrate how much the Episcopal Church depended upon the charismatic qualities of the individual priests. Their world was a local one in which the doings of the national church were of limited concern and those of the Church of England of no interest. At the same time, they promoted a message of denominational distinctiveness that kept their dealings with other Protestant groups within strict boundaries. There was little in the early Episcopal psyche to promote excessive lay initiative, and parishes that received only fleeting attentions from a priest frequently dissolved. That any sort of ecclesiastical infrastructure emerged must ultimately be credited to John Henry Hopkins, who, before there was a bishop for western Pennsylvania, performed every episcopal office that a priest of the church could perform. As Hopkins departed the region, a new fight was brewing that would pit Pennsylvania's Evangelicals against the emerging High Church party. The resolution of that conflict would have significant implications for the future Diocese of Pittsburgh.

70. Ibid., September 6, 1830.

2

Ritual, Righteousness, and Rebellion

The Establishment of the Diocese of Pittsburgh, 1833–1881

ONLY A FEW YEARS after John Henry Hopkins departed Pittsburgh for Boston, word began to filter into the United States of a seismic shift in worldwide Anglicanism. The occasion was the preaching by Anglican divine John Keble of a sermon on "National Apostasy" on July 14, 1833, in which he denounced the prevailing tendency to view the church as a merely temporal institution. The rise of what would later be termed the "Oxford Movement," which endeavored to reassert the importance of patristic theology within the Anglican tradition, was received with some sympathy in American circles. Not only do Hopkins's liturgical changes at Trinity Church attest to this, but even more significant was the decision of Bishop Hobart of New York to establish the High Church General Theological Seminary (GTS), whose first building was erected in 1827.[1]

Historian Robert Mullin has outlined what he terms a "Hobartian Synthesis" that governed the thinking of most American High Churchmen until at least the 1860s. For Hobart, the true marks of the church were external and the sacraments direct agents of personal transformation. High Churchmen insisted that Anglican liturgical practice represented continuity with the witness of the primitive church. "The church and its ordinances," writes Mullin, "were the chief vehicles of piety: the liturgy spurred on the growth of individual piety, while the catechism continued the work of instruction. Baptism, as the regenerative new birth, gave to all the chance of salvation and the ordinances of the church aided in the process of making that potential a reality." High Churchmen thus defended a form of devotional piety that was far less corporate than that of their

---

1. Chadwick, *Spirit of the Oxford Movement*. For the American experience of Tractarianism, see DeMille, *Catholic Movement*.

Evangelical counterparts, and they lacked the latter's interest in social reform.²

Throughout the 1830s, American churchmen debated the value of the Oxford Tracts (the doctrinal justification of the positions espoused by the Tractarian party published in the London *Times*) to the life of the Episcopal Church, and bitter exchanges took place about the nature of theological teaching at GTS. Leading Evangelical bishops denounced what they viewed as incipient Romanist tendencies at the seminary, and even Bishop Hopkins of Vermont entered the fray with a denunciation of Tractarianism that took many High Churchmen by surprise. However, the new Anglo Catholic party also boasted some impressive leaders, one of the most notable being William Rollinson Whittingham, elected bishop of Maryland in 1840. From that office, Whittingham promoted the doctrines of apostolic succession and baptismal regeneration in the face of open hostility from the Evangelical clergy in his diocese. Several of Whittingham's clerical protégés would be prominent in western Pennsylvania history, including the first bishop of Pittsburgh, John Barrett Kerfoot. Another High Church success story of the 1840s was Nashotah House, the first Anglo Catholic seminary, founded by students from GTS.

At the 1844 General Convention, church leaders refused to take an absolute position on the prevailing controversies, but Evangelicals were loud in their denunciations.³ Such tensions had repercussions for Episcopal congregations in western Pennsylvania. Although several of the more prominent parishes in Pittsburgh upheld a tradition of strong Evangelicalism that reflected the majority opinion within the Diocese of Pennsylvania, many of the rural parishes were served by Bishop Whittingham's men. Such circumstances gave western Pennsylvania the guise of a High Church refuge, something that would hinder efforts to erect a separate western diocese over the next thirty years.

THE GROWTH OF PITTSBURGH, 1833–1849

During the first half of the nineteenth century, ecclesiastical power in the Diocese of Pennsylvania was concentrated in Low Church Philadelphia. In 1845, the election of a successor to Bishop Henry Onderdonk (suspended from his office on a charge of intemperance) featured a contest

2. Mullin, *Episcopal Vision*, 60–96 (quotation on 72–73).
3. Chorley, *Men and Movements*, 209–17, 219–24, 237–45, 252–54, 263–64.

between Samuel Bowman of Lancaster and Stephen Tyng, the outspoken Evangelical rector of Philadelphia's Church of the Epiphany. After six ballots failed to yield a result, the convention turned to Alonzo Potter of New York.[4] The 1850s, historian Diana Butler has pointed out, were the period when Episcopal Evangelicals began to lose faith both in their nation and in the church in which they had hitherto enthusiastically participated.[5] Potter was necessarily suspect by virtue of his previous residence in a High Church diocese, but he would prove as committed to such Evangelical causes as temperance and abolitionism as his predecessor. He also had reservations about the focus of many High Churchmen. "The mournful experience of the past few years," he told the diocesan convention of 1846, "both in England and this country, shows the danger of that rash and presumptuous tone of speculation which is sometimes most rash when employed in advocating the abstract claims of authority; and which, beginning with harsh and unfilial animadversions on the reformers and founders of our church, terminates but too frequently, in renouncing their guidance for the spurious Catholicism of Rome."[6]

With his frequent visits to all parts of the state, Bishop Potter more than compensated for the earlier episcopal neglect of western Pennsylvania. In later years, Potter placed great emphasis on clergy convocations, which he hoped would promote regional unity. Only a year after his election, he traveled to Pittsburgh, where, at the request of the local community, he delivered a public address on "Popular Education" at the University of Western Pennsylvania. That Potter was so well received testified to the extent to which the Episcopal Church now enjoyed social respectability. Between 1820 and 1900, the consistent beneficiary in religious affiliation among Pittsburgh's founding families was the Episcopal Church, largely at the expense of the Presbyterian churches.[7]

The new Episcopalians included John Bindley, who came to Pittsburgh to launch a career as a successful builder. An early trustee of the Dollar Savings Bank, the English-born Bindley belonged to St. Peter's, Pittsburgh. Another member of St. Peter's (who began his church

---

4. *Convention Journal of the Diocese of Pennsylvania,* May 20–23, 1845, 33–34, 36–42.

5. Butler, *Standing against the Whirlwind,* 136–58.

6. *Convention Journal of the Diocese of Pennsylvania,* May 19–22, 1846, 32–33.

7. *Convention Journal of the Diocese of Pennsylvania,* May 18–21, 1847, 28–29; Rishel, *Founding Families,* 166–68.

life at Trinity Church, Pittsburgh, and served on its vestry) was Calvin Adams, the inventor of the hand coffee mill. Ulsterman John Harper, boyhood friend of Edwin Stanton—the future secretary of war to Abraham Lincoln—joined the Bank of Pittsburgh in 1832 and was the first president of the Pittsburgh Clearing House. Finally, in Pittsburgh's emerging industrial sector, we find an early Episcopal notable in the person of Abraham Garrison, a founding member of St. Andrew's, Pittsburgh. Born in New York, Garrison arrived in Pittsburgh in 1826, where he entered the iron foundry business and helped establish the domestic chilled-roll industry in the United States.[8]

Outside the City of Pittsburgh, church planting depended on the energy and enthusiasm of the priests appointed to serve. The Society for the Advancement of Christianity in Pennsylvania continued to be the principal instrument for fostering missionary activity, but even here the west continued to be shortchanged. In 1832, six of the society's thirteen missionaries were based west of the Alleghenies, but this number had declined to a mere four out of nineteen by 1835. By 1838, the number of western missionaries had increased only to five, despite the fact that the total number in Pennsylvania had grown to twenty-two.[9] During the 1830s and 1840s, new churches were more likely to be located in urban settings. The first new mission in Allegheny County was St. John's, Lawrenceville, founded in 1833, soon followed by St. Paul's, Laceyville (in the Hill District), in 1835, and St. Andrew's in the Strip District in 1837. Each of the remaining counties (Beaver, Fayette, Washington, and Westmoreland) gained a new mission, apart from Armstrong, which gained two. Notable among these were St. Michael's, Wayne Township (1834); St. Peter's, Uniontown (1838); and Trinity, Washington (1843).

The quality of the early priests varied considerably. At one extreme was the Butler clergyman, who, when he found that his far-flung congregation had difficulty assembling in the same location every Sunday, preached at a variety of locations around the county in the course of a month.[10] A less attractive record was compiled by William Johnston Bakewell, a former Unitarian minister ordained a deacon at Trinity Church on March

8. *History of Pittsburgh*, 3:870–72, 858–60, 4:165–66, 186–87.

9. *Convention Journal of the Diocese of Pennsylvania*, May 15–17, 1832, 15–16; *Convention Journal of the Diocese of Pennsylvania*, May 19–21, 1835, 20–21; *Convention Journal of the Diocese of Pennsylvania*, May 15–17, 1838, 19–20.

10. *Convention Journal of the Diocese of Pennsylvania*, May 19–21, 1840, 79–80.

5, 1844. An Episcopal priest before becoming a Unitarian in a Pittsburgh school subsidized by one of his cousins, Bakewell sought restoration to Anglican orders when his relative died in 1844. He later became a Roman Catholic, before returning to the Episcopal Church for the third—and final—time. Such behavior did nothing for the reputation of the Episcopal Church in the wider community.[11]

The Bakewell case demonstrates the poverty into which many Episcopal clergy frequently fell, a circumstance that Bishop Potter constantly deprecated.[12] At the 1834 diocesan convention, George Upfold, rector of Trinity, Pittsburgh, introduced a resolution urging all congregations to acquire lands for a parsonage to alleviate the straitened circumstances in which many rectors lived, but many congregations were slow to respond.[13] Four years later, the rector of Christ Church, Brownsville, complained that another congregation to which he was ministering had had no scruples about allowing him to pay for repairs to their church "out of his own famished purse."[14] Some clergy sought to solve their financial problems through teaching. The rector of Christ Church, Greensburg, oversaw a girls' school in the town; the rector of St. Peter's, Uniontown, was employed at Madison College; and the incumbent of St. Paul's, Laceyville, taught at the University of Western Pennsylvania.[15] Parishes could still be sanctioned for the neglect of their clergy. In 1842, the diocesan convention stripped St. James, Venango Furnace, of the right to send delegates, on the grounds that it had made no parochial or mission report in the

11. *Convention Journal of the Diocese of Pennsylvania*, May 21–24, 1844, 23; Rishel, *Founding Families*, 109.

12. Declared Bishop Potter: "Any diocese or parish, therefore, which is content to maintain a relatively low standard of ministerial compensation, will have no just cause to complain, if in the end it find itself indifferently served... I should be wanting, I conceive, in my duty to the laity, if even at the risk of being charged with vain repetitions, I did not remind them again and again that the best welfare of their respective congregations and families, requires that they should desire liberal things towards those, who, on entering the ministry of Christ, cut themselves off from secular pursuits, and often from almost all means of eking out a scanty salary." *Convention Journal of the Diocese of Pennsylvania*, May 18–21, 1852, 45–46.

13. *Convention Journal of the Diocese of Pennsylvania*, May 20–22, 1834, 60–61.

14. *Convention Journal of the Diocese of Pennsylvania*, May 15–17, 1838, 53–54 (quotation on 54).

15. *Convention Journal of the Diocese of Pennsylvania*, May 21–23, 1839, 51; *Convention Journal of the Diocese of Pennsylvania*, May 16–18, 1843, 40; *Convention Journal of the Diocese of Pennsylvania*, May 21–24, 1844, 66.

past three years and had neither employed a clergyman nor requested a missionary from the bishop. Six years later, St. John's, Lawrenceville, suffered the same fate.[16]

Most of the region's Episcopal congregations were flimsy organizations at the best of times. Although St. James, Franklin, was chartered in 1826, the building was abandoned after the roof and walls were completed. Six years later, a group of Cumberland Presbyterians took possession of the unfinished building for a six-year period on condition it finish construction, but the Presbyterians in turn abandoned the structure in 1838. The church building was closed from 1840 to 1859, when Samuel Lord attempted to revive the congregation, but in 1852 the building was again closed and remained in that condition until 1862.[17] At Kittanning, the church building was a joint venture between Lutherans and Episcopalians. In 1835, the latter secured title by offering the Lutherans compensation. Their problems were not over, however, for the assigned deacon soon discovered that the Sunday school had, until then, been jointly conducted with the local Methodist church on the understanding that no clergyman could address the students except by invitation. Fearing that this would deny the Episcopal children exposure to sound Anglican doctrine, the deacon abruptly severed the relationship.[18]

By the mid-1830s, clergy were beginning to report some successes. "There has been an increased attendance upon the services of the church during the year past," reported the clergyman in Brownsville, "and a growing attachment to her liturgy is indicated on the part of the congregation by their audible and prompt responses . . . Episcopacy also, which indeed was but a scarecrow when I first came among them, has become not only tolerable in their estimation, but a matter of fact which cannot

---

16. *Convention Journal of the Diocese of Pennsylvania*, May 17–19, 1842, 26; *Convention Journal of the Diocese of Pennsylvania*, May 16–18, 1848, 47.

17. Rev. Martin Aigner, "The History of the Church in the Diocese of Pennsylvania and Especially of the Western Counties from the Beginning of the American Church, in the Province of Pennsylvania in 1695, to the Eve of the Erection of the Diocese of Pittsburgh in 1865," read before the Historical Society of the Diocese of Pittsburgh, December 8, 1912, 25–26, 29, 37, RG5/1.1, box 1DP, Archives of the Episcopal Diocese of Pittsburgh, Pittsburgh, Pennsylvania (hereafter referenced as EDP).

18. *Convention Journal of the Diocese of Pennsylvania*, May 19–21, 1835, 46. The rector of St. Peter's, Waterford, abandoned conventional Sunday school altogether in the mid-1840s, preferring to undertake catechetical instruction in the chancel of the church. *Convention Journal of the Diocese of Pennsylvania*, May 19–22, 1846, 93.

be refuted, a divine institution, which cannot be departed from with safety."[19] Attendance was not the same as membership, however. At St. Paul's, Fairview, in Beaver County, many of the worshippers belonged to other denominations and gave no indication that they wished to become Episcopalians.[20] Six years after the first report from Brownsville, the local clergyman lamented that "so few have been brought, by means of his labours, into the fold of Christ" despite good attendance and participation in worship.[21]

The western missions necessarily relied upon the generosity of wealthy subscribers, both local and national. In Brownsville, an 1841 drive for funds to build a parsonage netted $2,000, including individual donations of $1,100 and $650.[22] Another local priest conducted a fund drive in New York and Philadelphia on behalf of the missions in Freeport and Wayne Township that yielded $140 from St. Ann's, Brooklyn, and a set of Communion vessels from a donor in Philadelphia.[23] Perhaps the most noteworthy donation of the period came from a subscriber in Uniontown, who advanced $2,000 to St. Peter's to assist in the erection of a house of worship. In this case, the donor was not even a communicant of the Episcopal Church, but trusted that the growth of the congregation and support from friends of the church would ultimately lead to his reimbursement.[24]

The objectives for any good Evangelical priest (to which party many of the western clergy belonged) were less the erection of buildings than the conversion, instruction, and formation of their congregants. The interest of many congregations in the erection of fine Gothic churches was to Bishop Potter an example of misplaced priorities. "I should deprecate as unfriendly alike to the extension and simplicity of our faith," he declared in 1848, "the growth of a taste which demanded gorgeous and magnificent structures for worship."[25] By contrast, he had nothing but praise for those parishes that maintained a spiritual library for their members. That

---

19. *Convention Journal of the Diocese of Pennsylvania*, May 20–22, 1834, 33–34.
20. *Convention Journal of the Diocese of Pennsylvania*, May 16–18, 1837, 35.
21. *Convention Journal of the Diocese of Pennsylvania*, May 19–21, 1840, 53–54.
22. *Convention Journal of the Diocese of Pennsylvania*, May 18–20, 1841, 53–54.
23. *Convention Journal of the Diocese of Pennsylvania*, May 16–18, 1837, 61.
24. *Convention Journal of the Diocese of Pennsylvania*, May 16–18, 1843, 39–40.
25. *Convention Journal of the Diocese of Pennsylvania*, May 16–18, 1848, 29.

same year, Christ Church, Brownsville, was able to report that its library was much used by the congregation of 125 adults and 85 children, with forty volumes in circulation at any one time.[26]

CIVIL WAR DIVISIONS, 1850–1865

From its beginnings, the Episcopal Church—or at least the High Church party—had prided itself on standing apart from secular political disputation. Memories of its lack of "patriotism" during the eighteenth century were slow to die, and many church leaders thought it unwise to compromise ecclesiastical security by involvement in worldly concerns. The mood of the 1850s was hardly conducive to such ambivalence, however. A historically Democratic state that would send a favorite son to the White House in 1856, Pennsylvania was coming to terms with its new status as the industrial and financial linchpin of the nation. The national debate over the future of slavery—and the related issue of free black citizenship in the North—had also begun to make itself felt.

It was to the inclusion of African Americans in the councils of the church that the Diocese of Pennsylvania was forced to turn during the 1850s. An early harbinger of that struggle came in 1849, when, by almost two-to-one margins in both the clergy and lay orders, the diocesan convention refused to seat representatives from the Church of the Crucifixion. This Philadelphia mission had been admitted to union in 1847, only for it to be revealed that its lay delegates had been elected by the largely black congregation. Of the eighteen clergy employed west of the Alleghenies, just six attended the convention, and only one—William Hilton, a missionary assigned to Kittanning—voted to seat the delegates. The rectors of Christ Church, Brownsville; Christ Church, Meadville; St. Paul's, Erie; and Trinity, Pittsburgh; as well as the missionary assigned to Mercer County, sided with the majority.[27] Three years later, a second attempt to seat the delegates carried in the clergy order but failed narrowly among the laity. This time there were nine western clergy present, but only one of them, William Hilton, had attended the 1849 convention and he still voted in the affirmative. He was joined by some of the newer missionary priests: Samuel Clements of Trinity, Washington; Thomas Crumpton of

26. Ibid., 67–68.
27. *Convention Journal of the Diocese of Pennsylvania*, May 15–18, 1849, 18–20, 42–46.

Christ Church, Allegheny; William Paddock, an itinerant missionary; and Charles Quick of St. Andrew's, Pittsburgh. The opposition was now represented by Theodore Lyman of Trinity, Pittsburgh; Richard Smith of St. Peter's, Waterford; and Joseph Taylor of Christ Church, New Brighton.[28]

In 1850, the opponents of racial segregation in ecclesiastical life began to turn their guns on the Eighth Revised Regulation of 1795. This instrument permitted St. Thomas African Church in Philadelphia to limit access to parish offices to African Americans in exchange for surrendering the parish's right to send delegates to the diocesan convention. The committee exploring the issue recommended retention of the regulation, arguing that there was no absolute right of participation in the government of the church. "[Can] there be any doubt, with dispassionate persons," its members concluded, "as to the incompetency of the parties in question, for the post of advisers and legislators in the concerns of this portion of the American Church? Are they qualified for it, either by education, cultivation or social position?" Evidence of a clear division in opinion can be seen from the split in the clergy order (the vote was 44–42) in defense of the Eighth Revised Regulation, with Bishop Potter voting with the minority. (The parishes backed it by the more substantial margin of 51–16). Only five western clergy were present and two of them—William Hilton and Thomas Crumpton of Christ Church, Allegheny—voted with their bishop. The other three—William Carmichael (Christ Church, Meadville); William Flint (St. Paul's, Erie); and Richard Smith (St. Peter's, Waterford)—shared the majority's distrust of the ability of African Americans to engage in church affairs. Of the three western parishes represented by lay delegates, Trinity, Pittsburgh, and Christ Church, Meadville, voted with the majority, but St. Andrew's, Pittsburgh—a bastion of Evangelicalism—did not.[29]

Opinion steadily swung against the Eight Revised Regulation; in 1854, the clergy embraced the call for repeal by a vote of 70–28. The western clergy proved no exception in this respect, voting 8–2 for repeal, with Benedict Lyman of Trinity, Pittsburgh, and Richard Smith of St. Peter's, Waterford, opposed. Among those backing repeal was Joseph Taylor of Christ Church, New Brighton, who had opposed seating the delegates

---

28. *Convention Journal of the Diocese of Pennsylvania*, May 18–21, 1852, 76–79.

29. *Convention Journal of the Diocese of Pennsylvania*, May 21–24, 1850, 49–62, 64–67 (quotation on 54). Carmichael, Flint, and Smith had all voted in the negative in 1849.

from the Church of the Crucifixion just two years before.[30] Under Bishop Potter's gentle prodding, Pennsylvania Episcopalians finally repealed the regulation in 1863, with solid majorities in both orders. A few holdouts remained to the bitter end, most notably Trinity, Pittsburgh, whose rector, Cornelius Swope, and lay delegate, John Shoenberger, both voted in the negative. The other clerical opponent was Edwin Van Deusen, rector of St. Peter's, Pittsburgh, a daughter church of Trinity Church.[31]

St. Peter's had become a source of conflict within the diocese as early as 1855, when its proposed parish charter drew criticism not only for the autonomy that it gave the vestry but also because it explicitly restricted membership to white males. On this occasion, Bishop Potter—having previously expressed his concerns to the rector of St. Peter's—formally declared that a segregated congregation only reinforced existing prejudices in the wider society. Only nineteen of the eighty-eight clergy present proved willing to admit the parish with such a charter, though Benedict Lyman (Trinity, Pittsburgh), Richard Smith (now a missionary), and William White (St. Peter's, Butler) all joined Van Deusen in defense of parish autonomy.[32]

Such debates did not remain confined to the ecclesiastical realm. During the 1840s, Episcopalians—who represented almost a third of candidates running for public office—were evenly split between the Whig and Democratic parties (in contrast to the strong preference of Presbyterians for the Whigs and the almost uniformly Democratic profile of Catholic candidates).[33] A decade later, the Episcopal pendulum had swung radically towards the Whigs' successors in the new Republican Party. Ardent Evangelical William Baum, a self-educated merchant who came to Pittsburgh from Baltimore in 1812, was an abolitionist who helped organize the Republican Party in Pittsburgh. George Whitten Jackson, Irish-born and a member of St. Andrew's, Pittsburgh, was equally committed to that cause. Active in the region's mercantile, packing, and cotton industries, Jackson became a director of the Mechanics and Manufacturers Bank of Pittsburgh in 1837 and helped launch the Allegheny Valley Railroad during the 1850s. Initially a Democrat, Jackson was a vocal critic

---

30. *Convention Journal of the Diocese of Pennsylvania*, May 16–19, 1854, 59–62.
31. *Convention Journal of the Diocese of Pennsylvania*, May 26–29, 1863, 71–76.
32. *Convention Journal of the Diocese of Pennsylvania*, May 15–18, 1855, 63–71.
33. See table 14 in Holt, *Forging a Majority*, 326.

of slavery who joined first the Free Soil Party and then the Republican Party. He later formed part of the Pennsylvania delegation to the national Republican convention that nominated John Fremont as its presidential contender in opposition to Pennsylvania's favorite son, James Buchanan.[34]

Commitment to the abolitionist cause did not in any way lessen Evangelical concerns about the threat posed by the growing Anglo Catholic party. "The earliest approaches to an insidious will-worship and a disguised Romanism should be guarded against," warned Bishop Potter in 1853. "Habits of thinking and speaking which are but too prevalent, in which the church is more prominent than her Head—sacramental grace more insisted upon than holiness of heart and life—zeal for shibboleth, substituted for zeal in doing and suffering God's will—outward unity put before fellowship of the spirit in the bond of peace—the liberty wherewith Christ has made us free, repudiated for a bondage to ordinance, and for prostration of mind and soul before some imaginary or self-constituted viceregent of Heaven."[35] Despite such warnings, the influence of Bishop Wittingham's protégés in the west was clearly evident by the early 1860s. While St. Andrew's, Pittsburgh, raised funds for Virginia Theological Seminary, the parishes of St. Paul's, Erie; Christ Church, New Brighton; and St. John's, Lawrenceville, all earmarked contributions for Nashotah House.[36]

Overall, the 1850s were a period of parochial expansion, marked by the establishment of seventeen new congregations, six of them in Allegheny County. Among the more notable Pittsburgh parishes were Grace (1851); St. James Memorial (1851); St. Mark's (1852); and Calvary (1855). Calvary's future rival, St. Stephen's, Sewickley, by contrast, was not organized until 1861. Other churches in the rural hinterland included Christ Church, New Brighton (1850); St. Mark's, Johnstown (1855); and St. Paul's, Monongahela (1860). Many of these new congregations served the growing industrial base of southwestern Pennsylvania. Writing on

---

34. *History of Pittsburgh*, 4:175–76, 182–83.

35. *Convention Journal of the Diocese of Pennsylvania*, May 17–19, 1853, 36–37.

36. *Convention Journal of the Diocese of Pennsylvania*, May 22–24, 1860, 64, 125; *Convention Journal of the Diocese of Pennsylvania*, May 28–30, 1861, 88, 142. The Evangelical presence had by no means vanished, however. The topic for discussion at an 1860 clergy meeting was reported as "the memorial movement in our communion, the liturgic movement in some others." Minutes of the Western Convocation of Pennsylvania, March 13, 1860, RG4A/1.12, box 18DSC, EDP.

behalf of Christ Church, New Brighton, the local missionary commented that the same energy that underpinned local businesses could also be witnessed in the life of the church, for $1,800 of the $3,000 in subscriptions for a church building had been raised within the parish.[37]

At Etna—a community composed largely of Irish and German Catholics—Episcopalians benefited from the munificence of a local company, whose owners underwrote the erection of an Episcopal church for the benefit of their Protestant employees (this phenomenon increased in the course of the nineteenth century).[38] Excessive reliance on a population drawn from manufacturing industry could have its downside. Many attendees at Christ Church, Allegheny, were not regular worshipers, let alone communicants, and rarely rented pews because of their constant shifting from job to job.[39] That many priests struggled to reach such audiences is clear from an 1864 paper at a clergy conference on how best to reach the laboring classes.[40]

Many missions still reported signs of spiritual growth despite such handicaps. In 1855, Bishop Potter applauded the fact that the number of Sunday schools in the diocese had almost doubled during his episcopate and urged parishes without them to remedy that deficiency. "Schools are opening the intellectual capacities of our people," he declared, "and creating an appetite for mental employment and gratification, which must be fed from the tree whose fruit is for the healing of the nations, or it will sate itself with garbage."[41] The rector of St. Paul's, Kittanning, noted that the Bible class that he had organized had revealed newfound interest "in the study of the Word of God," while the clergyman assigned to St. Michael's, Wayne Township, reported how nine of his most recent confirmation candidates had walked twelve miles for the ceremony and then walked the same distance back home again in order to be at work the next day.[42] Jubal Hodges, a missionary appointed in 1861 to visit isolated congregations, described a visit to a couple near Uniontown "seeking the way of

---

37. *Convention Journal of the Diocese of Pennsylvania*, May 20–22, 1851, 98.

38. *Convention Journal of the Diocese of Pennsylvania*, May 15–18, 1855, 124.

39. *Convention Journal of the Diocese of Pennsylvania*, May 17–19, 1853, 80.

40. Minutes of the Western Convocation of Pennsylvania, April 20, 1864, RG4A/1.12, box 18DSC, EDP.

41. *Convention Journal of the Diocese of Pennsylvania*, May 15–18, 1855, 25, 27 (quotation).

42. Ibid, 103, 106.

redemption." "We knelt in prayer," he later testified. "And gathering around some of the neighbors I opened the Scripture concerning Philip and the Eunuch and preached to them Jesus and baptism into his death."[43]

Missionaries like Hodges were still in short supply west of the Alleghenies, prompting a variety of alternative strategies. Sometimes, a prominent local layman would act on his own initiative, as was the case for a three-year period in northern Jefferson County, when John Robinson conducted services and held Sunday school in his cabin.[44] Established congregations that lost their minister could spend long periods without a resident clergyman until a new appointment could be made. When Trinity, Washington, appealed to the bishop for a new rector in 1856, Potter appointed its senior warden a "lay reader and catechist with provisional charge of the parish," until such time as he could find a replacement.[45] The work of laymen was equally essential in urban church planting. Hill Burgwin, who came to Pittsburgh in 1851 as a twenty-six-year-old lawyer, helped establish the Dollar Savings Bank and was influential in persuading the City of Pittsburgh to acquire Schenley Park for public use. He proved equally active in the life of the church, making house-to-house visitations to Pittsburgh's South Side that ultimately resulted in the establishment of St. Mark's, Pittsburgh, in 1851. In 1855, Burgwin was a founding member of St. Peter's, Pittsburgh, and served as senior warden and Sunday school superintendent. Four years later, he helped organize the Church Home, a centerpiece of Episcopal institutional life in Pittsburgh.[46]

The drive to establish church-run institutions to serve the public weal was a hallmark of the Diocese of Pittsburgh during the nineteenth century. With monetary resources concentrated in southeastern Pennsylvania, it was hardly surprising that most examples of church welfare were located in Philadelphia, but some effort was put into building up such entities in Pittsburgh. In 1853, the Locust Grove Seminary for young women opened; within a year, attendance had more than doubled. In New Brighton, the Kenwood School for Boys performed a similar service for Episcopalians in western Pennsylvania, and there were frequent calls for

---

43. Minutes of the Western Convocation of Pennsylvania, December 12, 1861, February 27, 1862 (quotation), April 20, 1864, RG4A/1.12, box 18DSC, EDP.

44. *Convention Journal of the Diocese of Pennsylvania,* May 16–19, 1854, 110.

45. *Convention Journal of the Diocese of Pennsylvania,* May 25–27, 1857, 99.

46. *Church News,* December 1898.

similar institutes to be established in Pittsburgh.[47] In November 1858, a group of clergy and laity (many of them attached to Calvary Church, Pittsburgh) met to discuss the establishment of a home for the aged and infirm in Allegheny County. The following year the group adopted a charter and in April 1859 the Church Home Association was launched.[48] Endeavors like the Church Home differed significantly from those establishments that would be organized during the early twentieth century, when the focus was on centralization of functions. Bishop Potter was a great believer in the voluntary principle and opposed to centralization, even objecting to efforts to vest control of national missionary funds in the General Convention, "which in attempting to legislate for all parts of a vast country at once, must necessarily overlook the peculiar wants and capabilities of each different section of it."[49]

Centralization and nationalization were nevertheless the secular wave of the future. On April 12, 1861, Confederate troops opened fire on Fort Sumter in Charleston Harbor; the following day, its garrison surrendered, the first engagement in over four years of civil war. Six weeks later, Samuel Bowman, assistant bishop of Pennsylvania, rallied the state's Episcopalians to the national cause: "But yesterday, and we should have thought that 'ten thousand swords would have leaped from their scabbards to avenge even a look of insult' offered to the flag of our country. But we have lived to see that flag assailed by disloyal hands, and openly dishonoured. War, with all its horrors is upon us—now a *civil*, soon perhaps, which God forbid, to darken into a *servile* war. Our consolation is, to know that we have not sought it—that we have striven to avoid it—that we have submitted to everything but absolute dishonour to avert it."[50]

War would reshape the daily life of Pittsburghers in many ways, for their region provided the industrial power that sustained the Union armies. Local Episcopalians joined the army, served in wartime agencies, and prayed for the success of the federal government. The rector of Calvary, Robert Peet, recalled how on one occasion members of the vestry

47. *Convention Journal of the Diocese of Pennsylvania*, May 16–19, 1854, 87; Minutes of the Western Convocation of Pennsylvania, September 12, 1860, July 19, 1862, RG4A/1.12, box 18DSC, EDP.

48. *Convention Journal of the Diocese of Pennsylvania*, May 24–27, 1859, 126; Edsall, "Three Generations," 12A.

49. *Convention Journal of the Diocese of Pennsylvania*, May 16–19, 1854, 35.

50. *Convention Journal of the Diocese of Pennsylvania*, May 28–30, 1861, 47.

went straight from a meeting to drill as home guards at the railway station in East Liberty. John Arunah Harper (the son of the first president of the Pittsburgh Clearing House) joined the Union army in 1863, while Felix Brunot was one of a number of physicians and nurses who offered their services to the military after the battle of Shiloh. Brunot endured confinement in Libby Prison and, after his release, presided over the Pittsburgh Sanitary Fair in 1864.[51]

The disruptions of the Civil War gave fresh impetus to demands for the establishment of a new diocese in western Pennsylvania. Although Bishop Potter had accepted the possibility as early as 1855, he was determined that no new diocese would lack the resources adequate to maintain its bishop. Without that guarantee, the only candidates for such bishoprics would be men of independent means. "There is no danger," he ruefully admitted, "that wealth should not be held in sufficiently high estimation in this country, and in our brand of the Christian world. It will bode only evil if it shall ever come to be considered as a necessary qualification for the highest office and honor of a Diocese. Disqualification it surely ought not to be."[52]

Despite numerous petitions, appeals from the west encountered little sympathy prior to 1862,[53] when the diocesan convention agreed to appoint a committee to examine the possibility of dividing the diocese. The committee's 1863 report stated that western support for a separate diocese stood at 20–5 in favor among local clergy and 20–8 in favor among local parishes. Since seventeen of those parishes were able to meet their ordinary expenses without outside help and two others were close to that point, the committee was optimistic that the necessary funds could

---

51. Edsall, "Three Generations," 14; *History of Pittsburgh*, 3:858–60; Slattery, *Felix Reville Brunot*, 55–81, 92–101. An unusual dissent from this general solidarity was recorded in 1864 by the clergy of the Western Convocation of Pennsylvania, when they protested national and state legislation that allowed for ministers to be drafted for military service. Those present pledged moral and material support to any member of the convocation who might be so drafted. Minutes of the Western Convocation of Pennsylvania, September 15, 1864, RG4A/1.12, box 18DSC, EDP. See also Fox, *Pittsburgh*.

52. *Convention Journal of the Diocese of Pennsylvania*, May 15–18, 1855, 30–37 (quotation on 36).

53. Bishop Potter noted in his 1860 convention address that a committee had been appointed to consider the matter in 1859, but that the will of the convention had not yet shown itself in favor, and division was deferred in 1861 because of the unrest in the country at large. *Convention Journal of the Diocese of Pennsylvania*, May 22–24, 1860, 39; *Convention Journal of the Diocese of Pennsylvania*, May 28–30, 1861, 56.

be raised for an endowment. Indeed, one wealthy parish pledged to quadruple its assessment if a new diocese was erected, while another small parish indicated that it would increase its pledge tenfold.[54]

The following year, an enlarged committee reported to the diocesan convention, meeting for the first time in Pittsburgh, that the basic conditions for establishing a new diocese had now been defined. Fifteen self-supporting parishes and fifteen presbyters were to be the minimum for any new diocese and at least thirty self-supporting parishes and thirty presbyters had to remain in the residual territory of the diocese from which the new diocese had been carved. Committee members argued that Episcopal Pennsylvania consisted of three regions: the southeast—which could easily form an independent diocese; the west—which currently fell just short of the requisite numbers but desired to separate; and the center—which had the potential of the southeast but no interest in separation. "Any division of the diocese," they warned, "which, for the sake of meeting the numerical conditions of the Constitution of the Church, should take a few [parishes in the central valley] and associate them with a western diocese, would be unnatural, in conflict with the habits of the people, and of necessity only temporary." Many of those in the western region also qualified their support for a separate diocese, expressing a desire for continued missionary support, concern about the need to build up an episcopal fund, and even a readiness to abandon their call for a separate diocese if a coadjutor bishop were to be based in the west.[55]

By the time of the 1865 convention, fifteen western parishes had relinquished all claims on the diocesan board of missions. The committee on the division of the diocese reported sixteen parish memorials in support of a new diocese and eighteen favorable memorials from resident clergy. They also reported two hostile parish memorials, one from St. James, Pittsburgh, with fifty-four signatures, and another—without reported affiliation—with thirty-four signatures. Deputy William Walsh then introduced the resolution to erect a new diocese with its eastern border at McKean, Cameron, Clearfield, Cambria, and Somerset counties,

---

54. *Convention Journal of the Diocese of Pennsylvania,* May 26–29, 1863, 66–70. "We hesitate not to say, that in the county of Allegheny alone, the laymen of our Church *could* sustain that charge, in addition to all other calls they are required to meet, without denying themselves even of a single *luxury,* they are accustomed to enjoy" (69).

55. *Convention Journal of the Diocese of Pennsylvania,* May 24–27, 1864, 247–58 (quotation on 251–52).

provided that $30,000 were raised to provide support for a new bishop. On May 26, 1865, the Walsh resolution was approved by 102 votes to 42 among the clergy and 62 votes to 17 among the parishes. There was not complete unanimity in the west, however, as three parishes—St. Andrew's and St. James, both in Pittsburgh, and Trinity, Washington—all voted in the negative.[56]

In June 1865, Bishop William Stevens (who had succeeded Bishop Potter) responded to the convention's action by appointing a twelve-man committee to prepare documentation and secure funds for the diocesan endowment. Within three months, the committee had raised $35,000, but on September 28 its members addressed a remonstrance to Stevens in which they objected to the imposed financial requirement. This had not been a prerequisite for any previous diocese, they argued, and could frustrate future attempts at diocesan division by raising the requirements to an impossible level. Committee members further argued that it placed an undue emphasis on the material rather than the spiritual aspects of the episcopate. The bishop curtly responded that he could not accept the remonstrance, which called into question the judgment of the diocesan convention and of his predecessor. When the letter was reluctantly withdrawn, Stevens announced that a primary convention would take place in Pittsburgh on November 15.[57]

A DIOCESE IS ESTABLISHED, 1866-1881

The eighty-eight clergy and laymen gathered in Pittsburgh's Trinity Church in November 1865 faced a daunting task. Only a few months earlier, the nation had welcomed the conclusion of four bloody years of conflict, and at the General Convention that year, the Episcopal Church—in stark contrast to most of the other large Protestant denominations—had welcomed delegates from the states of the former Confederacy back to its counsels. Reconciliation, then, was a guiding theme, as Episcopalians in western Pennsylvania met to select the man who would be their first bishop. "Better make any sacrifice of personal preference or party views or political tastes," Bishop Stevens warned the assembled delegates, "than

---

56. *Convention Journal of the Diocese of Pennsylvania*, May 23-26, 1865, 85-88, 93-96. The rectors of St. Andrew's and St. James, along with the clergyman assigned to St. Michael's, Wayne Township, also voted in the negative.

57. *Primary Convention Journal*, November 15-16, 1865, 1-14.

launch your Diocese upon a sea of troubles, with a divided crew and discordant helmsman ... Seek to be of one mind in this house of God, for a house divided against itself cannot stand."[58]

Convention delegates had two very different candidates from which to choose. From Massachusetts came Frederic Dan Huntington, rector of Emmanuel Church, Boston. Born in 1819, Huntington was a graduate of Amherst and Harvard Divinity School. A former Unitarian, he had served as pastor of the South Congregational Church of Boston before becoming Plummer Professor of Christian Morals at Harvard.[59] His rival was another convert, the president of Trinity College in Hartford, Connecticut, John Barrett Kerfoot. Three years older than Huntington, Kerfoot had been born in Dublin and baptized a Presbyterian, before his family moved to Lancaster, Pennsylvania, when he was three years old. Schooled under William Augustus Muhlenberg at the Flushing Institute on Long Island, he studied for Holy Orders and was ordained a priest in 1840. Kerfoot headed St. James's College in Hagerstown, established by Bishop Whittingham of Maryland, until this work was interrupted by the Civil War, moving to Hartford in 1864.[60] The following year, as a clerical delegate to the General Convention, he distinguished himself by moving the tabling of a resolution introduced by Pennsylvania layman Horace Binney, which proposed a series of thanksgiving services for the reestablishment of national authority over the South and the demise of slavery. Kerfoot later explained that while he shared the sentiments of the resolution, he felt its passage would needlessly offend the Southern delegates.[61]

Robert Coster, a student at St. James's College who subsequently became a priest in the Diocese of Pittsburgh, was one of Kerfoot's greatest admirers. "His sound scholarship; his through acquaintance with Anglican theology, particularly with everything related to the Roman controversy; the judicial character of his mind; his loyalty to the Anglican Church; his deep simplicity, his true sincerity and his entire consistency of conduct; made him a great Bishop and a noble Churchman," he declared eighteen years after Kerfoot's death, and many agreed with him. John Norman, who

58. Ibid., 35.

59. He later refused the bishopric of Maine, but was elected to the Diocese of Central New York in 1868.

60. Harrison, *Life of Kerfoot,* 1:1–65, 102–20, 126–301.

61. Ibid., 2:390–97. On the Binney Resolution, see *Convention Journal of the Diocese of Pennsylvania,* May 23–26, 1865, 61–62.

grew up in Centre County, Pennsylvania, and graduated as a physician in 1859, returned to southwestern Pennsylvania after service as an army surgeon in the Civil War. During the late 1860s, his community received a number of visits from Bishop Kerfoot who "surprised us with his gentle and affectionate manner and his love of children." With the bishop's encouragement, Norman was ordained a deacon in 1872 and subsequently became a missionary, first in Monongahela and then in McKeesport.[62]

Kerfoot's candidacy was also championed by Cornelius Swope, another graduate of St. James, the former rector of Mount Calvary Church, Baltimore—an Anglo Catholic stronghold—and the rector of Trinity Church, Pittsburgh. Impressed by Kerfoot's General Convention address, Swope worked to overcome residual antipathy to the High Church party, with the result that Pittsburgh's clerical delegates cast 19 votes for Kerfoot and only 9 for Huntington, a decision ratified by the laity (the parish delegations voted 19-8 in favor, with one divided).[63] On January 25, 1866, Pittsburghers flocked to Trinity Church for the consecration of Bishop Kerfoot. Seven bishops were present, including the former rector of the church, John Henry Hopkins, bishop of Vermont, and Cleveland Coxe, bishop of Western New York, supplied the mandate for the first bishop of Pittsburgh:

> To illuminate a city, to make the Church strong at the heart of any region, was to secure, in process of time, the evangelization of the surrounding country. Alas! Why have we been so slow to adopt this policy in doing our work in America? . . . Our Missions have often been wasted villages of the West, where the cheerless labors of an isolated Presbyter have been almost unfelt, and where, unsupported by the society of his Bishop and unconsoled by that of brethren, he has often pined and failed and died. Meanwhile great cities have been left, festering with corruption, to the kites and crows of infidelity and Romanism.[64]

Coxe's message spoke to the industrial shift already under way in western Pennsylvania (see chapter 3). It also anticipated the increas-

---

62. *Church News*, April 1897; Personal Sketch—Life of Reverend John P. Norman, n.d., RG5/1.1, box 1DP, EDP.

63. Harrison, *Life of Kerfoot*, 2:398–424; *Primary Convention Journal*, November 15–16, 1865, 31–32.

64. Harrison, *Life of Kerfoot*, 2:425–31; *Primary Convention Journal*, November 15–16, 1865, 146.

ing projection of the national church into public life and into the work of civic reform (one of the few aspects of early nineteenth-century Evangelicalism to be preserved by their Broad Church successors). Under Kerfoot, however, the model for the 1870s was not dramatically different from that of the 1850s. New church plants continued to appear across the region, and of the twelve congregations organized in Kerfoot's first five years, eight were located in Allegheny County. The latter included Emmanuel, Allegheny City (1867), St. Stephen's, McKeesport (1869), and Good Shepherd, Hazelwood (1870). Another sixteen missions followed in the early 1870s, with a somewhat greater focus on Fayette County. Notable parishes from this period included Ascension, Pittsburgh (1871) and St. Cyprian's Mission, the founding mission of the black parish of Holy Cross (1875). The final years of Kerfoot's episcopate witnessed the establishment of a further fourteen missions, with a shift to Somerset and Butler counties. The most successful parish of this period was that of St. Stephen's, Wilkinsburg (1879).

During the 1870s, the Episcopal Church devoted much time to articulating the nature of the faith it professed. Bishop Kerfoot had come to his diocese as a High Churchman and an admirer of James Lloyd Breck, the founder of Nashotah House. "He was my mate and friend in early school and college life," he declared at the time of Breck's death in 1876, "and the tie of affection was never severed... To many of us who have watched his course all these years, it seemed as though this American Church of ours, without Lloyd Breck at work in it, was hard to think of."[65] He was all too aware, however, that many members of the Evangelical party viewed the increasingly ritualistic approach of the *Protestant* Episcopal Church with alarm.

At the first General Convention following his consecration, Evangelical delegates submitted proposals for no fewer than twenty new canons, including the Connyngham Canon on the Manner of Conducting Divine Worship, which barred most vestments, the use of incense, elevation of the elements at the consecration, candlesticks, or crucifixes. This measure was only narrowly defeated in the House of Laity. Leading the fight in opposition to the Connyngham Canon at both the 1871 and 1874 General Conventions was Father James DeKoven, whose efforts cost him election successively as bishop of Massachusetts, Fond du

---

65. *Convention Journal*, June 14–15, 1876, 36.

Lac (Wisconsin), and Illinois. Even so, the High Church party successfully blocked efforts to revise the American Book of Common Prayer and Evangelicals increasingly lost heart as they saw their efforts at achieving a common front with other Protestants come to nothing. Such incidents as the 1868 trial of Stephen Tyng for preaching at a Methodist church and the deposition of Charles Cheney from the rectorship of Christ Church, Chicago, in 1871, for omitting the word "regenerate" from the baptismal service all prompted a steady exodus of Evangelicals from the Episcopal Church. When Bishop George Cummins of Kentucky finally organized the Reformed Episcopal Church in 1873 to accommodate the remaining dissenters, it was already too late to turn back the tide.[66]

Bishop Kerfoot proved an eloquent advocate of a middle way in the House of Bishops. Assigned to the General Convention's Committee on Uniformity in Matters of Ritual—which produced the Canon on Ritual in 1868—he fully participated in the General Convention of 1871.[67] Central to the debate was an attempt to revise the Book of Common Prayer to remove the phrase "One Baptism for the Remission of Sins." Baptism, however, was a matter of personal significance to Kerfoot, for whom the validity of his Presbyterian infant baptism had so concerned him that he had requested a conditional baptism before his ordination in 1840.[68] "My Brethren," Kerfoot warned his diocesan convention in 1870, "stability of doctrine is the very life of the Church ... changes that bear on doctrine are changes that cut some of the cables that anchor the ship ... Doctrine, the teaching of the Gospel, must come from the Church which speaks not in varying phrases." He was also unwilling to concede the efficacy of the notion of baptismal regeneration. "We see in our own land the foreign-born babe born anew into the nation by the same official act of naturalization that makes his alien father a citizen," the bishop pointed out. "Both become equally citizens, children of the State, and thenceforth have protection, privileges and obligations equal to those of the native-

---

66. Butler, *Standing against the Whirlwind*, 178–212; Guelzo, "Ritual, Romanism and Rebellion"; Slocum, "Romantic Religion."

67. Harrison, *Life of Kerfoot*, 2:510–13.

68. "Not that I slight the pious dedication of my pious parents in my infancy," he noted in his diary, "but I desire to fill up what they did desire for me, the Episcopal and truly catholic character of my baptism." Ibid., 1:27.

born citizen. Why, in all reason, should it be otherwise in the Kingdom of Christ?"[69]

The battle over ritualism would have ramifications for Pittsburgh. As early as 1867, Bishop Kerfoot had been obliged to request the rector of All Saint's Chapel, a man recommended by his mentor Bishop Whittingham, to refrain from his practice of reverencing the altar during services. The latter's refusal to do so (on the grounds that it would compromise his belief in the Incarnation) provoked a demand at the diocesan convention for an investigation of the chapel's forms of worship before delegates voted on admitting it into union with the diocese. While the clergy were almost evenly divided on this matter, the lay delegates endorsed it by a margin of almost 3-1. Two years later, after Kerfoot had fruitlessly issued a "godly admonition" for the rector to desist from his ritualistic practices, the diocesan convention rejected the mission's application, with only eight clergy and two parish delegations (those of St. Paul's, Kittanning, and Emmanuel, Allegheny) dissenting. The bishop's refusal to accept candidates for confirmation from All Saints Chapel and the death of its lay benefactor soon assured its demise.[70]

Such incidents helped demonstrate that even Kerfoot's High Church sensibilities had their limits. Reverencing the altar, he told the diocesan convention, "is not the private act of devotion done by unofficial members of a congregation, but the public act, most openly done in the view of all, by the official leaders of the worship. It is not an act of general reverence to God, done on entering His house. It is done in the midst of hymns and just before the Altar, before and after services . . . It is an act representative and typical of a whole system of doctrine and worship which, as every one knows, is claiming a place never before conceded to any such system in our Communion since the Reformation."[71] Only three years later, Kerfoot cautioned a High Church acquaintance that any candidate that the latter might recommend for Pittsburgh "must have none of the new fancies. Out here, such a man would be as likely to succeed as a box of Lucifer matches in a powder-mill. Hearty Prayer-Book teaching and modes are everywhere here acceptable, but 'advanced' ideas and gestures make

---

69. *Convention Journal*, June 14–16, 1870, 61–66 (quotations on 63–64, 65). See also *Convention Journal*, June 12–13, 1872, 43–47.

70. Harrison, *Life of Kerfoot*, 2:514–20; *Convention Journal*, June 9–11, 1868, 19–20, 25–26; *Convention Journal*, June 8–10, 1869, 27–31, 73–78.

71. *Convention Journal*, June 8–10, 1869, 74–75.

mischief right off. Such a man as *you* would call a little 'Low' who would be loyal to the Church and to this Diocese, and who is earnest and industrious, would do well."[72]

Challenges from the Evangelical wing of the Church also materialized, for Kerfoot remained perfectly ready to defend moderate ritualists like the rector of Christ Church, Meadville, whose vestry tried to dismiss him because his services were insufficiently Low Church.[73] As the Evangelical holdouts prepared to join Bishop Cummins, the rector of Calvary Church, Joseph Wilson, endeavored to persuade his flock to follow him into the Reformed Episcopal Church. Although many members were sympathetic, the vestry immediately surrendered spiritual charge of the parish into the bishop's hands, rejecting a petition from a large number of parishioners. Wilson initially organized a separate congregation to which many Calvary parishioners—including almost all the Sunday school—followed, but after he was called away from Pittsburgh the secessionist group dissolved. "A more causeless schism," Kerfoot told the diocesan convention of 1874, "no Church history can show. It alleges evils that do not exist; and it devises unlawful remedies that can correct no evils, but that will beget very many." That same convention rejected an amendment that would have admitted ministers of other denominations to its deliberations, clearly demonstrating that it did not regard the ministerial orders of its Protestant neighbors as identical with those of the Episcopal Church.[74]

Bishop Kerfoot made no secret of his belief that there should be at least a monthly celebration of Holy Communion in every congregation. In 1867, he lavished praise on one congregation that offered Morning and Evening Prayer on a daily basis and a weekly celebration of the Eucharist. Ten years later, the introduction of weekly Communion at St. Paul's, Kittanning—a departure from former practice—was welcomed by most parishioners.[75] The bishop urged his pastors to stress the value of

---

72. Rt. Rev. Dr. John Kerfoot to Rev. Dr. Dix, November 1872, quoted in Harrison, *Life of Kerfoot*, 2:493–94.

73. Harrison, *Life of Kerfoot*, 2:509.

74. *Convention Journal*, June 10–11, 1874, 17–18, 52–53 (quotation); Harrison, *Life of Kerfoot*, 2:479, 510; Edsall, "Three Generations," 18–21. On the wider context of the schism, see Guelzo, *For the Union*.

75. *Convention Journal*, May 21–23, 1867, 79–81; *Convention Journal*, June 12–13, 1878, 62–63.

confirmation to potential candidates through sermons, lectures, and personal interviews. He expected that the latter would be willing to receive Communion on a regular basis and to continue with classes and spiritual reading throughout their lives.[76]

Kerfoot was equally concerned that Pittsburgh's Episcopalians understand the organic nature of the Christian community. "The 'Diocese' is not a name for a compact by which a Bishop may be got and paid to come around, oftener than formerly was the case, to confirmation," he warned in 1872, "[but rather] means that the Bishop is to seek out the weak and needy Church, and the vacant and promising points, and give them his own ministrations, and find for them the more constant ministrations of the resident, or the frequently and regularly visiting Pastor. He is to stir up the Rectors of the stronger Churches to spare, now and then, some of their time and labor for such points."[77] He believed that the laity needed to be actively involved. Throughout his years in Pittsburgh, he constantly called for lay evangelists to read services and teach Sunday school, and was wont to remark on the fact that there was much more lay activity in Erie and the northern part of the diocese than in Pittsburgh.[78]

Before the great Catholic influx of the 1890s, the religious life of western Pennsylvania was exceedingly diverse. "[T]he effects of schism in these small towns is very manifest and truly lamentable," the rector of St. Peter's, Uniontown, declared in 1866. "With a population of only 2,500, we have nine places of worship, all struggling for existence, and we are threatened with the establishment of two more."[79] In reaching out to this pluralistic community, Bishop Kerfoot's priority was given to those immigrants who hailed from the British Isles and brought with them a historic and familial attachment to the Anglican way. Many of these "old-country church people" (Kerfoot's phrase) had been drawn to the region

---

76. *Our Diocese*, January 1877. The bishop recommended Bishop Hobart's "Candidate for Confirmation Instructed," and Bishop Meade's "Candidate for Confirmation Self-Examined."

77. *Our Diocese*, May 1872. It was not always easy to get the wealthier parishes to look beyond their immediate concerns. At the diocese's first annual convention, the Committee to Increase the Episcopal Fund of the diocese reported that while it had raised over $40,000 from nineteen parishes, another eighteen had failed to respond (including the principal opponents of erecting a diocese in the first place, the Pittsburgh parishes of St. Andrew and St. James). *Convention Journal*, May 16–18, 1866, 51–52.

78. *Our Diocese*, November 1874.

79. *Convention Journal*, May 16–18, 1866, 78.

by the promise of work in the iron and coal industry. Kerfoot frequently implored clergy in the Church of England to warn parishioners bound for America of the need to sustain their religious observances abroad and of the fact that the Episcopal Church—as a constituent member of the Anglican family—could serve them in that regard. In the mid-1870s, he directly negotiated an arrangement with the archbishop of Canterbury, whereby letters commendatory would be issued by the English clergy to immigrants to America, with instructions to seek out a religious community akin to those of the Church of England.[80]

Such work was not solely confined to English-speaking immigrants. During an episcopal visit to Wood's Run near Allegheny City, Kerfoot encountered a congregation of Welshmen who taught Sunday school in their own language. At worship, although the sermon and service were in English, the hymns were sung in Welsh. "The Bishop told them ... of his knowledge of the fact that the Welsh in Wales, as well as here in America, felt their native tongue to be the *language of their religion*, whatever other tongue they might use in their common life and business," the diocesan newspaper reported. Kerfoot also expressed the hope that laymen would be found to read the services and teach children their catechism in Welsh.[81]

The bishop took his responsibility to the isolated rural missions of his diocese extremely seriously. "We had a very weary ride over, or rather through, very bad roads to Waynesburg," he wrote of an 1867 visitation, "where at long intervals some ministers of ours held services years ago. We held service and I preached in the Court House, where we had a large and reverent congregation. We were guests of a family once ours, in which ... the Prayer Book, and the memories of the early Church home, hallowed and taught by it, still kept their hold. Time has been sadly lost in that south-western part of the Diocese."[82] Mission, the bishop warned the diocesan convention of 1870, needed to be focused on support for former residents of Great Britain working in the lumber, oil, iron, and coal regions who were used to an established church that did not depend on the voluntary support of its members. Funding for diocesan missions in southwestern Pennsylvania needed to be of the same order as that

---

80. *Convention Journal*, June 8–10, 1869, 40; *Convention Journal*, June 9–10, 1875, 51.
81. *Our Diocese*, March 1879.
82. *Convention Journal*, May 21–23, 1867, 69.

provided for missions in the Great Plains and Rocky Mountains, until the new Episcopalians had adjusted to the need to support their own congregation directly.[83]

The new industrial missions presented a unique set of problems for Episcopal clergy. In Camelsville, George Easter established the Dunbar Furnace mission to serve around four hundred ironworkers at a facility run by a local businessman who reportedly paid good wages and provided comfortable homes. While Easter initially had to hold services in a schoolhouse, the manager promised to build a chapel as soon as possible.[84] Such missions also contributed to better general understanding of the Episcopal Church. "Already there exists a more intelligent appreciation of the Church's stability in the community and of her Protestant as well as Catholic character and history," the priest conducting the monthly services at Immanuel mission in Washington County reported in 1878.[85] Many missionary clergy had vast areas of territory to cover and a rigorous schedule of preaching, and they continued to be plagued by underfunding. Throughout Kerfoot's episcopate, the diocesan board of missions made frequent requests for additional contributions because local parishes could not afford to supplement the missionary subsidy.[86]

Some problems were common both to the humble mission and the established parish. Many people, especially in large towns and cities, were reported to no longer be attending church on a weekly basis and those who did were not necessarily better off. "Scores of people that sit before us every Sunday," reported one priest in 1876, "do not know when we make a quotation, unless we give chapter and verse, and many can not tell whether we quote from Tupper, or Solomon and Isaiah." Irregular attendance led to indifference to the sacraments and other ordinances.[87] As congregational life grew more sophisticated, even the parish choir could become a source of contention. Bishop Kerfoot admitted in 1873 that a thwarted choirmaster could be a source of parish conflict, but warned

---

83. *Convention Journal*, June 14–16, 1870, 55–58 (quotation on 56).

84. *Our Diocese*, November 1872.

85. *Convention Journal*, June 12–13, 1878, 94.

86. *Our Diocese*, March 1874; *Convention Journal*, June 9–10, 1880, 34–35.

87. *Our Diocese*, December 1876. While one cannot say with authority who "Tupper" might be, Henry Allen Tupper (1828–1902) was a prominent Baptist clergyman who became corresponding secretary of the board of foreign missions of the Southern Baptist Convention in 1872.

rectors not to tolerate such behavior. "The only course for a Rector," he explained, "is to assume and act upon his rights and give his orders... He may wisely give his choir some scope for artistic music... But on ordinary Sundays the canticles should be chanted and the hymns should be sung to plain congregational chant."[88]

Financial instability was also a cause for concern. During his first year, Kerfoot was obliged to address the case of a church in Fayette County, which had been erected and consecrated several years previously on the understanding that it was debt-free. Subsequently, most of the founding families moved out of the district, with the result that an $800 loan made by one parishioner remained outstanding. Since the building was already consecrated, the bishop refused to abandon it, but chose to transform it into a mission to the unchurched. Of equal concern to him was the situation in Etna, where it was unclear who actually owned St. Matthew's Church, leading Kerfoot to urge those who contributed to the erection of a church to make sure ownership was always vested in the vestry.[89]

In 1870, the bishop established an incorporated board of trustees for the diocese (chosen annually by diocesan convention) to which gifts of land and money for future parishes could be entrusted, so that no potential gift would be lost because a local organization did not exist to make use of it.[90] Two years later, St. Paul's, Monongahela City, had to be saved from a sheriff's sale after getting into excessive debt. The board of trustees sold off the rectory but retained the church building for future use. By contrast, the parishioners of St. Stephen's Church, Sewickley, methodically acquired land for a parish plant, successively erected an inexpensive church building, an adequate rectory, and a schoolhouse, and swiftly cleared themselves of outstanding debt. Other parishes, the bishop concluded, could "get timely lessons [from St. Stephen's] in the prudence, correct taste, economy and efficiency, which are—too often—only learned too late, if at all, from experience."[91]

The lack of uniformity in financial matters was equally evident when it came to the matter of parish government, since the secular courts generally issued parishes whatever form of charter they requested. Kerfoot

88. *Our Diocese*, February 1873.

89. *Convention Journal*, May 16–18, 1866, 21–22; *Convention Journal*, May 21–23, 1867, 47–48.

90. *Convention Journal*, June 14–16, 1870, 53.

91. *Our Diocese*, May 1872; *Convention Journal*, May 21–23, 1867, 40 (quotation).

encouraged vestries to follow a common standard in order to promote a uniform body of parish law. He also welcomed the emergence of free churches, which had abolished pew rents and substituted a universal pledge system, of which Allegheny City's Emmanuel Church was an early pioneer. "There is no compulsion," the rector of Emmanuel explained, "other than that of conscience constraining all to be true to their own freely-offered pledge," but being a contributor of record was a necessary prerequisite to enjoying full rights of participation. In 1875, an amendment was proposed to the model parish charter allowing parishes to extend the franchise to all members (contributing and noncontributing) who acknowledged the authority of the church. The clergy were evenly divided on the issue, with sixteen joining the bishop in opposition and sixteen supporting it, but among the parish delegations only five were willing to endorse the change, while seventeen opposed it and another two were divided.[92]

Institutionally, Pittsburgh Episcopalians also made some progress, although constrained by financial considerations. Bishop Kerfoot was a strong promoter of Christian education, praising the work of Pittsburgh's Bishop Bowman Institute for girls and the Kenwood School for boys in New Brighton.[93] Two years later, the diocesan committee on education offered a more ambitious plan, calling for every parish to establish a parochial school and for the diocese to organize high school academies. If parishes could not afford to do this, committee members declared, then local clergy and laity should be involved in public school board elections and cooperate with other Protestant bodies to resist the Catholic threat. From such a position, they could ensure that public school teachers were at least Christian—if not Anglican—and that Protestant ministers could give moral and religious instruction in the schools.[94] Although religious schools with an Anglican veneer did not materialize, some parishes did separate themselves from the pan-Protestant phenomenon of Union Sunday school classes, which they thought diluted doctrine. The Sunday school of St. Stephen's, Sewickley, was replaced by Prayer Book–centered

---

92. *Convention Journal*, June 8–10, 1869, 58–59; *Our Diocese*, February 1872, November 1872 (quotation); *Convention Journal*, June 9–10, 1875, 17–19, 26–27.

93. *Convention Journal*, May 16–18, 1866, 24, 29.

94. *Convention Journal*, June 9–11, 1868, 63–69.

catechetical services, involving recitation of portions of the catechism followed by catechizing of those children present.[95]

The Episcopal Church also aspired to works of corporate mercy, but again its resources in this part of the state were limited. The Church Home endured, but was heavily dependent on annual donations. By 1879, it supported sixty-four children and seven aged women and was taking on maturing boys as apprentices for various Pittsburgh firms.[96] A more dramatic development had come in 1866, when the Pittsburgh Church Guild was established to unite city laymen in charitable acts that could not be undertaken by one parish. With 250 students in 1867, it offered organized classes in arithmetic, geometry, and mechanical drawing in both English and German and maintained a free reading room. In 1871, some of these classes were replaced with free public lectures on scientific and practical subjects. In 1869, the guild opened a dispensary available to all regardless of creed, to which city doctors gave their services free for one hour, six days a week. Medicines were furnished to those unable to pay for them and the guild also funded home visits by a physician where necessary.[97]

Beyond Pittsburgh, Bishop Kerfoot asserted the Anglo Catholic view that Christian unity was most likely to be achieved through Anglican solidarity and greater contact with the more liturgical churches. In 1874, he attended the Old Catholic Congress and met the movement's leading theologian, Joseph Von Döllinger, in Bonn.[98] He was also deeply impressed by the spirit of the first two Lambeth Conferences. "These rapidly growing and multiplying Anglican Churches of ours, are too much *one*

---

95. *Convention Journal*, June 12–13, 1878, 61.

96. *Convention Journal*, June 11–12, 1879, 104–5.

97. *Our Diocese*, August 1872. In 1874, a group of deaconesses was brought in to occupy the refurbished home for the Pittsburgh Church Guild, from whence the deaconesses would lead mothers' meetings, visit the poor and the sick, and hold Bible classes. Some had been trained at the Bishop Potter Memorial House in New York. *Our Diocese*, March 1874.

98. Harrison, *Life of Kerfoot*, 2:562–78; *Convention Journal*, June 9–10, 1875, 52–53. "The struggle there is to break off chains from intellect and conscience, and from freedom, civil and religious. The lesson to us here, is to see to it in time, that the like chains be not wrought craftily, and fastened on us and our children. No wise man will overlook the peril. American forges may be worked by foreign muscle and skill, in this sense as in others; and in this age and land of ours, even faster than in other and older ones, the manacles supposed to be discarded and renounced, might be reproduced and locked, before Americans wake up" (52).

to live and work apart comfortably; and are too strong and spreading to work apart safely; and too brave and independent to fear each other in a blessed co-partnership under Christ, in their holy task of winning souls and building up the kingdom," he told the 1879 diocesan convention. "We need each other's counsel, and the united effort that not only joins hand to hand, but gains tenfold fresh might from the union. Such Conferences not only bring out to our glad sight the wonderful unity this church begets in all essential truth and worship, but they also keep the one Faith written out brightly in the old lines of catholic Truth; these old lines traced afresh in living colors, which the truthful and obedient shall hereafter see with thankful memories of our counsels, when we shall have gone where the Truth and its sunlight shall never grow dim."[99] It was to be one of his last convention addresses, for in 1881 the first bishop of Pittsburgh died, exhausted by the toll that life in western Pennsylvania inevitably took.

99. *Convention Journal*, June 11–12, 1879, 29; Harrison, *Life of Kerfoot*, 2:446–74, 579–613.

PART TWO

Mission to America, 1882–1943

3

Proclaiming the "National Church Idea"

Cortlandt Whitehead and Industrial America, 1882–1909

For many in the Diocese of Pittsburgh, the mood in 1881 was far from upbeat. "Within the past few years," one Washington County resident explained, "the diocese has fallen continually behind what it used to be. Its contributions for missions . . . are not up to what they were during the most stringent times of the most recent panic. The clergy are generally low church, but poorly educated and indifferent men, quite lacking in energy or spirit; they are contented if they get their own salaries and the affairs of their parishes are tolerable. A spirit of Congregationalism pervades the whole diocese. There is not much going on of any sort; the diocese, clergy and laity alike, are dead spiritually and this seems to be generally admitted."[1]

Despite these concerns, no fewer than thirteen clergymen vied to succeed Bishop Kerfoot, including two missionary bishops, John Spalding of Colorado (formerly a priest in Erie) and Daniel Tuttle of Utah. Other strong contenders included William Hitchcock of Trinity Church, Pittsburgh, and Cortlandt Whitehead of Church of the Nativity in Bethlehem, Pennsylvania. Born in New York City in 1842, Whitehead attended Yale University and then studied at Philadelphia Divinity School from 1863 to 1867 (with a year of service on the U.S. Sanitary Commission in 1864). He was called as a missionary to Colorado, where his achievements led his missionary bishop to appoint him to the diocesan stand-

---

1. J. K. Mendenhall to Rev. Cortlandt Whitehead, October 30, 1881, RG2/2.1, box 2BP, Archives of the Episcopal Diocese of Pittsburgh, Pittsburgh, Pennsylvania (hereafter referenced as EDP).

ing committee only a year after his ordination. Returning to Bethlehem in 1870, Whitehead became rector of Church of the Nativity, where he helped plant both an independent daughter church and a mission and began work on a church hospital. While his name may not have been on the lips of every Pittsburgh Episcopalian, it was at least familiar to the members of St. Paul's, Erie, which offered him the rectorship only a year before he was elected bishop of Pittsburgh.[2]

The episcopal candidates were also subject to more scrutiny than in 1865, with a conference of clergy (lay delegates were not invited) discussing their merits prior to the vote. Although the heavyweight local candidate (Hitchcock) declined his nomination, some of his clerical colleagues were determined to select a Pittsburgher. Hitchcock received the votes of 7 of his fellow presbyters, compared to 8 for Whitehead, 6 for Tuttle, and the rest divided among the other candidates. Subsequent rounds became a two-man contest, with Whitehead receiving 16 votes to Hitchcock's 10 on the fourth ballot. After a motion for the clergy to retire for further consultation failed, the delegates elected Whitehead on the fifth ballot. The hour being late, the lay delegates adjourned for the night, a move interpreted by the press as heralding Whitehead's rejection. The following day they spent some time in secret session and even called in two of the clergy delegates for questioning, but ultimately emerged to announce their approval of Whitehead by a vote of 25–6.[3] Whitehead's admirers later assured him that no electioneering had been involved in the vote and that the clergy who favored other candidates had done so out of personal affection, not party spirit.[4]

Forty years later, Whitehead could afford to be magnanimous. "Only two men in the Diocese, I was told," he wrote in 1921, "had ever seen me—one a clergyman and one a layman—neither of whom voted for me—men of sense and fine discernment."[5] The new bishop of Pittsburgh

2. Ibid.; Rt. Rev. George M. Randall to Rev. Cortlandt Whitehead, July 21, 1869, Secretary of the Vestry of St. Paul's Parish, Erie, to Rev. Cortlandt Whitehead, January 22, 1880, RG2/2.2, box 3BP, EDP.

3. Rev. W. R. MacKay to Rev. Cortlandt Whitehead, October 24, 1881, RG2/2.1, box 2BP, EDP; *Special Convention Journal*, October 19–20, 1881, 40–45.

4. Rev. A. B. Putnam to Rev. Cortlandt Whitehead, October 22, 1881, J. K. Mendenhall to Rev. Cortlandt Whitehead, October 25, 1881, RG2/2.1, box 2BP, EDP.

5. *Church News*, September 1921. This was part of a series of episcopal reminiscences published in the *Church News* to celebrate Whitehead's forty years in office.

also registered the lay dissatisfaction with an electoral process that limited lay involvement to simple confirmation or rejection of the clergy's selection. Only seven months later, he suggested that it might be necessary to revise the process so that the clergy and lay orders might exercise their electoral rights conjointly.[6] Ironically, given Whitehead's long tenure in office, it would be forty years before Pittsburgh laymen would be granted that privilege.

THE END OF THE GILDED AGE, 1882–1892

"You will not find it hard to succeed Bp K[erfoot]," John Henry Hopkins Jr. assured the bishop-elect in October 1881. "He was not popular. Your genial and pleasant manners will make you more friends there in one year than he made in fifteen."[7] Whitehead nevertheless still had something to learn about diplomacy. His request for a schedule of parish visitations before he had even arrived in Pittsburgh alarmed members of the diocesan standing committee, accustomed to a less intense style of oversight.[8] Consecration day also proved far from auspicious. "It was a day to be long remembered," the bishop recalled in 1892, "for the mingling of fog and smoke and sleet and rain. Heavy clouds obscured the sky and a curtain of mist hung over our heads in the Church itself. It was one of the worst of what we call 'Pittsburgh days'—really the worst I ever saw."[9]

Whitehead was certainly aware of the limitations under which his predecessor had labored, not least the lack of facilities for a bishop. In his first convention address, he urged delegates to provide funds for the erection of a building to house his office, a reading room for clergy, and a place where diocesan committees could hold meetings.[10] Four years later—during which time, various city parishes made their facilities available to the diocesan leadership—the "hard-headed businessmen of the Diocese" finally succumbed to his pleas and set aside money to rent rooms, first at the Jackson Building on Penn Avenue and Sixth Avenue and later in the

6. *Convention Journal*, May 10–11, 1882, 44.

7. Rev. J. H. Hopkins to Rev. Cortlandt Whitehead, October 31, 1881, RG2/2.1, box 2BP, EDP.

8. Rev. Robert Coster to Bp. Cortlandt Whitehead, January 5, 1882, RG2/2.1, box 2BP, EDP.

9. *Convention Journal*, June 8–9, 1892, 21.

10. *Convention Journal*, May 10–11, 1882, 45–46.

Lewis Block on Smithfield Street and Sixth Avenue, not far from Trinity Church.[11] One perceptive (and anonymous) observer viewed such delays as indicative of undue episcopal dependence on wealthy urban elites. The sooner the diocese erected a cathedral to provide the bishop with an independent institutional resource and facilities, he concluded, the better. Absent such a provision, the situation in the rural districts would be that of a Fayette County Episcopalian who was told by her neighbor that "she had heard of Episcopalians, but had never seen any of 'em about these parts."[12]

Bishop Whitehead also lamented the absence of Episcopal schools and hospitals in southwestern Pennsylvania, blaming the generosity of local Episcopalians toward nondenominational charities. Compared with the Church of England, the Episcopal Church had a poor record of service.[13] Such neglect was all the more disturbing, he felt, because local Episcopalians appeared to have no qualms about trusting their health and the education of their children to those acknowledging a very different religious authority. "Our own people send their children to Roman schools," the bishop declared in 1888, "and permit the sick to lie within Roman hospitals, ministered to by those of an alien faith, while our own schools, where are they? And our own hospitals are unbuilt."[14]

Some Episcopalians did endeavor to address Whitehead's concerns. Trinity Hall in Washington, Pennsylvania, already provided schooling for boys, and a new school for girls was opened at Brookville in 1888 (the latter promoted its academic excellence by promising a certificate of proficiency that would ensure unconditional acceptance to Wellesley College).[15] In 1889, staunch Episcopalians Dr. Felix Brunot and his wife opened a boardinghouse for "the better class of working women"

---

11. *Convention Journal*, June 9–10, 1886, 41–42; *Church News*, October 1921. Whitehead later complained that his suggestions that either a building be erected and the remaining space leased (as the Methodists had done) or that Trinity Church add a third story to its parish house were both ignored.

12. *Church News*, August 1887.

13. *Church News*, Septuagesima 1886. The bishop encouraged the greater consecration of wealth to the establishment of parish endowments. "No man," he said, "has the right before God or man to make a will or settle an estate without a definite and equitable recognition of God's share in the property they have acquired."

14. *Convention Journal*, June 6–7, 1888, 61.

15. *Convention Journal*, May 10–11, 1882, 43; *Convention Journal*, June 6–7, 1888, 60; *Convention Journal*, June 5–6, 1889, 66.

employed as shopgirls and clerks in Pittsburgh. This house offered rooms at a weekly charge of between $3 and $3.50 and guaranteed medical care for any resident who fell ill.[16] Even more enduring—in terms of its wider impact on the City of Pittsburgh—was the $550,000 legacy bequeathed by John Shoenberger in 1890 for the erection of a public hospital. Under the bequest, nine Episcopal laymen served as hospital trustees, a provision that sparked one of the last open confrontations between the High and Low Church factions in the diocese. Evangelicals made every effort to elect "safe" men to serve on the board and to block any attempt to build a hospital chapel or appoint a chaplain (whom they feared would be a closet Romanist), but their declining influence in the counsels of the diocese ensured their defeat on both points.[17]

A more immediate concern to the bishop was the continued failure of the diocese to provide adequate financial support for local missions. Shortly after his arrival, Whitehead was obliged to circulate a letter begging for contributions because his treasury was empty.[18] Ironically, one cause of this shortfall appears to have been formerly mission-minded urban Evangelicals, many of whom viewed the domestic mission field solely as a device for bringing more Anglo Catholics into the diocese and preferred to focus their energies on foreign missions. As one local observer put it, they constantly asserted "the evil of High Churchmanship and solemnly affirmed their opinion that every High Churchman was nothing more or less than a Jesuit in disguise."[19] Hostility to local mission work could also be found among the laity, though for different reasons. "Why should the Church be sending men to new places to start new parishes and erect new church buildings," one critic demanded in 1889, "when there is a parish with a nice little church building free from debt and tastefully fitted up and with a small but, from the evidence before me, an energetic and earnest congregation, ready and willing to support the rector to the extent of their means and by their personal efforts, and all going to waste for want of a proper man to fill the place? It would seem to the mind of the layman

16. *Church News,* June–July 1889.

17. The margin by which the convention voted to consider the bequest was only 48–42. *Convention Journal,* June 11–12, 1890, 30, 38–42, 45–46; Rev. George Rogers, "Recollections of the Church in Pittsburgh Thirty Years Ago," 8–9, June 15, 1915, RG5/1.1, box 1DP, EDP. See also Brignano, *Story of St. Margaret's.*

18. *Convention Journal,* May 10–11, 1882, 40.

19. Rogers, "Recollections of the Church," 15.

that the Church should first strive to hold on and strengthen what she has, and after that, if able, to occupy other and new fields."[20]

Such views cut little ice with diocesan missionaries, many of whom doubted the effectiveness of outreach to the unchurched by established parishes. Many of the latter reported paltry rates of growth. Between 1876 and 1890, for example, the three parishes in Erie increased their total membership from 513 to 523 (with a *decline* from 543 to 523 between 1885 and 1890), despite a doubling of the local population. "This means," explained one Erie clergyman, "that the efforts of clergy and laity for fourteen years, spending men and money, have brought us as return a gain of only ten souls."[21] Rural missions, especially in areas where churches were as yet thinly distributed, offered much greater prospects of success. Between 1884 and 1892, no fewer than thirty-eight missions were established in southwestern Pennsylvania, of which twenty-one were organized outside Allegheny County, most notably in Armstrong, Cambria, and Westmoreland counties. Apart from St. Mary's, Charleroi (1891), however, most of the enduring parishes were located within the jurisdictions of Pittsburgh and Allegheny City. Amongst these were included Atonement, Carnegie (1884); St. Matthew's, Homestead (1884); All Saints, Brighton Heights (1889); and St. George's, West End (1890).

The struggle between parish and mission came to a head at the diocesan convention of 1884. Although convention delegates reaffirmed the existing rule that unincorporated missions (regarded as "minors" in legal terms) should not be given representation at convention, a strong minority report observed that in the previous year twelve missions with a total of 495 members had contributed $519 to church work, while twelve parishes with 183 members had contributed only $139. Was it equitable, lawyer Hill Burgwin demanded, for the latter to send thirty-six representatives to convention and the former to send none? The idea of equal lay representation for all incorporated parishes also disfranchised many of the laity in large parishes and ran counter to the principle of "representative democratic government."[22]

Burgwin's observations can arguably be viewed as an early temporal marker of the shift from the countercultural model of the separatist era

---

20. *Church News*, January 1889.
21. *Church News*, July 1890.
22. *Convention Journal*, June 11–12, 1884, 26–35 (quotation on 32).

to the more accommodating style of the institutionalist era. For Burgwin and his supporters, church polity was intended to be organized on the same basic lines as the secular political system, responsive to the general will of those who constituted its membership. Burgwin also enjoyed the backing of his bishop, who, a couple of years later, argued the case that well-organized missions should be able to petition for admission to convention if they had fifteen adult communicant members and were able to contribute $200 to support a clergyman.[23]

Serving a mission was no more of a sinecure for clergy during the 1880s than it had been during the 1850s. Many were obliged to adopt Methodist methods of circuit riding if they were to reach all those for whom they were nominally responsible.[24] The rector of Good Shepherd, Hazelwood, also had responsibility for St. Stephen's mission in McKeesport. His "parish" was forty miles in length, and included 170 families—most of them mechanics, barge builders, mill men, and coal diggers—with whom the clergy made contact at no fewer than thirty individual "stations." In confirmation of the fact that missions frequently attracted greater loyalty from their members than did parishes, St. Stephen's reported more communicant members than Good Shepherd.[25] An equally daunting task faced the rector of St. Mark's Church on Pittsburgh's South Side, who was responsible for a more modest eighteen square miles of territory. Evangelism—in the form of revival meetings, special services, and public lectures—proved an unending struggle. The parish also incurred significant debts in erecting a building to serve as headquarters for its most successful undertaking, a church guild devoted to social and devotional outreach. When St. Mark's proved unable to finance its indebtedness in 1891, the diocesan standing committee was sympathetic but unable to provide any assistance.[26]

---

23. *Convention Journal*, June 9–10, 1886, 62–63.

24. See Whitehead's commendation of circuit riding in *Convention Journal*, May 10–11, 1882, 42.

25. The mission was known for its enthusiastic worship: "Every one who attends these services feels, nay, knows, that he or she has a voice, and they are not ashamed to use that voice in the response and amens. The amens, by the way, are sung, and I for one wish that it could be made the custom in all the churches." *Diocesan Chronicle*, March 1883.

26. *Diocesan Chronicle*, May 1884; Standing Committee Minutes, May 11, 1891, RG4A/1.8, box 9DRB, EDP.

Not every mission was subject to such financial insecurity, and some clergy were singularly favored. In the town of Foxburg, which had a population of only eight hundred, there was but one religious institution—the Church of Our Father—and this was overseen by an Episcopal priest. This singular state of affairs could be traced to the economic dominance of one family, which owned all the land in the community and refused to sell or lease any other building for religious purposes.[27] Episcopalians in Townville did not have such a sweeping monopoly on public worship, but the local mission did enjoy the patronage of a wealthy woman and her family. While it had few communicant members, the heartiness of the mission's worship drew many "sectarians" to its services. Indeed, 85 percent of those who attended were something other than Episcopalian.[28]

In the absence of a wealthy patron, missions had to resort to other expedients if they did not wish to worship in the open air or the local schoolhouse. Appeals to employers to provide land for the erection of chapels for their employees were sometimes successful, but came at the potential cost of clerical independence.[29] As noted above, appeals for diocesan support faced strong resistance from urban parishes. At the 1890 diocesan convention a bitter fight erupted over parish assessments in the amount of $6,500 for diocesan missions, with a resolution making such assessments "binding and obligatory" going down to defeat by a margin of 49-29. Only a year later, the bishop found it necessary to chastise most of his parishes for defaulting on their mission commitments.[30] In 1892, the diocesan convention finally responded to Whitehead's concerns by establishing a diocesan missionary committee (elected by the convention) and regional convocations (composed of all the local clergy and one lay representative from each parish), to assume responsibility for the missionary districts.[31]

Perhaps inevitably, the diocese continued to devote much of its attention to the cause of English immigrants, to which Bishop Kerfoot had first drawn attention. In 1886, Bishop Whitehead visited the hamlet of Fordyce,

---

27. *Diocesan Chronicle*, February 1884. The building was offered solely for Episcopal use, but was not owned by the church. *Convention Journal*, June 13-14, 1883, 43.

28. *Convention Journal*, June 13-14, 1883, 84.

29. *Convention Journal*, June 6-7, 1888, 53-54.

30. *Church News*, May 1890; *Convention Journal*, June 11-12, 1890, 37; *Church News*, February 1891.

31. *Church News*, May 1892.

eight miles from Waynesburg in Greene County, where he was introduced to an Englishman who had lived in Fordyce since 1856 but had never seen an Episcopal clergyman. On that day, the family's six adult children were baptized and subsequently confirmed in company with their mother, and the whole family then received Holy Communion.[32] Working-class immigrants could not always be relied upon to come forward with their letters of transfer, however, and many found the atmosphere of predominantly middle-class Episcopal parishes unappealing. One effort to bridge this divide was the afternoon service conducted solely by laymen (a practice common in much of the Church of England) established by Emmanuel Church in Allegheny City.[33]

Some workingmen proved much more accessible, as the 1884 request for regular services by a group of coal miners and their families in Banksville demonstrated. When St. Mark's, South Side, launched a mission for them, the rector took the opportunity to assure those attending that participation in the worship and service of the Episcopal Church was no different than "if they were worshipping in the lordly cathedral of Durham or the noble church of St. Nicholas, Newcastle-upon-Tyne, under whose shadow they, in common with himself, were nearly all reared."[34] Miners without families were not regarded as such a desirable commodity. The rector of St. George's, Irwin, complained in 1890 that the English miners living in the area provided little support for his mission.[35]

Outreach beyond the core English constituency was frequently limited by the linguistic skills of the missionaries, but ethnic groups from non-Anglican liturgical traditions did receive some attention. "We sadly need a licensed lay reader or permanent deacon," declared one parish report. "If Welsh-speaking we should at once secure a large Welsh contingent."[36] In Pittsburgh, St. Andrew's Church ran a mission to the German inhabitants of the Troy Hill district.[37] From the rural part of the diocese, a call

32. *Convention Journal*, June 8–9, 1887, 68–69.

33. *Diocesan Chronicle*, July 1884.

34. *Diocesan Chronicle*, August 1884. St. Nicholas had become a cathedral only two years before, following the carving out of the urban Diocese of Newcastle from the Diocese of Durham to serve the rapidly growing working-class population of northeastern England.

35. *Convention Journal*, June 11–12, 1890, 175.

36. *Convention Journal*, June 13–14, 1883, 68.

37. *Diocesan Chronicle*, May 1884.

to action came in 1888, when an Episcopalian living in McKean County reported that many local farmers had formerly been nominal members of the Church of Sweden (the only continental Lutheran body to maintain apostolic succession at the Reformation). Most Swedish immigrants, however, either attended no church after their arrival or preferred Methodist and Baptist congregations willing to provide services in their mother tongue. "None but those living in the northern part of the Diocese," the local correspondent concluded, "can realize how great, how urgent the need for [a Swedish General Missionary] is. It will not do to say that in this Diocese we have as much as we can do to take care of the English speaking people."[38]

If one bond united the Swedish farmer with the Welsh miner, the affluent parish with the humble mission, it was the American Book of Common Prayer and the liturgical practices that it sustained. Though not a High Churchman in the style of John Barrett Kerfoot, Cortlandt Whitehead demanded that his clergy be diligent in observing the authorized forms of worship. At his first diocesan convention he made very clear his disdain for a causal attitude toward the sacramental element of worship:

> We do not uphold the Church's teaching if the minister's surplice be ragged, patched, or spoiled, and his stole torn, its fringe all frayed and worn away. We fall lamentably below a right standard, and lend ourselves to the prevailing irreverence and irreligion, if the Communion vessels be not scrupulously neat, and the appointments of the Lord's House be not of the very best we can afford. And surely, to use the Lord's House for the unseemly wrangles of a Vestry or Parish Meeting, or the discussions of parliamentary practice, is to treat holy things profanely.[39]

Whitehead also strove to instill in the laity a willingness to receive the Eucharist frequently, something anathema to an earlier generation of Evangelicals. "To come but seldom to communion," he reflected in 1883, "is both ultra-Protestant and Roman and is the result of erroneous teaching, which causes men to look upon the Sacrament from afar and with

---

38. *Church News*, November 1888. Bishop Whitehead added his pleas on behalf of the Swedes at the 1890 convention. *Convention Journal*, June 11–12, 1890, 76–77.

39. *Convention Journal*, May 10–11, 1882, 50–51.

dread, rather than as the Feast of the Communion, of nearness, of gracious approach to God."[40]

Evangelical clergy repudiated Whitehead's views and frequently ignored the forms of service laid down in the Book of Common Prayer, preferring to make the sermon the center of their worship. One Pittsburgh clergyman went to the lengths of refusing to wear clerical garb, instead sporting a gray suit and either a felt hat (in winter) or a straw one (in summer).[41] Observance of Prayer Book rubrics was a frequent source of conflict, illustrated in an 1883 newspaper debate between two clergy of the diocese, William MacKay and William Wilson, on the subject of extemporaneous prayer. MacKay was a vocal opponent of according the minister any discretion in how to frame the prayers of the people. "[The people] are sure of the Prayer Book," he explained, "they know well that though the Pulpit may preach 'Rome,' 'Canterbury,' or 'Geneva,' the Prayer Book will always be true to Gospel Truth and to 'the Faith once delivered.'" The Book of Common Prayer embodied the life and teaching of the church, MacKay concluded, and should not be subject to individual ministerial whim. Wilson retorted that, in an era of increased liturgical knowledge, even priests who believed in the integrity of Prayer Book worship needed some discretion. There was, moreover, an ecumenical dimension: "Other bodies of Christians are drawn to us because of the catholicity of our creeds and doctrinal teaching and they will look for a corresponding breadth in our ritual. As the apostolic order and authority of the Church is seen apostolic liberty will be expected and required. We have Catholic creed and doctrine, let us not circumscribe them with sectarian form and practice."[42]

Wilson's desire for liturgical liberty had implications for Episcopal devotionalism, particularly as the choral element in worship grew more sophisticated. In 1888, Trinity Church, Pittsburgh, became the first congregation to maintain a vested choir. Other city parishes—including

---

40. *Convention Journal*, June 13–14, 1883, 45.

41. Rogers, "Recollections of the Church," 16.

42. *Diocesan Chronicle*, January 1883, February 1883. After the General Convention of 1889, Bishop Whitehead declared that the Prayer Book revision that ultimately resulted in the 1892 edition had been largely that of "restoring much that our American revisors a hundred years ago erased." While there had been few new additions to the Prayer Book, he wrote, much greater flexibility in its use had been achieved. *Church News*, November 1889.

St. Peter's; St. John's; St James's; St. Mark's; Grace, Mt. Washington, and Emmanuel, Allegheny City—soon followed suit.[43] Hardly surprisingly, such musical professionalism soon led to parochial rivalry, which often played out in the diocesan press. In May 1891, a correspondent styling himself "Dan Dore Ezekiels" proposed a choir festival, but one limited to only three choirs, those of Trinity, St. Peter's, and Emmanuel, and excluding female vocalists. One clergyman retorted that standards could be raised only by a program of festivals open to all those willing to practice, while another correspondent called the idea of excluding girls "selfish and prejudiced." Ezekiels remained unrepentant, however, arguing that the voices of women and boys did not mix and that most of the local choirs were unable to sing in harmony: "For, such as most of them are, they cannot sing one Amen, be the cadence plagal or radical, without unpleasant effect; because untrained or badly trained boys' voices, and girls' too, are harsh if they but utter a sound. It would be mistaken charity to admit all in their current status."[44] If the choir festival ultimately took place, there is no record of it in the diocesan press, but an Episcopal interest in musical niceties had evidently become the mood du jour.

Liturgical freedom had decided limits as far as Bishop Whitehead was concerned. When a number of parishes experimented with the innovation of the Sunday school, the bishop warned against special Sunday school liturgies not based on Anglican rubrics. Keeping this aspect of Anglican identity uppermost was all the more important in Pittsburgh, where many people had "strong prejudice against both [the Episcopal Church and the Book of Common Prayer]."[45] Many Pittsburgh clergy needed little encouragement to avoid the Sunday school model, which they considered to detract from the work of parents and priests. When the rectors of two large parishes proposed to disband their parish schools and instruct the children themselves, however, the diocesan newspaper urged caution, fearful about the exclusion of the laity from the process of Christian education.[46] One layman was even more incensed by the news, pointing out that any rector pursuing such a strategy would be obliged to teach children of all ages in the same class, an increasingly rare practice in

43. *Church News*, January 1890.
44. *Church News*, May 1891, June 1891, August 1891 (quotation).
45. *Convention Journal*, June 13–14, 1883, 47.
46. *Diocesan Chronicle*, August 1883.

the public school system. An even more obvious danger was that incensed parents might decide to send their children to Methodist, Presbyterian, or Baptist churches that still offered Sunday school instruction. "Is it impossible for our rectors to take all available lay-helpers and train them in churchly-ways and churchly-ideas," he demanded, "so that they may in our Sunday schools promote growth in grace and growth in the knowledge of God?"[47]

Sunday school might be contested ground, but parish ministries dedicated to evangelism and Christian service were universally accepted. Just before Whitehead arrived in Pittsburgh, the women of the diocese organized a local branch of the women's auxiliary to foster missionary activity.[48] In 1884, a similar organization—the Guild of the Good Shepherd—was established to provide a structure for worship and church work for children in the mission stations and to connect them with their counterparts in more established parishes.[49] By contrast, a men's auxiliary—the Brotherhood of St. Andrew—was not organized in the diocese until the early 1890s, when the Pittsburgh congregations of St. John's and St. James and Good Shepherd, Hazelwood, all formed parish chapters. Initially, their work consisted of establishing reading rooms for the benefit of their working-class neighborhoods, and organizing lay visitation. By 1892, there were twenty-five chapters of the Brotherhood, with a total membership of three hundred (half of them in Allegheny City and Pittsburgh).[50] The bishop also urged established parishes to identify potential lay readers whose ability to lead certain services would free their rector to hold services in neighboring towns lacking an incumbent clergyman.[51]

By the late 1880s, Whitehead had begun to appreciate the need to organize a more active lay auxiliary, which could substitute for the clergy in leading services in missions outside their home parish. In February 1889, the Laymen's Missionary League (LML) was born. Modeled on the

---

47. *Diocesan Chronicle*, September 1883.
48. *Church News*, March 1882.
49. *Convention Journal*, June 10–11, 1885, 89–92; *Church News*, January 1890.
50. *Church News*, September 1891; *Convention Journal*, June 8–9, 1892, 41–42.
51. *Our Diocese*, September 1882. Whitehead always stressed that lay readers should confine their duties to the reading of Morning Prayer, Evening Prayer, and the Litany, and that they should officiate only from the lectern or prayer desk, not the altar.

88   PART TWO: MISSION TO AMERICA, 1882–1943

Lay Evangelistic Association of the Diocese of Durham (England),[52] the LML provided lay volunteers to serve in both missions and public charitable institutions. Within a year, the LML boasted forty active members, including four "Evangelists" who—after passing an examination in the English Bible and the Book of Common Prayer—were free to preach their own sermons (as opposed to merely reading from the published sermons of clergy of the Church of England or the Episcopal Church). The LML provided a particularly vital service to English and Welsh immigrants in Woods Run, Temperanceville, Chartiers, Knoxville, and Sharpsburg, where local residents worked in the iron industry and were unable to commute to Pittsburgh for Sunday services. A similar service to Pittsburgh's small but growing black population was provided by St. Cyprian's mission.[53] The League, declared the bishop, "attracts attention to the need and the duty of Lay Help. It brings out the latent forces of the Church, and is a new bond of union between the Bishop and Clergy, and Laity. It can not fail to aid in promoting that Diocesan cohesion and organization, which is a want of the Church in our time."[54]

The influence of the Diocese of Durham on Pittsburgh's Episcopalians was not confined to the LML. Bishop Whitehead was warm in his praise of Bishop Lightfoot's part in establishing the White Cross Army to promote respect for women, encourage premarital chastity, and assert equal moral standards for both sexes. In the face of what he viewed as a rising tide of immorality, Whitehead invited the young men of his diocese to follow the same approach. "We can condemn everywhere—by word and act—and ought to condemn, with the quiet vehemence of infallible truth," the bishop declared in 1884, "the vicious, sensational, and demoralizing literature, which is flooding our land engulfing our youth, making its way even into the best homes, and ruining the souls of young men and maidens alike."[55]

---

52. During his visit to England for the Lambeth Conference of 1888, Whitehead attended a service in Durham Cathedral at which fourteen lay evangelists, fourteen lay preachers, and a lay missioner were all commissioned. *Church News*, January 1889.

53. *Church News*, January 1890, March 1890, December 1890. See also the flyer "The Laymen's Missionary League, Diocese of Pittsburgh," February 1901, RG5/2.2, box 2DP, EDP.

54. *Convention Journal*, June 11–12, 1890, 81.

55. *Convention Journal*, June 11–12, 1884, 57–62 (quotation on 61).

By 1890, however, many national church leaders had begun to link campaigns on behalf of morality to wider issues of social reform on behalf of the poor and indigent. Members of the LML were encouraged to champion programs for the working classes that mirrored the university extension system now established in England and of which Oxford University's Ruskin College was the shining exemplar.[56] The League also produced a report on nondenominational church-run workingmen's clubs in Boston, Philadelphia, and New York, which concluded that substantial investment and a willingness to keep rules to a minimum were the keys to success for such an undertaking. "The freedom of the saloon must be given," the report's authors explained, "but without its bad influences ... though under the direction of the Church, there must be no church and very little religion in the management of such a club." Such clubs should provide ample forms of recreation (billiards and a gymnasium, if possible) and a reading library with a balance between entertaining and purely instructional works. The more ambitious clubs boasted an even wider array of services, including savings banks, building associations, and even free legal advice.[57] Such institutional models were as yet premature for the Diocese of Pittsburgh, yet they marked a sea change in the prevailing Episcopal culture, which would be utterly transformed by the 1900s.

The changing understanding of the role of the laity in church life would ultimately have consequences for the clergy, yet at this time change in their status was minimal and the educational standards required of them were rarely relaxed. In 1886, the standing committee refused a request from a candidate seeking ordination to be exempted from examination in the Greek Testament.[58] A year earlier, two lay members of the committee blocked an attempt to shorten the period of the diaconate of the future bishop of Erie, Rogers Israel of Christ Church, Meadville (although one lay member and three clerical members voted in favor, a three-quarters favorable vote was required).[59] While the new generation of High Church clergy might be more inclined to respect Prayer Book rubrics, the

56. *Church News*, April 1890.

57. *Church News*, May 1890.

58. Standing Committee Minutes, January 8, 1886, RG4A/1.8, box 9DRB, EDP.

59. Standing Committee Minutes, October 2, 1885, RG4A/1.8, box 9DRB, EDP. There was more flexibility by the 1890s. The standing committee, on the bishop's recommendation, recommended at least one instance of dispensation from Latin and Greek examinations and also expressed a willingness to entertain requests for a shortened diaconate. Standing Committee Minutes, February 10, 1896, December 11, 1899, RG4A/1.8, box 9DRB, EDP.

resistance of the older Evangelicals still provoked numerous adjurations from the bishop. "So many of our laity are members of societies and orders in which obedience to rule and rubrics is *absolute*," Whitehead reminded his clergy in 1886, "that we can well understand their discomfiture, when loyalty to the authority of the Divine society reaches so low a standard."[60] It would be unfair to conclude, however, that Evangelical clergy were neglectful of other aspects of the pastoral obligations. In 1882, the rector of St. Paul's, Kittanning, begged the bishop to postpone a confirmation visit because he did not believe his parish's candidates were ready. "I am afraid the work will be improperly done," he confessed, "and that all of us will be dissatisfied with the result."[61] Another clergyman called for more explicit teaching of the covenantal relationship between God and man established in baptism and the lay obligation to be part of a worshipping community. "Morality and religion should not be separated," he concluded. "The means of grace the church supplies are essential to eternal life."[62]

A TIME OF INDUSTRIAL UNREST, 1893–1900

The shift of the diocese toward more socially responsive ministries owed not a little to the profound economic changes taking place across western Pennsylvania. The region had seen steady growth and the rise of numerous company towns in the years following the Civil War, but the benefits to the working-class population varied considerably. Industrial unrest—particularly on the railroads—had seriously affected the region during the economic depression of the 1870s, but this was as nothing compared to the unrest that accompanied the depression of 1893–97. Andrew Carnegie's first employment of the Bessemer steel process in 1875 heralded an increasing shift from skilled to unskilled labor that markedly changed the ethnic and religious complexion of Pittsburgh and its environs. In 1892, the Homestead Works, overseen by Carnegie manager Henry Clay Frick, witnessed a lockout that drew national attention, with the climate of hostility only heightened by the attempted murder of Frick by a Russian-born anarchist. Resolution of the "labor question," as it was frequently dubbed, became a preoccupation of many churchmen during

60. *Convention Journal*, June 9–10, 1886, 60.

61. Rev. William W. Wilson to Bp. Cortlandt Whitehead, January 12, 1882, RG2/2.1, box 2BP, EDP.

62. *Our Diocese*, March 1882.

the 1890s, as they strove to reconcile the prevailing class conflict with their sense of America as a Christian nation.[63]

The greater involvement of Pittsburgh's Episcopalians in matters of social reform was not solely a product of local circumstance. The battles between the Anglo Catholic and Evangelical parties that had preoccupied the Episcopal Church during the 1870s gave way to the relative calm of the 1880s and 1890s. Anglo Catholics did continue their campaign to remove the phrase *Protestant* from the denomination's official title (and from the title page of the Book of Common Prayer), but the debate lacked the passion of the past. Bishop Whitehead admitted that the minority vote in support of the "change of name" at the General Convention of 1886 had been greater than anticipated, but he felt that the proceedings had been "deliberative and conservative." One of Pittsburgh's clerical delegates to the same gathering noted that he had always been critical of the term Protestant Episcopal, but only because it seemed supererogatory. "It ought to be no more necessary for this Church to parade her Protestantism," he declared, "than for a gentleman to advertise his respectability."[64]

At the diocesan level, theological controversy also declined. Members of Pittsburgh's standing committee, which had refused to approve the election of James DeKoven as bishop of Illinois, confirmed the election of DeKoven's spiritual heir Charles Grafton as bishop of Fond du Lac (Wisconsin) in 1888, with only one clerical dissent and all four lay members approving. Three years later, it was the turn of Phillips Brooks to be confirmed as bishop of Massachusetts, though two negative votes (one clerical and one lay) were recorded in this instance.[65] Brooks was the most prominent figure in the Broad Church party, many of them the offspring of Evangelicals but who found the theology of their parents too constraining. Historian Gillis Harp has demonstrated how Brooks borrowed from Evangelicalism's commitment to the individual's subjective religious experience, but abandoned both confessional standards and ecclesiastical discipline. Repudiating the Evangelical belief in the centrality of the

---

63. On the region's industrial transformation, see Krause, *Battle for Homestead*; Warren, *Triumphant Capitalism*; Blatz, "Titanic Struggles."

64. *Church News*, November 1886.

65. Standing Committee Minutes, December 5, 1888, June 5, 1891, RG4A/1.8, box 9DRB, EDP.

Fall, Brooks championed an inclusive Anglican doctrinal position entirely contrary to confessionalism.[66]

The principal Broad Church forum was the Church Congress (modeled on a movement that began within the Church of England), at which Episcopalians from various theological positions debated the issues of the day, particularly the interaction of science and theology. Beginning as a series of regional forums, the first national meeting took place in New York (despite the opposition of Bishop Henry Codman Potter) in 1874, at which papers on the relationship between capital and labor were discussed. Later meetings drew such national clerical luminaries as James DeKoven, Alexander Crummell, and William Rainsford, but the acrimonious temper of meetings during the 1880s alienated many Episcopalians, not least Bishop Whitehead.[67] "We began by having all schools of thought in the Church—'advanced,' 'high broad,' 'Evangelical'—all represented," he complained in 1882. "Now the Congress seems to be managed almost altogether by men who as a contemporary aptly puts it, seem 'to regard God only as good natured.' They gloss over or explain away the sterner aspects of Jehovah, until fear seems to have but little place in religion ... They make much of 'modern thought' and 'nineteenth century progress,' but they do not show us very clearly whither all this advance is leading them."[68] Six months later the diocesan newspaper—which usually echoed the bishop's views—defended the appropriateness of bringing presentment charges against the modernist clergyman Heber Newton.[69]

Despite episcopal reservations about the Church Congress, the institutional church movement continued to grow, particularly in the Diocese of New York. With the encouragement of Bishop Potter, men like William Rainsford came to the fore. Rainsford, who became rector of St. George's Church in New York City in 1883, was an early champion of the free church principle and created a lending library and a children's choir to appeal to the working-class children on New York's East Side. He later developed an industrial school and a gymnasium to be located on church premises for the benefit of families in the neighborhood, many of which did not belong to the parish. "I believed then and believe still that both in

---

66. Harp, *Brahmin Prophet*, esp. 207–17. See also Butler, *Standing against the Whirlwind*, 224–35.

67. Spielman, "Neglected Source."

68. *Diocesan Chronicle*, December 1882.

69. *Diocesan Chronicle*, June 1883.

cities and in country [the institutional church] must supersede the older form of religious organization," he wrote many years later. "The latter dealt with the family, provided for the family, had its family pew, and depended on patriarchal family ideas. Those ideas worked well in their time, but that time is not our time. The sort of church I was striving for should appeal to the community as well as the family."[70]

During the 1892 Homestead strike, Rainsford came to Pittsburgh to lead a mission. Stopped and searched on a city street by a Carnegie-employed detective, he was disturbed to see the families of strikers evicted from their homes and sitting on the grass verge: "I can still see the pinched despairing faces of the women, the sullen anger in the faces of the men, as they sat homeless, night coming on, in the mud . . . It was an amazing spectacle. It was not Christian, and it did not look even American to me. Next day in the church and the theatre I said so, and gave my reason for saying so."[71] Two years later, Rainsford returned to Pittsburgh to address an anniversary celebration of the Laymen's Missionary League.[72]

One of Rainsford's early disciples was George Hodges, who came to Calvary Church as an assistant in 1881. Deeply committed to parochial ministry (he had a map of the parish in his study that showed the location of every parish family), Hodges's first venture into social outreach was a day nursery for working women in the Mayflower mission district. Sadly, this came to nothing after the local Roman Catholic priest objected to what he saw as an attempt to indoctrinate the children, and only two women brought their babies. This failure led the sheepish clergyman to wonder if he could hire some children to escape the wrath of the ladies who helped establish the nursery![73]

After Hodges became rector of Calvary in 1889, he laid increasing emphasis on the civic and social responsibilities of Christians in the parish. He had also learned from the Mayflower debacle that cooperation with other denominations was an essential element of social outreach. Together with Father Morgan Sheedy of St. Peter and Paul Catholic Church, he organized a series of musical performances for families living in the tenements of the Point district. As Calvary's organist directed a

70. Rainsford, *Story of a Varied Life*, 211–15, 228–41, 249–55 (quotation on 230).
71. Ibid., 323–24 (quotation on 324).
72. *Church News*, March 1894.
73. Hodges, *George Hodges*, 60–95.

chorus of two hundred and an orchestra of thirty-five, Hodges and Sheedy jointly led devotional exercises. Hodges also promoted greater understanding between the Protestant churches, making the case for a Union Sunday school in Pittsburgh's East End, organizing a ministers' meeting, and creating a common parish paper for local churches. This last endeavor won Hodges approval from no less prominent a figure than William Reed Huntington, author of the Chicago-Lambeth Quadrilateral, the principal American contribution to Anglican self-definition during the nineteenth century. "Yours," Huntington told Hodges, "is the most practical attempt yet made within my knowledge, toward the construction of a 'Working Model' of Church Unity."[74]

In 1893, Hodges embarked upon his most ambitious project to date. Turning to leaders in the English and American settlement house movements, Samuel Barnett of Toynbee Hall, London, and Jane Adams and Robert Woods of Boston's Andover House, Hodges planned a similar undertaking for Pittsburgh. Kingsley House was organized in consultation with other local religious leaders and its first director was Kate Everett, a pupil of Jane Adams. The new settlement house undertook social research of communities in the East End and provided the local community with space for clubs and recreational facilities.[75] According to historian Roy Lubove, it "embodied two key aspects of the national settlement movement: religious idealism and dependence on the social elite for funding and support." It also set a precedent for social involvement that future generations of the Calvary Episcopal elite would feel obliged to emulate.[76]

Further north in Erie, the rector of St. Paul's Church, Franklin Spencer Spalding, endeavored to cater to the needs of the working-class population. A parish house—on the Rainsford model—was opened in 1898, providing a gymnasium with baths, an auditorium seating five hundred, a kitchen, a game room for boys, and a reading room.[77] Spalding proved to be more than just a builder, however. He spoke publicly for penal reform and against prizefighting and achieved local notoriety for a Labor Day ad-

---

74. Ibid, 96–107, 115–24 (Huntington quoted on 107). On Huntington, see Northup, "William Reed Huntington."

75. Hodges, *George Hodges*, 108–14. The settlement was named after Charles Kingsley, the English social reformer who "emphasized religion in preference to theology [and] cared a great deal more for things Christian than for things ecclesiastical" (110).

76. Lubove, "Pittsburgh," 308.

77. Melish, *Franklin Spencer Spalding*, 63–64, 69–70.

dress to workingmen in which he sympathized with their economic plight but also rebuked them for sending their wives and children out to work so that their families could afford luxuries. When the men responded by withdrawing their family members from the factories, Spalding was accused by some in his congregation of encouraging the workers to strike. Such criticism in no way dampened his enthusiasm and he shortly afterward organized a parish social science class and delivered many public addresses on social problems.[78] One interesting development at St. Paul's was the establishment of a regular gathering of society people to discuss social morality as it applied to their particular situation, including such topics as drinking, theatergoing, gossip, and divorce. However, while this group sometimes attracted as many as three hundred attendees, most of them were Presbyterians. Personal renewal was evidently something that Erie's Episcopal elite did not view as a priority.[79]

Elsewhere in the diocese, reform proved a more piecemeal undertaking, even though the spirit was undoubtedly willing. One Erie clergyman set up a factory in the city during the depression of the early 1890s, which he allowed the unemployed to run on a cooperative basis.[80] In Pittsburgh, St. James's Church opened a store for secondhand goods in 1895 and provided classes for the unemployed in the art of manufacturing saleable goods, for which it was praised by the Society for the Improvement of the Poor.[81] Even in rural areas like Clarion County, some Episcopalians sought to revivify community life. For example, the Episcopal priest in Foxburg helped organize the Foxburg Village Association, which maintained a facility similar to that built by Franklin Spalding in Erie, but overseen by a board of management composed of representatives from all sections of the community.[82] By the late 1890s, the Church Army had also become active in the area, running missions in Pittsburgh and Allegheny City for the care of released hospital patients and for homeless women and children.[83] Even Bishop Whitehead took a hand in the institutional church movement when he transformed a mission in Pittsburgh's Oakland dis-

---

78. Ibid., 82–86. In 1904, Spalding was elected bishop of Utah.
79. Ibid., 88–93.
80. Ibid., 61.
81. *Church News*, January 1895.
82. *Church News*, February 1900.
83. *Church News*, July 1897.

trict into his personal chapel in 1894.[84] The parish house of the new St. Mary's Memorial Church—dedicated in 1900—offered a variety of social programs to Oakland's working-class population.[85]

This new Episcopal interest in what was coming to be known as the Social Gospel did not deflect Bishop Whitehead from his earlier preoccupation with church planting. For all the praise earlier lavished on the vitality of missions, compared with established parishes, they still occupied a precarious existence. "There is no Parish organization," the 1895 parochial report from All Saints, Johnstown, ruefully admitted. "The large loss in membership is due to the removal of the Johnson Company's Rolling Mill and is not due to anything that could have been prevented by either the congregation or the Minister in charge."[86] Even though directly subordinate to the bishop, moreover, many missions were wont periodically to assert their independence. On one occasion a mission treasurer aroused concern by his refusal to furnish detailed financial reports. The archdeacon of the diocese consequently requested an audit and, when the treasurer threatened to resign, took him at his word. Although two other members of the mission's executive committee then resigned in protest at the bishop's "dictation," indicating that many mission leaders lacked appreciation of the legal distinction between parish and mission, the archdeacon refused to be swayed.[87] Given such structural problems, it is impressive that thirty new missions were still added to the diocesan roll call in the course of the 1890s, two-thirds of them in Allegheny County, with a lesser focus on Cambria, Westmoreland, and Fayette counties. Perhaps the most notable parishes founded during this era were St. Mary's Memorial Church in Oakland (1894) and Church of the Redeemer in Squirrel Hill (1900), both located in Pittsburgh.

Isolation and neglect of rural localities continued to be a problem. An infuriated resident of McKean County complained that while the

---

84. Whitehead may have been influenced by his 1888 visit to various English episcopal chapels: "The private chapels of the Bishops caused much envy on the part of their American brethren. Some of them would make for us quite respectable Cathedrals to begin with, and yet they are but private oratories for the Episcopal households." *Church News*, October 1888.

85. *Church News*, April 1900.

86. *Convention Journal*, June 12, 1895, 161.

87. Ven. D. F. Cole, "Recollections of an Archdeacon," read before the Historical Society, March 26, 1912, RG5/1.1, box 1DP, EDP.

number of places of worship in Kane had increased from two to eight between 1885 and 1893, none of these were Episcopal. Were people simply expected to stand by and watch their baptized brethren join sectarian bodies? he demanded.[88] The situation in Latrobe, where the mission was maintained by "three zealous churchwomen," testified to a similar problem. One Sunday, only one of these ladies was available and the assigned lay reader was absent. Unfazed, the teacher opened and closed the Sunday school with a hymn and prayer, gave a simple address to the children on the life and death of Christ, and even persuaded those adults who had planned to leave when they heard they would be no regular service to remain for extemporaneous worship, which she led using an essay from George Hodges's *Christianity between Sundays*.[89]

Missions of this type frequently requested the services of the Laymen's Missionary League.[90] At times, though, this need could prompt an exercise of lay initiative that went beyond what the bishop considered acceptable. In June 1900, Mortimer Starling inquired of the League's chaplain if he might—if requested at short notice—lead a service at a neighboring mission without further reference to ecclesiastical authority. So agitated by this inquiry was Bishop Whitehead that he wrote directly to Starling. "I could not understand, and do not understand how a license which is given for a specific location can be stretched to suit any locality," he expostulated. "If any city Rector desires the services of a Lay Reader, he should either obtain a Lay Reader for himself among his own people, or should make his request through the Bishop."[91]

Whitehead's sensitivity on this matter was not uncharacteristic. "The Bishop may not be wiser than anyone else," he insisted in 1893, "just as a judge may not be any more learned in law than many lawyers in his court. But the judgment pronounced is *official*, and is the result of quiet consideration of precedents and circumstances and consequences, bound to be unbiased by personal and partisan feeling, wider in its outlook and bearing than that of the single Clergyman or Layman is likely to be."[92] The

88. *Church News*, August 1893.

89. *Church News*, April 1893.

90. Executive Committee of Church of the Incarnation, Knoxville, to Rev. John R. Wightman, March 9, 1900, RG5/2.2, box 2DP, EDP.

91. Mortimer Starling to Rev. John R. Wightman, June 8, 1900, Bp. Cortlandt Whitehead to Starling, June 15, 1900, RG5/2.2, box 2DP, EDP.

92. *Convention Journal*, June 14, 1893, 88.

following year, Whitehead rebuked the "unnecessary and factious inquiries of unauthorized persons" directed to the chancellor of the diocese. This officer, he reminded convention delegates, could not serve as a court of appeal against the bishop's decisions.[93]

Episcopal authority was most at issue when it came to matters of finance. Whitehead was particularly concerned by the fact that many parishes neglected to pay mission support in installments, and were then obliged to whip up a hasty collection at the end of the year.[94] In 1896, he blamed the failure of three-quarters of his parishes to contribute either to foreign or domestic missions on the ambivalence of many clergy and the much vaunted envelope system, which, he said, encouraged "parochial selfishness" and worked against the principal of free-will offerings.[95] In 1900, when the diocesan convention modified the canons to constitute itself as the board of missions, delegates responded to Whitehead's concerns by giving the bishop greater discretion to appoint and reassign missionary clergy.[96]

The reluctance of the established parishes to fund central diocesan machinery was not confined to missionary assessments but extended to the permanent episcopal fund (the episcopal endowment), which, as a result of a depreciation in property values, had declined from a high of $51,000 in 1875 to just $44,000 in 1891.[97] Three years later, Bishop Whitehead recommended adoption of the plan pioneered in the Diocese of Milwaukee, under which the outstanding balance still owing on the fund (in Pittsburgh's case, roughly $5,000) was apportioned to the parishes on the basis of four criteria: communicant membership; number of souls; value of offerings for all church purposes; and value of real estate. The apportionment was then treated as an outstanding loan to the parish from the diocese at 5 percent interest. Once it had been paid off, the parish would be exempt from further responsibility for the bishop's salary.[98] The Milwaukee plan was not well received by the large parishes, however. In 1899, the bishop noted with frustration that the missions at Kittanning,

93. *Convention Journal*, June 13–14, 1894, 99.
94. Ibid., 40.
95. *Convention Journal*, June 10, 1896, 7.
96. *Convention Journal*, May 17–18, 1899, 71–72; *Convention Journal*, May 16–17, 1900, 56–57, 111–13.
97. *Convention Journal*, June 10–11, 1891, 12–13.
98. *Convention Journal*, June 13–14, 1894, 96–97.

Uniontown, and Foxburg had all contributed generously to the fund but their resentment toward their wealthier neighbors who refused to give proportionate to their means was increasing.[99]

Money might be the most pressing concern, but missions and parishes also sought to develop a distinct community identity, whether in as simple a matter as their name, or the basis on which they were organized and administered. Even such a simple action as naming a mission could be a controversial exercise. In the early years of the diocese, Pittsburgh Episcopalians tended to emphasize the "mysteries" of their Lord's life, adopting such names as Ascension, Nativity, Epiphany, Atonement, Incarnation, and Transfiguration. By the mid-1890s, however, Bishop Whitehead was insisting on a greater focus on the Apostles and on English saints, a trend confirmed by the establishment of St. Alban's Church, Erie, in 1894.[100] A few months later, Cross and Crown, Erie, adopted the name of St. Vincent's (a fourth-century Spanish martyr).[101] The mission in Woods Run, Allegheny City, changed its name from St. John the Baptist to All Saints, but this was largely because its members wished to end the confusion caused by the prevailing belief that it was a "Baptist mission."[102] The standing committee set the seal on this shift in nomenclature in 1898, when it stated that a parish could be formed in Wilkinsburg, provided that it "shall adopt some name other than that of 'Grace' Church, and, as far as possible different from the name of any parish in the city of Pittsburgh or immediate vicinity."[103]

Debates over parish governance also produced a fresh interest in the virtues of pew rents. These had already been abandoned by many institutional churches, especially those in New York; local advocates could point to the doubling of parish income and a threefold increase in attendance at St. John's, Pittsburgh, after it abandoned pew rents in 1888.[104] Support for abolition was not simply a class issue. John Shoenberger left $100,000 of his 1890 hospital bequest to Trinity Church, Pittsburgh, on

---

99. *Convention Journal,* May 17–18, 1899, 121–22.
100. *Church News,* June 1894.
101. *Church News,* September 1894.
102. *Church News,* January 1896.
103. Standing Committee Minutes, December 6, 1898, RG4A/1.8, box 9DRB, EDP.
104. *Church News,* December 1888.

condition that it became a free church within three years.[105] Several years later, some members of the congregation of St. Paul's, Erie, demanded the right to establish a new parish on the free church principle, arguing that they favored a vestry elected by all communicant members, not just pew renters. They pointed out that every seat at St. Paul's was presently taken and many were still waiting for an opportunity to rent a pew. In 1894, the standing committee authorized the erection of St. Alban's, Erie.[106]

Such pressure from below to abolish pew rents foreshadowed even greater participation by ordinary Episcopalians in the process of parish government. For all his autocratic style, Bishop Whitehead welcomed such involvement. Parishes were encouraged to consult their charters, prepare registries of voters, and determine the eligibility of any candidate for office at least a month before any parish meeting. In 1894, the bishop made an unusually liberal defense of the right of female parishioners to participate in parish elections, if not specifically excluded by statute. He also hinted that parishioners of either sex who were denied the right to exercise the franchise by parish cliques would be justified in taking the matter to civil court![107]

Occasionally, proposed parish charters would still be sent back for revision. An interesting example is the 1897 standing committee decision to reject the charter for Trinity Church, New Castle, because it lacked a requirement for vestry members to be baptized Christians. On inquiry, it became apparent that this provision reflected less the presence of incipient modernism in the parish than an objection on the part of the rector to the Episcopal Church's excessive focus on baptism. "I believe in baptismal regeneration," he told a fellow clergyman, "but a baptism that is not followed by confirmation and communion, either in fact or in purpose, I believe to be a still birth; and to have it expressed in a Church charter that vestrymen shall be baptized men, but that they need not be confirmed or communicants, is to my mind giving countenance to a deadly heresy . . . Therefore I could not conscientiously approve of a charter which would give qualification to *merely* baptized men, if they need not be communicants."[108]

105. *Convention Journal*, June 11–12, 1890, 41.

106. Standing Committee Minutes, April 23, 1893, June 12, 1894, RG4A/1.8, box 9DRB, EDP.

107. *Church News*, March 1894; *Convention Journal*, June 13–14, 1894, 100–101.

108. Standing Committee Minutes, April 26, 1897, RG4A/1.8, box 9DRB; Rev. J. D. Herron to Rev. Amos Bannister, April 29, 1897, RG4A/1.7:1, box 6DSC, EDP.

The New Castle affair pointed to a residual Evangelical spirit in the diocese, but by the late 1890s clergy disregard of Prayer Book rubrics was more the mark of an Anglo Catholic presbyter. "I have myself in one of our congregations heard the *Ave Maria* sung in English," Bishop Whitehead told the 1898 diocesan convention, "not as a quotation from St. Luke's Gospel merely, but with the addition many times repeated, 'Pray for us, pray for us, now and in the hour of our death.'"[109] Clerical defenders of liturgical change—such as the rector of Emmanuel, Corry—retorted that candles and incense were in conformity with the English Book of Common Prayer of 1549 and that the American Prayer Book adopted in 1892 included the prayers of humble access and consecration that implied a real and actual presence in the Eucharist: "Why," he demanded, "should we not, instead of being timid and careless of our rightful inheritance, bravely maintain all those things, which of right do belong not only to the Protestant Episcopal Church, but to the Holy Church throughout all the whole world?"[110]

As Roman Catholic immigrants flooded into southwestern Pennsylvania during the late 1890s, Episcopal identity increasingly came to be defined as much by what it was not as by what it was. "An alien faith and an alien sovereignty have no claims upon us," Bishop Whitehead warned the diocesan convention of 1887.[111] A few years later, an Episcopalian in Sharon, Pennsylvania, attacked the notion of a special primacy accorded to the Apostle Peter: "Whatever degree of supremacy came to the Bishop of Rome was by reason of his prominent position as ruler of the Diocese where the Emperor had his throne, in the chief city of the Empire. An analogous position belongs to the Bishop of New York in the American Church today, and yet the prominence of the Bishop of New York makes him not one whit different from his humblest brethren in spiritual functions or Episcopal jurisdiction."[112] Any hope of reconciliation or even dialogue was largely ended with the 1896 papal bull declaring Anglican orders invalid. Episcopalians needed to understand "what the true Catholic posi-

---

109. *Convention Journal*, May 11–12, 1898, 116.

110. *Church News*, March 1898.

111. *Convention Journal*, June 8–9, 1887, 64. "Eloquent these ancient ruins are of an historic faith," Whitehead wrote of his 1888 visit to Iona, "a continuity of organic life in the Church, and that so far independent of Papal Rome as to be a standing, undying protest against her claims." *Church News*, October 1888.

112. *Church News*, October 1893.

tion is," Bishop Whitehead warned in response, "as opposed to Romanism and Papalism, and understanding also what true Protestantism is, *against what* we protest and *for what reasons.*"[113]

Relations between Episcopalians and other Protestants could be equally strained at times. In 1888, a visiting Episcopal clergyman was required to sign a guarantee that in the services he conducted "nothing should be done contrary to the Christian religion," before being permitted access to the community's union chapel (available to most Protestant groups in the town). In another instance, a contribution toward the erection of a new church was withdrawn because it was felt that an Episcopal church would not be "conducive to morality."[114] It was evident that the issuing of the Chicago Quadrilateral by the House of Bishops in 1886, which sought to define Anglicanism's core doctrines—namely, the Old and New Testaments as the revealed word of God; the Nicene Creed as a sufficient statement of Christian faith; the two sacraments of Holy Baptism and the Lord's Supper; and the Historic Episcopate, locally adapted—as a point of departure of discussions surrounding Christian unity had fallen short of expectation.

The Chicago-Lambeth Quadrilateral (as it was termed after its adoption by the Lambeth Conference of 1888) was, observed Bishop Whitehead, a declaration of the church's desire for unity "on the basis of absolutely divine essentials, setting aside whatsoever is of merely human ordering, and waiving its own preferences."[115] Other Protestants contested the definition of "divine essentials." Most considered pulpit exchange to be a natural courtesy and considered Episcopal opposition to the practice a slight to their ministry. Many Episcopalians retorted that their objection was merely a commitment to the ecclesial integrity of their ministry.[116] Protestant resentment was arguably displayed in the reaction of the residents of Ludlow, who blocked Episcopal attempts to use the union chapel in 1898. Even here, the diocesan newspaper found some consolation in persecution. "It makes our Church primitive and Apostolic," the editor

---

113. *Church News*, May 1897.
114. *Convention Journal*, June 6–7, 1888, 64.
115. *Convention Journal*, June 8–9, 1887, 54.
116. *Church News*, May 1894.

concluded, "thus to meet with persecution at the hands of those who 'call themselves Christians.'"[117]

The 1890s marked the triumph in Episcopal circles of what came to be known as the "national church idea." First promoted by William Reed Huntington in 1870,[118] the notion of the Episcopal Church as a "national church" that would provide the basis for Protestant reunion gained fresh traction as the century drew to a close. "Though many non-Episcopalians were sympathetic to the idea of inter-denominational cooperation in the area of social reform," writes Paul Phillips, "the supporters of the National Church idea tended to be liberal Episcopalians (or American Broad Churchmen)."[119] In Pittsburgh, the 1898 diocesan convention saw lawyer Hill Burgwin secure diocesan endorsement of a proposal that the Episcopal Church should adopt the name "The National Church of the United States."[120]

Just as the Episcopal Church's origins owed much to the climate of nation-building that pervaded the 1790s, so the national church idea achieved center stage as the United States made its first projection of global power with the seizure of Spanish colonies in the Philippines, Cuba, and Puerto Rico during the Spanish-American War. That same year, 1898, Bishop Whitehead delivered a powerful convention address asserting solidarity with the McKinley administration, an attitude far removed from the general anti-Erastian stance that had previously characterized the church: "*Loyalty* must needs characterize that Church whose daily petition arises for the President, the Governor and all who are in authority. And loyalty is all the more possible since already one grand result has already been attained, for which we should be devoutly grateful, *the complete unification* of our whole people under the one Flag; so that the sense of *Nationality* has developed as could not have been predicted or expected a few months or even weeks ago."[121]

One diocesan priest—Walter Lowry of Emmanuel, Corry—served as an army chaplain during the Spanish-American War. From Puerto

117. *Church News*, May 1898.
118. Huntington, *Church-Idea*.
119. Phillips, *Kingdom on Earth*, 162–85 (quotation on 169). One of the most active proponents of the national church idea was the future bishop of Arkansas, William Montgomery Brown. See Brown, *Church for Americans;* Carden, "Bolshevik Bishop."
120. *Convention Journal*, May 11–12, 1898, 38–39.
121. Ibid., 106–8 (quotation on 108).

Rico, he reported his admiration for the bravery of the Spanish troops and horror at the injuries inflicted by modern rifles, but his principal concern was to speculate on what the Episcopal Church might do to minister to a local population whom the Catholic Church had largely failed to reach. Lowry also expressed the view that the church could play a role in helping to industrialize the island and develop its economy.[122] The imperial ambition of the United States had evidently struck a responsive chord in Episcopal circles.

REALIZING THE DREAM OF THE NATIONAL CHURCH, 1901–1909

As the twentieth century dawned, Episcopalians adjusted to their new quasi-establishment status, both abroad [123] and at home. A new Episcopal readiness to speak out on matters of public concern had become evident at the highest levels of the church. In 1893, Bishop Whitehead took the authors of the Geary Act of 1892, which restricted Chinese immigration to the United States, to task, calling the legislation "unjust, inhuman, dishonoring to our good name and cruel towards innocent victims."[124] In Pittsburgh, however, the prevailing concern was the promotion of civic reform, the impetus for which came from a group of energized laymen at Calvary, who sought to promote the vision of George Hodges after he departed for a teaching post at the Episcopal Theological School in Massachusetts.

Among the leaders of this movement was Henry David William English, an insurance salesman (and founder of the underwriting firm of English and Furey) whose first foray into politics involved the preparation of voters' guides on candidates for public office and the prosecution of vote fraud. Elected president of the chamber of commerce in 1905, English joined forces with another Calvary vestryman, George Wilkins Guthrie, to elect the latter (a reformist Democrat in a Republican town) as mayor of Pittsburgh in 1906, on a platform of municipal reform and anti–machine politics. English led the drive for improvements in the city's milk supply and the establishment both of a water filtration plant and a national testing laboratory for mines. Together with Guthrie, he spon-

---

122. *Church News*, October 1898.
123. See, for example, Douglas, *Fling Out the Banner!*; Norbeck, "False Start."
124. *Convention Journal*, June 14, 1893, 96 (quotation).

sored the Pittsburgh Survey, one of the most far-reaching investigations of urban social problems in the early twentieth century. Both men were active in numerous reform activities, serving on the board of Kingsley House and supporting the Greater Pittsburgh movement that led to the merger of Pittsburgh with Allegheny City in 1907.[125]

The activities of the "damned Calvary crowd" (as the machine politicians irritably referred to them) led some to wonder if the Pittsburgh model had application elsewhere. The Church Club of the Diocese of Pittsburgh offered a forum through which laymen could be initiated into more active participation in community projects.[126] That the Diocese of Pittsburgh was seen as a pioneer in some fields of social endeavor may be deduced from the fact that the principal men's organization in the Episcopal Church—the Brotherhood of St. Andrew—located its national headquarters there in the early 1900s.[127]

Perhaps the most dramatic change took place at the mother church of the diocese. In 1891, Trinity Church elected Alfred Arundel as its new rector. Arundel brought the same perspective to Trinity that Franklin Spalding had earlier brought to St. Paul's, Erie. "When our wealthy church members went to the suburbs, to New York and to Europe," Arundel explained in 1911, "I went into this downtown district of our parish to fill the empty pews, among underpaid and underfed laborers, in the slums and the tenderloin, I saw the results of extortionate capitalism—the undue enrichment of the few and the underserved poverty of the many."[128] Following in the footsteps of William Rainsford,[129] Arundel supervised the erection of a new parish house. Completed in 1906 at a cost of over $70,000, the parish house hosted a kindergarten for slum children and

---

125. *Church News*, February 1910; *History of Pittsburgh*, 3:847–51, 4:239–40; Bauman and Spratt, "Civic Leaders"; Bauman and Muller, *Before Renaissance*, 36–41, 51–101.

126. *Convention Journal*, June 13–14, 1894, 103.

127. *Convention Journal*, May 13–14, 1903, 119–20.

128. *North American*, November 23, 1911.

129. Rainsford insisted that all who used the parish house be members (not necessarily communicant members) of St. George's and he viewed the parish house as the place where the lines of class disappeared: "The Parish House was open on Monday nights to everyone, and meet there we did, from Pierpont Morgan to the last adopted Armenian refugee... If the old Avenue A folks of the early 1880's seldom put in an appearance here, their children did in throngs, and as they did so, insensibly they changed class; for here all were in their own house, for all did something to support it." Rainsford, *Story of a Varied Life*, 293–309 (quotation on 295).

boasted a gymnasium, a boys' brigade, and sewing and cooking classes for young women.[130]

Other Pittsburgh parishes offered similar institutional programs, ranging from boys' clubs at Calvary and Ascension to weaving classes at St. John's, St. James, and St. Mary's to a night school at St. Mark's.[131] Two new diocesan institutions also began to make their mark: the House of the Merciful Savior, organized by the parishes of Calvary, Ascension, and St. Mary's Memorial in 1900, cared for infirm women and those deserted by their husbands, for abused children, and for women suffering from addiction to alcohol or drugs.[132] Such work was complemented by the work of the Brothers of St. Barnabas, a lay order formed in 1901 to care for men leaving hospital care without home or friends.[133] Some priests sought to promote a better understanding of the corporate nature of Christian life. The rector of St. Stephen's, McKeesport, for example, issued members of each year's confirmation class with a corporate name and motto and a card with the names of members of that class and prayers specific to that group. Each class held an annual reunion that included a corporate Communion.[134]

The expansion of the institutional church movement had implications for other areas of parish life. Some observers had second thoughts about the earlier rejection of the modern Sunday school model. Parochial Sunday schools, the diocesan newspaper opined in 1905, were marked by "an air of general dilapidation, or of invalidism." What was needed was a model that not only reflected the public schools' emphasis on punctuality and grades but also stressed the study of the Bible and the Book of Common Prayer, rather than books *about* them.[135] In 1910, St. Stephen's,

---

130. *North American,* November 23, 1911; Trinity Church Vestry Minutes, April 30, 1906; Alfred Arundel to Edward T. Dravo, October 15, 1907, RG3/2.2, box 3T, EDP; Harriss, *Trinity and Pittsburgh,* 83–87, 99–104.

131. *Church News,* April 1902.

132. *Convention Journal,* May 14, 1902, 114–17; *Convention Journal,* May 13–14, 1903, 115–17.

133. *Convention Journal,* May 14, 1902, 118–19. See also Calvin, *Barnabas in Pittsburgh.*

134. *Church News,* May 1904.

135. *Church News,* November 1905. It was notable that a greater proportion of the members of missions attended their Sunday schools than did those of established parishes. *Convention Journal,* May 13–14, 1903, 123–25.

Sewickley, adopted graded lessons and required state certification of its Sunday school teachers.[136]

In a related development, Bishop Whitehead's involvement in the national commission that produced a new marginal readings Bible in the early 1900s led him to take a peculiar interest in his diocesan priests making use of it. In 1904, the bishop urged his clergy to study the new Bible during Lent, compare it with the Revised Version, and discuss the contrasts between the two in their sermons. He also defended greater use of the new Bible as a stimulus to more profound thought and reflection on the part of both clergy and laypeople, but was shrewd enough to invoke the democratic principle when he opined that churchwardens had a duty to acquire such a lectern Bible, so that people "may not be defrauded their rights given by vote of General Convention."[137]

Even as support for national church idea swelled, Anglo Catholics renewed their struggle for the "change-of-name" with a vengeance. Many of them—including Frederic Morehouse of the *Living Church*— appealed to the bishop of Pittsburgh for support in their attempt to substitute the name American Catholic Church. Whitehead was initially more favorable to the arguments advanced by his chancellor Hill Burgwin, who argued that Episcopalians had better cause than most American denominations to consider themselves a national ecclesiastical organization. Furthermore, the name *Protestant* Episcopal, Burgwin contended, "seems to have been dropped upon us without authority, by a mere heading prefixed to the memoranda of an informal meeting of twenty-six most excellent praiseworthy clergymen and laymen at New York in 1784, assembled, not in legislative convention, but simply to suggest some general plan of ecclesiastical government for the faithful few, who still adhered to the faith and liturgy of this then independent branch of the Holy Catholic Church."[138]

---

136. *Church News*, January 1910.

137. *Church News*, January 1902, February 1904 (quotations). One advocate of the marginal readings Bible was Robert Benton of Sewickley. Benton noted that criticisms in the religious press were generally mild and he urged that it be given a fair trial (many clergy, by his testimony, were intentionally *not* using it). Benton, however, was an advocate of even greater flexibility, advocating occasional use of both the Modern American Bible and the Twentieth Century New Testament. *Church News*, May 1904.

138. Hill Burgwin to Editor of *Church Standard*, April 16, 1898, RG2/2.2, box 3BP, EDP. According to Burgwin, the Presbyterians and the Methodists had no national organization, the Congregationalists and Baptists no national *territorial* organization, and the Roman Catholics were still a missionary church.

Men like Morehouse argued that use of a title like "National Church" or "American Church" might run afoul of probate law, especially given the U.S. Constitution's prohibition on any one denomination being designated the church of the nation. It was the judgment of those who drafted the Milwaukee Memorial, Morehouse told Whitehead, "that the only safe way was to find an adjective to apply to the Church, and in doing so to select the adjective that savored least of sectarianism and would be the least objectionable of any that could be found."[139] Morehouse protested too much. The adjective in question had decidedly sectarian and objectionable qualities for all too many American Protestants. Another Whitehead correspondent put the matter succinctly: "Those who seek a change propose to introduce the word 'Catholic' into the new name. I apprehend that a large number of the members of our church, while appreciating the word in its proper sense, as used in the Prayer Book, would dislike it as a church name for the reason that it is associated with a church whose errors in faith they deplore and with a party in our own communion which, as they conceive, represents narrowness of view, intolerance of spirit and disregard of Episcopal authority."[140]

Anglo Catholics made considerable progress at the General Convention of 1904. "I believe we have reached the stage of the argument that was reached in the Fifth Century," a delegate from Wisconsin told Bishop Whitehead, "when many divisions had arisen among Christians, and in one of the Fathers we read an instruction that when going from one city to another we should not ask simply where is the Church, but where is the Catholic Church. So now I believe if we are to stand for historic Christianity, the historic continuity of its ministry, sacraments and faith, we should take the same stand—not simply the Church, but the Catholic Church."[141]

Bishop Whitehead still maintained that any change should come through an open and democratic process. "The opinion of the Diocesan Conventions is asked this year," he told the 1903 diocesan convention. "I

---

139. Frederic C. Morehouse to Bp. Whitehead, January 19, 1903, RG2/2.2, box 3BP, EDP. Morehouse subsequently assured Whitehead that if the latter's "territorial" name was better received, the *Living Church* would give it greater prominence, since it was better for the advocates of change to rally around a single objective. Frederic C. Morehouse to Bp. Whitehead, February 5, 1903, RG2/2.2, box 3BP, EDP.

140. Joseph Packard to Bp. Whitehead, January 19, 1903, RG2/2.2, box 3BP, EDP.

141. B. Jacob Rogers to Bp. Whitehead, November 3, 1904, RG2/2.2, box 3BP, EDP.

should be glad if the opinion should be sought of each clergyman separately, and each Vestry separately. And, because Vestries are not always representative, I should be in favor of universal consideration on the part of all our people in congregational meetings."[142] Correspondents like Morehouse were aghast at the bishop's naiveté, telling him that the decision made at that level "would tear parishes all to pieces," and Whitehead lost much of his earlier enthusiasm as the lack of support for the move in Pittsburgh became clear.[143] He later refused to give countenance to the American Church Union, telling one of the leaders of this Anglo Catholic pressure group that its vocal opposition to modernistic theology might do more harm than good. It would be far better, he said, to allow individual bishops to exercise discipline on an informal basis.[144]

Whitehead also took a personal interest in debates over the issue of Christian unity and the role that worldwide Anglicanism might play. As early as 1888 he was in correspondence with the Presbyterian John De Witt, an instructor at Lane Theological Seminary (Presbyterian) in Cincinnati, concerning the desirability of pulpit exchange between denominations. Whitehead agreed with De Witt that his church had neglected its Protestant brethren. "I am rather disposed to think that the High Anglican Sacramentarian (such as I consider myself to be) will find no difficulty with your position," he concluded, "in comparison with the more 'moderate' Episcopal minister and the layman will be the hardest of all to convince."[145] As the 1889 General Convention approached,

---

142. *Convention Journal*, May 13–14, 1903, 135.

143. Frederic C. Morehouse to Bp. Whitehead, January 11, 1904, RG2/2.2, box 3BP, EDP. Commenting on the defeat of a change-of-name proposal three years earlier, the diocesan newspaper urged all those who voted "no" to be more earnest in carrying the Protestant banner to every town and village and upholding the bishop in all his plans for expansion. "He is a poor Protestant who makes no objection to a *diminution* of the Faith, while loudly declaiming against all *additions* to the Faith," it concluded. "'Protestant Episcopal' ought to be an outward and visible sign of an inward and spiritual conviction, earnestness, devotion and staunch Episcopalianism." *Church News*, February 1906.

144. Rev. Charles M. Hall to Bp. Whitehead, January 28, 1907, Whitehead to Hall, March 20, 1909, RG4A/1.7:1, box 6DSC, EDP. "The Crapsey trial has done good already," Whitehead wrote in 1907. "The Cox matter is by no means finished. Note the brave statement and Charge of Bishop Vincent, this week published . . . There will be other manifestations of the Church's position." Whitehead to Hall, January 31, 1907, RG4A/1.7:1, box 6DSC, EDP.

145. Bp. Cortlandt Whitehead to John De Witt, n.d., 1888, RG2/2.2, box 3BP, EDP. De Witt argued that allowing non-Anglican clergy to preach in Episcopal churches should

Whitehead dismissed concerns that there was too diverse a range of motives and approaches to Christian unity and helped organize a breakfast at which the work of various ecumenical societies was discussed.[146]

The Anglican contribution to Christian unity became all the more significant as relationships developed between Anglicans worldwide. In 1888, Bishop Whitehead attended the third Lambeth Conference. "It was not a Synod or Council," he later assured a Pittsburgh audience. "It had no legislative function. It was not summoned by authority ecclesiastical or civil. It was exactly what its name imports—a 'Conference'—the voluntary 'bringing together' of men representing diverse interests and yet one overmastering interest, that they might mutually and interchangeably contribute something of their experienced wisdom to the common treasury and to each other."[147] While he remained convinced of the ecumenical possibilities inherent in the Lambeth experience, Whitehead was also clear that the American bishops had a rather different relationship to the "Mother Church" than the colonial bishops by virtue of their "independent national" status. "If [a bishop] had 'strings to his hat' and wore the gaiters," reported the diocesan newspaper, "he was at once recognized as an English or Colonial Bishop . . . If [a bishop] wore trousers, and had on *any* sort of a hat and without rosette or strings—sometimes with rather a well-worn coat, as if the purse had not been very full when in London, then it was easy to see that he was an American Bishop."[148]

The evidence for or against a developing global understanding of Anglicanism in Pittsburgh is conflicting. The diocesan standing committee directed that a parish's articles of association, which defined it as being in Communion with "the Church of England or the Church of Ireland," should be changed to "all churches in Communion with the Protestant Episcopal Church."[149] Commenting on the ruling by the

---

not be seen as an implicit concession to the validity of non-Anglican orders. "[Your] Church," he added, "by its Theological Comprehensiveness, is nearer to most of the Protestant Churches than they are to each other. Up to this time, your Church seems to have failed to recognize this nearness, and to have emphasized only the distance between itself and them." See John De Witt to Bp. Cortlandt Whitehead, March 5, 1888, RG2/2.2, box 3BP, EDP.

146. Bp. Cortlandt Whitehead to Rev. G. Woolsey Hodge, August 8, 1889, RG2/2.2, box 3BP, EDP.

147. *Church News*, January 1889.

148. *Church News*, October 1888.

149. Standing Committee Minutes, April 26, 1897, RG4A/1.8, box 9DRB, EDP.

archbishops of Canterbury and York in 1899 against incense and processional lights, Bishop Whitehead stressed that the American church was in no way bound to take note of opinions generated by Lambeth Palace (some American parishes, he remarked, might even be tempted to use incense for the first time to demonstrate their national independence). He further noted that the most recent General Convention had rejected a proposal to establish a board of arbitration under the presidency of the archbishop of Canterbury to consider questions submitted by the national churches.[150]

That said, Anglican identity would continue to preoccupy Whitehead in his declining years. "[One] does not belong to St. Peter's, St. John's, St. Matthew's parish; nor yet to the Diocese of Pittsburgh; nor indeed to the 'P.E.C. of the U.S.A.,'" declared a 1908 diocesan newspaper editorial on the Pan Anglican Missionary Congress of that year. "We are not baptized into these puny and ephemeral bodies, but into [the] great Holy Catholic Church." Many Episcopalians, the editorial added, failed to appreciate the debt they owed to the missionary efforts of the Church of England. Where English colonists had gone, the church and the Prayer Book followed.[151]

The rector of Christ Church, Greensburg, expressed a similar sentiment in 1903, while discussing the change-of-name issue. Why, he inquired, "should this comparatively small branch of the one great Anglican Communion be the only branch that holds on to an epithet which ... gives her a sectarian or denominational name?"[152] The essential unity of all Christians—as embodied in such gatherings as the Lambeth Conference—remained a frequent topic of conversation.[153] James McIlvaine, rector of Calvary, preaching at a 1905 ordination, made this very clear. "In no narrow, selfish spirit," he declared, "but in the spirit of a great large-hearted yearning for the reunion of Christendom, we must hold distinct and definite both the Catholic Faith and Historic Ministry."[154]

At home, the missionary dynamism of the early years of Whitehead's episcopate was fading. Though nineteen new missions were established between 1901 and 1910, this figure was two-thirds that of the 1890s

150. *Church News*, October 1899.
151. *Church News*, March 1908. See Bosher, "Pan-Anglican Congress."
152. *Church News*, April 1903.
153. *Church News*, April 1908.
154. *Church News*, October 1905.

and only half that of the 1880s. The bulk of new activity was confined to Allegheny County, with its eleven missions, but there were also three in Washington County. Success rates were also declining. Nine missions folded quickly; another seven lasted no more than thirty years; while St. Margaret's, Wilmerding, endured until 1960, when it was absorbed into All Soul's, North Versailles. The only extant parishes founded in this period (both in 1904) were Advent, Brookline, and Transfiguration, Clairton. Such failures could hardly be blamed on a lack of enthusiasm by the Laymen's Missionary League. In 1902, all missions were requested to appoint a committee to canvass their local neighborhoods for "persons belonging to our Church," while those in industrial areas were encouraged to extend their efforts to the mills. LML members placed cards with the location and service times of missions in hotels and railroad stations and also provided this information to local newspapers. In Uniontown, the rector of St. Peter's Church took things a stage further by leading the men of his parish through the center of the town and preaching sermons to audiences of up to four hundred that included bankers, lawyers, and physicians.[155]

Established parishes could not deny that they befitted from the work of missionary priests. One rector admitted in 1904 that he had recently received twelve new members from one particular mission. Even though the parish now enjoyed an increased income of $100, in addition to the many practical contributions that the new members were giving to parish programs, his parish had paid a grand total of $5 in support of the mission throughout its existence.[156] Missions were also exceedingly economical. In 1901, the fifty-three diocesan missions were maintained at an average annual cost of $100, while missionary priests were, on average, paid $200 per year. The total monthly cost of $500, diocesan officials pointed out, could easily be met if every member of the diocese subscribed just 2¢.[157]

The less than wholehearted support of missions was not solely the result of parochial indifference. The economic recession of the 1910s—which had serious implications for southwestern Pennsylvania—affected

155. "Resolutions Adopted at Meeting of the Laymen's Missionary League, November 4, 1902," RG5/2.2, box 2DP, EDP; *Church News*, April 1906.

156. *Convention Journal*, May 25–26, 1904, 48.

157. *Convention Journal*, May 14, 1902, 55–57. In 1908, St. Stephen's, Sewickley was praised for consistently raising $1 per communicant member for missionary purposes. *Convention Journal*, May 13–14, 1908, 70.

the financial well-being of the churches. As early as 1903, diocesan leaders demanded that parishes provide details of any project under consideration before they would give consent to loans that used the parish property as security.[158] When Waynesburg's bank failed in 1907, it took with it the building fund of the local Episcopal mission. The diocesan standing committee responded by offering the mission a $500 grant, provided its members were willing to match it dollar for dollar.[159] A year later, when St. Stephen's, Wilkinsburg, applied for diocesan assistance, the board of trustees declared that it could not assist it in renegotiating the parish's mortgage because the deed was not in the name of the board of trustees. It did, however, offer the parish a loan of $4,000, to be repaid over five years, so that it could reduce its obligations at the bank, most of them personally underwritten by members of the vestry.[160]

As Pittsburgh Episcopalians battled these financial setbacks, they also found themselves facing a subdivision of the diocese. In 1906, a committee on division of the diocese recommended the separation of the northern and southern portions of western Pennsylvania into separate dioceses. Growth in the north had stagnated since 1900, falling from 25 percent to only 1 percent, even as the south grew by 28 percent. The northern parishes were reported to play little part in the affairs of the diocese, with only 57 percent of elected delegates present for the 1903 diocesan convention and no clergy or laymen from the north serving on a diocesan committee. Any division "would make practically no change whatsoever in the conduct of the affairs of the Diocese of Pittsburgh."[161] While the mechanics of separation would take four years to accomplish, the final achievement of division in 1910 would mark the beginning of an entirely new phase of existence for Episcopalians in southwestern Pennsylvania.

---

158. Standing Committee Minutes, September 28, 1903, RG4A/1.8, box 9DRB, EDP.

159. *Church News*, April 1907; Standing Committee Minutes, December 10, 1907, RG4A/1.8, box 9DRB, EDP.

160. Board of Trustees Minutes, November 7, November 24, 1908, RG4A/3.3, EDP.

161. *Convention Journal*, May 9–10, 1906, 48–49 (quotation on 49), 67–69.

4

Division, War, and Depression

The New Face of the Diocese of Pittsburgh, 1910–1943

THE DIOCESE OF PITTSBURGH that emerged in 1910 was a more compact—and more urban—Episcopal entity than had hitherto existed in western Pennsylvania and proved increasingly responsive to those trends within the Protestant mainline that bound its member churches to the cause of Progressivism.[1] The age called for a structured response from the church, a commitment to institutional centralization and the establishment of new mechanisms to cope with the challenges posed by industrial society. For Episcopalians this response would culminate in the Nation-Wide Campaign (NWC) of 1919, which was intended to establish a stable basis for funding national church institutions. For Cortlandt Whitehead, the iconic father figure of the diocese,[2] this institutional centralization was something completely outside his experience. His death in 1922 would mark the beginning of a period of ecclesiastical stasis, as the comparative economic tranquility of the 1920s was succeeded by the economic crisis of the 1930s. His successor, Alexander Mann, would have the unenviable task of holding together the administrative apparatus of a diocese in transition. Only with the coming of the Second World War

---

1. On the connection between religion and politics, see McWilliams, "Standing at Armageddon."

2. "Wherever I go in this portion of Pennsylvania which I have inherited from you," the Bishop of Erie told Whitehead in 1915, "I find your name revered and honored. Everywhere I have been obliged to make my own place, nowhere being able to take your place in the hearts of the people. Many times, could spirit have ministered to spirit, your heart must have warmed within you as the people expressed to me their love and devotion for 'the old Bishop.'" Rt. Rev. Rogers Israel to Bp. Whitehead, May 7, 1915, RG2/2.2, box 3BP, Archives of the Episcopal Diocese of Pittsburgh, Pittsburgh, Pennsylvania (hereafter referenced as EDP).

would Pittsburgh embark on a radically different course from the rest of the national church.

WHITEHEAD'S LAST YEARS, 1910–1922

In 1910, the question of dividing the Diocese of Pittsburgh had been under review for almost twenty years.[3] Almost thirty years of service had left the aging Bishop Whitehead exhausted by his hectic round of parish visitations and he therefore laid two options before the diocesan convention of 1910. Either it should immediately proceed with a division of the territory, he said, or it should elect a coadjutor bishop—as the Dioceses of Maryland and Virginia had recently done—to prepare the northwest for eventual separation in 1913 (the next year that a General Convention could ratify such a change). Fearful of the costs involved in electing a coadjutor, delegates pressed for immediate division, on the understanding that at least $30,000 (over and above any monies that would be realized from a division of existing diocesan assets) were raised for an endowment for the new diocese.[4]

By the time the General Convention met in October 1910, $34,000 had already been raised in subscriptions and no further objections were raised. At a primary convention in November, Scranton clergyman Rogers Israel (a former resident of the Diocese of Pittsburgh) was elected bishop of the Diocese of Erie. Three months later, Pittsburgh's board of trustees transferred $37,732.50—representing exactly half the amounts contained in the Episcopal Fund and the Christmas Fund—to the Diocese of Erie, and forty-five years of union with the Episcopalians of southwestern Pennsylvania came to a close.[5]

---

3. The rector of Trinity, New Castle, read a paper at the 1893 Northern Convocation in which he argued that the church in the apostolic era had been on a small and intimate scale until the "worldly principle at centralization" overcame it. The division of a diocese, he said, conserved the energy and lengthened the life of the bishop, strengthened the church's influence in local communities and demonstrated to non-Anglicans how the episcopate might be "locally adapted." Rev. J. D. Herron, "The Division of the Diocese of Pittsburgh," February 8, 1893, RG5/1.2, box 2DP, EDP. See also the five-part series on the mechanics of division, *Church News*, September 1906–January 1907.

4. *Convention Journal*, May 18–19, 1910, 126–27, 57. The rector of Ascension, Bradford, had been in the field seeking funds for a diocesan endowment since January. *Church News*, January 1910.

5. *Church News*, November 1910; Board of Trustees Minutes, February 7, 1911, RG4A/3.3, EDP; *Convention Journal*, May 17–18, 1911, 35–36.

The new Diocese of Pittsburgh proved highly responsive to the new reform impulses pulsing through church and society, impulses increasingly driven less by parish-based programs and more by the actions of dedicated churchmen serving as Christian leaven in the social lump. At the 1911 diocesan convention, a committee assigned to consider the Irwin coal strike in Westmoreland County proposed the establishment of a committee on social service, a move endorsed both by the bishop and by convention delegates.[6] Such a proposal was in line with the desire of national church leaders, who had been pressing for some time for the development of a professional social service apparatus at the diocesan level.

Statistics from the national church reveal that the number of American dioceses with a social service commission grew from seventeen in 1911 to a staggering forty-six in 1912.[7] The Diocese of Pittsburgh formed its social service commission in June 1912. Its first undertaking was a canvass of rectors regarding the nature of social service work in their parishes.[8] Clergy responses varied. Some rectors—those in Oakmont and McKeesport, for example—reported high standards of public health, good relations between labor and management (though whether they had many working-class congregants was debatable), and considerable interdenominational cooperation on social service issues.[9] For such clergy, it was doubtful if they saw the point of additional institutional machinery. In the poverty-stricken Manchester area, blighted by the ill effects of "vile dance halls" and saloons, the rector of the North Side's Emmanuel Church reported that few members of his parish had much understanding of

---

6. *Convention Journal*, May 17–18, 1911, 86–93, 147–48. The committee report stated that few workmen (the class to which Jesus had belonged) or laborers (the class that had most enthusiastically received his message) were represented in the Protestant churches, finding their sense of community in unions or lodges. Of course, many of the region's laborers were members of Roman Catholic or Eastern Orthodox parishes.

7. Frank M. Crouch, "The Work of the Joint Commission on Social Service: Report of the Field Secretary to the Executive Committee, June 6, 1912." *Churchman*, July 20, 1912, 86–87. Crouch, the field secretary of the joint commission on social service, contacted the Pittsburgh social service commission in June asking it to conduct a survey of conditions. Rev. Frank M. Crouch to Rev. Joseph Speers, June 18, 1912, RG4A/2.3:1, box 6DC, EDP.

8. Standing Committee Minutes, May 31, 1912, RG4A/1.8, box 9DRB, EDP; Rev. Joseph Speers to "Revd. and Dear Sir," September 17, 1912, RG4A/2.3:1, box 6DC, EDP.

9. Rev. C. M. Young to Rev. Joseph Speers, September 25, 1912, Rev. Lewis N. Tucker to Rev. Joseph Speers, October 11, 1912, RG4A/2.3:1, box 6DC, EDP.

social problems, but equally no one had criticized him for the views he expressed. "I preach constantly on social matters and constantly allude to them by way of illustration," he wrote.[10] Some clergy were more positive in their assessment. The rector of St. Andrew's, New Kensington, reported that his parish had no social service committee but that he would support the establishment of one.[11] Robert Meade of Church of the Redeemer—an influential figure in the diocese—also declared a willingness to establish a committee, but only "provided it is more than a name after formation."[12]

For all that it reflected the spirit of the age, the social service commission was dependent on the cooperation of individual parishes. In 1913, its request that ten parishes host speakers on issues of social concern elicited only two favorable responses. Indeed, the commission's principal success was the preparation of a form for use by clergy preparing parishioners for marriage. Fully congruent with prevailing standards of social hygiene, it required both parties to the forthcoming marriage to obtain a doctor's certificate indicating that they suffered from no communicable or incurable disease. Diocesan clergy were encouraged to endorse legislation barring the "morally and physically unfit" from obtaining marriage licenses.[13] The commission also lobbied on pending state legislation dealing with housing standards, safeguards for women working in industry, and child labor, in all of which the church was considered to have a very real interest.[14] Even so, the social service commission continued to bemoan its lack of funds and general parochial unresponsiveness well into the First World War. "The problem," commission members declared in 1915, "which confronts your Commission—and this diocese—is to devise some method to convince our people that the Church has entered upon a period in which the

---

10. Rev. George B. Richards to Rev. Joseph Speers, October 12, 1912, RG4A/2.3:1, box 6DC, EDP.

11. Rev. Herbert A. Grantham to Rev. Joseph Speers, September 23, 1912, RG4A/2.3:1, box 6DC, EDP.

12. Rev. Robert N. Meade to Rev. Joseph Speers, September 27, 1912, RG4A/2.3:1, box 6DC, EDP.

13. *Convention Journal*, May 14–15, 1913, 34–38; Rev. Joseph Speers to "Revd. and Dear Sir," March 19, 1913, RG4A/2.3:1, box 6DC, EDP. Speers was later invited to cooperate with an exhibit on mental hygiene put on in Allegheny County by the Public Charities Association of Pennsylvania. See Mrs. Enoch Rauh to Rev. Joseph Speers, April 14, 1913, RG4A/2.3:1, box 6DC, EDP.

14. Rev. Joseph Speers to "Reverend and Dear Sir," February 1913, RG4A/2.3:1, box 6DC, EDP.

social implication of the Gospel is receiving, and must receive, a growing emphasis, and that social service is indeed of paramount importance.[15]

One exception to the prevailing apathy was found at the mother church of the diocese. In November 1914, Trinity Church built upon the tradition established by its former rector by establishing Trinity Girls' Friendly Lunch Room. This provided a cheap but wholesome lunch to the overwhelmingly female—and underpaid—workforce of the downtown offices and department stores, who were generally denied access to the male-only eateries of the Point. Operating five days a week for nine months of the year, the lunchroom provided meals at a cost of 23¢ per person. Its customer base increased dramatically, from 40 customers on the first day to 90 on the second and 270 on the third. Daily attendance stood at 500 by the end of the first month and had reached 1,200 by 1921. Such outreach also benefitted the parish. Several of the women who ate in the lunchroom also attended the noonday services and a few became members.[16]

Another attempt at reviving the institutional church had less happy consequences, involving as it did the charismatic former rector of Trinity, Alfred Arundel.[17] Throughout his time at Trinity, control of the vestry had remained in the hands of the social elite and Arundel failed to achieve the "democratization" of the vestry that Rainsford had pushed through in New York.[18] Starting in 1909, Arundel became more outspoken in his views and embraced a more explicitly Christian Socialist idiom. In one sermon, he directed his wrath against the politics of the day:

> Pennsylvania has been the fortress of tariff protection and Pittsburgh has been the inner citadel. All our manifold industries have enjoyed the advantages of protection to the limit. We are an

---

15. Report of the Social Service Commission, 1915, RG4A/2.3:1, box 6DC, EDP.

16. *Church News*, September 1922.

17. I discuss the social context of the Arundel Affair at greater length in "Limits of Acceptable Behavior."

18. The dramatic account of Rainsford's confrontation with financier J. P. Morgan is described in Rainsford, *Story of a Varied Life*, 279–84. "The rector," Morgan told the vestry, "wants to democratize the church, and we agree with him and will help him as far as we can. But I do not want the vestry democratized. I want it to remain a body of gentlemen whom I can ask to meet in my study." Rainsford responded: "I want in this vestry [those] who would represent fittingly the very great number of wage earners that are now regular members of St. George's. These should be represented *by one of their own number and class*" (281–82).

industrial state, with an industrial civilization and an industrial political conscience that, on the whole, has not risen above the dollar mark ... Public servants of every grade, from the unintelligent and misled man in the city council up to the clever and calculating boss, and even higher still, have measured their responsibility from this estimate. We deplore municipal evils and denounce the knavery that has fleeced the city and the state; but these things have been put up with and winked at because, up to date, they have seemed to be part of the price of safety for the sacred ark of the protective tariff.[19]

The year 1910 marked the publication of Shailer Matthews' book *The Social Gospel* (the first such volume to use the expression),[20] and Arundel sought to advance the parish commitment to that objective by initiating a series of Sunday evening discussions on such topics as "The Morals of the Wage System," "The Aim of Twentieth Century Charity," and "Prevention of Non-Employment." Speakers included the rector of Trinity and Bishop Charles Williams of Michigan, a prominent Social Gospeler.[21]

Infuriated by such social activism, the vestry ruthlessly sought to reduce or eliminate Arundel's funds for mission work and otherwise hamstring his attempts to fund a parish secretary and staff for Trinity's new recreational and educational facilities, obliging him to appeal to the wider parish for supplemental assistance.[22] In April 1911, while Arundel was away from Pittsburgh, vestry members resolved to "accept" his resignation, with the offer of a severance package of $10,000 over three years. Although Arundel had authorized the meeting, it remains unclear if he knew what was to be discussed. He later complained that he had never expressed a desire to retire but that one vestryman had told him shortly before "that the unanimous sentiment of the vestry is that my present relation to the parish should cease." He also objected to the reputed personal attack on him by the senior warden at the meeting and the release of the news of his resignation by the junior warden before it had been

19. *North American*, November 23, 1911.
20. Gorrell, *Age of Social Responsibility*, 127–28.
21. *Church News*, November 1910.
22. *North American*, November 23, 1911; Alfred Arundel to "Members and Friends of Trinity Parish," March 8, 1910, RG3/2.2, box 3T, EDP.

formally tendered. Nevertheless, on April 17, the rector of Trinity Church offered his resignation and it was accepted.[23]

Within a year, however, Arundel—who had been preaching in various eastern states—came to Whitehead with a proposal. What he needed, he said, was an ecclesiastical laboratory in which to do for Pittsburgh what Rainsford had done for New York and what Arundel had ultimately failed to do for Trinity. He pressed upon Whitehead the desirability of taking in hand the South Side parish of St. Mark's, a former daughter church of Trinity. The increasingly blue-collar environment of the South Side offered possibilities for an institutional church, and he considered himself suitable to head such an effort.[24] Parishioners of St. Mark's were enthusiastic at the prospect and elected Arundel rector in June 1912. When the bishop informed them that they could not call a new rector while a clergyman was in charge, the vestry promptly asked for the current incumbent to be removed.[25] On July 6, 1912, they defiantly informed the bishop that they had issued a call to Arundel, which brought back an equally frosty reply from Whitehead that the parish had been a dependency of the diocese for thirty years, with its ministers supported by the missionary board: "Before assuming independence, it would have been businesslike, not to say courteous to the Bishop and the Diocese, for the Vestry to have given some indication of their ability to maintain themselves. And now it appears that the Vestry is content to transfer its dependence from the Diocese, and to make S. Mark's virtually a mission and appendage of Trinity, Pittsburgh; for it is well know[n] that the Vestry of Trinity Church are sustaining their former Rector for the current year and the next two years."[26]

The vestry of St. Mark's and Arundel himself were unmoved, and Arundel agreed to take up residence in October 1912.[27] At this point, the bishop took legal advice from Calvary lawyer George Guthrie, who

23. Trinity Church, Vestry Minutes, April 4, 11, 17, 1911, RG3/1.3:1, box 1TVM, EDP. Alfred Arundel to the Vestry of Trinity Parish, April 7, 1911, Alfred Arundel to Edward T. Dravo, September 1, 1911, RG3/2.2, box 3T, EDP.

24. Bp. Whitehead to Alfred Arundel, March 12, 1912, Arundel to Whitehead, March 15, 1912, RG3/2.2, box 3T, EDP.

25. George P. Robinson to Bp. Whitehead, June 15, 1912, Whitehead to Robinson, June 19, 1912, Robinson to Whitehead, June 22, 1912, RG3/2.2, box 3T, EDP.

26. George P. Robinson to Bp. Whitehead, July 6, 1912, Whitehead to George P. Robinson, July 9, 1911, RG3/2.2, box 3T, EDP.

27. George P. Robinson to Bp. Whitehead, August 3, 1912, Rev. Alfred W. Arundel to Bp. Whitehead September 7, 1912, RG3/2.2, box 3T, EDP.

responded with the embarrassing revelation that short of bringing Arundel up before an ecclesiastical court—something the bishop was reluctant to do—his options were quite limited. Since Arundel had retained canonical residence in the diocese, the bishop could exert no bar against him taking up employment in a parish. Furthermore, while Whitehead could refuse to visit St. Mark's, he had no legal authority to dissolve it or interfere with administration of its property. "The Parish in this state," wrote Guthrie, "is not the child of the Convention. It does not require for its existence any authority from the Convention. It is not entitled to representation in the Diocesan Convention until its charter and by-laws have been approved by the Convention. But its existence and operation is not dependent on such recognition, so far as the civil law is concerned." Worse, still, from Whitehead's point of view, once Arundel took up his post, he would be entitled to a seat at the convention. Guthrie also doubted if any bill for an injunction against St. Mark's would succeed unless brought by a member of the parish having a property right to be protected.[28]

The new rector laid out expansive plans for institutional development. His teaching series on "Socialism as a Moral and Religious Force" proved equally controversial. "Socialism guides far better than the Bible," he told his listeners on one occasion, "because it make a man cleaner in his daily life by holding up a constant example before him. A supposed Christian will not lift his hand to right an economic wrong but a supposed atheistical Socialist will endanger his daily bread for his cause." Such statements led to public protests and did nothing to warm the bishop to the rector of St. Mark's.[29] When Arundel wrote asking the bishop to make a visitation for the purposes of confirmation and—rather naively—sought permission from the diocese to borrow "a few thousand" on the property, Whitehead sent back the note with the simple inscription, "What would be your reply if you were in my place?"[30] Fortunately for the bishop's blood pressure, Arundel's Christian Socialist experiment proved of short duration, and in March 1913 he resigned, citing his health as the cause.[31]

28. George W. Guthrie to Bp. Whitehead, September 7, 1912, RG2/2.2, box 3BP, EDP.

29. See the mounted, undated clipping subscribed "If the Protestant Episcopal Church is catholic as it claims to be why does not it discipline this heretic?" RG3/2.2, box 3T, EDP.

30. Cortlandt Whitehead to Alfred Arundel, November 27, 1912, RG3/2.2, box 3T, EDP.

31. Rev. Alfred W. Arundel to Bp. Whitehead March 7, 1913, RG3/2.2, box 3T, EDP.

Three months later, St. Mark's apologized to the bishop and asked to be taken back under his pastoral care. A stormy chapter in diocesan history had come to a close.

For most Episcopalians, attitudes to the Social Gospel fell somewhere between the extremes of apathy and outright defiance of authority. One option for those unhappy with the pace of change was to look outside the denomination for ecumenical initiatives.[32] Thus, in 1913, the secretary of the Allegheny County Federation of Bible Classes invited the participation of the social service commission in a pre-election meeting in Wilkinsburg at which it was hoped that a ticket could be agreed upon such that "the strongest Christian man may receive support of the Christian men as one body for the respective office which he is seeking."[33] Two years later, a committee from the Presbytery of Pittsburgh approached the rector of Trinity Church, Pittsburgh, asking him to publicize the downtown Market Street mission, something "worthy of the confidence and support of all evangelical churches in the community."[34] Such endeavors may well have influenced the social service commission in its 1918 recommendation for full cooperation with the Pittsburgh council of churches. "These war times have made men impatient with those who frivol with realities," commission members explained. "Why prate of 'unity' if we can not meet with our brethren of other Communions on the common platform of civic and social service? Unless we can cooperate with our brethren we fail to grasp the need of the hour."[35]

It was not simply the social service commission that favored a greater spirit of public service. Cortlandt Whitehead's confrontation with Alfred Arundel had as much to do with episcopal authority as with politics, and he in no way refrained from political observations of his own.[36] In a 1911

---

32. For more detail on this point, see Zahniser, *Steel City Gospel*.

33. Henry Gilchrist to Rev. Joseph Speers, February 21, 1913, RG4A/2.3:1, box 6DC, EDP.

34. William L. McEwan et al. to Rev. Edward S. Travers, October 16, 1915, RG3/1.2, box 2T, EDP.

35. *Convention Journal*, January 22–23, 1918, 44.

36. "[In] the last ten years," Whitehead told Bishop William Guerry of South Carolina in 1912, "there has been in spiritual matters retrogression [at Trinity], and a growing dissatisfaction which Dr. Arundel tried to meet by adopting what he called Christian Socialism, which won popularity in certain directions, but was not attractive to the people who really composed the parish. From my standpoint, his position was in itself entirely harmless, and I doubt if there was anything that he preached, or in the position which he

Ash Wednesday sermon indicting urban corruption, he urged the people of Pittsburgh to make a choice "between Barabbas and Christ—between bossism and political chicanery and clear, clean upright administration." A committee of Episcopal clergy and laity took heart from this adjuration to demand that all Christians make an effort to discern the moral principles underlying political and economic issues. The committee pledged support for the Pittsburgh Plan and urged citizens to "unite as one man, and defeat, if possible, the unrighteous manipulations and machinations of the selfish problems whose mis-called 'interests' are at stake."[37] Nor did Pittsburgh Episcopalians overlook the moral aspects of the Progressive crusade. In 1919, the social service commission opposed efforts to permit professional baseball games or movies on Sunday.[38] Though Episcopalians were generally cooler to Prohibition than other Protestant groups, even Bishop Whitehead came out in support of the Nineteenth Amendment in 1922. "[Every] thoughtful person," he wrote, "recognizes the necessity of some control, and the majority have believed in the ultimate expediency of Prohibition as to the manufacture and prevalent use of that which can intoxicate."[39]

Civic reform and the regulation of moral behavior were intimately connected, in Progressive eyes, with greater gender equality. Just as the Progressive movement enjoyed some of its strongest successes in the western United States, so it was in that region that women first secured the franchise. This shift in secular life had implications for the mode of governance of many American Protestant churches. Initially, Episcopal efforts to give women a greater say in the life and work of the church took the form of a special House of Churchwomen with the diocesan convention, an initiative particularly popular with many dioceses in the Pacific and Mountain states. However, such a body provided women only with a forum for discussion of ministries peculiar to their sex. As early as 1915, a committee considering whether a House of Churchwomen would be

---

assumed, which would not be entirely agreeable to your view of what the Gospel means when applied to Civic and Social matters. My judgement is, that it was simply too large a subject for Dr. Arundel's abilities, and he could not carry his people with him." Bp. Whitehead to William Guerry, March 9, 1912, RG3/2.2, box 3T, EDP.

37. *Church News*, June 1911. The text of Whitehead's sermon can be found in *The Parish Directory*, 8–10, RG2/2.2, box 3BP, EDP.

38. *Convention Journal*, April 22–23, 1919, 31–33.

39. *Church News*, June 1922 (quotation).

appropriate for Pittsburgh instead recommended a constitutional change to allow one female convention deputy for every self-sufficient parish. Women represented a majority in every congregation, committee members pointed out, and deserved the right to shape diocesan policy directly. Deputies disagreed with the recommendation and tabled the resolution by a distinct margin of 45-18.[40]

The following year, however, the diocesan convention did approve an amendment that gave parishes the option of selecting a woman deputy.[41] In so doing they were responding to very clear signs that their bishop favored the move. As Cortlandt Whitehead reminded deputies in 1919, even the national church had come round to this point of view, and the national board of missions was preparing for the advent of female members. "The matter is having consideration in England," the bishop warned. "It is looming up before the minds of the people who believe in Democracy. It should find its ready solution in the vestries of our parishes and in the delegates to our Convention."[42] Local option would remain the standard for over half a century, however, and while Pittsburgh deputies to the General Convention over the next few decades would be vocal advocates of women's right to representation at the national level, by no means did every parish adhere to that standard.[43]

As discussed in the previous chapter, Cortlandt Whitehead had pleaded for a permanent episcopal headquarters since the beginning of his episcopate. Rented rooms in downtown Pittsburgh, though preferable to being hosted in a parish building, clearly had little appeal to him. The rise of the national church idea brought with it a corresponding American interest in the erection of cathedrals, which would serve not only as episcopal seats but also as hubs for planning different aspects of the institutional church in a diocesan context. The cathedral movement also represented an effort by the advocates of greater national central-

---

40. *Convention Journal*, May 13-14, 1915, 57-58, 85. Most houses of churchwomen had no legislative power and were restricted to discussing missions, education, and charitable works.

41. *Convention Journal*, May 17-18, 1916, 67, 69.

42. *Convention Journal*, April 22-23, 1919, 100-102.

43. In March 1921, Bishop Whitehead drew attention to the recent Lambeth resolution urging that women be admitted to all church councils to which laymen had access. It was hard to see any objection to their admission to vestries and conventions, the bishop concluded, and he noted that the removal of the word "male" from the diocesan constitution gave any parish the option of electing female deputies. *Church News*, March 1921.

ization to vest authority in the office of bishop sufficient to counteract the influence exerted by the powerful rectors of wealthy urban churches. "A noteworthy feature in the Church's life in this country at present is the extraordinary interest in Cathedrals and pro-Cathedrals," the bishop of Pittsburgh commented in 1912, "and this means centralization ... the Institutional Church is groping towards this ideal of a central unifying executive force, gaining for the Diocesan Episcopate a local institution as well as a name."[44]

Members of the committee appointed in 1912 to explore the possibility of establishing a cathedral pointed out that Pittsburgh (the nation's eighth-largest city) was one of the few metropolitan dioceses not to have considered the issue. "Christianity, as represented in the Diocese," they argued, "should be appropriately clothed as a witness for Christ by housing it in an imposing Cathedral. The need of this is evidenced by the great banks, commercial and educational institutions and the State, all of which are clothed in magnificent outward form."[45] They stressed, however, that it would be wrong to understand a cathedral purely in terms of imposing worship space. A cathedral, they argued, should also serve as an educational institution (an analogy here was drawn with the Carnegie Library) and should be a "a people's Church ... not a church for the satiated church-goer, nor located in a fashionable or populous community."[46]

Such lofty sentiments notwithstanding, it remained unclear just how the project was to be accomplished. Funds for a new structure seemed unlikely while the pro-cathedral strategy (utilizing an existing parish church) relied on the willingness of the parish to sacrifice its independence. For various reasons, Trinity Church, Pittsburgh, was the obvious choice, but churches in the Oakland district, such as St. Peter's and Ascension, were also considered to possess "equipments of sufficient character and dignity, compatible with the importance of a cathedral church." Some consideration was also given to the suburban solution, reflecting the population shift away from the city to the suburbs and the consequent popularity of suburban cathedrals, with Calvary, St. Andrew's, and St. James Memorial in the East End all considered suitable.[47]

44. *Convention Journal*, May 22, 1912, 97–98.
45. *Convention Journal*, May 14–15, 1913, 42.
46. Ibid., 43.
47. Committee on the Diocesan Cathedral—Report of Subcommittee on Parish Relations, n.d. (prob. 1913), RG4A/1.7:2, box 6DSC, EDP. Bishop Whitehead suggested

In the event, there was little prewar enthusiasm for the cathedral project. One committee member resigned in 1913, saying that he felt that any available funds should be devoted to liquidating outstanding obligations to the national church.[48] Another Pittsburgher complained that most people with whom he had communicated viewed a new cathedral as an unrealistic proposition.[49] In December 1913, an attempt was made to counteract the negative publicity by inviting Alfred Harding, bishop of Washington, in whose diocese the National Cathedral was already under construction, to deliver a public lecture on the great cathedrals at the Carnegie Lecture Hall, but such efforts proved in vain.[50] Trinity declined the honor in May 1914, and a subsequent approach to St. Peter's elicited no response.[51] "I do not expect myself to see a Cathedral or Pro-Cathedral inaugurated," the bishop reluctantly admitted in March 1914, "but I am sure that gradually the proper spirit will be developed."[52] It must have been extremely galling for him later that year when the Diocese of Erie announced that it had accepted the offer of St. Paul's, Erie, to serve as its diocesan pro-cathedral.[53]

The failure of the cathedral scheme and the struggle with Alfred Arundel left Bishop Whitehead very concerned that his office continue to be respected. Writing to one of Trinity Church's lay leaders, as the parish began its search for Arundel's successor, the bishop made it very clear that he would not tolerate another individualist in such a prominent position:

---

that a pro-cathedral might be formed by the merger of St. Paul's with either St. Mary's Memorial or St. Peter's. Minutes of the Committee on the Diocesan Cathedral, November 11, 1913, RG4A/1.7:2, box 6DSC, EDP.

48. Edwin S. Craig to Bp. Whitehead, June 9, 1913, RG4A/1.7:2, box 6DSC, EDP.

49. Harvey Childs to Rev. John R. Wightman, June 20, 1913, RG4A/1.7:2, box 6DSC, EDP.

50. Herbert M. Wilson to "Dear Sir," December 24, 1913, RG4A/1.7:2, box 6DSC, EDP.

51. Minutes of the Special Committee on the Relation of the Cathedral to the Diocese, December 16, 1913–May 4, 1914, RG3/1.2, box 2T, EDP. The only recorded offer during Whitehead's episcopate was made by St. Stephen's, Wilkinsburg. See *Convention Journal*, January 22–23, 1918, 86.

52. Bp. Cortlandt Whitehead to Rev. Rudolph E. Schulz, March 6, 1914, RG3/1.2, box 2T, EDP.

53. *Church News*, November 1914.

The first purpose of a parish is to build up people in Christian lives, not to provide entertainment for the boys in the Brigade, young men in gymnasiums, young girls in the Girls' Friendly Society, and things of that sort. All these things should be the result of a deeply religious tone first established in the parish; and I tell you, from my rightful place as Bishop, that your first need is a deeply spiritual, and earnestly devout clergyman. The men that you have had in mind ... are not to be so characterized; good men, active, full of the "time-spirit," emphasizing the institutional and external and manifest, but themselves not posing as men in which the deeply religious element is most present ... I have been told that Mr. Sturges is considered by those who understand him best, to be "virtually a Unitarian," full of German rationalistic theology, preaching over the heads of his present congregation; which would indicate that he would be far afield in ministering to the multitude whom it should be the passion of Trinity to reach.[54]

Eight years later, the bishop even went to the length of denying permission for lay readers and clergy to hold services at St. Paul's, Laceyville, after the congregation reneged on a promise to waive its parish status and put itself under diocesan authority as a result of seriously going into arrears.[55]

Whitehead also continued to impress upon parishes the need for fiscal and administrative transparency. Treasurers were instructed to post a weekly report of contributions and expenditures and to present an itemized report at every vestry meeting. The results of the annual audit were also to be announced to the congregation on the Sunday before parish elections.[56] The bishop encouraged parishes to use a blank ballot for elections so that write-in votes were a possibility and parishioners could indicate their view of significant financial initiatives. "Our Parishes," Whitehead complained in 1914, "are frequently governed by an oligarchy, a few men who virtually form a close corporation, and the great mass of the people attend the service, pay the bills and support the institution, but have really nothing to say in the administration of affairs."[57] Similar indictments were frequently made of diocesan government. "The Diocesan Convention meets in a small circle of the more favored Parishes,"

54. Cortlandt Whitehead to Southard Hay, April 24, 1912, RG3/1.2, box 2T, EDP.
55. Committee on Established Work—Missionary Committee Minutes, November 23, 1920, RG4A/2.5:1, EDP.
56. *Church News,* January 1910.
57. *Convention Journal,* May 27–28, 1914, 135–38 (quotation on 135).

concluded the committee on the state of the church in 1915, "and all of its proceedings are more or less colored by that favored circle."[58]

Wealthy parishes had their own complaints about the standard of leadership elsewhere and the burdens they were expected to bear. Predominantly working-class congregations, such as St. Stephen's, Wilkinsburg, frequently sought their assistance. In 1910, St. Stephen's requested a $50,000 loan from Trinity Church, Pittsburgh, to liquidate its outstanding debt, since members could not afford to finance the interest payments. Trinity refused but agreed to be part of a consortium arrangement under which five Pittsburgh parishes—Calvary, Trinity, Ascension, St. Peter's, and St. Andrew's—all agreed to contribute a total of $2,000 a year for five years (or $10,000), to liquidate the outstanding principal.[59] St. Stephen's at least performed active ministry to Wilkinsburg's working-class population, but some other missions were both poor and apathetic. Members of the board of trustees were peculiarly frustrated with the situation in Monessen. "The congregation," they complained, "consists of about ten or a dozen families, who are dissatisfied that they have not a church of their own but seem to be in no shape to do much towards this end, for themselves, their attitude being that they expect Churchmen in Pittsburgh to provide a church building and a permanent rector."[60]

The weakness of missions like that at Monessen was compounded by the relatively thin distribution of Episcopal congregations across the region, for fewer than 15 percent of communities with more than five hundred residents enjoyed the presence of an Episcopal parish or mission. The pace of mission planting was far less than during the nineteenth century. Of the fifteen new missions established during the 1910s and early 1920s, seven were located in Allegheny County and all had closed by 1929. The only enduring parishes formed during this era were St. John's, Donora, organized in 1915—the only church from this period to survive to the present day—and All Saints, Aliquippa, formed in 1915 and closed in 1999.

By the mid-1910s, then, the pace of life in the Diocese of Pittsburgh appeared to have slowed. Even the outbreak of war in Europe in 1914 did not greatly alter the situation, though it brought much-needed employ-

58. *Convention Journal*, May 13–14, 1915, 110.

59. John T. Mackenzie to H. Lee Mason Jr., October 8, 1910, Mason to Mackenzie, February 4, 1911, Theodore Myler to Mason, April 29, 1911, RG3/1.2, box 2T, EDP.

60. Board of Trustees Minutes, December 5, 1916, RG4A/3.3, EDP.

ment to many working-class Pittsburghers. In 1917, however, President Woodrow Wilson's fateful decision to intervene in the conflict on the side of the Allied Powers posed a host of conundrums for Americans of all classes and creeds. Intervention appears to have won general Episcopal approval, if only because many church members still had close ties to the United Kingdom. Pittsburgh's diocesan convention passed resolutions supporting the U.S. government and stressing the altruistic nature of America's participation in the conflict, while Bishop Whitehead delivered a hawkish address to convention delegates: "If ever there was a war justifying the name, this is indeed 'A War of the Lord,' such as is mentioned in Holy Scriptures... With unfaltering confidence in the Lord God Almighty, this people is girding itself for a battle which must end in victory for the right, not because of the biggest guns or the greatest battalions, but because righteousness must surely conquer at last."[61]

Members of the diocese responded accordingly. Younger Episcopalians, including the son of a prominent Calvary vestryman, joined the armed services, and in September 1917 members of St. Stephen's, Wilkinsburg, watched as soldiers of the Eighteenth Infantry Division and their families received Communion together. A Red Cross workroom was opened at Trinity Church, Pittsburgh, which produced sweaters, socks, and bandages, while diocesan leaders urged local Episcopalians to pray for the soldiers, send letters, and contribute to soldiers' aid societies.[62] A women's war committee of the diocese was later organized to care for the 1,500 women brought to Swissvale to work in the expanding munitions industry.[63] In April 1918, Cosmo Lang, archbishop of York, visited Pittsburgh as part of a tour of thanks to the United States for its assistance. "You and I stand united together," he told a mass meeting at the Syria Mosque in Oakland, "and say 'Without liberty we cannot live and for liberty we shall die.'"[64]

---

61. *Convention Journal*, May 22–23, 1917, 35–36, 93 (quotation). Whitehead later composed an editorial on the "privilege" of being conscripted and the opportunity for men "to bear high witness, to do noble deeds, radiate courage, manifest their manhood, and to stand for their Country against injustice and wrong." *Church News*, September 1917.

62. *Church News*, June/July 1917, October 1917.

63. *Church News*, April 1918.

64. *Church News*, May 1918.

This newfound patriotism did nothing to reverse the steadily eroding financial position of the diocese. At the time when the Diocese of Erie separated from Pittsburgh, Bishop Whitehead had expressed some concern about the low level of the diocesan endowment, but subsequent efforts to solicit additional funds from wealthy churchmen came to nothing.[65] In December 1919, the board of trustees reported a deficit of over $5,500 and warned that urgent measures needed to be taken.[66] The financial crisis was not merely a local but a national issue. Earlier that year, Pittsburgh had become the first diocese to be briefed on the Nation-Wide Campaign (NWC), an ambitious attempt by the national church to raise $20 million over three years to stabilize its finances and establish the institutional machinery needed to address contemporary social problems.[67]

"We were a congregational Church [in the years prior to 1919]," an official at the General Board of Missions later admitted. "The diocese was pretty much a legal fiction, and every specialist board or agency was responsible for securing its own funds, even though there was General Convention or Diocesan Convention authorization behind them." At the initiative of Bishop Arthur Lloyd of the General Board of Missions, who expanded the limited mandate given him by the General Convention of 1916, a detailed national budget for mission, religious education, and social service was drafted, and a national every-member canvass, based on models already developed for parochial and citywide fund-raising, was endorsed by the General Convention of 1919.[68]

At Pittsburgh's 1920 diocesan convention, the local NWC committee announced that the proposed general financial canvass of all members of the diocese was only part of a wider program designed to make churchmen more aware of their corporate responsibility to the church: "The agencies of the Church are being centralized in the hope of a more efficient conduct of the affairs of the Church and a nearer measuring up to the demand of her Mission. We speak no longer of the Mission of the Church, but of the Church's Mission. We must, then, in this Diocese

---

65. *Church News*, April 1911; Bp. Whitehead to George C. Burgwin, February 23, 1912, RG4A/1.7:2, 6DSC, EDP.
66. Board of Trustees Minutes, December 9, 1919, RG4A/3.3, EDP.
67. *Church News*, June/July 1919.
68. "Reminiscences of Bishop R. Bland Mitchell," 234.

conform, if not in every respect in our Diocesan machinery, to the spirit of this new endeavor."[69]

The 1920 every-member canvass was not all that its proponents desired, however. Diocesan conferences on the issue drew representation from fewer than half the parishes (one conference organized for laypeople drew no attendees and had to be cancelled), and the opening service for a preaching mission on the subject was so poorly attended that it had to be postponed.[70] In October 1920, the diocesan missionary committee urged the NWC committee to stress the educational and spiritual aspects of the program.[71]

By January 1921, diocesan ambivalence had become even more evident. While almost $98,000 had been raised on behalf of the national church—compared to $45,000 the previous year—only half of the congregations had met their quota. Moreover, twenty-seven of the forty-one congregations that met their quota were missions rather than self-supporting parishes (assisted congregations supplying over 10 percent of direct receipts). By the fall of 1921, returns were even more disappointing, especially compared with similar efforts being undertaken by the Methodists and Presbyterians. An extreme case was reported of a congregation with parochial expenses of $8,000 that allocated less than 1 percent of its income to the national campaign. Overall, Pittsburgh had fallen behind about half the dioceses in the nation.[72]

Even as the Nation-Wide Campaign got into gear, parallel efforts to reorganize the diocese were under way. The committee appointed to study executive reorganization recommended the establishment of permanent committees on finance, established work (the selection of clergy for mission stations), church extension, and publicity and education. The standing committee, meanwhile, proposed the creation of a new post of administrative secretary to coordinate the work of all boards, committees,

69. *Convention Journal*, January 27–28, 1920, 39–58 (quotation on 45).

70. Committee on the Nationwide Campaign to the Missionary Committee, December 10, 1920, RG4A/2.5:1, EDP.

71. Minutes of the Missionary Committee of the Diocese of Pittsburgh, October 8, 1920, RG4A/2.5:1, EDP.

72. *Church News*, January 1921, September 1921. Fifteen parishes and four missions were delinquent in their NWC pledges in 1919 and seven parishes and four missions in 1920. Report of the Finance Committee to the Missionary Committee, January 14, 1921, Missionary Committee of the Diocese of Pittsburgh, RG4A/2.5:1, EDP.

and other diocesan organizations. The committee nominated a local clergyman, Homer Flint, for the post.[73] Secretary Flint entered upon his work with gusto, but expressed reservations about the degree of zeal evident in the diocese: "We need, however, one thing more than is at our present command, and that is a clearly defined, highly idealized, organized Diocesan spirit . . . It is embarrassing, therefore, to be obliged to report that there are yet some few clergy, some groups of laymen who have not seen the new glimpse which our Church has of its world-wide responsibility—the splendid new chance that has opened in this Diocesan-wide opportunity."[74]

The most radical changes proposed at the diocesan level affected the spheres of Christian education and foreign missions. As early as 1914, the Sunday school committee successfully pressed for the creation of a diocesan board of education, whose members were drawn from all parts of the diocese. Four years later, the board of religious education announced a plan to work with the boards of the Dioceses of Erie and Ohio to establish the Conneaut Lake Summer School. It also appointed a specialist in religious education to make regular visits to parish schools to advise rectors and Sunday school teachers.[75] In the sphere of foreign missions, the Nation-Wide Campaign had been specifically designed to provide an improved system of funding. Pittsburgh's close association with mission work in China before the First World War endured into the 1920s. In early 1919, funds were requested for $4,000 to erect a home for American women doctors and nurses in Wuchang and $25,000 for a center for young men in the business section of Nanking.[76] When a devastating earthquake inflicted heavy damage on Anglican institutions in Japan in 1924, almost forty parishes subscribed to the Japan Reconstruction Fund, as did many church schools and altar guilds. The diocese ultimately pledged $40,000, making it the fifth diocese in terms of giving, despite being the twelfth in terms of numerical strength and financial wealth.[77]

---

73. Report of the Committee on Plan and Scope, n.d., Missionary Committee of the Diocese of Pittsburgh, RG4A/2.5:1, EDP; Standing Committee Minutes, March 22, May 25, 1920, RG4A/1.8, box 9DRB, EDP.

74. *Convention Journal*, January 25–26, 1921, 47.

75. *Convention Journal*, May 14–15, 1913, 44–49; *Convention Journal*, January 22–23, 1918, 33; *Convention Journal*, January 25–26, 1921, 43–44.

76. *Church News*, August 1912, January 1919, February 1919.

77. *Church News*, June 1924; *Convention Journal*, January 27–28, 1925, 39.

A new area of concern for Pittsburgh Episcopalians—as for the Progressive movement in general—was the Americanization of immigrants from eastern Europe. "It will not do any longer to permit our non-English speaking residents to go their own way, to cherish ideals which are not ideals," warned the committee on missionary survey in the diocese in 1918. "The moment a man steps foot on our soil, from whatever other land, at that moment he must begin to become an American. With the new and less restricted opportunity that is presented to him, must go also our insistence upon new modes of thought for him and new ways of physical and moral and spiritual life."[78] Such outreach was relatively unknown before 1914. In 1918, Archdeacon Charles de Coux lambasted the attitude of the regular congregation in Braddock toward a mission to the local Italian community: "Until now the Mission has been carried on in the basement of the parish church. One would think that men and women naming the name of Christ and banded together in a corporate way, would welcome the opportunity of being host to a band of foreigners who come seeking our Christ; yet we regret to say that on the part of some of the people it is far otherwise; they look upon their being in the basement of their church as a veritable thorn in the flesh."[79]

The following year, Father Sisto Noce was commissioned to undertake a survey of local communities with substantial Italian populations. Noce concluded that, except in areas where they had the numbers to dominate a parish, Italians were second-class citizens in the Catholic community. "It seems that the Roman Priest [a Croat] lets his national feelings get the best of him in his attitudes towards [Italians]," Noce wrote of a visit to Rossiter, but the Italians would not attend the local Presbyterian church "because it does not answer to their idea of a Church." The same appeared to be true in Brownsville, where, according to Noce, half the Italians stayed away from the German and Hungarian Catholic churches because of the greediness of the priests and their contempt for Italians. In Sagamore, where the local priest reportedly refused to administer the sacraments without payment, Noce offered his services for free, baptizing a newborn and administering last rites to a dying woman. He also worked with the Italians excluded from the German and Irish churches on Pittsburgh's South Side and urged St. Mark's, Pittsburgh, to start evening classes in English and citizenship.

---

78. *Convention Journal*, January 22–23, 1918, 75.
79. Ibid., 65.

"The men especially look with favor upon our Church," he explained, "because while it keeps the dignity and sacred character of the Roman Church to which they have been used, it does away with its objectionable features—the compulsory confession and unmarried Priests."[80] St. Mark's already enjoyed a reputation for making its parish house available to the local community, and its members were proud of the fact that people of all denominations attended services and that there were Roman Catholic and Presbyterian members of the choir.[81]

Another previously neglected Episcopal constituency was Pittsburgh's African American community. The diocese maintained two black missions: St. Philip's and St. Augustine's. The latter had 150 communicant members in 1913 and was rapidly outgrowing its premises. "The colored like our Church," reported the diocesan newspaper, "and are very loyal to its discipline, doctrine and worship, and we have a most intelligent congregation."[82] Appeals for money for a larger facility bore fruit, and in 1917 the two black missions were merged into one congregation—Holy Cross. The new congregation had a widely dispersed membership, with parishioners from as far away as Sewickley. Its Sunday school reported 248 students, and every student over fourteen was a confirmed member of the church.[83]

Holy Cross apart, missions of the early 1920s were obliged to take on a different character from that of their predecessors. Some changes could be beneficial, as many established parishes began to develop formal relationships with struggling missions. In 1920, Calvary Church established a partnership with St. Alban's mission in Duquesne, the rector of Calvary calling this an opportunity to give productive work to the "wasted"

80. *Church News*, May 1921; Executive Council—Missionary Committee Minutes, April 8, 1921, Reports of Rev. Noce, n.d., Committee on Survey and Church Extension, Missionary Committee, RG4A/2.5:1, EDP. All the quotations are from Noce's reports.

81. Report on St. Mark's Parish, December 7, 1920, Committee on Established Work—Missionary Committee, RG4A/2.5:1, EDP.

82. *Church News*, January 1913. The paternalism of diocesan leaders is clear from a report of the model kitchen, dining room, and living room maintained by the mission. "The orderly, dignified ways of the Church ought also to characterize the work which many of our young colored people are called upon to perform," the paper recorded. *Church News*, February 1913.

83. *Convention Journal*, May 22, 1912, 103; *Church News*, March 1921. Even after the establishment of Holy Cross, "colored work" continued to be of interest to diocesan leaders. Committee on Established Work—Missionary Committee Minutes, October 27, 1920, RG4A/2.5:1, EDP.

manpower that Calvary's guilds and societies failed to absorb. A similar connection was formed between Grace Church, Mt. Washington, and St. George's in the West End.[84]

However, the administrative secretary of the diocese warned that other changes might be more radical in their effects. "Not today, not quite tomorrow, but within the day of many of us ... our Church will enter no new field unless and until it is prepared to enter that field fully equipped both to render service and to educate," he warned in 1922. "This I fear will be a bitter pill for the Episcopal Church to swallow; it has no sugared coating."[85]

Missions were increasingly seen as existing to serve their local community more than to make good Episcopalians. Of the Red Bank mission, one observer wrote: "A small hamlet of railroad people with no other Church for several miles ... There are no amusements in the village, no fire equipment, no community organizations of any kind and the Missionary here by tact and progressiveness could soon become a leader and could make the Mission the center of the whole village life."[86] At St. Luke's, Georgetown, attempts to increase membership were suspended for a two-year period, so that the parish might be made a welcoming place for the whole community. Evening forums, a stereopticon lecture, and celebratory events were all promoted, while members of the congregation also formed a community club and helped secure a public library for the town.[87] Similar considerations no doubt informed the decision of the rural missionary in Armstrong County to participate in a community church in Chickasaw rather than form a separate Episcopal mission.[88]

A FRESH START, 1923–1929

On September 18, 1922, the bishop of Pittsburgh suffered a fatal heart attack while in Niagara Falls, New York, for rest and recuperation. Three days later, the mortal remains of Cortlandt Whitehead were borne to

---

84. *Church News*, May 1920, February 1921.

85. *Convention Journal*, January 25–26, 1922, 88.

86. Report of the Rev. M. S. Kanaga, June 1920, Missionary Committee of the Diocese of Pittsburgh, RG4A/2.5:1, EDP.

87. *Convention Journal*, January 25–26, 1922, 87–88, 147–49.

88. Report of the Committee on Established Work, n.d. (January 1921), Missionary Committee of the Diocese of Pittsburgh, RG4A/2.5:1, EDP.

Pittsburgh's Church of the Ascension, where he lay in state as laypeople and clergy from both the city and the far-flung diocesan missions came to pay their respects. "So he passed," wrote a clerical veteran of the Whitehead years, "and so those who knew him most bore his body to its final rest, without ostentation or pomp, but with the dignity that comes of deepest grief and the sincerest reverence."[89] The legacy that Whitehead bequeathed his successor was a mixed one, and the economic decline of southwestern Pennsylvania in the years that followed would only exacerbate underlying problems. The new bishop of Pittsburgh had a difficult task before him.

Whitehead's high public profile and the reputation for social witness enjoyed by the diocese nevertheless ensured that there would be much vying for the episcopal title. Many local clergy favored the selection of a candidate from among their own ranks. Their strategizing was seen by some observers as little less than the work of a political caucus, though Homer Flint, administrative secretary of the diocese, earnestly sought to dispel such notions. "They acted openly," he assured Pittsburgh lay leader H. D. W. English of Calvary, "not in any closed meeting of any sort ... They were not discussing men, and I doubt if a single one of the Clergy (except two or three who appear to have been involved by their over-anxious friends in a seemingly aggressive campaign for notice) has a very definite idea yet of the 'best man for the job.'"[90] Flint, who, it should be remembered, had been the leading proponent of a new mission strategy, also had some advice for the new bishop. While many peripheral parishes were reporting dramatically higher rates of growth, the focus of the diocese continued to be on Allegheny County. "For one to view the job (using the vernacular) as being that of the 'Bishop of Pittsburgh,'" the administrative secretary warned, "will be to find himself with only a city and its suburbs for a Diocese, and the rest a problem which he does not and can not and never will understand."[91]

While Flint's name was briefly floated as a candidate, he showed little interest in the office.[92] Serious local contenders included Alleyne

89. *Church News*, October 1922.

90. Rev. Homer A. Flint to H. D. W. English, October 18, 1922, RG3/1.2, box 2T, Trinity Church/Cathedral Papers, EDP. Flint encouraged English to organize a similar meeting for the laity to think (and pray) about what qualities the next bishop should have.

91. *Church News*, November 1922.

92. "I should regret above measure if any person should permit his regard for me, his appreciation for what he sees me trying to do for the work or for the city, the fact

Howell of St. Stephen's, Sewickley; John D. Hills, president of the standing committee and rector of Epiphany, Bellevue; and Frederick Budlong of Ascension, Pittsburgh. Among the laity, who, for the first time, would directly cast a vote—by orders—for the nominee, the preference remained for an outsider. Two established bishops were contenders—David Ferris, bishop of Western New York (a former assistant at Calvary) and Herman Page, missionary bishop of Spokane—but many laypeople also expressed interest in the candidacy of Alexander Mann, rector of Trinity Church, Boston. A son of the manse, Mann had studied at Hobart College and the General Theological Seminary, from which he graduated in 1886. After service in Buffalo and Orange, New York, he moved in 1905 to Trinity, which had previously served as a preaching station for the legendary Phillips Brooks. Over the next fifteen years, Mann expanded the parish plant, built homes for the elderly and for boys, and introduced a parish financial budget system. He also became part of the fabric of Boston civic life, served four times as president of the Episcopal House of Deputies, and declined election as bishop of the Diocese of Washington in 1900 and of the Diocese of Western New York in 1917.[93]

Mann enjoyed the active support of Edwin van Etten, rector of Calvary, who had previously served as Mann's assistant in Boston, and he undoubtedly moved minds among the influential Episcopalians of his parish.[94] At the special diocesan convention in November 1922, Alleyne Howell led on the first ballot in both the clerical and lay orders, but both Bishop Page and Alexander Mann ran close behind. By the third ballot, Mann had secured a narrow majority of the lay delegates, but only a quarter of the clergy, demonstrating the fundamental division within the diocese. On the fifth ballot, Howell enjoyed a majority among the clergy, but Mann still led by 78 votes to 33 among the lay delegates, with 22 scattered among other candidates. The impasse continued until the eleventh ballot, when the clergy stampeded to John Hills in an effort to break the

---

that I happen to be one of the local Clergy, or the mere circumstances of my position in the Diocese, to obscure to the slightest degree the clearness of judgment as to the man needed for the highest results to the Church in the Diocese." Rev. Homer A. Flint to H. B. Rust, October 21, 1922, RG3/1.2, box 2T, Trinity Church/Cathedral Papers, EDP.

93. *Church News*, December 1922, February 1923.

94. After the election, Henry Scully of Calvary wrote to Mann telling him that the Scully family was 100 percent behind the new bishop and that he had prayed for Mann's election at the convention. Henry R. Scully to Rev. Alexander Mann, November 15, 1922, RG2/3.1, box 6BP, Bishops' Papers, EDP.

deadlock, but though Mann lost some ground among the laity, his lead could not be broken. Voting continued until the sixteenth ballot, when, with ten clerical abstentions, Mann finally secured the elusive clerical majority.[95]

It was not the most propitious start for a man charged with stabilizing the diocese. Nor was the new bishop, accustomed as he was to the civic amenities of Boston, overly impressed with what he found in his see city. Pittsburghers, he declared soon after his arrival, "are not greatly concerned over what I may call the recreational side of life. The very nature of the industries does not tend to make the town beautiful or attractive. And to the eye of the New Englander, there is a certain drab cheerlessness about them. All this no doubt will be remedied in time, with the growth of community spirit and community pride. When Pittsburgh gets rid of its smoke and covers its barren hillsides with foliage it will be one of the most picturesque as well as the most virile and industrious cities of the world."[96]

If disappointed in Pittsburgh's cultural scene, Bishop Mann had no such reservations about developing the social vision forged during the 1910s. He encouraged participation in a new conference on social welfare that brought together representatives from all of Pennsylvania's Episcopal dioceses to develop a consensus on social service issues, an initiative that he hoped would convince professional social workers that the church was genuinely interested in their work.[97] In 1925, the joint heads of the diocesan social service department (Henry English and Julius Sauber) attempted further to stress that they understood their mission as complementary to that of the state. "The Department [of social service]," they declared, "feels that it is not the purpose of the Church in the Diocese to set up separate and distinct social organizations but rather that it is our purpose to pour its contribution of thought, inspiration and service into the channels of agencies already existing, so that instead of becoming a competitor of any, we become the co-worker of all."[98] Sauber proved no laggard in this regard, for he served as president of the Social Workers Club of Pittsburgh, chairman of the Conference on Immigration Policy,

95. *Special Convention Journal*, November 8, 1922, 14.

96. Rt. Rev. Alexander Mann, Address to the Scotch-Irish Society of Pennsylvania, n.d., RG2/3.1, box 6BP, Bishops' Papers, EDP.

97. *Church News*, May 1925.

98. *Convention Journal*, January 27–28, 1925, 99.

and a member of the Federation of Social Agencies.⁹⁹ Later in the decade, the department conducted a number of surveys of parish programs and a social survey of Carnegie, which was intended to reveal to local Episcopalians how best they might contribute to social improvement.¹⁰⁰

The shift away from the institutional church model also had significant implications for other areas of diocesan life. In 1923, the diocesan Conneaut Lake Summer School offered a number of relevant courses to interested students, including "Social Service in the Parish"; "Social Service and the Individual"; "The Mind of the Worker"; and "The Foreign-Born in Western Pennsylvania." Trinity Church, Pittsburgh, also served as a venue for discussion of such issues with its "Friday Night Conferences," at which a leading figure in the field of social work would be the principal speaker. For the nonspecialist, Trinity also provided a number of Trinity Institutes—noonday lectures on social principles.¹⁰¹ Smaller parishes were urged to follow in Trinity's footsteps. "A Parochial Discussion Group would be a new venture in most Parishes," the department of social service admitted, "but one quite in keeping with the trend of the times. The technique of Discussion Groups is developing and the popularity of the method is increasing in other circles."¹⁰²

Some parishes took up the challenge. "Housing, health, thrift, education are but a few of the big problems of the Negro in this community," the rector of Holy Cross reported, "but this does not mean that the parish is to become another of the many social agencies and launch out into welfare work. Competent agencies are already engaged in this work." Instead, Holy Cross would encourage its members to participate in secular welfare work.¹⁰³ Kingsley House, though now detached from its Episcopal roots, continued to provide services to the Italian American community of East Liberty, including workshops, nursing and maternity services, and facilities for social and musical organizations.¹⁰⁴ The bright shining star of the era, however, was the rector of Christ Church, New Brighton, who

99. *Convention Journal*, January 26–27, 1926, 99–100.

100. *Convention Journal*, January 27–28, 1927, 160–61.

101. *Church News*, April 1923. This issue also carried articles by a case supervisor of the Associated Charities of Pittsburgh and a town planner and member of the Citizens' Committee on the City Plan of Pittsburgh.

102. *Convention Journal*, January 24–25, 1928, 114–15 (quotation on 115).

103. *Church News*, September 1924.

104. *Church News*, February 1925.

helped establish a child study bureau and a children's aid society in his local community. He also served on the Beaver County Safety Council and was active in encouraging leading local citizens to find work for the unemployed. "[The] work in this parish," the department of social service concluded, "offers an example of service which may be rendered to the community in which we live."[105]

Episcopalians were also active in the political arena. "[One] has but ... to study the names on our Diocesan Boards and Departments," mused Homer Flint,

> or to read over the directorship lists of charitable, educational, social and political institutions, or of the banking, manufacturing, commercial, transportation, and publishing enterprises, or to look into the "Who's Who" of the professions, the rosters of the fraternal associations, the patron list of any civic or patriotic or other community undertaking, to understand that there really is a "force" exerted by our Church in the Diocese ... which is surpassed by that of no other group, large or small, within our borders. It is so in the cities, in the industrial centers, in the small towns.[106]

In 1922, Calvary Church celebrated the election of one of its members, David Reed, to the United States Senate.[107] Even the bishop did not neglect political issues, delivering an address in 1925 at Trinity Church in support of American participation in the World Court. "[The] United States," Mann explained, "with its vast and heterogeneous population drawn from all races and religions of the world will show the world that the spirit of brotherhood is capable of embracing all peoples and creeds. It will be a picture in miniature of what the world under the Spirit of Peace may become."[108]

---

105. Department of Social Service Minutes—Diocesan Council, Report for 1929, RG4A/2.5:2, EDP.

106. *Church News*, May 1923. Bishop Mann argued that these business connections could provide an excellent basis for erecting a Church House on the site of Trinity House, which would not only serve as a diocesan headquarters but could pay for itself by leasing to downtown businesses in search of additional office space. *Convention Journal*, January 22-23, 1924, 113.

107. Edsall, "Three Generations," 148A.

108. Bp. Mann address at Trinity Church, December 30, 1925, RG2/3.1, box 6BP, EDP. The following year the diocesan convention urged Pennsylvania's two senators to vote in favor of participation in the World Court. *Convention Journal*, January 26-27, 1928, 30.

Like Cortlandt Whitehead, Alexander Mann devoted much of his time to the maintenance of stable diocesan finances. His constant lament was that his diocese did not exert the same influence in the affairs of the national church that the region played in national affairs (all the more sobering when one considered the number of Pittsburgh's business leaders who were members of Episcopal parishes).[109] The lukewarm response to the Nation-Wide Campaign in the early 1920s told its own tale. In 1921, twenty-one parishes reported that their contribution to the national church program exceeded a quarter of their parish budget. Nine such parishes had more than three hundred members, including St. Andrew's, Pittsburgh (46 percent of parish budget); Advent, Pittsburgh (44 percent); St. Stephen's, Wilkinsburg (42 percent); and Calvary, Pittsburgh (41 percent). Twenty-four parishes, on the other hand, allocated less than one-tenth of their budget to the national church, including seven who gave nothing at all. Three of the latter had more than three hundred members: St. Matthew's, Homestead; St. Mark's, Pittsburgh; and Incarnation, Knoxville.[110] These disparities did not bode well for expansion of the national church's administrative machinery.

In March 1923, Bishop Mann warned of the looming crisis facing the national council of the Episcopal Church, still reeling from a deficit of $400,000 in 1922. Pittsburgh, he noted with pain, had subscribed only $43,703 out of a quota of $159,370, a truly "mortifying figure."[111] That many parishes were lukewarm is self-evident; but whether the lack of enthusiasm arose from a failure of clerical leadership or genuine lay disaffection is unclear. In one instance, the rector of St. Stephen's, Sewickley, Alleyne Howell, charged Homer Flint—as administrative secretary of the diocese—with wrongfully claiming that Howell had refused to allow his vestry to canvass for the Nation-Wide Campaign, despite the parish's "untold wealth," when it was members of the vestry who had been unenthusiastic. "I do not of course see great numbers of persons from the Sewickley parish," Flint responded. "But of those who have ever talked to me about the interest of the Sewickley people in the Church's program,

---

109. *Church News*, May 1923.

110. Statistics derived from summary table in *Convention Journal*, November 8, 1922.

111. *Church News*, March 1923.

you yourself are the only one who has ever intimated that there was any lack of enthusiasm on the part of the people."[112]

Alexander Mann constantly urged the national church to adopt a realistic approach to its financing, criticizing the tendency of some to put as much emphasis on new projects as on existing work. "Men feel and rightly that there is a moral urgency to pay our share of the cost of the work which the Church is actually doing," he pointed out, "which does not attach in the same degree to work which the Church would like to do if it had the money."[113] In 1925, Mann called for a national budget based on a reasonable expectation of diocesan receipts, even if this led to a reduction in overall expenditures.[114] To Mann's gratification, the national council responded by adopting a pay-as-you-go approach, and the bishop of Pittsburgh then undertook to raise almost $35,000 from wealthy members of his diocese to help liquidate $1.4 million of national church debt.[115] Mann did recognize that commitments from below were as important as those from above, and he chastised parishes that tried to hold back diocesan and national assessments until the end of the year, when they needed to be remitted on a monthly basis.[116]

As economic prosperity returned during the mid-1920s, the national funding shortfall slipped from the headlines. In Pittsburgh, diocesan leaders actually revealed a willingness to allow established parishes to go into debt. From the $9,000 mortgage secured by Church of the Messiah, Sheraden, for its new rectory and choir room to the $15,000 mortgage for the new parish house for St. Paul's, Monongahela, and the $20,000 mortgage for St. Mary's, Beaver Falls, to pay off what it owed on its parish house and enlarge the church building, a climate of rising expectations

---

112. Rev. Alleyne C. Howell to Rev. Homer A. Flint, March 14, 1923, Flint to Howell, March 16, 1923, RG3/1.2, box 2T, EDP.

113. *Convention Journal*, January 22–23, 1924, 39.

114. *Convention Journal*, January 27–28, 1925, 36–37. Some of those reductions came all too quickly. Later that year, the national council rescinded grants that it had planned to make to Episcopal colleges because of the failure of many dioceses to meet their apportionments. "It will tend inevitably to create the impression that the Episcopal Church does not care for higher education under Church auspices," Mann commented, "an attitude which is certainly not that of the other great Christian Communions." Bp. Mann to Editor of the *Churchman*, 1925, RG2/3.1, box 6BP, Bishops' Papers, EDP.

115. *Convention Journal*, January 26–27, 1926, 38, 41.

116. *Convention Journal*, January 24–25, 1928, 48.

overwhelmed any sense of fiscal restraint.[117] A reinvigorated Alexander Mann spoke glowingly of the diocese's financial standing in January 1929 and emphasized its need to make a full pledge for national missionary work, complete the endowment, and raise the salaries of clergy in the smaller parishes. "The Diocese is out of debt," he explained, "the country is prosperous. We are facing the new administration of national affairs with confidence—is it then unreasonable to believe that we can put this Diocese in the one hundred per cent class, if we really care to do so."[118]

Symbolic of the new prosperity was the movement of middle-class Pittsburghers from the city to the suburbs, a phenomenon identified early in Mann's episcopate by the field secretary of the diocese, Milton Kanaga:

> In increasing numbers, men of small means or average salaries are building their homes beyond the limits of the city along the railways, interurban lines and paved roads. Small villages have come to count their populations in thousands such as Dormont, Beechwood, Corliss, Coraopolis and West View. In addition to these each year sees new communities of smaller populations, with stores and schools and too often with no Church of any kind. Sunday after Sunday, these people "listen-in" by radio to the services of the city Churches but they are deprived of the whole development that comes through corporate worship and service.[119]

The flagship parish of this suburban transformation was St. Paul's Church, which relocated from Laceyville to the automobile suburb of Mt. Lebanon in 1925 and within four years was poised to begin work on a church building.[120] Bishop Mann took an unusual degree of interest in this particular church plant, especially after the mission's executive committee invited him to choose the site. After driving through the borough, Mann recommended a location near the geographic center of the com-

---

117. Board of Trustees Minutes, June 9, 1924, November 10, 1925, January 11, 1927, RG4A/3.3, EDP. Of the Beaver Falls mortgage with the Dime Savings and Loan Association, the chancellor warned that placing a mortgage with a building and loan association made one a stockholder and, if that institution failed, the mortgager would be in the position of being both creditor and debtor: "It was stated also, however, that under normal circumstances the contingency above suggested was a very remote one."

118. *Church News*, January 1929.

119. *Church News*, May 1923.

120. Board of Trustees Minutes, November 14, 1924, RG4A/3.3, EDP. On the growth of Mt. Lebanon, see Hoffman, "'Plan of Quality.'"

munity and close to the site of the future high school. "The growth of Mt. Lebanon has been phenomenal and there is no sign of lessening activity," he told the diocesan convention. "It is the great new residential district [for] the City of Pittsburgh and it is being filled with a class of people to whom the Episcopal Church makes a strong appeal."[121]

Suburban sprawl also produced new approaches to ministry and mission. In 1921, Calvary Church hosted the first radio broadcast of a church service in the United States. Evening broadcasts of Calvary's services became a regular feature, with the addition, five years later, of a half-hour prelude during which hymn tunes requested by listeners (many of them from non-Episcopal sources) were played.[122] In 1930, St. Peter's, Pittsburgh, held its first "screen services," consisting of a popular film accompanied by an act of worship. Films shown included *Quo Vadis*, *The Little Minister*, and *Tale of Two Cities*.[123] For isolated families living far from a place of worship, the department of missions prepared special "sermonettes," which also contained an order of service, to be mailed out twice a month, and also provided every family with a copy of the new version of the Book of Common Prayer, authorized in 1928.[124]

Outside the booming suburbs, smaller congregations increasingly looked to each other for solace and support. In 1924, a meeting was held on Pittsburgh's North Side, at which members of Christ Church, North Side; Emmanuel, North Side; Nativity, Crafton; Epiphany, Bellevue; and St. Stephen's, Sewickley, all met for fellowship and discussion of common problems.[125] The notion of merging small parishes was also tentatively explored, despite the predictable resistance that most parishes expressed to surrendering their own building. In 1929, St. Mark's on the South Side—for many years supported by the diocese—agreed to unite with Incarnation, Knoxville, to become St. Mark's, Knoxville. "Such mergers do

---

121. Department of Missions Minutes, Diocesan Council, January 8, 1929, RG4A/2.5:2, EDP; *Convention Journal*, January 22–23, 1929, 43. St. Paul's was one of the few successful church plants of the period. Only three new missions were planted during the 1920s, two in Armstrong County—St. Andrew's, Cadogan (1925) and St. Thomas, Furnace Run (1926)—and one in Somerset County—St. John's Meyersdale (1926). All were closed between 1934 and 1946.

122. Edsall, "Three Generations," 141–42; *Church News*, February 1926.

123. *Church News*, February 1930.

124. *Convention Journal*, January 28–29, 1930, 119.

125. *Church News*, March 1924.

not easily come about," Bishop Mann admitted. "There is on both sides a natural and rightful local pride and affection, and it means self-control, and a willingness to sink personal preferences in a common effort for the good of the Church to effect such a merger."[126] Diocesan leaders were less impressed by the sort of attitude displayed by members of St. Margaret's, Wilmerding, when they inquired how much aid their mission could expect from the diocese, even though they had yet to conduct an every-member canvass to determine the mission's capacity to support itself. "Your people are not assisting the Diocese to do something," a diocesan official explained. "The Diocese is trying to assist your people to maintain the Missions. Naturally, therefore, the people will do and will want to do all they can before they ask for help."[127]

Like the national church, the Diocese of Pittsburgh generally escaped the worst of the theological controversies that tore asunder the Protestant mainline denominations during the 1920s.[128] Conflict over the declarations of William Montgomery Brown, bishop of Arkansas, and William Lawrence, bishop of Massachusetts (most notably Lawrence's contention that many Episcopal clergy did not accept the doctrine of the Virgin Birth) did provoke agitated debate, though neither bishop enjoyed a dedicated following. Even so, U.S. senator George Wharton Pepper of Pennsylvania went to the lengths of leading a delegation to Bishop William Manning of New York protesting the growing strength of liberal Protestant theology within the Episcopal Church. In 1925, Manning engineered a compromise in the House of Bishops—which still required that all Episcopal clergy and laity must accept a literal interpretation of the Virgin Birth and physical resurrection of Jesus Christ—and spearheaded moves to depose Bishop Brown, who had declared that he believed the creeds only in a symbolic fashion.[129]

Bishop Mann refused to take sides in the debate. Arguing that theological scholarship was something better suited to "quiet thought in the study rather than for excited declamation in the pulpit,"[130] he made it clear

126. *Convention Journal*, January 22–23, 1929, 42.
127. Secretary Treasurer to Fred B. Sheldon, December 10, 1929, RG1/1.11, box 10PP, EDP.
128. See, for example, Furniss, *Fundamentalist Controversy*; Hart, *Defending the Faith*.
129. Prichard, "Place of Doctrine," 28–35; Katerberg, "William T. Manning."
130. *Church News*, January 1924.

that he had no desire to stifle exchanges. "Let the liberal and conservative continue the debate to which they are drawn by their very natures, their whole intellectual and moral prepossessions," he remarked. "But let them argue as members of a common family, bound together by a common family tradition, breathing the common atmosphere of mutual trust and mutual good-will, and recognizing in each other, as a matter of course, the same honesty of purpose, the same loyalty to the common cause, the same devotion to the common Lord."[131]

A visible aspect of the emerging sense of common mission was the successful establishment at Trinity Church, Pittsburgh, of the diocesan cathedral long dreamed of by Cortlandt Whitehead. At the heart of the city's financial and commercial district, Trinity was much involved in outreach to the business community.[132] In 1927, the parish offered its facilities as the basis for a cathedral, an offer unanimously approved by a meeting of junior and senior wardens of diocesan parishes in December.[133] "It is a frank and generous offer," Bishop Mann declared. "It contemplates a real cathedral, owned and controlled by the Diocese, not a Parish Church camouflaged under that title."[134]

At a congregational meeting in January 1928, the rector, Percy Kammerer, reminded his audience that Trinity had already ceased to be solely a parish church:

> [We] have for five years been conducting in this Church what is in reality Diocesan work. We have not the limited work of the average Parish. We have here in the downtown section of Pittsburgh a peculiar form of work, a work which does not center in the Sunday services, but covers every day of the [week]. Our Noon-Day Services meet the spiritual needs of thousands of our fellow-citizens. We are indeed a Diocesan Church already and ever since my coming to you as Rector I have striven to shape the policy of

---

131. *Convention Journal*, January 22–23, 1924, 40–41. At the close of the decade, the Episcopal Church adopted a revised version of the Book of Common Prayer. "[The New Prayer Book] has been enriched," declared Bishop Mann; "its rubrical provisions have been made more flexible, archaic expressions have been eliminated, especially in the Office of Holy Baptism, and the whole Book has been made more intelligible and so more acceptable to our day and generation." *Convention Journal*, January 22–23, 1929, 38.

132. *Church News*, December 1923.

133. Minutes of Laymen's Meeting, December 19, 1927, RG3/1.2, box 2T, EDP.

134. *Church News*, January 1928.

this Church so that should the Cathedral idea come up, the change could be made with a minimum of friction and with great ease.

Kammerer assured his congregation that cathedral status would in no way undermine its existing organizations, but would actually stimulate an increase in membership. The new cathedral would not accept letters of transfer from other parishes in the city, he promised, to avoid competition with other clergy, but would rather seek to minister "to those thousands of people who walk up and down our city streets." The congregation endorsed the move by an overwhelming 100 votes to 2.[135]

Bishop Mann pledged that the building would be a visible symbol of unity for the diocesan family. "It will be a house of prayer for all people who care to come here to pray," he promised at the cathedral's dedication. "We hope they will enter here as they enter the Public Library or the Museum of Art with the feeling that it belongs to them."[136] Within two years, Trinity had hosted a visit by the Methodist missionary to India, E. Stanley Jones, and also offered an Armistice Sunday service for the community.[137] It is "the centre of all civic religious movements," the bishop insisted, "and we have already established a very cordial understanding between ourselves and the other Christian Communions ... Also, we are in touch with the trained social workers of the City and they look to the Cathedral as their spiritual home."[138]

HOLDING THE LINE, 1930–1943

The consecration of Trinity Cathedral in many ways proved to be the high point of Alexander Mann's episcopate. The following year, the economic downturn that followed the Wall Street Crash brought to an abrupt end many of the bishop's more expansive plans for the diocese. In February

---

135. Transcript of congregational meeting at Trinity Church, Pittsburgh, January 4, 1928, RG3/1.2, box 2T, EDP.

136. Mann address at the opening service of Trinity Cathedral, June 3, 1928, RG2/3.1, box 6BP, EDP.

137. *Convention Journal*, January 28–29, 1930, 47.

138. Rt. Rev. Alexander Mann to Rev. William A. Lawrence, May 14, 1930, RG3/1.2, box 2T, EDP. Some saw the new cathedral chapter structure as a means of mollifying diocesan parishes. In 1934, there was discussion of making the former rector of St. Stephen's, Sewickley, an honorary canon to propitiate the parish's pro-Howell vestry, which was still resentful of the fact that he had been obliged to retire. Hill Burgwin to Rt. Rev. Alexander Mann, August 15, 1934, RG2/3.1, box 6BP, Bishops' Papers, EDP.

1930, it became clear that the diocesan pledge to the national church would be $1,500 less than that pledged in the previous year. While he admitted that the national church would have to curb its spending, the bishop still urged his parishes not to adopt a "pay as you please" philosophy.[139] The following month, the board of trustees began to discuss whether the diocese should cease to take a direct interest in building new churches.[140] October brought the news that the treasurer of the diocese lacked the money needed to pay that month's salaries, leading Mann to urge that any parish economies should not be made at the expense of the diocese.[141]

In January 1931, Bishop Mann delivered a somber assessment of the economic situation. The diocese had met its pledge to the national church only because wealthy individuals had made up a shortfall of $13,000. While substantial grants had been made to support the erection of new churches in Aliquippa, Mt. Lebanon, and Carnegie, existing reserves had had to be mortgaged to meet the promised payments. Striving to make the best of bad circumstances, the bishop noted that hard times economically might serve to reinvigorate the church. "A long period of uninterrupted material prosperity," he declared, "has usually had the effect of dimming the spiritual vision and enfeebling religious effort."[142]

By the close of 1931, material prosperity showed no sign of returning. The treasurer reported that forty-one congregations now had outstanding debts and that the diocese had assumed responsibility for those parishes whose deeds it held.[143] "It is apparent," he told the board of trustees, "[that] the Churches in the Diocese hold a privileged position so far as credit [is concerned and this] is due mostly to the fact that our congregations are closely integrated in the organization of the Diocese. In other words the

139. *Church News*, February 1930.
140. Board of Trustees Minutes, March 14, 1930, RG4A/3.3, EDP.
141. *Church News*, October 1930.
142. *Convention Journal*, January 27–28, 1931, 44.

143. Parishes that undertook major construction during the early twentieth century were increasingly required to surrender their deed as a condition of the diocese underwriting their endeavors. In 1931, the board of trustees entertained a request from All Saints, Aliquippa, which offered to transfer all property from the parish to the board if the latter would mortgage that property to the Fidelity Trust Company of Pittsburgh for $23,000. "The request," the board noted, "is really a transfer of indebtedness, the property being already mortgaged to Woodlawn parties for $19,000 and a note still due Contractors for $4,200." Board of Trustees Minutes, October 13, 1931, RG4A/3.3, EDP.

basis of credit is the good will and integrity of the Diocese." Given the numerous failures of banks that held church mortgages, it might be possible to spread repayment of total liabilities over a period of years. However, the treasurer warned, even the church could not expect the financial sector to forgive its debts. He recommended the establishment of a temporary finance corporation, independent of both the board of trustees and the diocese, which could handle all mortgage repayment issues.[144]

Repayment of outstanding financial obligations increasingly took second place to the more immediate need to provide direct relief to destitute Episcopalians. As early as 1928, Bishop Mann, though taking no stand on the merits of the dispute, had urged local Episcopalians to contribute to the Clergyman's Fund for Miners' Relief, which sought to relieve suffering in the strike-torn coal districts of West Virginia.[145] By 1931, his calls for relief were more directed to the needs of those of his coreligionists whose jobs had been terminated by the recession. A first step in that process was an initiative of the social service department that provided rectors with lists of employers matched to the skills of their unemployed parishioners.[146] Declining employment rolls soon undermined this approach, leading to new plan under which members of wealthy parishes, who might have odd jobs to be done, were linked with parishes with a more working-class demographic. Such marriages of convenience included Church of the Ascension with St. James Memorial, and St. Paul's, Mt. Lebanon, with St. Mark's, Knoxville.[147] Even this solution had limits, as became clear in November 1932, when Bishop Mann delivered a radio broadcast in which he explained that about half of the $2.5 million needed to assist the needy in Allegheny County had been raised from the well-to-do and the balance must be obtained from "the great mass of citizens who are neither very rich nor hopelessly poor."[148]

144. Board of Trustees Minutes, December 8, 1931, RG4A/3.3, EDP. The 1932 convention authorized the board of trustees to use diocesan funds to meet the indebtedness of parishes and missions. *Convention Journal*, January 26–27, 1932, 28–29.

145. *Convention Journal*, January 24–25, 1928, 56.

146. *Church News*, February 1931. On the appointment of that committee, see Department of Social Service Minutes—Diocesan Council, March 25, 1930, RG4A/2.5:2, EDP.

147. Department of Social Service Minutes—Diocesan Council, December 18, 1931, RG4A/2.5:2, EDP.

148. Address by the Rt. Rev. Alexander Mann, D.D., in behalf of the Welfare Fund, Station KDKA, November 16, 1932, RG2/3.1, box 6BP, Bishops' Papers, EDP.

Some parishes chose to take direct action. Members of St. Peter's, Pittsburgh, chose to repaint the parish church in 1930 "because we know that there is very serious unemployment at the present time and we feel that if we can give work to men nowadays we are doing a little bit towards helping to solve one of the great social problems of the country."[149] Calvary, East Liberty, organized its own emergency committee in 1931, under whose auspices the women of the parish sewed clothes and obtained shoes and household supplies for indigent families. The following year, the sewing work was offered to local women as a form of paid employment.[150] Emmanuel Church on the North Side had twenty-five unemployed families in its midst in 1932. "Visits paid to families in distress often reveal the fact that the families were once active in some church, but fallen fortunes, changes in living conditions made them sensitive," one report concluded, "and they do not make themselves known to the Rector although there is always a welcome and friendly hand extended to all who come." In response, Emmanuel hired twenty unemployed parishioners to refurbish the church basement. Outside Pittsburgh, the women's guild of St. Paul's, Kittanning, served "soup luncheons" to between 150 and 200 needy schoolchildren.[151]

A presidential election year brought a new consciousness to many Episcopalians that they might have to participate directly in the search for a solution to the prevailing economic crisis. The diocesan department of social service encouraged parish vestries to adopt a resolution requesting the state legislature to make full and adequate relief available to the unemployed.[152] Some of Pittsburgh's Episcopalians entered the political arena, though eyebrows were raised throughout the diocese when the minister-in-charge of St. Andrew's, New Kensington, was nominated in the 1931 primary election for treasurer of Westmoreland County.[153] In Pittsburgh, the failures of the city administration helped elect two mayors

---

149. *Church News*, March 1930.

150. Edsall, "Three Generations," 192; *Church News*, December 1931, June 1932.

151. *Church News*, January 1932.

152. Department of Social Service Minutes—Diocesan Council, June 3, 1932, RG4A/2.5:2, EDP.

153. Department of Missions Minutes, Diocesan Council, June 2, 1931, RG4A/2.5:2, EDP. A majority of the parish approved of his candidacy.

of Pittsburgh—William McNair and Cornelius Scully—who were members of Calvary Church.[154]

There was an altered tenor to Bishop Mann's 1932 convention remarks, as he commended his clergy's cooperation with local relief agencies and social workers: "You will agree with me that it is not for the Church, as such, to endorse officially methods of public relief. That is the business of the State, but of one thing I am sure, and that is that the Christian citizen's attitude towards the various schemes of relief that are proposed must be determined, not by the politician's concern for votes, nor by the selfish fear of increased taxes, but by those unforgettable words of Jesus Christ—'I was hungry and ye gave me meat, I was naked and ye clothed me.'"[155]

In Kittanning, Louis Perkins, rector of St. Paul's Church, served as the elected chairman of the general relief committee of Armstrong County, which cooperated with relief organizations to gather and distribute surplus fruit and farm produce to the needy.[156] Parishes such as St. Peter's, Pittsburgh, and St. Timothy's, McKees Rocks, hosted local community councils,[157] while Emmanuel, Pittsburgh, offered its parish auditorium as a place to store clothing for the Red Cross, even as its parish workers helped distribute four thousand sacks of flour throughout the Manchester district.[158] "We have learned by bitter experience," admitted Bishop Mann in a sermon preached in New York in 1933, "that we cannot be individually Christian and nationally and economically pagan."[159]

Most parishes experienced a severe decline in income during the 1930s. The finance committee of St. Stephen's, Wilkinsburg, sent out a letter and budget statement to every parish family at the close of 1931. "Each case is taken on its merits," the committee explained, "and especially are parishioners, whose incomes have been reduced or who are out of work,

---

154. Edsall, "Three Generations," 199, 213A.

155. *Convention Journal*, January 26–27, 1932, 53.

156. *Church News*, September 1931.

157. *Church News*, May 1932, November 1932. St. Peter's hosted the community council for the city's Fourth Ward, which assigned vacant garden lots in Oakland to the unemployed and supplied them with seed.

158. *Church News*, December 1932.

159. Rt. Rev. Alexander Mann, "Sermon Preached at the Consecration of Trinity Church, Geneva, NY," Memorial Day, 1933, RG2/3.1, box 6BP, EDP.

to be reminded that payment of worship has prior claim."[160] The fall in parish income had a corresponding effect on contributions both to the diocese and the national church, and periodic—if futile—appeals for assistance went out from the board of trustees. In response to complaints about its failure to meet its 1933 quota, Church of the Messiah, Sheraden, declared that its pledge income was less than $1,200, while expenses ran at $2,500, with the balance raised by church organizations "who twice a month during practically the entire year engage in some money making activity."[161] Widespread unemployment in the mill town of Aliquippa took its toll on the members of All Saints Church, who were forced to appeal to the board of trustees for help with overdue taxes.[162]

Financial stringencies continued to handicap members of the Diocese of Pittsburgh well into the 1930s. Bishop Mann was eloquent in his appeals to the diocesan convention of 1934, noting that parish pledges for mission work had fallen from over $100,000 in 1930 to little more than $50,000 in 1933. He urged Pittsburgh Episcopalians to focus on restoring the life of the church: "It is a call to restore God and His Will to their rightful place in the life of our day, in politics, in business, in society, and in the home ... It calls for no new organizations, it makes no financial appeal, it furnishes no universal methods. All it asks is that in public Worship, in Sacrament and Service and Sermon and in the work of Guilds and Societies and other parish agencies, the effort be made to hold high the great purposes of God in which we hold a place as His Children." Neglect of assessments could have practical implications, the bishop pointed out. He reported the case of a clergyman whose parish had always paid its pension premiums. On retirement at the age of sixty-eight, the clergyman assumed that he would be entitled to the full pension of $1,000 per annum, but discovered that as a number of parishes in the diocese had failed to keep current, he was entitled only to the minimum of $600 per annum.

---

160. *Church News*, January 1932. St. Stephen's was better off than many parishes. It assumed a mortgage of $75,000 in 1930 to build a new parish house and the costs of building a new rectory were simultaneously assumed by a parishioner as a memorial gift. Board of Trustees Minutes, May 13, 1930, RG4A/3.3, EDP.

161. Committee of the Vestry of Church of the Messiah to Department of Missions, Diocese of Pittsburgh, March 27, 1934, RG1/1.17, box 21PP, EDP.

162. Board of Trustees Minutes, September 12, 1934, RG4A/3.3, EDP. The board offered to furnish half the amount if the congregation could raise the rest.

While the back assessments had now been paid, the dangers of such a situation were obvious.¹⁶³

The board of trustees constantly wrestled with the dilemma of reduced income. In 1935, the treasurer recommended a parish assessment schedule that would reduce the obligations of forty-five parishes, but warned that if payments were not made more promptly than in 1934, total indebtedness would be $3,000 greater by the end of the year. While diocesan deficits did fall in 1935, the deficit to the national church doubled compared to 1934. At the close of 1936, the diocese was still directly responsible for five large mortgages on the properties of parishes in Aliquippa ($22,000) and Monessen ($18,000), which were single-industry towns, and Carnegie ($31,000), Monongahela ($14,000), and Donora ($10,595).¹⁶⁴ By 1940, however, most mortgages were within the carrying and paying ability of their respective congregations. In the exceptional cases of Carnegie and Aliquippa, the treasurer urged the diocese to focus on Carnegie, since the diocese did little other business with the parish's mortgage carrier, and to switch to Aliquippa once Carnegie's debt had been redeemed.¹⁶⁵

If nothing else, the Great Depression strengthened the hand of those who favored a more coordinated approach. In November 1932, the vestries of the congregations in Charleroi, Donora, Monessen, and Monongahela formed an organization similar to that organized in the Pittsburgh area during the 1920s.¹⁶⁶ The successful merger, which created St. Mark's, Knoxville, in 1929, only heightened the bishop's desire to increase central authority. At the 1936 diocesan convention, Mann thanked the delegates for passing a resolution inviting the chancellor to draft measures to allow the standing committee, board of trustees, and bishop greater authority to consolidate parishes:

> All of us are familiar with the haphazard way in which parishes have been established in the past, especially in the large cities of

163. *Convention Journal*, January 23–24, 1934, 37–49 (quotation on 42).

164. Board of Trustees Minutes, January 11, December 10, 1935, November 9, 1936, RG4A/3.3, EDP.

165. Board of Trustees Minutes, May 14, 1940, RG4A/3.3, EDP.

166. *Church News*, November 1932. During the war years, Emmanuel Church and Christ Church, North Side, reached an agreement whereby they would "share" a clergyman, but both parishes maintained separate vestries and remained responsible for their own finances. *Church News*, May 1943.

the country. We can also see clearly how parishes that had a reason for existence before the days of the automobile and consequent good roads are no longer needed, and might well be merged with some other parish to the real strengthening of the Diocese. But under present canonical regulations, it is not easy to bring about such mergers, and we face the spectacle of parishes that are leading a precarious existence, disheartening alike to rector and to people, when by combination with some other parish a strong and growing center of Church life and work might be established.[167]

If Episcopal parishes learned the art of cooperation during the 1930s, many Christian denominations were not so far behind. From the time of his consecration, Bishop Mann was a pioneer of ecumenical dialogue, aided by his former protégé, Edwin van Etten, rector of Calvary Church. A 1922 ordination conducted at Calvary by the bishop of Ohio was noteworthy for the participation of Frederick Emrich, a Congregationalist minister. This was the first such involvement by a representative of the Reformed tradition in an Episcopal ordination; the Calvary ceremony made manifest the expressed hope of the recent Lambeth Conference for closer ties with the Congregationalists.[168] When Calvary launched its famous radio broadcasts in the early 1920s, one of van Etten's parishioners even complained: "The trouble with Mr. van Etten's sermons is that they are just as good for the Baptists as they are for us!"[169]

Bishop Mann frequently exhorted members of his diocese to remember the contribution of the Episcopal Church to the revitalization of liturgical practice within mainstream Protestantism.[170] "[Our] influence is out of all proportion to our numbers," he declared in 1933,

> and when the Episcopal Church speaks in her corporate capacity, no Christian Communion in the country commands more truly the attention of thoughtful men. We are one per cent of the popu-

---

167. *Church News*, February 1936.
168. *Church News*, January 1923.
169. Edsall, "Three Generations," 142. At the tenth anniversary celebration of van Etten's ministry at Calvary, a Jewish rabbi, a Catholic priest, and a Baptist pastor all praised the friendliness of the rector. *Church News*, December 1927.
170. "I believe that our influence extends far beyond the confines of our membership, that the increasing reverence and beauty of Public Worship, the growing observance of the Christian Year, the tendency towards a simpler statement of the Christian faith, among all Christian communities, are largely due to the Episcopal Church." *Church News*, May 1923.

lation, we are thirty per cent of college and university students ... We are too Catholic for some of our members and we are too Protestant for others. We are told that our position is illogical, but after all what is it but the position of the family, where one son is an extreme radical and one is an ultra conservative, but where all the children are held together by the bond of a common loyalty, a common love and trust.[171]

Mann also expressed admiration for southwestern Pennsylvania's leading Protestant denomination. "The Presbytery of Pittsburgh is probably the strongest and wealthiest in the world," he declared in 1923, "and their Churches are known throughout the world for their missionary zeal and generosity."[172] He joined other Protestant leaders in opposing a 1928 plan for a community chest for the city, evidently fearing that such a civic institution would be under the control of Roman Catholic politicians.[173] At the same time, his department of missions pledged not to undertake new mission work in any community adequately served by existing Protestant congregations.[174] Mann remained guarded in his appreciation of more widespread ecumenical initiatives like the Faith and Order Conference of 1927. "The great Communions of Christendom must learn to know one another better," he declared at the time, "to appreciate more intelligently what each one is doing for the uplift of human life, before conferences on questions of Faith and Order are likely to lead on to practical action looking toward reunion."[175] In practice, relations with other Protestant groups

171. Rt. Rev. Alexander Mann, "Sermon Preached at the Consecration of Trinity Church, Geneva, NY," Memorial Day, 1933, RG2/3.1, box 6BP, EDP.

172. *Church News*, May 1923. After attending the service celebrating the consecration of King George VI of England, the general secretary of the United Presbyterian Board of Missions praised the service as "a great, religious, patriotic pageant, timely and appropriate." R. A. Hutchison to Rt. Rev. Alexander Mann, May 17, 1937, RG2/3.1, box 6BP, Bishops' Papers, EDP.

173. *Church News*, March 1928. In 1931, Mann delivered an address to the General Assembly of the Presbyterian Church as it met in Pittsburgh. "It was that unhappy union of Church and State, with its consequent legislation, which in the 17th Century, drove those hundreds of godly ministers out of the Church of England, and led to the formation of the Presbyterian Church of Scotland," he told the audience. "An impressive warning, may I say in passing, to all well meaning but misguided religious enthusiasts who would seek by lobbies in Washington to effect an informal union of Church and State, and to advance the Kingdom of God by the use of political methods." *Church News*, June 1931.

174. Department of Missions Minutes, Diocesan Council, Report for 1928, RG4A/2.5:2, EDP.

175. *Convention Journal*, January 24–25, 1928, 27–28.

experienced something of a decline during the 1930s. So unimpressed by the proceedings of the 1936 meeting of the Pennsylvania Council of Churches were the Episcopal delegates that they recommended that the diocese sever its connection with that body.[176]

Relations with the Orthodox churches, by contrast, only strengthened during the 1930s. A decade earlier, the department of missions had encouraged priests in communities with large Orthodox communities to offer whatever pastoral care would be accepted, on the premise that Anglicans were part of a sister communion. At Christ Church, Indiana, the rector baptized, married, and buried members of the Greek, Syrian, and Russian Orthodox communities and taught their children in his Sunday school, while churches at Latrobe and Clairton offered services according to the Syrian rite.[177] One of the most striking examples of ecumenical cooperation came in 1926, when Father Chrysostom Trahatias of the Greek Orthodox church in Pittsburgh's Oakland district appealed to the Episcopal Diocese of Pittsburgh for advice on organizing a modern Sunday school for his congregation. Officials from the Christian education department helped translate English textbooks into Greek and worked with teachers at the church to instruct them in contemporary education methods.[178]

After the onset of the Great Depression, warm relations with the Orthodox churches continued. The performance of Russian Orthodox Great Vespers by the choir of St. Mary's Russian Orthodox church at St. Andrew's, Pittsburgh, in 1933 provided a forum for Bishop Mann to preach on the good relations between Anglicanism and Orthodoxy.[179] An attempt was later made to loan the facilities of St. Mary's Memorial to a Russian Orthodox group based in Carnegie, though this ultimately proved unsuccessful.[180] More satisfactory was the enduring relationship between Transfiguration, Clairton, and the local Syrian Orthodox community, which Bishop Mann permitted to use its own liturgy. When a bishop from the Syrian Orthodox church conducted Holy Week services

176. Department of Social Service Minutes, Diocesan Council, June 8, November 30, 1936, RG4A/2.5:2, EDP.

177. *Convention Journal*, June 25–26, 1923, 132–33.

178. *Convention Journal*, June 27–28, 1927, 157.

179. *Church News*, April 1933.

180. Department of Missions Minutes, Diocesan Council, December 4, 1934, January 8, 1935, RG4A/2.5:2, EDP.

in Clairton, he took the opportunity to praise the Episcopal parish for the sound instruction and pastoral care that it had provided to his people.[181]

The skilled assistance provided by the department of education to the Greek Orthodox Church was not an isolated event, but reflected the increasingly advanced standard of Christian education provided in many parishes of the Diocese of Pittsburgh. One stimulus to excellence was the Conneaut Lake Summer School, the second-largest of its kind in the Episcopal Church in 1925, with 336 registered students. "Think what it means," enthused Bishop Mann, "to have these boys and girls from strong city parishes and weak country missions live together, worship together, study together and play together for ten days." It would help establish a new generation of leadership for the diocese, he insisted.[182]

After 1928, general responsibility for oversight of Christian education fell to the diocesan superintendent of religious education, Evelyn Buchanan, who had previously been a church worker at St. Stephen's, Sewickley. Trained at the New York Training School for Deaconesses, the University of Pittsburgh, and Columbia University, Buchanan specialized in religious drama.[183]

Under her direction, Sunday school instruction in the diocese was increasingly informed by modern educational methods.[184] At Church of the Ascension, Pittsburgh, Elizabeth Hopkins pioneered the idea of a "Children's Corner," a devotional space furnished with books, a prayer desk, chairs, and pictures, where unsupervised children were left free to experience the presence of God in their own way.[185] At Calvary Church, Hilda Shaul oversaw the creation of a motion picture film by church school pupils that developed the idea of God from Abraham to Jesus, as depicted in the Old and New Testaments. So successful was this endeavor that the film was later shown at a number of seminaries throughout the nation.[186] Many schools also introduced the innovation of classes for

---

181. *Church News*, May 1938.
182. *Convention Journal*, January 26–27, 1926, 43–44 (quotation on 44).
183. *Church News*, October 1928.
184. See the discussion in Gillespie, "What We Taught," 53–59.
185. *Church News*, January 1930.
186. *Church News*, June 1930; Edsall, "Three Generations," 189.

preschoolers and also provided parents with advice on the religious training of their children.[187]

For Buchanan, it was essential that religious education include a worship component. "This emphasis," her department's 1930 report warned, "implies provision for training the devotional life through practice and precept and is a challenge to every spiritually minded person to share in a forward movement in the field of Religious Education."[188] Nor was religious education confined to the city. In 1932, Buchanan organized a vacation church school at St. John's, Donora, a mill town noted for steel wire and zinc galvanizing facilities, but completely lacking in civic amenities. An average of one hundred children from six nationality groups participated in devotions, crafts (such as making scrapbooks for children in hospitals), stories, songs, and games.[189]

The department of religious education welcomed initiatives that made for greater uniformity of teaching and strengthened bonds with the public schools. As early as 1930, it agreed to cooperate with the Allegheny County Sabbath School Association to set up district training schools and also organized regional meetings for Episcopalian religious educators.[190] In 1941, its regional organization was strengthened by the establishment of four vice-chairmanships to cover Allegheny Valley, Beaver Valley, Monongahela Valley, and the Pittsburgh district.[191] Regarding the public schools, the department held to the view that teachers of religion should be permitted to come into the schools and teach religion as part of the regular curriculum, thus avoiding "divorcing it from the routine of life as so many other plans do."[192] When the board of education of the City of Pittsburgh agreed to grant high school credit for religious education provided by the city's churches and synagogues, the move was enthusi-

---

187. Department of Religious Education Minutes, Diocesan Council, Report, January 1930, RG4A/2.5:2, EDP.

188. Ibid.

189. *Church News*, September 1932.

190. Department of Religious Education Minutes, Diocesan Council, Report, January 1930, RG4A/2.5:2, EDP.

191. Department of Religious Education Minutes, Diocesan Council, March 14, 1941, RG4A/2.5:2, EDP.

192. E. L. B. Pielow to Rt. Rev. Douglas H. Atwill, March 15, 1939, Department of Religious Education Minutes, Diocesan Council, RG4A/2.5:2, EDP.

astically welcomed by local Episcopal clergy.[193] Among the latter was the rector of Messiah, Sheraden, who helped plan a religious education course for students at his local high school.[194]

Religious education also laid the foundation for the only successful church plant of the 1930s. Beginning in 1930, lay leaders from Calvary helped establish a church school in Fox Chapel for Episcopal families in Aspinwall and Fox Chapel who felt that Calvary was located too far from their homes for Sunday worship. The school met at Shadyside Academy and had sixty pupils by 1932. Just as a number of nineteenth-century parishes had begun as Sunday schools, so the Fox Chapel endeavor would lead to the establishment of a formal parish structure during the 1940s.[195] Fox Chapel proved the exception rather than the rule, however. Particularly galling for Bishop Mann was the fact that, as the economic situation improved, the stronger parishes continued to make low pledges. "To care so little for the Church that we have no interest in extending work," the bishop warned in 1936, "means simply that we are on the road to decay."[196] Mann continued to urge his clergy to preach more mission-oriented sermons and to distribute informative literature on missions, noting that most laymen no longer read the church papers or the mission journal, the *Spirit of Missions*.[197]

Mann's concerns were shared by the treasurer of the diocese, who issued a warning of his own in 1940:

> The fact which faces the Diocesan Council is that the Diocese as a group of congregations, as a body of clergy leaders and lay members, is neither meeting nor apparently seriously attempting to meet the Budget proposed year after year by the Council ... It is time that the Council took this matter seriously. In all good faith you asked the congregations for $57,000.00 for 1940. There

---

193. *Church News*, January 1940.

194. Vestry Minutes, Church of the Messiah, Sheraden, MsS-1-15, box 1 (unprocessed), EDP.

195. Department of Missions Minutes, Diocesan Council, June 3, 1930, RG4A/2.5:2, EDP; Edsall, "Three Generations," 191; *Church News*, June 1932. A church school was also the basis for the 1941 organization of St. Peter's parish in Brentwood.

196. *Church News*, June 1936. The diocesan treasurer reported in 1937 that canvasses had become increasingly ineffective since 1929. A 1936 visitation of six leading parishes saw four keep their pledges constant and one actually implement a reduction. Diocesan Council Minutes, January 13, 1937, RG4A/2.5:2, EDP.

197. *Church News*, June 1939.

isn't a padded item in the list. There are only trivial overhead items of expense. The congregations responded with, including the children's offering, an approximate $37,000.00[,] slightly over 60% of the amount asked. And the response is incidentally less than that of year ago for a smaller budget. It is no service for the Council to recommend a budget to the Convention without a very definite and assured plan for meeting it. The Convention will pass any budget ... and then pass also the buck about the income to meet it.[198]

But how was the diocese to be reenergized? Unlike his predecessor, Bishop Mann took a comparatively "low" view of episcopal authority and a correspondingly "high" view of lay responsibility.[199] For Mann, the solution to the problem of lay apathy was to be found in the Forward Movement, a national initiative to stimulate the lay members of established parishes and missions to evangelize their communities. An early diocesan move in that direction came from Atonement, Carnegie, where the men's Bible class sponsored the mailing of church bulletins to every parish family and of special pamphlets on discipleship for the 1935 Lenten season. The latter proved particularly successful, with the sermon delivered at the Wednesday Lenten services being based on the pamphlet topic for that week.[200]

The full force of the Forward Movement was unleashed in Pittsburgh in 1940, when a number of conferences were held in the diocese and a copy of the pamphlet *Building a Parish Program* was mailed to every layman who attended them. Two parishes that promptly acted on the Forward Movement's recommendations were Church of the Redeemer, Pittsburgh, and St. Mary's, Beaver Falls, but other parishes did make use of the *Half Hour Papers* published by the Forward Movement. At St. Stephen's, Wilkinsburg, the Reverend William Porkess distributed *Forward Day-by-Day* to parish families, with supplemental information relating to their parish, while the rector of St. Stephen's, Sewickley, Louis Hershon, was the chair of the Forward Movement committee.[201]

---

198. Diocesan Council Minutes, January 11, 1940, RG4A/2.5:2, EDP.

199. After the 1937 General Convention, Mann praised its decisions not to permit individual bishops to make the decision as to whether to marry divorced persons and its refusal to make the House of Bishops a final court of appeal on matters of faith and doctrine. *Church News*, November 1937.

200. *Church News*, April 1935.

201. *Church News*, April 1940.

Alone, the Forward Movement would have had but limited impact, had it not been for the international mood. As war clouds gathered in Europe, William Porkess introduced a resolution at the diocesan convention of 1939 expressing "grief and dismay at the persecution of the Jewish People in Central Europe," and urged all present to "work for a larger measure of justice and consideration for all Jews and other minority groups in our national life."[202] Bishop Mann, by contrast, sounded a mildly isolationist tone later that year. "What we need above all at this time is to cultivate the temper of peace here at home," he insisted, "the strong sense of equity, the steady self-control. We can put away from us all radical contempts and hatreds. We can refuse to be carried away by any wave of popular hysteria. We can bear in mind that this war must end sometime and that when that day comes a strong and peaceful United States can better serve an exhausted and suffering world than if we had been one of the combatants."[203]

It was not easy for Pittsburgh's Episcopalians to feel detached, however, as was demonstrated by the service at Trinity Cathedral in May 1937 in celebration of the accession of King George VI.[204] In January 1941, the diocesan convention passed a resolution authored by Father Frederick Kempster of St. Mark's, Pittsburgh, "extending its deepest sympathy with the Mother Church of the Anglican Communion in its titanic struggle to preserve Christianity for the world" and pledging "our constant prayers and whatever material aid we can render during this unparalleled crisis."[205] As war preparations continued, the department of religious education paid careful attention to the needs of young Episcopalians entering the military and invited young people's groups to establish contact with them.[206]

---

202. *Convention Journal*, January 24–25, 1939, 16.

203. *Church News*, October 1939.

204. One Wilkinsburg resident praised the service, declaring that the new British consul would help cement "good fellowship between the peoples of America and the British Empire." Nancy K. Pushee to Rt. Rev. Alexander Mann, May 16, 1937, RG2/3.1, box 6BP, Bishops' Papers, EDP.

205. *Convention Journal*, January 28–29, 1941, 14.

206. Department of Religious Education Minutes, Diocesan Council, November 18, 1940, RG4A/2.5:2, EDP.

With Japan's attack on Pearl Harbor, the diocese moved to a war footing.[207] Several clergy volunteered their services as military chaplains and those who remained in Pittsburgh adopted a generally patriotic stance. "Too much [superficial pacifism]," mused Arthur Kinsolving, rector of Calvary, in January 1943, "served only to destroy confidence in religion and throw members of the Naval and Military establishments into the arms of the Roman Catholic Church."[208] Later that year, the diocesan war commission issued a book of occasional services, including liturgies for the presentation of war crosses to men entering the armed forces and for the dedication of a roll of honor, and prayers for special occasions.[209]

Local parishes also responded to wartime needs. St. Mary's, Beaver Falls, offered nursery facilities for up to ten hours per day to the many women with small children who had moved into the region to work in local plants. Church leaders tried to persuade local personnel managers to put such women on day shifts and offered to provide a school with trained teachers for only a nominal fee.[210] Trinity, Washington, offered its facilities to Washington and Jefferson College for its officer training school, with the church available for daily prayer, a room in the parish house transformed into a reading room, and frequent organized dances, while Christ Church, Greensburg, set aside a chapel for prayer for those on active service.[211] The steady influx of servicemen into Pittsburgh colleges provided an unprecedented opportunity for evangelism and chaplaincy work. Special services were offered at Heinz Chapel at the University of Pittsburgh and the Pittsburgh parishes of Church of the Ascension and Church of the Redeemer, and many church members supported the United Services Organization canteen near the Pennsylvania Railroad Station, whose chaplain was Dean Moor of Trinity Cathedral.[212]

---

207. The board of trustees adopted a war damage insurance policy for $15,000 on the episcopal residence in 1942. Board of Trustees Minutes, September 8, 1942, RG4A/3.3, EDP.

208. *Church News*, January 1943.

209. Diocesan War Commission, *Services and Prayers for Use in Time of War* (1943), RG2/4.1, box 7BP, Bishops' Papers, EDP.

210. *Church News*, January 1943.

211. *Church News*, March 1943; "Chapel of Our Savior, Christ Church, Greensburg—Set Apart for Prayer for Those in the Service of Our Country," RG2/4.1, box 7BP, Bishops' Papers, EDP.

212. Department of Religious Education Minutes, Diocesan Council, March 15, 1943, RG4A/2.5:2, EDP; *CJ*, January 18, 1944, 60–61.

The Episcopal Church in southwestern Pennsylvania had come a considerable distance from the early days of Alexander Mann's episcopate first arrival. These changes owed much to the economic and social transformation of the region, something to which the administrative secretary of the diocese drew attention in 1933. Never again, he declared, would Pittsburghers enjoy their "placid, cocksure, self-promoting, Bourbonistic state of perennial bliss."[213] Organized labor was now a force in southwestern Pennsylvania of which Episcopalians were wise to take note. In 1931, Trinity Cathedral welcomed representatives of labor unions to a service addressed by William Green of the American Federation of Labor, and the board of trustees was treated to an address on the subject of "The Labor Union in the Steel Mill" in 1938.[214] At the same time, an increasing number of Episcopalians belonged to the white-collar professions. "Offsetting the fact that the laboring men are receiving increased incomes," warned the diocesan council in 1941, "federal taxation for this year is requiring from the 'white collar' families amounts that are already serious, and will become in succeeding years greater burdens, without any or only nominal salary increases. This group numerically is the main support of the Church, and with the rapid dwindling of the number of larger givers, is the group to which we must largely look for our future missionary as well as parochial income."[215]

"We know that there will be more of loss and sacrifice and suffering," admitted Alexander Mann in his final convention address in January 1943. "We know that taxes at home will be much heavier, and that battles abroad will be greater and will involve heavier losses. We know that many of our sons will make the supreme sacrifice, and many homes will be desolate. But we know also that we are contending for a righteous cause for all that makes life honorable and lovable and worthwhile. And so with trust in God we will carry on."[216] In the postwar era, that trust would be sorely tested.

213. *Convention Journal*, January 24–25, 1933, 104.

214. Ibid., 60; Department of Social Service Minutes, Diocesan Council, January 17, 1938, RG4A/2.5:2, EDP.

215. Diocesan Council Minutes, Budget for Diocesan Council, 1941, RG4A/2.5:2, EDP. In 1929, the executive secretary noted that since he had arrived in Pittsburgh in 1916, eight parishes outside Allegheny County had become dependent on diocesan aid and no such parish had become financially independent. Since no industrial resurrection could be anticipated, towns that failed to diversify their industry would only continue to decline. *Convention Journal*, January 22–23, 1929, 130–32.

216. *Convention Journal*, January 26–27, 1943, 21.

Portrait of William White, the first Episcopal bishop of Pennsylvania, together with a letter written to his son on the occasion of his sole visitation to the Pennsylvania backcountry in 1825. In the letter, White laments the loss of a pair of spectacles, which he plans to replace upon arrival in Pittsburgh.

Founded in 1765, St. Luke's Church in the Chartiers Valley became a target of local hostility after its patron John Neville accepted the post of federal tax inspector. After the Whiskey Rebellion of 1794, the congregation underwent a decline that would not be reversed until the 1850's. No record exists of any regular clergy serving St. Luke's until 1852, when the Rev. Theodore Benedict Lyman, rector of Trinity Church in Pittsburgh, began services in the area.

John Barrett Kerfoot, first bishop of Pittsburgh (1865–1881). Born in Dublin, Kerfoot was headmaster of the College of St. James, a boys' preparatory school in Maryland, from 1842 to 1864. Elected to serve the newly established Diocese of Pittsburgh, he worked to pull together a widely dispersed flock and helped calm the tensions among the various church parties in western Pennsylvania.

Children and elderly residents on the steps of the Episcopal Church Home in 1931. Established in 1859 to shelter the aged and infirm, it also took in many children orphaned by the Civil War. As the county began turning to foster care in the 1920s, the need for children to be taken into the Home became less and by 1948 it had returned to care for the elderly. Independent living for men and women of moderate means was added in the 1980s and the name of facility was changed to Canterbury Place.

Cortlandt Whitehead, second bishop of Pittsburgh (1881–1922), in the diocesan offices in the Lewis Block Building on the corner of Smithfield and Sixth in downtown Pittsburgh, where they were located between 1895 and 1913. To his right is Archdeacon Charles J. de Coux and to his left their secretary, Miss Jane Cuddy. An imposing Pittsburgh personality, Whitehead oversaw one of the most fruitful periods of church planting in diocesan history.

The choir of St. Augustine's Mission, forerunner of Holy Cross Church in Homewood, circa 1899. Located on Pittsburgh's North Side, St. Augustine's was one of two predominantly African American Episcopal missions in the Diocese of Pittsburgh in the late nineteenth century.

The dispensary of St. Margaret's Memorial Hospital, sometime during the 1930s. Before his death in November 1889, John H. Schoenberger arranged for a legacy to be used to build a hospital in memory of his wife, Margaret, who had died several years previously. Bishop Cortlandt Whitehead laid the cornerstone in October 1896 and the hospital continues to serve western Pennsylvania today as a regional branch of the University of Pittsburgh Medical Center.

Alfred W. Arundel, rector of Trinity Church from 1891 to 1911. An avid proponent of the Social Gospel, Arundel was a constant thorn in the side of Bishop Cortlandt Whitehead, who objected to his independent cast of mind.

Because young women working and living in downtown Pittsburgh were not permitted in the men's eating establishments, Trinity Church's chapter of the Girl's Friendly Society instituted an inexpensive lunchroom in 1914. The church also provided a place where they could relax, exercise in the gym, sing in the chorus, as well as attend classes and noon prayer in the Chapel.

Alexander Mann, third bishop of Pittsburgh (1922–1943), with Edwin van Etten, rector of East Liberty's prestigious Calvary Church. At five feet in height, Mann never spoke from the pulpit because he felt he couldn't be seen, and reportedly said of his bishop's staff, "I can't handle this crozier; it's too big." Mann's episcopate overlapped the Great Depression, and the stress took its toll. He retired in 1944 and died in 1948.

The Erie-Pittsburgh Summer Conference—one of the largest summer schools in the Episcopal Church during the 1920s—traditionally held at Conneaut, was held for the first time at Kiskiminetas School in Saltsburg, only 35 miles from Pittsburgh, in 1930. The program included 15 educational sessions as well as church services, exhibits, recreation opportunities, and evening lectures.

Bishop Alexander Mann delivers a sermon over the radio. The first radio station in the United States was established in Pittsburgh by Westinghouse International Radio Company (now KDKA) in 1920. They supplied the technology to broadcast the first Christian church service from Calvary Church's sanctuary on January 2, 1921, covering a distance of 1000 miles.

Austin Pardue, fourth bishop of Pittsburgh (1944–1968), with Quentin Huang, exiled bishop of Yunkwei in China, who settled in Pittsburgh after the Nationalist defeat. Pardue brought a passion for prayer and evangelism to Pittsburgh's moribund congregations that led to new departures in mission and ministry during the 1950s and laid the foundations for the rise of the renewal movement during the 1970s.

Clergy of the Diocese of Pittsburgh on a field trip on behalf of the Society for the Promotion of Industrial Missions (SPIM). The brainchild of Bishop Austin Pardue, SPIM represented an effort to reach out to the blue-collar communities of the Mon Valley, which had seen little evangelism by Episcopalians up to that point. One of the most successful new mission fields was headed by former Roman Catholic priest, Joseph Witkofski, in Charleroi.

Samuel Moor Shoemaker, rector of Calvary Church. Invited to Pittsburgh by Bishop Austin Pardue in 1952, Shoemaker helped build an active prayer culture throughout the diocese and founded the Pittsburgh Experiment—which served the downtown business community—in 1955. A strong believer in personal transformation through prayer, Shoemaker had a lasting impact on a generation of Pittsburgh Episcopalians.

Robert Bracewell Appleyard, fifth bishop of Pittsburgh (1968–1979), launches an Episcopal tradition by pitching the first baseball for a Pittsburgh Pirates' game. Taking office at a time of heightened social tension, Appleyard steered his diocese with a puckish sense of humor through the troubled waters of the civil rights debate and the conflict over whether to ordain women to the priesthood.

Beryl Turner Choi, the first ordained woman priest from the Diocese of Pittsburgh. Born in the United Kingdom, Choi was accepted as one of the first two female postulants for the diaconate from the Diocese of Pittsburgh, ordained in 1973 as the first Episcopal woman deacon in southwestern Pennsylvania, and priested in 1977. A passionate spokeswoman for progressive causes, she served as an assistant at Church of the Ascension (1973–76) and Calvary Church (1976–83).

Alden Hathaway, sixth bishop of Pittsburgh (1980–1997) brandishes his broom at the launch of the SWEEP (Service Worship, Evangelism, Education and Pastoral Care) program in 1983. A prominent Evangelical, active in the Fellowship of Witness, Hathaway oversaw the emergence of a cadre of clergy trained at Trinity Episcopal School for Ministry in Ambridge, who helped transform Anglican and Episcopal culture in southwestern Pennsylvania.

Robert William Duncan, seventh bishop of Pittsburgh (1997–present), blesses the water for the annual Easter Blessing of the City of Pittsburgh from the top of Mt. Washington by members of the Christian Leaders Fellowship. Presiding over Pittsburgh's Episcopal life during a period of acute stress in the life of the Episcopal Church and the Anglican Communion, Duncan has emerged as the spiritual leader for conservative Anglicans throughout the United States and Canada.

During the November 1999 diocesan convention, the Diocese of Pittsburgh voted to form a five-year partnership with the Diocese of Rwanda and World Vision to assist the children orphaned through the genocide in that country. More than 800 children were sponsored through diocesan parishes, the largest group in World Vision's history. Shown here are Emmanuel Mbona Kolini, Archbishop of Rwanda, his wife and members of the Rwandan delegation, together with Theresa Newell and Jeanne Hungerman of World Vision.

PART THREE

Mission to the World, 1944–2006

5

New Men and New Methods

Austin Pardue, Sam Shoemaker, and the Civil Rights Debate, 1944–1969

IN MAY 1963, AUSTIN Pardue, bishop of Pittsburgh, announced that he was rescinding his 1943 instruction to the diocesan clergy not to join Anglo Catholic and Evangelical societies. At that time, clergy morale had been low and parish conflicts extensive. In some extreme cases, priests had been locked out of their churches for being too High or too Low in their liturgical practice.[1] Twenty years later, the situation had altered. "If you want to be a member of a liberal, or an evangelical, or an Anglo-Catholic Society," Pardue declared, "this is wisely allowable. The reason I feel this way is because many other groups throughout the Church have developed in the last number of years . . . I hope we will do everything possible to emphasize the Episcopal Church as a whole and learn to move together in unity."[2]

Pardue erred in only one particular. The "new" groups to which he referred would prove to have even less attachment to the notion of the unity of the church than had their nineteenth-century predecessors. Beginning in the 1960s, catholicity would increasingly give way to "prophecy," as a number of bishops—most notably John E. Hines (presiding bishop from 1965 to 1974)—sacrificed episcopal collegiality for social justice. "If a movement of justice or a trend, such as the feminist movement, is of God, the Church should become part of it," wrote Paul Moore (bishop of New York from 1973 to 1989) some years later. "This is true not only of

---

1. Edwards interview.
2. *Convention Journal*, May 14, 1963, 23.

feminism, but of the peace movement, the ecological movement, and even the demands for gay rights."[3]

POSTWAR GROWTH, 1944–1960

Believing that a younger man was needed to develop the full potential of the diocese, Alexander Mann submitted his resignation in 1943, thus becoming the first bishop of Pittsburgh not to die in office.[4] As in 1922, the question immediately arose as to whether to elect as a successor an influential local clergyman—Nathaniel Moor, dean of Trinity Cathedral, and Arthur Kinsolving, rector of Calvary Church, being the strongest contenders—or an outsider. The latter category included two cathedral deans, Arthur Lichtenberger of Newark (the future presiding bishop) and Austin Pardue of Buffalo. While Kinsolving and Moor both led Pardue on the first ballot, and their combined vote on the second would have been sufficient to elect a Pittsburgh candidate, many of Moor's lay supporters switched to the man from Buffalo on the third ballot and Pardue was duly elected.[5]

Hitherto, the bishops of Pittsburgh had hailed from the northeastern United States. In Austin Pardue, Pittsburghers had their first midwestern bishop and one, moreover, who had by no means always felt a sense of religious vocation. In his early years, Pardue admitted, he had been less interested in religion than in athletics. "I am not interested primarily in boys who show proclivities that are overly pious at a youthful age," he remarked in a 1954 appeal for young men to consider the ministry. "As a matter of fact, some of the worst rascals make the finest priests."[6] Pardue had been a chorister at St. Peter's, Chicago, in large measure because it gave him access to the church's athletic equipment, swimming pool, and summer camp. "I began to feel that the church had done so much for me that I might go into the ministry," he explained in 1951. "There was nothing pious about it."[7]

Pardue never completed high school, joined the army in 1917, and was three times rejected by liberal arts colleges during the 1920s before

3. Moore, *Presences,* 258. On Hines, see Kesselus, *John E. Hines.*
4. *Convention Journal,* January 26–27, 1943, 29.
5. *Special Convention Journal,* October 19, 1943, 9.
6. *Convention Journal,* May 11, 1954, 20.
7. *Time,* December 31, 1951.

being admitted to New York's General Theological Seminary. Graduating in 1923, he moved to Minnesota's Iron Range in 1926 to become rector of St. James Church in Hibbing and spent most of the next decade in Minnesota, latterly as rector of Gethsemane Church in Minneapolis. Twelve years later, he was called to be dean of St. Paul's Cathedral in Buffalo, where he developed close ties with steelworkers and labor organizers and acquired a reputation as a national broadcaster. Between 1940 and 1944, his radio program *Our Morale* was broadcast on Monday nights on over a hundred stations across the nation.[8]

Arguably, it was Pardue's radio broadcasts that gave him a high profile in Pittsburgh. Richard Davies, who was ordained by Pardue in the 1950s, recalls listening to *Our Morale* as a teenager. "That voice was captivating," he admits. Though Pardue was greatly loved, he had a very individual style. Davies remembers how Pardue tested his commitment to vocation by telling him at his first interview that he planned to send him to join the Brotherhood of St. Barnabas. When Davies returned a few weeks later to insist that he still wanted to be a priest, Pardue cheerfully complied.[9] Peter Moore, a Neo-Evangelical (see below) educated at Yale, whose first parochial responsibilities were undertaken in the Diocese of Pittsburgh, also attests to Pardue's solid devotional life. He liked the company of the well-to-do, says Moore, but "he once said to me: '[The wealthy] are great people to have as friends but you don't always want to minister to them because they're hard to minister to.'"[10]

Another postulant, Walter Righter, was warned by his rector not to enter the ordination process until Pardue had been installed "because [Bishop Mann] will insist you have an income of $2,400 a year or he won't accept you." Obediently following this advice, Righter soon discovered that the new bishop had his own condition for postulancy—all his clergy candidates would spend time working in a mill or factory. The purpose was to gain an understanding of working-class culture. "Don't preach,"

---

8. Ibid; *Bulletin Index*, March 29, 1945, RG2/4.1, box 7BP, Bishops' Papers, Archives of the Episcopal Diocese of Pittsburgh, Pittsburgh, Pennsylvania (hereafter referenced as EDP). In November 1944, the board of trustees voted the new bishop $100 per month to cover the costs of his radio broadcasts until June 1945. Board of Trustees Minutes, November 14, 1944, RG4A/3.3, EDP.

9. Davies interview.

10. Moore interview.

Pardue told him. "You're there to learn about the mill; you're not there to convert people."[11]

Austin Pardue brought to the Diocese of Pittsburgh a stronger commitment to High Church liturgical practice than had Alexander Mann and frequently bemoaned the failure of the Protestant churches fully to subscribe to the catholic and apostolic faith. "We do not claim to be personally better than other denominations nor are we claiming to be spiritually superior," he observed in 1945, "but we have got a more full and historic belief."[12] Such a perspective was sustained by an understanding of the Eucharist that was at least as strong as that of Cortlandt Whitehead. "You are not approaching a mere symbol," he wrote in an adjuration to regular reception of Holy Communion, "you are approaching the heart of universal reality. God has come down to meet you."[13]

Nevertheless, Pardue was far from being a straightforward Anglo Catholic. He was a prolific and popular devotional writer, most of whose publications were in the nature of general Christian apologetic and tended to emphasize universal Christian themes rather than an explicitly Anglican theology.[14] "Scholars agree that Jesus founded a religion based on the claim of His own divinity," he wrote in 1947. "It is quite evident that you cannot accept Jesus as a great and good man while at the same time you reject Him as the Son of God. No great and good man could be merely that and make such preposterous claims."[15] The following year, he attacked what he called the distinctively American problem of constructing one's faith for oneself: "Modern destructive liberalism has contributed much toward this individualistic attitude concerning things that belong to God. The debunking of faith, the Bible, the Prayer Book, the Creeds, theology, the Sacraments, and the Church, have all made us more and more disrespectful toward the eternal verities and therefore we have created inadequate little philosophical codes of transitory values which we claim to be 'a religion of my own.'"[16]

---

11. Righter interview.
12. *Church News*, April 1945.
13. *Church News*, March 1948.
14. See, for example, *He Lives; Prayer Works; Create and Make New; The Single Eye.*
15. *Church News*, December 1947.
16. *Church News*, January 1948.

Theological values were not the only things in flux. The economic prosperity induced by the military buildup during the Second World War and the superpower confrontation of the Cold War had consequences for the Episcopal Church. Under the leadership of Henry Knox Sherrill (presiding bishop from 1947 to 1958), the national church developed ties with government leaders and expanded its administrative apparatus.[17] In Pittsburgh, the suburbanization that had begun in the 1920s redoubled during the 1950s, boosting congregations based in the suburbs. "When I started my Ministry in All Saints Church, Aliquippa, in 1927," Pittsburgh's suffragan bishop, William Thomas, remarked in 1959, "not over 20% of the families rode to church in automobiles. Today at least 90% of the people, attending All Saints, Aliquippa, ride to church, for the simple reason that they have moved away from the blast furnaces, into areas where there is greater breathing space."[18] Successful bishops across the nation redoubled their efforts to plant churches in virgin territory to attract their well-educated, fecund, and affluent inhabitants. Parochial and diocesan income also grew dramatically as these new Episcopalians became committed to the church.[19]

Bishop Pardue was no laggard in promoting new church plants. Two years into his episcopate he called for the establishment of a $125,000 diocesan reconstruction and advance fund. Some of the programs Pardue sought to fund were a theological internship, university courses for clergy, a city missionary, portable churches, and a part-time publicity agent.[20] In 1947, the bishop pledged to start at least one mission every year and put Archdeacon William Thomas in direct oversight of this venture.[21] By 1958, both Pardue and Thomas could speak with pride of a dramatic diocesan transformation. The fifty missions and twenty-two parishes that had existed at the commencement of Pardue's episcopate had been transformed into fifty-seven parishes and twenty-three missions. Much of this success the bishop attributed to the services of unpaid volunteers in diocesan departments; despite a significant expansion of the diocesan machinery, the number of paid staff members had *decreased* by one dur-

17. Douglas, "Whither the National Church?"; Sherrill, *Among Friends*, 225–34.

18. *Convention Journal*, May 12, 1959, 22.

19. For an example of dramatic postwar diocesan expansion, see Booty, *American Apostle*, 52–57.

20. Board of Trustees Minutes, September 11, 1945, RG4A/3.3, EDP.

21. *Convention Journal*, January 21, 1947, 22.

ing the 1950s.[22] Pardue was equally convinced that support for the national program of the church should not be qualified. "There are things in the national budget that I am not happy about," he admitted in 1962, "but Christ's Catholic faith, as represented by the Episcopal Church, is a democracy and so stands in the manner in which He originally founded The Faith."[23] In 1966, he had the satisfaction of seeing members of his diocese oversubscribe a $1 million fund drive for a new diocesan endowment—the Centennial Episcopal Advance Fund (CEAF)—by 50 percent.[24]

As suburban parishes contributed an ever-increasing proportion of diocesan income, they assumed a position in diocesan affairs similar to that enjoyed by the wealthy urban parishes of the nineteenth century. Some suburban Episcopalians even viewed the small rural parishes and missions as a positive hindrance to the work of the church, as was demonstrated in a letter to Bishop Pardue from Gordon Wright of Fox Chapel Church concerning the Sharpsburg mission: "Even before you came to Pittsburgh, we in Fox Chapel, with the Archdeacon and others, were trying to find some way to deliver the coup de grace to the Sharpsburg Church so that there would be one less dying mission to worry about and so that Fox Chapel might get some cash and equipment out of the liquidation. Just a couple of weeks ago, the same thought came up during a meeting in Fox Chapel."[25]

Fox Chapel Church was the crown jewel of the revivified diocese. Formally recognized as a diocesan mission in May 1945, it appealed for further support from the department of missions the following year because of "the enthusiasm of the people and the growth of both the congregation and the Church School, averaging 100 and 80 respectively; also the necessity for the Episcopal Church to establish itself in the community before the Presbyterians do so."[26] The board of trustees approved the

22. *Convention Journal*, May 13, 1958, 22.

23. *Convention Journal*, May 18, 1962, 18.

24. *Convention Journal*, May 11, 1965, 14, 20, 29; *Convention Journal*, May 24, 1966, 14–15, 27. Parishes that raised at least double their quota were St. Thomas, Barnsboro; Holy Cross, Pittsburgh; St. Philip's, Moon Township; Trinity, Beaver; St. Stephen's, Sewickley; Transfiguration, Clairton; St. Bartholomew's, Scottdale; and Trinity, Monessen.

25. Gordon E. P. Wright to Bp. Pardue, October 19, 1948, RG1/1.11, box 10PP, EDP. Interestingly, Wright changed his opinion after Pardue preached at Fox Chapel and spoke in support of more missions for the mill and mining towns. Some of his fellow parishioners may have been less convinced.

26. Department of Missions Minutes, Diocesan Council, May 8, 1945, May 14, 1946, RG4A/2.5:2, EDP.

purchase of a $45,000 property in Fox Chapel and $30,000 in improvements to the property in 1946.[27] Shortly after Fox Chapel Church's acceptance into union with the diocese in 1951, the parish confirmation class stood at well above the level of 10 percent of the active communicant list recommended by the diocese.[28] At an episcopal visitation, Bishop Pardue described it as "the church of the doctors, surgeons and physicians, for I think proportionately we have more medical men in this parish than in any other in the Diocese."[29]

Such missionary dynamism was not confined to Fox Chapel. Between 1948 and 1960, ten new congregations were established and three other Pittsburgh parishes relocated outside the city.[30] Although these included St. Michael's, Ligonier (Westmoreland County), St. David's, Peters Township (Washington County), and St. Francis, Somerset (Somerset County), most development occurred in suburban Allegheny County. Beginning with St. Thomas, Gibsonia, the diocese embarked upon a steady round of church planting that saw Christ Church on the North Side move to the North Hills in 1952 and St. James Memorial in Homewood move to Penn Hills in 1954. New missions sprang up in Monroeville in 1954 (St. Martin's), in Moon Township in 1955 (St. Philip's), and in Warrendale in 1956 (St. Christopher's). In 1958, St. Stephen's, McKeesport, planted a mission in Liberty Boro (Good Samaritan), and St. George's in the West End relocated to Jefferson Boro. Finally, in 1960, two composite missions were established: Church of Our Savior in Glenshaw (which absorbed the former congregation of Trinity, Sharpsburg) and All Souls, North Versailles (a merger of St. Mary's, Braddock; St. Margaret's, Wilmerding; and a few members of St. Alban's, Duquesne).[31] With these developments in southern Allegheny County, the period of expansion came to a close, but it had been the most fruitful decade of church planting in over forty years.

27. Board of Trustees Minutes, May 14, 1946, RG4A/3.3, EDP.
28. *Church News*, November 1951.
29. *Church News*, January 1954.
30. Some urban congregations did recover ground in the 1950s. When Pardue first arrived in Pittsburgh, he did not expect St. Peter's, Pittsburgh, to survive, but by 1951 it had a large local congregation at the heart of one of the largest concentrations of hospital facilities in the city. *Church News*, December 1951.
31. The national church contributed to the establishment of All Souls with a 1954 allocation of $3,500 for an experimental mission in which members of all three congregations participated. Department of Missions Minutes, Diocesan Council, December 14, 1954, RG4A/2.5:2, EDP.

New congregations were quick to make use of any available space. "Route 22 Mission had an attendance of about 60 people representing forty families," reported the department of missions in 1953. "A place has been found for holding services, namely, the Police Station which seats 100 people; and has a second floor where the Church School will hold sessions."[32] In Ligonier, the first services were held in the sitting rooms of young couples who had grown up in Pittsburgh, Sewickley, and Fox Chapel; later, they moved to a former railroad station.[33] In 1955, members of the department of missions discussed the merits of mission work in three different communities, but ultimately agreed to focus on Monroeville, where there were thirty-eight interested families.[34] Pleasant Hills, where thirty Episcopal families temporarily worshiped at the local Presbyterian church, became the diocesan objective for 1958. The new mission (ultimately located in Jefferson Boro) absorbed a few former members of St. George's in the West End, now seeking a more suburban location, but mainly attracted new residents of the Pleasant Hills area.[35]

Middle-class departures from the City of Pittsburgh reflected the new Episcopal demographic. The starkest illustration of this change can be seen in the case of St. James Memorial. As African Americans (including former members of Holy Cross in the Hill district) flooded into Homewood, Archdeacon William Thomas urged the vestry of St. James Memorial to make its church building available to a black congregation on Sunday evenings. Bishop Pardue supported this initiative but admitted that it was a potentially "difficult program." The vestry raised no objection, and even made the church building available on two additional weekday evenings.[36] By 1953, however, so many white parishioners had moved from Pittsburgh to Penn Hills that both parishes concluded that the best course would be for the Holy Cross congregation to purchase the church building in Homewood, thus providing capital for the erection of a new

---

32. Department of Missions Minutes, Diocesan Council, March 10, 1953, RG4A/2.5:2, EDP.

33. Nimick interview.

34. Department of Missions Minutes, Diocesan Council, January 11, June 14, 1955, RG4A/2.5:2, EDP.

35. Department of Missions Minutes, Diocesan Council, February 12, 1957, March 11, 1958, RG4A/2.5:2, EDP.

36. Department of Missions Minutes, Diocesan Council, February 8, March 8, 1949, RG4A/2.5:2, EDP.

church in Penn Hills. In March 1954, the transfer was formally put into effect, despite the fact that Holy Cross had yet to sell its old property on the Hill district's Center Avenue.[37]

Relocated parishes did not rest on their laurels. In the North Hills, parishioners of the former Christ Church, North Side, soon settled into their new surroundings. "The secret [of their success]," the bishop explained, "is that [Father William] Bradbury has trained his people to be missionaries, but he himself sets a fabulous pace. They tell me that he is at the doorstep of every new home before the moving van arrives and that he ceaselessly and constantly rings doorbells and talks to everybody within miles of the church."[38] Bradbury's approach comported with Pardue's insistence that his parishes be mission-oriented. Many established parishes proved rather less innovative. A 1948 survey reported that while parish leaders served on other community organizations, only half of the parishes made their facilities available to community and nonsectarian groups on a regular basis.[39] Parish leaders were also fiercely protective of their autonomy. For a two-year period, the vestry of Trinity, Connellsville, resisted the efforts of William Thomas, Pittsburgh's suffragan bishop, to persuade them to sell its building and move to a more suitable area. In 1956, Thomas accepted defeat and, against his better judgment, recommended that a remodeling project proceed.[40]

Bishop Pardue had little time for such "leaders" and had harsh words for the "lay-popes" who dominated the life of many parishes.[41] In 1952, he formed a commission on evangelism—chaired by the future dean of Trinity Cathedral, Dixon Rollit—to develop materials for lay visitation and help raise up a new generation of parish leaders. The commission sent out teams of laymen "who have experienced a transformation in their lives by Christianity" to visit parishes and discuss that experience. These

---

37. Department of Missions Minutes, Diocesan Council, September 15, 1953, March 9, 1954, RG4A/2.5:2, Board of Trustees Minutes, April 21, September 15, 1953, March 9, 1954, RG4A/3.3, EDP; *Church News*, May 1954.

38. *Church News*, May 1954.

39. *Church News*, March 1949. One-third of parishes lacked an adult education class, with potentially serious consequences for the forthcoming decade.

40. Department of Missions Minutes, Diocesan Council, September 11, 1956, RG4A/2.5:2, EDP.

41. Department of Missions Minutes, Diocesan Council, October 12, 1954, RG4A/2.5:2, EDP.

presentations frequently led to the establishment of prayer and Bible study groups at the parish level.[42] Another innovation of the 1950s—the parish life conference—became popular in Pittsburgh, as testified to by the wife of the rector of Nativity, Crafton, who reluctantly attended one in Uniontown. "What I found," she later confessed, "was the Church as a living, freedom-giving, heart-warming Reality—something I always knew existed but which I had never experienced with such intensity."[43] In 1961, there were thirteen parish life conferences in the Diocese of Pittsburgh, to which at least eighteen parishes sent delegates.[44]

Austin Pardue demanded spiritual rigor in his parishes, but he was by no means a liturgical formalist and was even willing to permit the introduction of a family celebration of the Eucharist. While the standard morning service was too formal for many suburban families and prevented them from making family excursions, Pardue explained, those families with small children could not be expected to attend the early celebration. The family service, in the bishop's view, had "grown up to meet a need in a social situation characterized by larger families, the development of the automobile, and the evergrowing popularity of the golf-course." It should have a straightforward character, with singable hymns and with the homily not an "abstract theological presentation" but "a 'homey' message marked by story, simile and illustration."[45]

Even those parishes that shied away from a family service were still capable of considerable liturgical diversity. At Pardue's first parish visitation to Church of the Epiphany in Avalon, he was obliged to borrow a cope and miter from the local Orthodox church in order to appear as the rector desired. That experience led Pardue to request that in future all parishes should communicate their liturgical style to him in advance.[46] He praised the liturgical flexibility of St. Thomas, Gibsonia, which had "types of ritual and service from those of ornate tradition to those of virtual Quaker experience meetings."[47] "[The] thing I liked almost best of all," the bishop declared after worshiping at Church of the Advent, Brookline, "was

42. *Convention Journal*, May 11, 1954, 41.

43. *Church News*, May 1957.

44. *Church News*, November 1961.

45. *Church News*, November 1956. On the cultural context of the family service, see Moriarty, *Liturgical Revolution*, 89.

46. Edwards interview.

47. *Church News*, February 1951.

the fact that they worshiped like Episcopalians and sang like Methodists."[48] Homilies, he added, in advice to the clergy of the diocese, should be geared to what was talking place in the world around them. "Remember, boys," he told them on one occasion, "the newspaper is the new New Testament. Don't ever stray from current events. Make the Gospel relevant to someone new."[49]

Liturgy was not the only aspect of diocesan life in transition. Suburban parents also demanded a religious education curriculum reflective of the concerns of the day. In 1944, there were actually three hundred fewer children under instruction than in 1882 when Bishop Whitehead took office; the following year, the system suffered a loss of forty-three teachers and 561 pupils. Pardue was not willing to permit continued drift and appointed a committee chaired by Demas Barnes—a history professor at the University of Pittsburgh and a member of the Laymen's Missionary League—to develop a new education program. Later known as the Pittsburgh Plan, the four-year series developed by Barnes approached Christian education from the perspectives of "The Life of Christ"; "Prayer Book and Sacraments"; "History of the Church"; and "Great Stories of the Bible." Tested in a number of pilot parishes in 1945, the Plan relied upon the careful training of teachers, regular attendance by pupils, and considerable parental involvement.[50]

The following year, the pilot parishes progressed from "The Life of Christ," to "Prayer Book and Sacraments," while many additional parishes embarked upon the Pittsburgh Plan, increasing the total number of students receiving instruction to around two thousand. Students were given their weekly lesson prior to the class and were encouraged to work on it with their parents (parent-teacher groups were formed to promote parental participation).[51] By 1950, the number of Pittsburgh students using the Pittsburgh Plan exceeded four thousand. As communities outside the diocese began to express interest, Esquire Press assumed responsibility for distribution of the Plan, with the diocese receiving one-quarter of the gross income from sales.[52]

48. *Church News*, May 1951.

49. Davies interview.

50. *Church News*, March 1944; *Convention Journal*, January 23, 1945, 67–68; *Church News*, September 1945.

51. *Church News*, September 1946; *Convention Journal*, January 21, 1947, 61.

52. Department of Missions Minutes, Diocesan Council, April 11, 1950, RG4A/2.5:2, EDP.

Although the national church subsequently embarked upon its own education plan (with Pittsburgh's archdeacon serving on the committee that helped draft it), interest in the Pittsburgh Plan did not dissipate. Sales had generated $500,000 by 1958, including an order from as far away as the Diocese of London (England).[53] Some Pittsburgh priests did welcome the national church's Seabury Program, among them Don Gross, a Pittsburgh clergyman with an interest in psychology (in which he earned a master's degree from the University of Pittsburgh in 1959). Gross praised the way in which the Seabury Program emphasized a practical application of Christian faith to the problems of modern life. It encouraged the teacher, he said, to help students identify their problems and find faith-based solutions, a great improvement over the older model of Christian education, which emphasized knowledge.[54]

The growing affluence and fecundity of Pittsburgh's Episcopal population prompted some parents to press for a more systematic approach to juvenile education. In 1947, parishioners at Church of the Ascension, Pittsburgh, organized a parochial school—Ascension Academy—with six teachers and sixty children. So popular was the school that it soon outgrew its facilities. Initially, the younger classes relocated to Calvary Church and the graded classes to Church of the Redeemer, but this proved only a temporary remedy. The school was only saved from oversubscription by the gift of Redeemer parishioner Pauline Mudge, who offered land for a school building adjacent to the church in 1952. The new St. Edmund's Academy (for boys only) adopted the English public school system as its model. Its first headmaster was Edward Izod, formerly a schoolteacher in McKeesport and the part-time choirmaster at Redeemer. "[To] make sure that Christian values are presented to the students," Izod explained in 1954, "teachers are selected not only for their educational ability, but also for their character, personality and interest in the boys. Moreover, chapel services, to which parents are always invited, [are] a regular part of the curriculum."[55]

It was not only suburban children whom the church sought to reach during the 1950s. One local woman worried about the fact that her older children had become religious skeptics after going away to college. "Last

---

53. *Church News*, November 1959.

54. *Church News*, January 1958. On the Seabury Series, see Booty, *Episcopal Church in Crisis*, 28; Gillespie, "What We Taught," 67–73.

55. *Convention Journal*, May 13, 1952, 43; *Church News*, January 1954 (quotation).

Sunday," she told Bishop Pardue, "as I watched the youngest one walk down the aisle in his vestments carrying the symbol of his religion, with his eyes fixed on the cross in the distance, I couldn't help but wonder with what nonsense he will be filled next year when he, too, leaves home and church, and I fully expect to hear the same story from him. I'm used to it now, but I heartily agree when you say the most urgent missionary work we can do is on the college campus."[56] The expansion of the universities and a generally higher standard of living had led to markedly increased student enrollments. Though a transient population, students were a community that many in the Diocese of Pittsburgh believed it was essential to reach, in the first instance by funding Episcopal chaplaincies at local universities.

The first signs of active student ministry became visible in 1946 when students at the University of Pittsburgh organized a Canterbury Club (the Episcopal student association), for which the rector of Church of the Ascension served as chaplain.[57] Two years later, Church of the Redeemer used a $10,000 loan from the diocese to purchase a house for a Canterbury Club at the Carnegie Institute of Technology.[58] By 1949, Episcopalians at the University of Pittsburgh could expect a monthly corporate Communion, followed by a buffet supper and discussion. They were also active in helping form a campus branch of the Student Christian Federation (an umbrella organization for Protestant Christian groups). The Carnegie Tech group was even more active, offering a regular weekly program and providing five licensed lay readers to serve different parishes in the diocese. Similar activities, though on a lesser scale, were also reported at Geneva College, Waynesburg College, and Indiana State Teachers College.[59]

In addition to general student ministry, Pittsburgh also promoted a special ministry to Chinese students attending colleges in southwestern Pennsylvania, in the hope that such students might not revert to Communism when they returned to China. In 1955, Bishop Thomas issued an urgent appeal for Pittsburgh to serve as the location for an Oriental Center for Episcopal work with Chinese students. The diocese

56. *Church News*, January 1949.
57. *Church News*, November 1946.
58. Board of Trustees Minutes, January 13, 1948, RG4A/3.3, EDP.
59. *Convention Journal*, May 10, 1949, 79–81.

recruited Quentin Huang, who had attended the University of Pittsburgh and Philadelphia Divinity School before the Second World War, to lead the ministry. The former bishop of Yunkwei, Huang had left China after the Communist victory in 1950.[60] By 1958, there were 212 Chinese students (including 150 non-Christians) involved in the work of the center, which provided a weekly service on Sunday afternoons and a monthly Eucharist.[61]

As the demands of ministry expanded, the bishop looked to his clergy to bear much of the burden. When Pardue first arrived in Pittsburgh, there were no fewer than twenty-five parish vacancies, a deficiency partly explained by the decision of many clergy to serve with the U.S. military. Pardue approved this turn of events and went so far as to refuse—for the duration of the war—to accept candidates for Holy Orders who were capable of being drafted, since he desired no priest who had used the ministry as justification for exemption from military service.[62] In the immediate postwar era, more would be demanded of diocesan priests than a military record. In 1949, the board of trustees requested Episcopal seminaries to mandate at least one course in business administration to give future priests a better understanding of parish finances.[63] Two years later, the board of missions pledged to "give psychological tests to the Clergy to determine their best aptitudes and fields of service, if the Clergy are willing to take them."[64]

Bishop Pardue was equally concerned for the material well-being of his subordinates. By 1960, most Episcopal clergy had an income only four-fifths that of all Protestant clergy, half that of lawyers, and less than a third that of doctors. The mean Pittsburgh clerical salary ranged from $5,426 in the industrial parishes of the Mon Valley to $6,521 in the suburban parishes. "There is an immediate need to raise the level of income of the established ordained clergy of the Diocese," a committee appointed to

---

60. Department of Missions Minutes, Diocesan Council, September 13, 1955, RG4A/2.5:2, EDP; *Church News*, December 1955.

61. Department of Missions Minutes, Diocesan Council, December 9, 1958, RG4A/2.5:2, EDP.

62. *Convention Journal*, January 23, 1945, 23; *Convention Journal*, January 21, 1947, 34.

63. Board of Trustees Minutes, February 8, 1949, RG4A/3.3, EDP.

64. Department of Missions Minutes, Diocesan Council, February 13, 1951, RG4A/2.5:2, EDP.

investigate the issue declared, "if we are to attract and keep good men, not only in the Diocese, but also in the ministry of the church as a whole."[65]

Perhaps Pardue's greatest concern was that many seminaries tended to produce priests more endowed with religious knowledge than with spiritual ability. "Most of us modern clergy," he declared in 1956, "come to the people as trained Biblical critics rather than fiery spiritual leaders steeped in the fabulous mysteries and powers of God." Preaching that emphasized the miraculous element of God's mercy was much to be preferred.[66] One attempt to provide practical gloss to the formal education imparted by the seminaries came from the rector of Calvary Church, Sam Shoemaker. In 1957, Shoemaker offered a house near his church for a group of recently ordained men working in local churches, hospitals, and industrial plants (both Episcopalian and Presbyterian) to serve a theological "internship" under the supervision of a former assistant at First Presbyterian Church.[67]

While Pardue approved of practical cooperation with the Protestant churches, he nevertheless shared with his predecessor a natural interest in rapprochement with liturgical churches. In 1945, the diocesan convention passed a resolution noting that closer ties between Anglicanism and Orthodoxy would produce a "large Catholic body of non-Roman authority."[68] By 1957, this had come to represent the new paradigm for the Episcopal Church in Pittsburgh. "No longer do we feel that our mission is merely to those of English background from which we spring," mused the bishop, "but rather that we are a part of the true and historic Church of God which reaches whole-heartedly to all nationalities."[69]

Outreach to such groups began during the 1940s. A 1947 meeting between Orthodox and Episcopal clergy at McKees Rocks was followed by the launch of a chapter of the Episcopal-Orthodox Fellowship, which

---

65. *Convention Journal*, May 10, 1960, 55–56 (quotation on 56).

66. *Church News*, February 1956.

67. *Church News*, February 1957.

68. *Convention Journal*, January 23, 1945, 21.

69. *Convention Journal*, January 21, 1957, 22. Surveying the unchurched Slavic and Italian communities of the Pittsburgh region, Pardue commented that they were generally attracted to the Episcopal Church: "Our Altars are often like the Altars they have known before and our worship has much of the dignity to which they have been accustomed." *Church News*, December 1946.

met for worship, reading, study, and the sharing of religious experiences.[70] Kenneth Waldron, rector of Church of the Epiphany, Bellevue, served as an expert witness in church history and canon law at court trials arising out of disputes between the Roman Catholic Church and the Orthodox Church, and was made a proto-presbyter by the latter for his efforts.[71] Close ties were also developed with the Polish National Catholic Church (PNCC), with the suggestion made that, since there was no PNCC church in Pittsburgh itself, an Episcopal parish should offer to share its space to allow the establishment of a PNCC pro-cathedral. One PNCC church shared its worship space with an Episcopal congregation after the latter had sold off its church building, while another Episcopal parish provided pastoral support to a Polish congregation that was temporarily without a priest.[72]

Relations with the Roman Catholic Church were understandably much cooler. "[Many] people want the benefits of the Roman Catholic system without paying for them," Bishop Pardue explained. "Frequently, Episcopalians would like absolute authority, power, and definiteness, while at the same time they desire to be free, and personally live in a laissez-faire atmosphere ... These are days when people are worshiping power. Roman Catholic power is impressive. Personally, I would rather struggle along for unity in the hard traditional Christian way. Episcopalians frequently bungle things badly but we do permit open speaking and democratic procedures."[73]

This notion of a Catholic threat to democracy remained a potent theme among the mainline Protestant churches. The appointment of an American ambassador to the Vatican provoked "heated discussion" at the 1950 diocesan convention, and when the Truman administration agreed to appoint such an ambassador a year later, Bishop Pardue denounced the move as an act that violated the historic separation of church and state and placed "a single religious denominational group in an exclusive preferential position in our capital at Washington."[74]

---

70. *Convention Journal*, January 21, 1947, 71–72; *Church News*, March 1947.

71. *Church News*, November 1957.

72. Department of Missions Minutes, Diocesan Council, March 12, 1946, RG4A/2.5:2, EDP.

73. *Church News*, May 1946.

74. *Convention Journal*, May 9, 1950, 31; *Church News*, November 1951.

A decade later, Pardue's views had moderated. "We thank God for Pope John XXIII," he told delegates to the 1963 diocesan convention. Invited by Pittsburgh's Catholic bishop, John Wright (appointed in 1959), to visit Rome the previous year, Pardue had been much impressed with the open discussion he witnessed. On his return he drafted a pastoral letter, in consultation with his clergy, responding to the pope's invitation to worldwide unity, which achieved international notoriety, not least because it was quoted by Cardinal Bea in his lectures on church unity at Harvard University.[75]

Relationships at the parochial level could be more strained. Kirk Hartman, rector of St. Mary's Memorial, found himself embroiled in a struggle with Bishop Wright over a case involving a male parishioner married to a Roman Catholic, who wished their marriage to be retroactively blessed by a Roman priest. When Hartman advised that it would be wrong for the father to make a pledge to bring up his children as Catholics, Wright denounced this as merely a personal opinion and not the perspective of the Episcopal Church as a whole. Hartman responded by quoting to the contrary from the deliberations both of the Lambeth Conference and the General Convention.[76] Clearly Anglican-Catholic relations had some way to go.

A NEW BASIS FOR MINISTRY, 1952–1960

A year's work experience in an industrial mill or mine was the single prerequisite that Austin Pardue demanded of prospective seminarians. From such experiences, he hoped to produce a band of dedicated priests willing to serve a much-neglected Episcopal constituency—blue-collar workers—in the industrial missions of the Mon Valley. The bishop had a record of contact with organized labor that dated back to his years in Buffalo and viewed Pittsburgh as an excellent laboratory for testing the principles of Christian evangelism in a working-class setting. He believed that such an initiative was vital given the bitter industrial disputes that had polarized the region since the 1930s (and indeed before). "If a revolution comes in

---

75. *Convention Journal*, May 14, 1963, 27–28.

76. "As a communicant of the Episcopal Church," Hartman concluded, "you cannot and must not ignore the moral issues involved, nor can you fly in the face of the stated position of the General Convention by signing the nuptial agreement of the Roman Catholic Diocese of Pittsburgh." Rev. J. Kirk Hartman to Edward J. Ellis, July 27, 1962, RG1/1.9, box 9PP, EDP.

America," Pardue warned in 1949, "it will explode in communities such as yours, and you cannot and dare not neglect the great mass of working people, where the Communists are constantly establishing new cells of operation ... There is no greater missionary work than that which exists among the millions of people who live on our industrial door-step."[77] The following year, the bishop accepted an invitation from Philip Murray of the United Steel Workers (USW) to attend his union's convention in New Jersey (the first official recognition of the Episcopal Church by the labor movement) and also addressed the USW's local (Allegheny County) district.[78]

Pardue frequently consulted with Episcopalian trade unionists, the most prominent of whom was Michael Budzanoski, an officer of the United Mine Workers and a member of St. Mary's, Charleroi. A war veteran, Budzanoski was well schooled in the theology of the Mystical Body of Christ so much in vogue among his Roman Catholic counterparts in the trade union movement. "In the social theory laid down by our Lord," he wrote in 1949, "each man is a member of every other man." Conceding a degree of culpability to both sides in industrial disputes, Budzanoski nevertheless took the view that without a living wage and improvement of working conditions, the attractiveness of Communism to many mineworkers could only increase. "We cannot say that one side has been completely good while the other was wholly bad," he admitted. "The modern historian knows there have been selfish men on both sides ... The threat of Communism may be having beneficial results among us. We're being forced to make our Christianity into a living ideology."[79]

Another prominent player on the labor scene was Budzanoski's rector, Joseph Wittkofski, popularly known in Charleroi as "Father Joe."[80] A former Roman Catholic priest, Wittkofski had become convinced of a call to Holy Orders in the Episcopal Church while studying biology at Fordham University. Mentored by Pardue in Buffalo, he accompanied the bishop-elect to Pittsburgh, where he ultimately took charge of the mission at Charleroi.[81] Here he became a standard-bearer for outreach to lapsed

77. *Convention Journal*, May 10, 1949, 26.
78. *Convention Journal*, May 8, 1951, 22.
79. *Church News*, May 1949.
80. Edwards interview.
81. For evidence that Pardue was instrumental in Wittkofski's conversion when he was dean of Buffalo Cathedral, see *Church News*, February 1953.

Catholics, securing independent status for his mission and transforming it into a bastion of working-class Anglo Catholicism. In 1946, he presented Pardue with a confirmation class of thirty-four—including fourteen former Roman Catholics—the largest in the parish's history.[82] A chaplain in the American Legion and an active member of Protestants and Other Americans United for the Separation of Church and State, Wittkofski achieved national recognition for his books on devotionalism.[83] In an article in the *Living Church*, Wittkofski described the first obligation of the Christian life as the development of a permanent "Christian conscience," and encouraged his readers to use the Pauline formula "I can do all things through Christ which strengtheneth me," on a daily basis.[84]

Men like Wittkofski were exceptional. The lifestyle of the Mon Valley was far removed from that of the middle-class Episcopalian living comfortably in Sewickley or Mt. Lebanon. In 1951, the department of missions called for the erection of a new rectory in Donora, "as [the current rectory] is now situated in the midst of an industrial section which is unhealthy to live in."[85] Some of the industrial towns not only lacked rectories but priests. In Wilmerding—a community of fifty thousand—a machinist employed by Westinghouse oversaw the tiny parish of St. Margaret's, which had never enjoyed the services of a resident priest.[86] In Tarentum, George McCormick, vice president of the local chapter of the Congress of Industrial Organizations, served on the vestry of St. Barnabas Church.[87] Such trade unionist involvement may well have dissipated working-class suspicion that their parish's activities were subject to middle-class dictation. When Pardue visited Donora, Michael Budzanoski invited him to be present at a mass meeting of ten thousand miners and their families.[88] Further proof of the commitment of Pittsburgh's blue-collar congregations to the work of the church came in 1952, when a lifelong steel worker

82. *Convention Journal*, January 21, 1947, 38. Walter Righter attests to the fact that it was Wittkofski who helped local Episcopal priests to understand the Catholic idiom. Righter interview.

83. *Church News*, December 1957.

84. *Church News*, March 1949. This was a reprint of the *Living Church* article.

85. Department of Missions Minutes, Diocesan Council, March 13, 1951, RG4A/2.5:2, EDP.

86. *Church News*, January 1951.

87. *Church News*, May 1951.

88. *Church News*, September 1951.

and member of a working-class parish bequeathed $50,000 to the diocese for the education of seminarians.[89]

Such encouraging signs led Pardue to declare industrial work to be the priority of his diocese. As early as 1945, members of the board of trustees had discussed how to raise money for mission work in industrial areas and to subsidize a salary increase for priests involved in such work.[90] On November 6, 1951, twelve Pittsburgh priests gathered to establish the Society for the Promotion of Industrial Mission (SPIM).[91] SPIM, the bishop explained the following year, "believes that the worship of the Church reaches out into the community through people and that ... Christ works over the desk; Christ works through executive positions; Christ works through the workers on the job; Christ works around the bargaining table; Christ travels with the salesman."[92]

SPIM drew immediate national attention both in church periodicals and secular journals such as *Time*, and national church leaders also took note. On February 28, 1952, Presiding Bishop Henry Sherrill visited Pittsburgh, where he toured the Mathies Coal Mine—the largest commercial mine in the world—and visited the parishes at Braddock, Charleroi, Donora, Duquesne, Homestead, McKeesport, Monongahela, and Wilmerding. At the conclusion of his visit, Sherrill was made an honorary member of SPIM, in the presence of the nineteen priests who served industrial communities.[93] It must have been something of a culture shock to the courtly Sherrill, who "was not really fit to be roaming around Duquesne, Pennsylvania," but so enthused was he by the experience that he persuaded the General Convention of 1952 to elect Pardue to chair the new joint commission on industrial work.[94] Nor did Pardue confine his industrial work to the Episcopal scene. His appreciation for the labor schools organized by the Roman Catholic Church led him to propose the creation of a labor institute sponsored by the diocese and

---

89. *Church News*, February 1952.

90. Board of Trustees Minutes, February 13, 1945, RG4A/3.3, EDP.

91. *Convention Journal*, May 8, 1951, 31; *Church News*, December 1951. The original name proposed for the organization was the Society for the Promotion of Industrial Territory, "which meant the initials would be quite different." Righter interview.

92. *Convention Journal*, May 13, 1952, 32.

93. Ibid., 32–33; *Church News*, April 1952.

94. Righter interview (quotation); Department of Missions Minutes, Diocesan Council, December 9, 1952, RG4A/2.5:2, EDP.

the Presbytery of Pittsburgh. In November 1951, he joined the board of the Industrial Areas Foundation, organized by Bernard Shiel, the Catholic bishop of Chicago, and labor activist Saul Alinsky to promote democracy and self-determination for those living in industrial areas.[95]

Pardue's commitment to industrial mission took on an added urgency in the wake of the strikes that rocked southwestern Pennsylvania during the early 1950s. In April 1952, he visited strike-torn Monongahela and confided his impressions to his diary:

> Tonight the great steel strike is on and it is an historic evening since the strike was called as the result of the decision of Judge Pine, who stated that the seizure of the steel mills was unconstitutional. While we were at the rectory, the phone constantly rang because workers in the mills were reporting in as to why they would not be able to be present at service. A number of them were maintenance men who were going to the mills to shut down the furnaces. While the service was beautiful, there was nevertheless an ominous and terribly tense feeling in all of the towns we passed through tonight. On our way home, we went to Homestead and watched the picket lines and passed the big union headquarters where crowds of people were thronging the streets in obvious tension over the decisions that were ahead of them.[96]

Later in the decade, a renewed burst of strike activity left many Mon Valley residents with time on their hands. Richard Davies, then rector at St. Paul's, Monongahela, organized repairs to the church to provide them with some form of activity. "The women," he recalls, "were ecstatic because the men had something to do."[97]

SPIM's leaders also sought to make the national church more aware of the industrial missions and to recruit able clergy. In 1952, they manned a display at the General Convention in Boston, led a clergy conference in the Diocese of Bethlehem, and prepared a book on mission work in industrial areas. The following year, twenty seminarians from five different seminaries attended a local conference directed by Richard Hardman, rector of St. Stephen's, McKeesport, and chairman of SPIM. In 1956, Hardman resigned to accept a position with the national church. Under

---

95. *Church News*, December 1951.

96. *Church News*, September 1952. On the industrial conflicts of the 1950s, see Hinshaw, *Steel and Steelworkers*, 105–71.

97. Davies interview.

his successors, there would be a shift toward the study of the problems of the "time-clock" communities, with a focus on preaching, laymen's activities, and making church services more meaningful.[98]

Complementing SPIM was an emerging Neo-Evangelical prayer culture. The two great innovations of the Pardue episcopate were united in the person of Dave Griffith, a member of the Congress of Industrial Organizations employed at the Homestead Works. In an effort to solve a looming strike, Griffith decided to pray for guidance and then act as the Holy Spirit moved him. The result was a committee to monitor workplace conditions involving representatives from the workforce, salaried employees, and management. Within four months, Griffith also brought together between 200 and 350 of his coworkers for a regular prayer meeting. Close to Sam Shoemaker, rector of Calvary Church (see below), Griffith brought fellow unionists to gatherings at Calvary, where they were introduced to the sons of privileged Episcopalians. At least for a moment, traditional class cleavages gave place to appreciation of the equality of all Christians before God.[99]

During the 1950s, a sophisticated apparatus of prayer ministries extending the length and breadth of the diocese was instituted. Bishop Pardue was thoroughly committed to prayer ministry and had been since at least the early 1940s, when he first recognized the importance of prayerful support to the soldier on the battlefield. "[Our fighting men] want God," he wrote in 1944, "they want Christ, they want faith, they want the Bible and they want prayer, but they do not want pious stuffiness, abstract theology, religious bigotry and a divided Christianity . . . Without the power of prayer there is no steam behind idealistic action. If we really want a better social and political day after this war, we must have the power of prayer behind our efforts."[100] In 1951, Pardue helped revive the Legion of Silence—first established during the Second World War—to pray for members of the armed services serving in Korea.[101]

For Pardue, prayer transcended the theological differences that separated the Evangelical from the Anglo Catholic and the Episcopalian from

---

98. *Convention Journal*, May 12, 1953, 45–46; *Church News*, December 1953; *Convention Journal*, May 14, 1957, 57.

99. Shoemaker, *I Stand by the Door*, 130–32.

100. *Church News*, February 1944.

101. *Convention Journal*, May 8, 1951, 23. Pardue later visited troops serving in Korea.

his Presbyterian and Lutheran neighbors. Jesus, he once suggested, had established "machinery"—in the form of the church—to convert God's spiritual energy into something that ordinary men and women could use. When they failed properly to utilize this energy, this was not a reflection on the design so much as a human misunderstanding of the mechanism. Thus, a High Churchman was always tempted "to add new gadgets, rules and systems, copying them from another great institution whose organization they crave but whose discipline they avoid." A Low Churchman, by contrast, believed that one could sustain "production" even if some of the basic industrial processes were omitted. Finally, those of a Broad Church disposition dismissed the machinery as outdated and frequently encouraged unskilled workers to tamper with the inner workings. Even allowing for the playful nature of the metaphor, Pardue's comment underscores how prayer ministries helped to overcome the limitations imposed by Anglican pluralism.[102]

Postwar Pittsburgh was fertile soil for prayer ministries, especially those devoted to healing. Indeed, the Episcopal connection with healing ministry could be traced back to 1920, when the rectors of Trinity Church and Calvary Church invited James Moore Hickson to lead healing missions at their churches. Hickson, an Anglican layman of English origins, had developed a ministry of healing prayer, which included encouraging parishes to form prayer circles that would make intercessory prayer for the sick. In the course of an eight-month tour, Hickson visited many cities—including Pittsburgh—and even won the support of New York clergyman William Manning (soon to be elected bishop of New York). Enthusiasm for Hickson's methods eventually waned, however, with Bishop Whitehead stressing that spiritual healing should be seen as complementary to the work of skilled physicians, not an alternative to it.[103]

Hickson's legacy was to be rediscovered during the postwar period. In 1948, Dixon Rollit, a clergy assistant at Calvary, reported that at least twenty parishioners were receiving prayers for healing each day.[104] That same year, Nancy Chalfant, a Sewickley Episcopalian struggling to come to terms with the birth of her handicapped daughter, visited Bishop Pardue. The bishop told her that, while he believed in the efficacy of

102. *Church News*, February 1945.
103. *Convention Journal*, January 27–28, 1920, 96–99; Cunningham, "James Moore Hickson."
104. *Convention Journal*, May 10, 1949, 48.

scientific medicine, he felt that there was a place for healing prayer. He encouraged her to read *The Healing Light*, a book first published in 1947 by Agnes Sanford, the daughter of Presbyterian missionaries to China, about her cure from depression through healing prayer.[105] As she read Sanford's account, Chalfant gained a new understanding of God's actions in the world:

> I knew it must be God's power, the power of the Holy Spirit, because that was what Mrs. Sanford was writing about. Oh, what hope I was filled with then! God's power was real, and I was actually feeling it as it burned in my heart. I knew that he loved me and Verlinda and wanted her to be whole and well. I saw that I could be a channel through which that power could work, and I didn't have to sit by helplessly as Verlinda grew in years but not in mentality. Jesus became real to me, no longer a shadowy figure living 2,000 years ago but a person to love and be loved now, today, a person who loved Verlinda, too, and who hurt when we hurt.[106]

Healing prayer ministries soon took root in Pittsburgh. In 1949, the rector of St. Luke's, Georgetown, successfully employed the Prayer Book service of anointing the sick for a parishioner of whose recovery doctors had despaired, while at St. Peter's, Uniontown, a group of twenty-five parishioners prayed daily for sick members of their community. One woman, paralyzed on her left side, was reported to have recovered the use of most of her faculties within four months.[107]

Perhaps the most innovative healing prayer ministry was to be found in Brentwood. Under Don Gross, the congregation of St. Peter's Church had already become experienced in healing ministry, but in 1959 his successor, Richard Davies, took it to a new level. While making the rounds of his parish to ask how the new church building might best be used, he became acquainted with a family with a Down syndrome child. "Do something for Debbie," her mother implored, and so the preschool for handicapped children was born. Marrying Gross's interest in prayer and unction to the work of two Philadelphia doctors who had worked with "patterning" the brain, Davies and retired social worker Elsie Wagner developed a program that blended a family-centered ministry with traditional social work and healing prayer. Such was its success that it was

---

105. Sanford, *Healing Light*.
106. Chalfant, *Child of Grace,* 29–30 (quotation on 30).
107. *Convention Journal*, May 9, 1950, 69; *Church News*, January 1949.

soon invited to carry out research by the United Mental Health Services of Allegheny County. Bishop Thomas described the school's work as a "vital demonstration of how an Episcopal Church can work so harmoniously with psychiatry and medicine, how willing volunteers can truly give of themselves in loving another man's children, and how the community has accepted and encouraged the work of the Episcopal Church in Brentwood."[108]

Bishop Pardue was a great enthusiast for such developments. "In religion today," he wrote in 1956, "we are victims of our own double thought and double talk. We read or listen to multiple stories in the Bible of healings and promises that God's forces shall be continued today but often we are scandalized by the thought that we can experience them. For example, the way we have fought against the revival of the healing movement in the Church you would think that Our Lord was against it instead of its Creator."[109] By the mid-1950s, almost half the parishes in the diocese scheduled regular healing services or hosted healing prayer groups, and Pittsburgh boasted one of only two diocesan healing commissions in the United States (the other was in the Diocese of Los Angeles). One of the commission's better-known members was Emily Gardiner Neal, author of *A Reporter Finds God* and a member of Church of the Advent, Brookline, who had shifted from a position of journalistic skepticism to a belief that there was indeed evidence for spiritual healing.[110] Another enthusiast was Pittsburgh clergyman Don Gross, who had a particular interest in Pittsburgh healer Kathryn Kuhlman and published a monograph on spiritual healing in 1958.[111]

Healing prayer was only one component of the new postwar emphasis on the Christian life transformed by the development of a personal relationship with Jesus, in many ways a return to the nineteenth-century Evangelical emphasis on personal regeneration. One of the more prominent leaders of this transdenominational movement, Billy Graham, conducted a number of his crusades in southwestern Pennsylvania in 1952, and took some time to address members of the University of Pittsburgh's

108. Davies interview; *Church News*, May 1960 (quotation).
109. *Church News*, February 1956.
110. *Convention Journal*, May 8, 1956, 61; *Church News*, April 1957; Neal, *Reporter Finds God*. Neal later became a deacon in the Episcopal Church.
111. Gross, *Case for Spiritual Healing*. See also Kuhlman, *I Believe in Miracles*.

Canterbury Club.¹¹² Bishop Pardue appreciated Graham's emphasis on the need for the mature Christian to develop a personal relationship with his Lord and Savior but believed that such a process required nurture in a group setting and should be overseen by someone who respected Anglican traditions. In 1952, therefore, he turned to one of the legends of Anglican devotionalism in the United States, Samuel Moor Shoemaker, and persuaded him to accept the call to become rector of Calvary Church, East Liberty.¹¹³

While at New York's Calvary Church, Shoemaker pioneered outreach to what he called the "happy ethical pagans." His evangelism sought to connect with those members of the comfortable middle class who believed revivalism had no message for them. In an effort to persuade people of the universal character of the conversion experience, Shoemaker downplayed the intellectual aspects of the religious life in favor of the purely experiential. For this reason, he would later be criticized by Neo-Evangelicals like Peter Moore—who served a clerical internship under him—because his message failed to impart a "rootedness" to new converts. For all that he was a liberal Evangelical, says Moore, he had "an evangelist's heart and an amazing gift of evangelism."¹¹⁴

Shoemaker's arrival in Pittsburgh heralded the beginning of a new phase for Anglicanism in southwestern Pennsylvania. As Bishop Pardue noted: "The young married crowd at Calvary ought not to be an unusual phenomenon, in present-day Christianity, but it is. The well-educated, intelligent, and sophisticated young people of today have generally not been led to experience religion in such a way as to make it natural, healthy and personal."¹¹⁵ Shoemaker and his wife, Helen, shattered all these perceptions. Within a year, there were nine Episcopal prayer groups—two at Trinity Cathedral; one at the Harvard-Yale-Princeton Club; one at the Homestead Works; and the rest in private homes—which sought by their

---

112. *Church News*, December 1952. Pardue was present for this meeting and later attended one of Graham's evangelistic rallies at Forbes Field.

113. Department of Missions Minutes, Diocesan Council, April 8, 1952, RG4A/2.5:2, EDP. "The Bishop welcomed Dr. Samuel M. Shoemaker to the Department of Missions, not only as a member but as a personal friend of long standing." For an overview of Shoemaker's career, see Shoemaker, *I Stand by the Door*.

114. Shoemaker, *Children of the Second Birth*; Sack, "Reaching the 'Up and Outers'"; Moore interview.

115. Shoemaker, *I Stand by the Door*, 129–30.

intercessions to care for the needs of the sick and the troubled, and to strengthen the local community, the diocese, and the world.[116] Shoemaker also encouraged student prayer groups across the denominational divide, and made Calvary a popular venue for the Christian youth movement. In 1953, the parish hosted a conference on Christian vocations that attracted 150 students from ten universities from as far afield as Iowa.[117]

The transformation of the culture of Calvary was only a small part of what Shoemaker had in mind. Far more all encompassing was his effort to transform the wider Pittsburgh community—particularly the business community—through corporate prayer. In 1955, therefore, the Pittsburgh Experiment—uniting five downtown churches—was incorporated. Participants in the Experiment, many of them influential members of the business community, focused on personal transformation affecting the totality of their lives through the mechanism of prayer. "For Shoemaker," says historian Michael Sider-Rose, "a primary achievement of the Pittsburgh Experiment was its existence as a Christian institution that invited rather than alienated people who did not identify with the church." It was a transdenominational undertaking very different from that of the National Council of Churches, and it marked the first entry of Pittsburgh's Episcopal community into a wider evangelical subculture.[118]

By 1956, there were seventy-five prayer groups (and a further seventy-five organized by other denominations) meeting in Pittsburgh.[119] Although Bishop Pardue welcomed these developments, he warned all Episcopal prayer groups to include a priest, though as an advisor, not a group leader. He encouraged them always to commence meetings with Holy Communion, and follow this with a book report (recommending Agnes Sanford's *The Healing Light* as a good preliminary text), the sharing of personal religious experiences, prayers, and silent meditation. Prayer groups, he said, should not be debating societies, and their primary focus should be on witnessing to the spiritual results achieved by prayer and action. They should use the power of prayer to assist the healing of others and to strengthen their members' faith and capacity for action.[120]

116. Ibid., 171–73; *Church News*, December 1953.
117. *Convention Journal*, May 12, 1953, 47; *Convention Journal*, May 11, 1954, 35.
118. Sider-Rose, *Taking the Gospel to the Point*, 19–24 (quotation on 23–24). See also Shoemaker, *I Stand by the Door*, 194–208.
119. *Church News*, October 1956.
120. *Church News*, June 1954.

Some prayer groups brought together the like-minded. Nancy Chalfant became part of such a group, many of whose members also had handicapped children. They met first in the chapel of St. Stephen's, Sewickley, and then, as numbers increased, were obliged to move into the sanctuary. "It was," she writes, "the high point of my week. We were all experiencing the newness of life that Paul wrote about in Romans. We were hungry for spiritual food and were being fed." She recalled how the group on one occasion prayed for the atheist husband of a member after he suffered a stroke; he, on his recovery, became a Christian and began to study for the ministry.[121] Some prayer experiments were less successful, however. When Peter Moore was assigned as deacon-in-charge to All Souls, North Versailles, he also sought to convince members of his blue-collar congregation of their need for personal conversion, but met considerable resistance. "They wouldn't have been able to say 'Jesus is my Lord and Savior,'" says Moore today. "A few of them might, but they wouldn't have known the full implications of that."[122]

Sam Shoemaker's activities contributed considerably to American Anglicanism's dialogue with evangelical Protestantism. Anglicanism, he wrote in 1956,

> believes as much in an ordered ministry, and is as emphatic about sacraments as Rome. It believes as much in conversion and personal religion and evangelism as Protestantism ... We believe this to be a more faithful representation of what our Lord gave to His apostles and to the world. We believe it to be a much richer blessing and help for human nature ... [While] all of us stand in debt to the Anglo-Catholics for their emphasis on the grace of God in the Sacraments, still the genuinely evangelical side of our Church needs greatly strengthening. We need to find again the actual and living power of the Holy Spirit, conversion, fellowship and Christian witness.[123]

Bishop Pardue enthusiastically agreed. "The article is wise as a serpent," he told Shoemaker. "I think it gives a wedge through which you

---

121. Chalfant, *Child of Grace*, 33–35 (quotation on 34).

122. Moore interview.

123. *Church News*, May 1956. Contrast this with Pardue's comments made seven years earlier: "As far as I am concerned, it makes little difference what a man's Churchmanship is, if he has walked with Jesus and can bring me closer to His life and grace." *Church News*, May 1949.

can enter the lives of many more people with your great and powerful emphasis."[124]

The work of SPIM and of Sam Shoemaker represented a shift—however subtle—away from the institutional church approach. While Bishop Pardue did establish a department of Christian social relations in 1945, it did not appear that diocesan leaders intended to resurrect the model adopted during the heady days of the 1910s.[125] In 1946, the diocesan convention defeated a resolution suggesting that the presiding bishop should speak out on moral questions pertinent to all Americans, not just Episcopalians, and a 1955 resolution condemning all forms of public gambling was tabled.[126] Moreover, when the charter of St. Margaret's Memorial Hospital was amended in 1959 to allow it to receive state aid, some delegates expressed concern that this presaged the advent of socialized medicine, or, at any rate, an excessive degree of oversight by the state.[127]

THE REDEMPTION OF THE CHURCH, 1961–1969

While Austin Pardue remained bishop of Pittsburgh until 1967, it is safe to say that his successor, Robert Bracewell Appleyard, proved a more paradigmatic episcopal leader for the turbulent changes that took place during the 1960s. Born in Jamestown, New York, and raised a Methodist, Appleyard graduated from Union Theological Seminary in 1943. While serving as a U.S. Navy chaplain during the Second World War, he became an Episcopalian (the only English-speaker in a sixty-member confirmation class in New Guinea). Ordained in 1947, he served Connecticut

124. Bp. Pardue to Rev. Samuel Shoemaker, March 6, 1956, RG2/4.1, box 7BP, Bishops' Papers, EDP.

125. *Convention Journal*, January 23, 1945, 78. In 1964, the department requested for the first time that it be accorded a line in the diocesan budget. Its focus by this point was heavily geared toward civil rights. Over the previous year it had assisted five parishes working on racial integration, lobbied in Washington for civil rights legislation, planned a Religion and Race seminar, and organized the diocesan chapter of the Episcopal Society for Cultural and Racial Unity. *Convention Journal*, May 12, 1964, 85–86.

126. *Convention Journal*, January 22, 1946, 18; *Convention Journal*, May 10, 1955, 16. On the other hand, a resolution calling for abolition of capital punishment in Pennsylvania passed in 1959 without much debate. *Convention Journal*, May 12, 1959, 18.

127. *Convention Journal*, May 12, 1959, 16–17. One clergyman went so far as to offer $1,000 with the hope of provoking enough similar contributions to obviate the need to seek state support.

parishes at Watertown and Greenwich before moving to Palm Beach, Florida, to serve as rector of Bethesda Church. He was elected on the second ballot, with a clear lead over his principal rival, Benedict Williams of St. Stephen's, Sewickley.[128] Appleyard's congeniality soon won him friends in the diocese, due, not the least, to his determination to attempt to remember the names of the many people he met during episcopal visitations.[129] A sensitive priest with a somewhat stylized manner of conversation (John Guest recalls his frequent use of the phrase "Your bishop thinks..."), he had strong pastoral convictions and deep personal piety.[130] Like Pardue, he believed in the necessity of individual Bible reading and personal prayer. "Prayer is the breath of the soul," he declared in 1973, "and without regular, disciplined, intelligent, costly prayer, the soul will shrink and wither."[131]

The devastating fire that swept through Trinity Cathedral in 1967 ensured that Appleyard would be the first Episcopal bishop consecrated in a Roman Catholic cathedral: St. Paul's Cathedral in Pittsburgh. The ceremony was also the first to be carried on all three local television networks. Presiding Bishop John Hines officiated, assisted by Bishop Pardue and Bishop Thomas, and the new bishop coadjutor was presented with a special crosier designed by Eliza Miller of Gibsonia, which incorporated aluminum, glass, and steel, reflecting the region's principal industries. A Roman Catholic monsignor attending the consecration was impressed by the liturgical similarities with the Catholic rite and with the degree of congregational participation. "Their responses were spontaneous and sincere," he marveled. "[I]t showed they had done this before. They put us to shame, because in too many cases in our liturgy we see people with book in hand but not taking part, or worse still with no book in hand or not paying attention."[132]

Appleyard soon demonstrated a commitment to social justice that more than matched that of his predecessor. At his first episcopal visitation

---

128. *Special Convention Journal*, November 14, 1967, 13–14. For Appleyard's biographical details, see the obituary at http://www.post-gazette.com/regionstate/19991027appleyard9.asp.

129. Little, "Historical Notes," 1.

130. Guest interview; Edwards interview; Fairfield/Rodgers interview.

131. *Convention Journal*, May 4–5, 1973, 49–50.

132. *Church News*, January–February 1968, March–April 1968 (quotation).

in April 1968, he stressed the essential connection between discipleship and action:

> The Church is all kinds and all conditions of people. Here in our worship, here in our fellowship, we receive God's friends to go out to the world, to go out to witness to the love, a love that we said in the Creed and in the Lord's Prayer—"Our Father." We are then willing to comfort the family existing in its slum tenement, its ghetto, terrified by guns, by fire, by riots, by cockroaches, by utter filth ... We can identify with those movements that have to do with good government, fair housing to all everywhere, equal rights and the highest standards of education for everyone. We can pray for those whose lives have become so bitter, so empty, so disconsolate, that they are not able to get down on their knees and pray. We can extend the fellowship of the Church into the lives and homes of those who have been rejected, those who have been forgotten, [those] who have been overlooked for years and years.[133]

Appleyard inherited a diocese in which the social cleavages were broad and deep. Most isolated, culturally and geographically, were those parishes located in the Mon Valley, a region beginning to feel the effects of the steady decline of the steel industry and rising levels of unemployment. Many members of these blue-collar congregations resented the fact that most social expenditures—secular and ecclesiastical—were lavished on areas of urban blight, while their own communities tended to be neglected or forgotten. The frustration of mill town Episcopalians at their lack of influence over the work of the church was given voice by Lynn Edwards, an Episcopal priest in Donora. "Nobody seems certain about who's doing what," he complained in 1969, "and where one council or committee ends and another begins."[134] "We say we belong to a diocesan family," lamented another Mon Valley priest. "We say we want to get together on common problems of the diocese, but our actions ... the rest of the year seem to belie what we have said in [the presence of our bishop]. We seem to act

---

133. *Church and Community: Christian Social Relations Bulletin*, May 1968, RG4A/2.3:1, box 6DC, EDP.

134. Rev. Lynn C. Edwards to Bp. Appleyard, March 8, 1969, RG4A/2.1:1, box 1DC, EDP. When Edwards first came to Donora and Monessen, the parish had gone years without a priest; within recent memory, one priest had stayed for one Sunday before departing again. Edwards interview.

as Congregationalists. I sometimes wonder if the structure of the Church forces us to act in this manner."[135]

Such disenchantment had implications for how clergy like Joseph Wittkofski of Charleroi would respond to the great cause of civil rights during the 1960s. While it is fashionable to dismiss white backlash as the product of irrational prejudice, in Pittsburgh's case this arguably fails to do justice to the clannish culture of southwestern Pennsylvania. Wittkofski's dedication to the people of his parish and of the Mon Valley in general was absolute. He was the sponsor of various resolutions defending the rights of the small parish, including an ultimately successful plea that the diocesan convention meet in different parts of the diocese to increase interest in its activities and foster parochial fellowship.[136] In 1968, however, the priest from Charleroi introduced a more contentious proposal: that any diocesan expenditure to improve inner-city housing should be matched dollar-for-dollar with spending on similar projects *outside* Pittsburgh. Given that four times as many people lived in substandard housing outside the city, Wittkofski argued, expenditures that disproportionately benefited the inner-city ghetto made nonsense of the implied equality of Christian outreach. The resolution failed, heightening tensions within the diocese and pushing Wittkofski further to the right in his church politics.[137]

Such disenchantment notwithstanding, Appleyard's commitment to racial equality built upon the record that had already been established under Pardue, who had warned of the severity of the racial problems confronting the United States as early as 1945, before even the national church was fully committed to the cause.[138] In 1957, Pardue publicized the statement issued by his Arkansas counterpart on the conflict over integration at Central High School in Little Rock.[139] He also supported the 1959 visit to Pittsburgh of Archbishop Joost de Blank of Cape Town. A vocal

---

135. Rev. Eugene J. Loughran to Bp. Appleyard, March 4, 1969, RG4A/2.1:1, box 1DC, EDP.

136. *Convention Journal*, May 8, 1962, 13–14, 16.

137. *Convention Journal*, May 14, 1968, 16, 31–32.

138. Board of Trustees Minutes, April 10, 1945, RG4A/3.3, EDP. For a general survey of the early phase of the civil rights movement, see Shattuck, *Episcopalians and Race*, 59–160.

139. *Church News*, December 1957.

critic of the South African government, de Blank preached at St. Mary's, Pittsburgh, under the auspices of the American Church Union.[140]

Some Pittsburgh Episcopalians took their cue from Pardue. Members of the Christian social relations department participated in a 1952 Race Relations Sunday service at East Liberty Presbyterian Church, where they heard the story of a black minister's experience of being called to serve a white congregation in Connecticut.[141] Six years later, the diocesan convention approved a resolution calling on members of the diocese to work to end housing discrimination.[142] Walter Righter had his first exposure to the issue while pastoring All Saints, Aliquippa, in the early 1950s. When post office official Garfield Shaw and his wife relocated from Massachusetts to Aliquippa, they came to All Saints and asked Righter to baptize their new baby. The Shaws were African Americans, however, and Aliquippa had been organized as a series of ethnically segregated communities (known as "plans"). There were black churches in Plan Nine, a vestryman observed when Righter reported that the Shaws wished to become members, to which the rector responded that none of them were an *Episcopal* church. "Well, Reverend," the vestryman answered, "you've got yourself a problem." Undaunted, Righter accepted the Shaws as members and, in the event, lost only one family as a result of his action. Shaw later became a deacon in the Episcopal Church.[143]

The assaults inflicted on civil rights activists by members of the police department of Birmingham, Alabama, in 1963, prompted an uncharacteristically strong denunciation from Bishop Pardue. Alarmed at the rising escalation of violence, the bishop unfavorably compared President Eisenhower's intervention at Little Rock (which Pardue had visited shortly after the confrontation) with the hands-off attitude of the Kennedy administration. He was also troubled that his pastoral letter on integration, while eliciting strong support from many people, had produced "many disturbing complaints."[144] In 1963, the diocesan convention passed a

140. *Church News*, October 1959.
141. *Convention Journal*, May 13, 1952, 72.
142. *Convention Journal*, May 13, 1958, 19.
143. Righter interview.
144. *Convention Journal*, May 14, 1963, 28–29 (quotation on 29). Pardue thanked Father Walter Parker of Holy Cross, Homewood, and Jessie Vann, a Holy Cross parishioner, who had succeeded her husband as editor of the nationally renowned black newspaper, the *Pittsburgh Courier*, for helping to damp down tensions in the black community.

resolution reaffirming its opposition to segregation and discrimination and endorsed the bishop's call to maintain civil peace. The convention's members also stood for a moment of silent prayer on behalf of all those involved in racial conflict.[145]

Within the diocese, the focus inevitably shifted to the new Christian social relations department, which urged the 1964 diocesan convention to support civil rights legislation. Despite the opposition of Joseph Wittkofski, who "made a passionate plea for us to be out teaching and doing civil rights and not relying on the state," most delegates agreed with Thomas Hayes, rector of St. Thomas, Gibsonia, that the time had come for action.[146] Only a few days earlier, a meeting at Trinity Cathedral had resulted in an agreement to form a diocesan chapter of the Episcopal Society for Cultural and Racial Unity (ESCRU), the principal Episcopal civil rights organization.[147]

Perhaps the most significant development, however, was the June 1964 decision of St. Stephen's, Sewickley, to be a pilot parish for the missionary-in-training program, which helped develop the skills of prospective missionaries in problematic settings in the United States.[148] St. Stephen's accepted Richard Martin (a Virginia Theological Seminary graduate) as its missionary-in-training and proposed that he conduct his work in Pittsburgh's Hill district, which had lacked an Episcopal presence since Holy Cross had left the neighborhood in 1954. Martin took up his position with enthusiasm and worked with local drug addicts, whose condition he blamed on weak family structures and high unemployment. He frequently attended court sessions to request that offenders be committed to treatment clinics rather than prison. From Martin's ministry developed an increasingly active Episcopal ministry to the African American community. During the summer of 1966, younger members of the parish helped coach their African American counterparts at the local YMCA. In August, six of the latter entered the Edgeworth Club Invitational

---

145. Ibid., 17–18, 21–22.

146. *Convention Journal*, May 12, 1964, 18 (quotation), 21.

147. *Church News*, April 1964. ESCRU was formed at St. Augustine's College, Raleigh, North Carolina, in 1959. On its establishment, see Shattuck, *Episcopalians and Race*, 98–102.

148. *Church News*, June 1964. The missionary-in-training program was developed in response to the decline in the number of large foreign mission stations that could offer apprenticeships to new missionaries.

Tournament, becoming the first African Americans to play in a junior tennis tournament in Pittsburgh.[149]

Priests like Richard Martin and Thomas Hayes, both of whom went on the Selma to Montgomery march, discovered that not every Pittsburgher was impressed by their witness. "You return home," Hayes later recounted, "to hear you have received disturbed phone calls, obscene letters, right-wing literature. One former friend now declares he is your enemy."[150] At the 1965 diocesan convention, Bishop Pardue, even as he praised the work of the local ESCRU chapter and expressed appreciation for the "obedience to conscience" of the four priests who had gone to Selma, stressed that no diocesan funds had been expended for their travel.[151] Such assurances did not mollify men like Horace Atkins of St. Mary's, Charleroi. Atkins even introduced a resolution barring the use of diocesan funds to groups (on either side of the issue) involved in racial and civil unrest, which, he argued, had *followed*, not preceded, the granting of the right to vote. He also accused Martin Luther King Jr. of contempt for the nation's laws. Thomas Hayes responded that the Atkins resolution "was not worthy of a vote," and even moderates like Philip Schaefer, rector of All Saints, Aliquippa—who accepted that there were people of goodwill on both sides of the issue—maintained that the church had to take a stand and must commit funds to sustain it. Walter Parker, rector of Holy Cross, set the seal on the debate with the comment that Christians could not be lukewarm or neutral on racial justice, and the Atkins resolution was summarily defeated.[152]

While Richard Martin's Hill ministry represented the most public face of Episcopal witness to racial equality in Pittsburgh, there were some other faltering steps. In the North Side's Manchester district, local residents nicknamed Emmanuel Episcopal Church—which had remained a white congregation in an increasingly black neighborhood—"The Bastille." In response, its rector, Thomas Cox, argued that the parish had a duty to promote community empowerment and provide essential services to minority residents of the North Side. Cox also put pressure on Allegheny General Hospital to strengthen pediatric care and mental health services

---

149. *Church News*, June 1965; *Church and Community: Christian Social Relations Bulletin*, November 1966, RG4A/2.3:1, box 6DC, EDP.
150. *Church News*, May 1965.
151. *Convention Journal*, May 11, 1965, 26.
152. Ibid., 15–16, 21.

for the community and challenged the local board of realtors to meet their responsibilities to tenants in substandard accommodation.[153]

In the Hill district, Richard Martin completed his missionary-in-training program in 1966 and departed for a post in Tanzania in 1966. His successor, Robert Hetherington, was a dedicated social activist with scant regard for the prevailing social order or the sensibilities of the middle-class whites who assisted him. "Our job as Christians," Hetherington insisted in 1969, "is not to condemn [ghetto residents] or force them to come up to our standards but rather to understand and try to give what we can so the system can function and so that fewer hungry tomorrows come about. The value system is indirectly the fault of the suburban community anyway. As more suburban people leave the city and assume less responsibility as to what happens there, as more and more of us move away, we leave an enormous cesspool where [the] key word of daily existence is survival."[154] A prime example of this new spirit of social empowerment was the establishment in 1967 of the Hill Cultural Center, Inc., a project overseen on a day-to-day basis by local artist Ed Ellis. Although partly funded with grants from the Mellon Foundation and the Heinz Endowment, 50 percent of the center's operating budget came from members of St. Stephen's, Sewickley.[155]

By 1967, the civil rights movement had begun to adopt a more confrontational approach to civil authority in its efforts to improve economic and social integration. Across the nation, resentment within the black communities of many of America's metropolises boiled over into rioting. In August 1967, as news of the civil unrest reached Pittsburgh, the Christian social relations department planned a program on the causes and effects of rioting. While members of the department acknowledged that little serious trouble had yet been reported in Pittsburgh, they expressed concern about increased sales of small arms at sporting goods stores. When minor disturbances did take place in the Hill district, the department was pleased at the news that Ed Ellis had been able to assist some of the victims with food and clothing.[156]

153. *Church News*, January–February 1967.
154. *Church and Community: Christian Social Relations Bulletin*, March 1969, RG4A/2.3:1, box 6DC, EDP.
155. *Church News*, Summer 1967.
156. *Church and Community: Christian Social Relations Bulletin*, August 1967, RG4A/2.3:1, box 6DC, EDP.

On the North Side, matters worked out rather differently, after the Pittsburgh school board announced its intention to institute a busing plan to desegregate Columbus High School. Members of All Saints, Brighton Heights, reacted badly to the news that their children might be denied access to the neighborhood school. In September 1967, the parish's rector, Alan Walbridge, announced that a private school would be opened in the All Saints parish house. This move led to vocal demands from most of the Episcopal clergy in the City of Pittsburgh that All Saints cooperate with the new busing plan. One dissent from the prevailing view came from Ralph Brooks, rector of St. Andrew's, Pittsburgh, who criticized his colleagues for being less concerned with strict justice than with disassociating themselves from Walbridge and proving their "progressive and liberal" credentials. "The issue," Brooks argued, "is quality education. If we fight or publish letters, let it be for that, because no mere relocation of bodies will solve the deep dilemma of the ghetto child who needs and deserves some clearer thinking and more courageous thought from us."[157]

The uneasy relationship between white activists and black militants presented problems of its own. The arrest of Ed Ellis, coordinator of the Hill Cultural Center, for possession of marijuana and a loaded revolver provoked a stormy meeting of members of St. Stephen's, Sewickley. At that meeting they learned for the first time that Ellis had received convictions for burglary in 1956 and 1958. Many were also troubled by the focus on black consciousness—including classes in Swahili and the making of Afro-American garments—that Ellis had promoted at the center, Why, it was asked, was Swahili being taught at the expense of instruction in practical skills?[158] A 1969 profile of the Hill mission portrayed Ellis as an artist, former civil rights worker, and "radical" community-builder: "[The radicals]," the diocesan newspaper reported, "want to see the ghetto as a place which will eventually stand on its own two feet, a place where initiative is encouraged and developed. They want to own the businesses in their community; they want a local school board made up of citizens in their community; they want job-training programs which will give people skills which in turn can be used in the community itself."[159]

157. *Church and Community: Christian Social Relations Bulletin*, August 1967, September 1967 (quotation), RG4A/2.3:1, box 6DC, EDP.

158. *Church and Community: Christian Social Relations Bulletin*, May 1968, RG4A/2.3:1, box 6DC, EDP.

159. *Church News*, October 1969.

Few Episcopalians quarreled with such objectives, but many questioned the means of attaining them. A 1968 convention resolution entitled "Dignity of Man" expressed support for lifting "the legal, sociological and psychological barriers to full expression of humanity of the Negro," but tempers flared in the ensuing debate over an effort to remove all references to color in favor of a more general expression of concern for human dignity. Junius Carter, the new rector of Holy Cross parish, was scathing in his observation that everyone knew what "White Power" was and insisted that Black Power simply meant equal opportunity.[160] White liberals were soon to learn the full implications of Black Power, however, for in November 1968, Holy Cross hosted a clergy conference on the theme "Black America Looks at the Church."[161]

The keynote address came from Baptist pastor C. T. Vivian, one of the first African Americans to attempt the integration of lunch counters in Nashville. Provocatively entitled "The Black Revolution in Transition," Vivian's address depicted the early civil rights achievements as a false dawn for black America and indicted the entire white power structure—including the white churches—as complicit in this failure. Institutional racism, he explained, "comes to us in such a form that individuals in America do not have to take a racist stand; all they have to do is go along with the institutions that the nation has formed and the institutions will do the acting-out of racism for them. And the church has not spoken to the fact that this is what we allow, and this is what we allow our parishioners to get by with."[162]

Arguing that the civil rights of individuals were respected only in relation to the power base from which they emanated, Vivian expounded on the necessity of "interdependence" on the black community's terms. Leadership groups needed to be formed *in* the black community (not selected by white leaders), which would control all programs, priorities, and processes. Through such control, African Americans might actually bring about the redemption of America:

> No matter what else you think about the ghetto, we've got Soul ... Let's contrast that for a moment. In the richest nation that the

160. *Convention Journal*, May 14, 1968, 17–18, 34–35 (quotation on 34).

161. *Church News*, December 1968.

162. Rev. C. T. Vivian, "The Black Revolution in Transition," November 21, 1968, 3, RG4A/2.1:2, box 2DC, EDP.

world has ever known—you know all those glorified things we like to say in the pulpit—in the richest, most mature nation the world has known, more ground to develop on than any other major nation has had, more technology, more ability to do: we take all our money and all our plans and all our expertise, and what do we build—to live in, to live in—is the last frontier of the non-human: the suburb. It tells us something about America: it does not know who it is.[163]

If the militant tone of Vivian' address were not enough, tempers were further exacerbated by the moderator, who periodically told the audience members that they were "going to get it straight" and should "feel fortunate we don't have any really mean Black brothers here!" While many diocesan clergy appreciated the tenor of Vivian's address when he touched upon the spiritual message of the black community for all Americans, they objected to the notion that whites were unable truly to empathize with blacks. In the group discussions that followed, some priests found the distinction between interdependence and separatism (the black community's complete control over its own affairs) hard to grasp. Others found objectionable the suggestion that there was "no difference between 'White Liberalism' and 'George Wallace,'" not least because some Episcopal priests had spoken up boldly for civil rights and had seen their parishes lose members and income as a result. While some priests felt that the whole experience had been somewhat cathartic, it was clear that there had not been a complete meeting of minds.[164]

If white liberals had reasons for resentment, more conservative Episcopalians had become completely alienated. Among the items of busi-

---

163. Ibid., 9. Note another telling passage from this address: "Integration is dead. Black people did not kill it, and if black people talk about separatism at all, it is because white people killed the concept of integration. And possibly the church was the most profound segregationist of all. Because even at the point where we found doctors and lawyers integrating, we did not find any of our priests and ministers integrating. We did not find our churches integrating. For that integration was on the basis of professionalism. But if the church was to integrate, it would have to take a man on the basis of his humanity, his problems, his family, his situation; but as we talked more profoundly about love as a church, we in fact were not able to act in a profound way, in terms of acceptance, and love. And integration then becomes a dead concept; it is an individual option, but it is no longer a group option" (5).

164. Rev. Everett I. Campbell, "Report by Observer," and Rev. Don H. Gross, "Comments on Conference at Holy Cross Church," RG4A/2.1:2, box 2DC, EDP. Both of these were confidential reports; the latter provided a slightly more balanced take on proceedings.

ness at the 1969 diocesan convention was an ominous resolution entitled: "Membership in Segregated Organizations." Its authors sought formally to condemn those societies, clubs, and fraternities that continued to bar persons from membership on grounds of race. Even as the resolution was introduced, there arose from the ranks of the delegation from Charleroi the senior warden of St. Mary's, Horace Atkins, to condemn the resolution as "pure political activity," and a diversion from the real business of cultivating personal holiness. Junius Carter promptly accused Atkins of a limited view of what constituted the "dignity of man." How could any real son of the church endorse membership in an organization that promoted racial segregation, he demanded?[165]

Atkins's rector, Joseph Wittkofski, now entered the fray. Conscious of the proclivity of white ethnics for fraternal organizations where membership was defined by their country of origin, he better appreciated the threat posed by the resolution than his more liberal colleagues who staffed white middle-class parishes in and around Pittsburgh. Blue-collar Episcopalians in the Mon Valley felt the same sense of social disconnection from the institutional ecclesiastical machinery that black Episcopalians experienced, but they also experienced a more acute sense of neglect. Poverty, unemployment, and lack of social amenities were not problems confined to the urban ghetto, but the decade of the 1960s had largely associated them in the public mind with the African American community, something hardly calculated to encourage class solidarity across racial lines.[166]

Determined to avoid being swamped by the clergy vote, the Charleroi delegation demanded a vote by orders (with a majority required in both the clergy and lay orders). While the clergy endorsed the resolution by a margin of 54-7, the lay delegates (with a substantial number of abstentions) rejected it by a margin of 78-69.[167] In the bitter hush that followed announcement of the result, Junius Carter rose to request the bishop's permission for the Holy Cross delegation to leave. The vote, he declared, represented a formal breaking of church fellowship. The bishop sadly agreed that the convention could not continue and forthwith led the remaining delegates in recitation of the General Confession. He deliberately omitted to administer an episcopal absolution at its conclusion, merely

---

165. *Convention Journal*, May 13, 1969, 16, 34.

166. Ibid, 34.

167. There were 69 clerical and 213 lay delegates registered on May 13. Thus, there were 8 clerical abstentions and 66 lay abstentions (one-third of the total).

stating that the second day of the convention would be held two weeks later.[168]

At the reconvened convention, Bishop Appleyard told delegates that while they might not agree "on all of the implications of the Gospel as it pertains to our time and our condition," it was essential to recognize that racism "denies the effectiveness of the reconciling work of Jesus Christ, through whose love all human diversities lose their divisive quality." He urged all parishes and missions to become more welcoming and to strive for human rights and freedoms in their communities. In response, John Baiz, rector of Calvary Church, presented a compromise resolution that condemned segregation apart from "associations of national origin." Most delegates, however, felt it better not to tamper with the results of the earlier vote, with Benedict Williams, rector of St. Stephen's, Sewickley, arguing that the process of confession and atonement at the earlier meeting had been far more valuable than any retroactive attempt to evade "guilt feelings."[169]

Many of Pittsburgh's Episcopalians still harbored reservations about the way in which the national church had chosen to respond to the demands of Black Power. There had been much criticism of the administration of the General Convention Special Project (GCSP), which had been created in 1967 at the prompting of Presiding Bishop John Hines to provide financial assistance to community-building groups in minority communities, and in 1969, Bishop Appleyard issued a pastoral letter defending the $200,000 grant made to the Black Economic Development Conference. "We tried to separate the constructive, concrete proposals of the Black Manifesto from its objectionable rhetoric which we rejected," he explained, "and which we had reason to think was used to shock the Church to action rather than as a serious statement of destructive purposes. A rejection of our black clergy and lay advice would have meant that we considered them wrong or disloyal to their Church and their country."[170]

At the 1970 diocesan convention, however, delegates voted with clear majorities among both the clergy (39–27) and the laity (127–55) to require Pittsburgh's deputies to the General Convention to seek further informa-

168. *Church News*, June 1969.
169. *Convention Journal*, May 27, 1969, 17–18, 42–43.
170. *Church News*, October 1969. On GCSP, see Holmes, "Presiding Bishop John E. Hines."

tion about the management of GCSP and to refuse to vote further funds unless this information was made public and diocesan bishops given a say in how funds were allocated within their jurisdictions.[171] Reports of financial mismanagement and the funding of controversial groups led to a significant decrease in pledges from Pittsburgh Episcopalians for work outside the parish and diocese, and St. Stephen's, Sewickley, hosted two debates on financial support for the national church addressed by a member of the executive council of the Episcopal Church and the director of the GCSP.[172]

Despite such setbacks, Bishop Appleyard remained committed to greater involvement of African Americans in the life of the diocese. In 1967, the diocesan council agreed to participate in Project Equality, under which church organizations would do business only with companies that had open-hire employment policies.[173] "The basic purpose of Project Equality," a Pittsburgh clergyman explained, "is to help establish a new moral climate of respect for the law."[174] The diocesan council renewed participation in Project Equality in 1969 (albeit with one dissenting vote), but made no formal request of parishes to comply with the reporting procedures, and few parishes formally committed to implementing Project Equality.[175]

Following the riots of April 1968, a number of parishes—including Trinity Cathedral; Calvary, East Liberty; Christ Church, North Hills; St. Thomas, Oakmont; and St. David's, Peters Township—formed urban crisis groups. Even more ambitious was St. Stephen's, Wilkinsburg, which requested funds from the Christian social relations department to pay the salary of a full-time African American clergyman to help bridge the racial gap in their community. The diocese also supported the United Black

---

171. *Convention Journal*, May 12, 1970, 17, 33–34. Another resolution passed by the same convention expressed opposition to funding organizations promoting prejudice against groups based on racial, ethnic, religious, or class distinctions or advocating violence.

172. Standing Committee Minutes, December 18, 1972, RG4A/1.8, box 10DRB, EDP; *Church News*, February 1973.

173. *Church News*, September–October 1967.

174. *Church News*, December 1968.

175. Project Equality proved inadequately funded to conduct business evaluations or distribute the results to parishes. Diocesan Council Minutes, June 10, 1969, RG4A/2.1:1, box 1DC, EDP; Rev. Cn. Robert E. Merry to Bp. Appleyard et al., October 19, 1971, RG4A/2.1:3, box 12DC, EDP.

Front Youth Program and the Interfaith Housing Corporation and sponsored a ten-week seminar to educate clergy and employees of the real estate industry on their part in addressing the racial crisis.[176] Such ventures were not achieved overnight or without struggle. The early meetings with community leaders concerning the housing corporation, Bishop Pardue reported, were a "confrontation with ghetto fury ... we took a blasting that was the worst I ever experienced."[177]

Perhaps the most significant contribution of the diocese to community relations was the financial support that it provided for the Homewood Supermarket. Purchased by Holy Cross parish and other Hill residents after the 1968 riots—when the number of independent grocery stores declined from forty-two to twelve—the former Vilsack-Ray Supermarket was capitalized through the sale of $10 shares to local residents. It provided a program for training local residents in all aspects of store operation and management. In April 1969, a gas leak leveled the building, obliging Junius Carter of Holy Cross to appeal for outside assistance. The diocese provided $6,000 to support the erection of a new facility, funding supplemented by a $10,000 grant from the GCSP.[178]

Bishop Appleyard also sought to engage with the Union of Black Clergy and Laity (UBCL), which he invited to conduct a survey of Pittsburgh's black community. If he had expected it to offer evenhanded advice he was sadly mistaken, for the UBCL observers had no patience for what they perceived as clerical temporizing. "Heretofore," they declared, "the total strategy of the Diocese of Pittsburgh, has been that of those sister dioceses who 'pretend' concern, that is, to pass resolutions concerning racial problems. These resolutions have not produced any measurable change because they were merely words without teeth. During the past six

---

176. Department of Christian Social Relations, Episcopal Diocese of Pittsburgh, Annual Meeting Report, April 29, 1969, RG4A/2.3:1, box 6DC, EDP. The Interfaith Housing Corporation was launched with the support of the Roman Catholic diocese and most of the mainline Protestant denominations. One of its vice presidents was Monsignor Charles Owen Rice (a famous name in Pittsburgh labor history), and its secretary was Father Stewart Pierson of Calvary. *Church News*, January–February 1968.

177. *Convention Journal*, May 14, 1968, 38.

178. *Church News*, September 1968; "Home Supermarket," n.d. (1969), Bp. Appleyard to Rev. Cn. Junius F. Carter, March 20, 1970, Leon E. Modeste to Carter, June 4, 1970, RG4A/2.1:3, box 12DC, EDP.

years, segments of the population have questioned the effectiveness of the church in the area of social relations."[179]

The UBCL insisted that the existence of only one black Episcopal parish and two black clergy in the diocese was proof of subconscious paternalism, aggravated by a low level of diocesan spending in the city compared to the suburbs. Even parishes that were "integrated," it concluded, were complacent about the lack of integration of their communities, and blacks were underrepresented on vestries and diocesan committees. Employment practices, the placement of diocesan missions, and the use of educational materials with a white middle-class bias also contributed to the perpetuation of "institutional racism." The UBCL urged the bishop to promote awareness of unconscious racism and encourage parishes and the diocesan office to hire black professionals and office staff. It also recommended the appointment of a black professional to coordinate missions in black neighborhoods, and of a black priest to lead Emmanuel on the North Side. Finally, in the spirit of the Holy Cross conference, it recommended investment by the Episcopal Church in black banks and businesses.[180]

In response, Bishop Appleyard established a diocesan committee to review the report and make recommendations. In doing so, he fell afoul of Junius Carter, after he failed to invite him to serve as committee chairman. When the bishop also requested several members of Holy Cross to serve on the committee without first consulting Carter, the latter denounced it as "a very poor and segregated committee."[181] Appleyard refused to be intimidated by such statements, and one of the fruits of the ensuing dialogue was a 1972 "Statement of Fair Employment," designed to enhance the prospects of women and racial minorities.[182] Black leaders like Carter and Lawrence Howard of Calvary, a professor at the University of Pittsburgh, continued to feel that something more radical was needed

179. UBCL Findings, Pittsburgh, n.d. (quotation on 3), RG4A/2.1:2, box 2DC, EDP.
180. Ibid.
181. Bp. Appleyard to Rev. Junius F. Carter, February 2, 1971, Carter to Appleyard, February 5, 1971, RG4A/2.1:2, box 2DC, EDP. Carter's resentment was very much in evidence when he wrote: "You have ignored my leadership as Rector of the Parish. I will not serve on any committee, nor will I allow the majority of my members to participate. I cannot control all the members on this committee, but I can influence the majority. I am sending this back to you, as I inform you I will not serve on a committee that demonstrates racism, which is an evil in our society."
182. Standing Committee Minutes, December 18, 1972, RG4A/1.8, box 10DRB, EDP.

to ameliorate the absence of African Americans from the diocesan leadership. At the 1974 diocesan convention, both men made vocal interventions, prompting passage of a special resolution authorizing the bishop to establish a task force on affirmative action.[183]

That same month, Appleyard met with Carter and Howard, who together presented him with a list of blacks and whites they considered suitable for such a task force (the bishop expressed concern about the absence of names of Episcopalians from outside the City of Pittsburgh) and urged him to formulate a program that gave "visual evidence of the joyfulness of a black-white communion."[184] At a December meeting of the task force, Howard emphasized the church's moral obligation to support affirmative action and warned that the level of communication between whites and blacks was deteriorating. He called for priority to be given to addressing the problem of hunger in poorer communities and the desegregation of the Pittsburgh school system before it became "another Boston."[185]

While civil rights remained the principal area of contention within the Episcopal Church during the 1960s, it is important to remember that this was also the era of liturgical experimentation, which would ultimately lead to the production of a new Book of Common Prayer in 1979. Conflicts over "Trial Use," as it came to be known, could be as divisive, in their way, as debates about greater inclusion of minorities, for they involved the adoption of a radically different set of liturgical premises. As Michael Moriarty has demonstrated, a commitment to apostleship *in* the world was an essential ingredient in the program of liturgical renewal upon which the Episcopal Church embarked in the postwar decades. From 1950 to 1963, the standing liturgical commission of the Episcopal Church generated sixteen volumes of *Prayer Book Studies*—texts of revised services for experimental use. The most active proponents of the new liturgy were to be found within Associated Parishes (AP), formed from a group of Episcopal clergy interested in the wider liturgical move-

183. *Convention Journal*, May 10–11, 1974, 20.

184. Lawrence C. Howard to Bp. Appleyard, May 16, 1974, RG4A/2.1:2, box 2DC, EDP. Despite his strong defense of black activism, Howard continued to stress the value of Appleyard's contribution: "It must be added that I personally—and I think most blacks—appreciate your efforts and respect your sincerity. It is unpleasant to be in disagreement with a person so full of love and openness." Lawrence C. Howard to Bp. Appleyard, December 19, 1974, RG4A/2.1:2, box 2DC, EDP.

185. Diocesan Special Task Force on the Black Presence Minutes, December 18, 1974, RG4A/2.1:2, box 2DC, EDP.

ment. AP's founders were keen to foster liturgical practices in parish worship more likely to instill worshipers with an understanding of how the mature Christian lives out his vocation in the secular world.[186]

One of AP's original board members, James Joseph, hailed from Pittsburgh, and the group made its first appearance in southwestern Pennsylvania in August 1947. The occasion was a meeting addressed by Dom Gregory Dix, the English Benedictine whose *The Shape of the Liturgy* had so influenced the modern liturgical movement, at St. Barnabas House in Gibsonia.[187] How far the movement extended its reach into the diocese prior to 1965 is debatable, but there is a report of a Labor Day Communion at All Saints, Aliquippa, in 1960, at which the offertory included symbols of local industries, including iron ore and a steelworker's hard hat. "I sincerely believe," the rector of All Saints explained, "that this gives us an appropriate opportunity to show the relevance of Christian teachings to an urban-industrial situation."[188]

The opening of the Second Vatican Council in 1962 and the radical liturgical changes proposed for the Roman Catholic Church gave fresh heart to the Episcopal liturgical movement. The 1964 General Convention approved a constitutional amendment to permit general "Trial Use" of alternative liturgies (it would only become effective in 1967) and made the standing liturgical commission responsible for oversight.[189] The latter encouraged dioceses to form their own liturgical commissions, and the Diocese of Pittsburgh complied with the request in 1965. One of its commission's first undertakings was to develop a dialogue between Episcopal and Roman Catholic clergy on the nature of eucharistic worship in their separate traditions.[190]

With Trial Use reconfirmed in 1967, the stage was set for a period of conflict that was frequently as intense as had been the debate over civil rights.[191] Some Episcopal parishes welcomed the new variety. St. George's, Jefferson Boro, for example, imitated its Catholic neighbors by experi-

---

186. Moriarty, *Liturgical Revolution*, 30–35.

187. On the early days of AP, see ibid., 40–57, 230n14. The account of Dix's visit is on 55.

188. *Church News*, October 1960.

189. Moriarty, *Liturgical Revolution*, 101–13.

190. *Convention Journal*, May 11, 1965, 26–27.

191. For an overview, see Moriarty, *Liturgical Revolution*, 113–55.

menting with the American Folk Mass.¹⁹² "As the people of God," Bishop Appleyard urged members of his flock in February of 1969, "we are developing the liturgy, and we ought to be a real part of this life in God process." He urged parishes and missions to employ Trial Use during the season of Epiphany and for at least half of the church year thereafter.¹⁹³

Many of Pittsburgh's clergy and laity were unconvinced, however, and their bishop conceded that adoption of a new liturgy would be a long and difficult process. Lynn Edwards, an Anglo Catholic priest of the diocese, denounced Trial Use in 1970 as "liturgical coercion."¹⁹⁴ More tolerant clergy still had to face the wrath of aggrieved parishioners. "We went through the Green Book, the Zebra Book and those books," says Richard Davies, "and [members of my congregation] were very flattering to me; they criticized me as though I wrote it."¹⁹⁵ Even Bishop Appleyard, who welcomed the "joyous mood" of Trial Use, accepted the need for a more penitential form of worship at certain seasons. He still felt it important to take Trial Use seriously as it is "the very form and substance through which we corporately and individually apprehend the very presence of the living God."¹⁹⁶

Some large parishes pursued their own forms of liturgical innovation. At St. Stephen's, Sewickley, four potluck suppers on Wednesday evenings were followed by Communion according to the new liturgy and a discussion of people's reactions to it. "The Passing of the Peace," one observer reported, "often a difficult point, became an easy and meaningful experience. Not all parishioners attended, and not all those who did were pleased, but for most it was a transforming experience."¹⁹⁷ At Christ Church, North Hills, Maundy Thursday was the occasion for a candlelit meal of lamb stew, bread, grapes, and table wine, followed by Scripture readings, hymns, prayers, and Holy Communion.¹⁹⁸ "In some parishes," Bishop Appleyard admitted in 1972, "Trial Use has caused confusion, others seem to enter upon Trial Use with ease and order. I am certain that

192. *Church News*, January–February 1968.
193. *Church News*, February 1969.
194. Moriarty, *Liturgical Revolution*, 152.
195. Davies interview.
196. *Church News*, April 1969. That year's diocesan convention adopted a resolution encouraging liturgical experimentation. *Convention Journal*, May 13, 1969, 16, 33.
197. *Church News*, April 1969.
198. *Church News*, June 1969.

one of the reasons we have a differing response is the preparation, the education that has taken place before use, before direct involvement in worship . . . The few parishes and missions who have not entered into this experience have cheated themselves out of this phase of the Church's growth."[199]

The essence of opposition to the changes would become clear in a 1978 diocesan convention debate on whether to allow continued use of the 1928 Book of Common Prayer after the new book had become official. In that debate, John Rodgers (dean-president of the new Trinity Episcopal School for Ministry in Ambridge) called the 1928 Book of Common Prayer an expression of "classical Anglican Elizabethan formularies" and argued that the Episcopal Church was the only national church planning to replace the Book of Common Prayer with a lesser book. Such a charge demonstrated where the battle lines were now being drawn.[200] In a denomination where creedal truths tended to be expressed through worship forms, liturgical revision had significant implications.

"The effectiveness of the Episcopal Church is hampered by its own peculiar faults," lamented Bishop Pardue in 1955. "In some quarters it bogs down in ritualistic trivialities and dissensions over unimportant issues. In other places, it becomes deflected from its goal by what amounts to an idolatry of scholarship and biblical criticism. Or again, the energies of the Episcopal Church become drained off by the belief that the future of the faith hinges upon new educational techniques and round table discussions. Or the Church may become so broad and liberal that it agrees with everybody and stands for nothing."[201] Fifteen years later, the struggle for civil rights had not excised such weaknesses but merely brought them into sharp relief, and the Diocese of Pittsburgh would soon form a key battleground.

199. *Convention Journal*, May 5–6, 1972, 29.

200. *Pre-Convention Journal*, October 20–21, 1978, 39; *Convention Journal*, October 20–21, 1978, 25.

201. *Convention Journal*, May 10, 1955, 22.

6

The Center Cannot Hold

The Neo-Evangelical Challenge to Modernity, 1970–1987

BY THE LATE 1960s, the theological compromise negotiated by Bishop Manning in the 1920s was proving increasingly difficult to sustain.[1] "Neither liturgy nor polity as previously understood and practiced by American Anglicans," concluded historian William Petersen in 1978, "can bear the burden of unifying the Church, much less providing alone or in combination for the requisite authentic renewal, ecumenical rapprochement, liturgical renewal or theological restatement."[2] Among those who dissented from the new orthodoxies arose the notion that those coming to adulthood in the 1960s and 1970s were part of a "lost generation."[3] Their byword was "renewal," a term popularized by the Second Vatican Council, but among American Anglicans generally applied to those who embraced a culturally accessible version of nineteenth-century Evangelicalism. In Pittsburgh, the movement would place particular reliance on an English-born Evangelical priest, John Guest, who, in 1980, would help promote the election of Alden Hathaway, another leader in the renewal movement, as bishop of Pittsburgh.

RESTRUCTURING THE DIOCESE, 1970–1979

At the beginning of the 1970s, many Episcopalians were still reeling from the tensions generated by the struggles of the 1960s. The membership gains recorded during the 1950s proved a false dawn, as the numbers of active Episcopalians began to inch steadily downward. This inevitably

1. See Prichard, "Place of Doctrine," 35–45.
2. Petersen, "Tensions of Anglican Identity," 452.
3. McGrath, *Renewal of Anglicanism*, 33–47.

put pressure on parishes that had vastly expanded their plants during the boom years yet now found it difficult effectively to utilize their property. When parish consolidation and team ministries were proposed as a solution, however, most parishes turned a deaf ear. Episcopalians, Pittsburgh priest Richard Barnes somberly observed in 1969, have "the mentality of the Church but the practices of a sect." Barnes was an advocate of the "larger parish" model of urban ministry in which parishes were organized into "clusters," each of which had an administrative headquarters, with directors of Christian education and Christian social action and a choirmaster responsible for *all* the parish choirs. "The idea of being a series of 'independent parishes' is an anachronism in our system," Barnes concluded. "The lay people who are involved deeply in the Church get all consumed with the matters of housekeeping and survival. And, in the meantime, the ministry of the Church gets forgotten."[4]

Progressive Episcopalians emerged from the battles of the 1960s with a heightened antagonism to episcopal and clerical authority. During the 1970s, they would press for reforms that would, as they put it, enhance the democratic nature of the government of the church and increase lay involvement in ministries and programs. Debates about the restoration of the permanent diaconate and the ordination of women would both be informed by this rhetoric of "democratic" participation. In Pittsburgh, many Episcopalians resented what they felt was the arbitrary nature of episcopal oversight. For some, Bishop Pardue was "autocratic" and "ran a tight ship," so disliking diocesan conventions that he tried to complete them in less than a day.[5] Under his successor, a series of conversations with members of the diocese about what they saw as the way forward produced the recommendation that a higher priority be given to Christian education for adults. The discussions also revealed the existence of two distinct bodies of opinion within the diocese: one group wished to continue the work of the previous decade and relate the church ever more closely to the concerns of secular society; the other viewed the church as

---

4. Rev. Richard Barnes, "Clustering of Pittsburgh Parishes," April 24, 1969, RG5/2.1, box 2DP, Archives of the Episcopal Diocese of Pittsburgh, Pittsburgh, Pennsylvania (hereafter referenced as EDP). A cluster parish was also proposed for the Mon Valley communities—Monongahela, Donora, Monessen, and Charleroi—but this met with little local sympathy. *Church News*, May–June 1968, Jack H. France to Bp. Thomas, January 20, 1969, RG4A/2.1:1, box 1DC, EDP.

5. Little, "Historical Notes," 1.

a body with a discrete program and an obligation to provide a haven for worship and fellowship distinct from secular society. The approach of the second group will be discussed below; here, we are concerned with the perspectives of the first. A diocesan report on the results of these conversations concluded that a stable parish should be characterized by "creative tension just short of chaos."[6] As a description of how the 1970s would unfold, this was not altogether inapt.

It was under Robert Appleyard that the Diocese of Pittsburgh underwent its most dramatic reorganization since the 1920s. That earlier restructuring involved the creation of an efficient centralized structure of operations. The 1975 restructuring, by contrast, was concerned with the creation of representative and responsive instruments of governance. Attempts to establish a regional structure during the 1960s that would foster ties between parishes had had a limited impact.[7] Furthermore, although social outreach by many parishes had increased, it did not seem to be drawing large numbers of new Christians into the Episcopal Church. "Every year I see fewer and fewer people come," lamented Ralph Brooks, rector of St. Andrew's, Pittsburgh. "The more involved we make ourselves in the world problem, the less people seem to come to church. So, don't feel that just because we are urging our friends to get involved in community life that this is going to mean that the pews are going to get filled up with eager people anymore the way they used to be [sic]."[8] Bishop Appleyard appreciated such warnings. "We should seek forms that emphasize interdependence," he told the 1971 diocesan convention. "Missions, parishes and a diocese are a family in Christ, through which the on-going life of Christ's Church is carried on, sometimes parochially, sometimes on a diocesan basis, sometimes through mutual action ... Mutual responsibility and inter-dependence in the Body of Christ should and must be built into the diocesan organization as well as into the mission and parochial organization and structure."[9]

---

6. Diocesan Committee on the Purpose and Goals of Parishes and Missions Minutes, November 9, 1969, RG4A/2.1:1, box 1DC, EDP.

7. *Convention Journal*, May 11, 1965, 15, 18–19. The regions were East Pittsburgh, South Pittsburgh, Allegheny Valley, Monongahela Valley, Ohio Valley, and Mountain and Greensburg.

8. Diocesan Committee on the Purpose and Goals of Parishes and Missions Minutes, January 4, 1970, RG4A/2.1:1, box 1DC, EDP.

9. *Convention Journal*, May 7–8, 1971, 26.

Given its preference for grassroots initiative, the new diocesan structure now envisaged the role of bishop as a facilitator rather than a chief executive officer. "It is still commonly expected," Bishop Appleyard explained, "that every Bishop should be a pastor, a counselor, an evangelist, a financier, an administrator, a business consultant . . . He is to be a charismatic figure who solves all problems and is all-knowing. That is too much for any one man to do and be, or at least it is too much for me to do, effectively and well."[10] Suiting his actions to his words, Appleyard sought the assistance of a number of leading Episcopalians to facilitate the restructuring, including lawyer Thomas Nimick. Disturbed by the absence of proper rules of procedure and of a deliberative process for shaping discussion at the diocesan convention, Nimick worked with Pittsburgh clergyman Richard Davies to devise a system of précis—draft formularies of proposed convention resolutions—that could be discussed prior to convention so that convention debates might not be bogged down with inessentials.[11] The desirability of this reform may be deduced from the remark of the rector of St. Stephen's, Sewickley, that 340 people had attended regional meetings to discuss resolutions for the 1970 diocesan convention; no fewer than thirty resolutions were subsequently debated![12]

The 1973 diocesan convention received the proposed reforms with enthusiasm, and laypeople were encouraged to express their opinion by means of a questionnaire printed in the diocesan newspaper. The convention appointed a commission on structure, which examined the reorganization plans already implemented in eight other dioceses and issued its preliminary report in May 1974. First discussed at that year's diocesan convention, and subsequently at regional meetings, the restructuring plan was finally adopted in 1975. It proposed the creation of an integrated planning apparatus and—apparently paradoxically—the strengthening of both the authority of the bishop and the democratic accountability of diocesan institutions. It also recommended the establishment of a diocesan planning commission and enhanced institutional support for parishes.[13]

---

10. *Convention Journal*, May 4–5, 1973, 51.

11. Nimick interview; Davies interview.

12. *Convention Journal*, May 12, 1970, 16.

13. *New Structures and Processes, Episcopal Diocese of Pittsburgh: The Final Report of the Commission on Structure* (March 1975), RG4A/2.1:2, box 2DC, EDP; *Church News*, January 1974.

The commission on structure recommended that the bishop and his staff function as the executive arm of the diocese with responsibility for program administration and development, a role previously performed by an unelected diocesan council. The latter was to be replaced with an elected body whose members would be chosen by the diocesan convention and would function as the convention's surrogate for the rest of the year. The diocesan council would review the program and budget proposed by the diocesan leadership and recommend changes where necessary. "This is the cry of Vestries and Regions," insisted Richard Davies.[14] A more controversial—and ultimately unsuccessful—suggestion was to give the diocesan standing committee the power to entertain appeals from executive decisions, including those of the bishop. The rector of St. Stephen's, Wilkinsburg, pointed out that such a move would make the standing committee the "final and ultimate authority" in disputes between parishes and clergy. Many of these disputes were pastoral in nature, he insisted, and, as such, should ultimately be resolved by the bishop alone.[15]

To improve the representative nature of the diocesan convention, the commission proposed revised rules for the election of convention deputies, which included staggered terms (to ensure a measure of continuity) and a maximum period of consecutive service of three years for any deputy (to promote regular turnover). Some laypeople still considered these measures inadequate. Helen Seager, a laywoman from Church of the Ascension, Pittsburgh, argued that the new measures permitted four people in a parish with three deputies to successively occupy their parish seats, with one rotating off every year. All elected diocesan bodies, she insisted, should be required to hold (and publicize) a minimum number of meetings each year and there should be procedures for calling emergency meetings and adding items to precirculated agendas. "Such provisions," she wrote, "prevent the evolution of a self-perpetuating elite."[16]

14. Rev. Richard W. Davies to Dupuy Bateman, June 12, 1975, RG4A/2.1:2, box 2DC, EDP.

15. Rev. Alex H. MacDonell to Christien Altenberger, November 5, 1974, RG4A/2.1:2, box 2DC, EDP.

16. Helen Seager to Christine Alteberger, n.d., (1974), RG4A/2.1:2, box 2DC, EDP. An earlier debate on democratic process had taken place in 1966 when it was proposed that a committee review all prospective resolutions and recommend acceptance or rejection. Initially rejected by the clergy because it was seen as too sweeping a form of oversight, the proposal was ultimately accepted after it was modified to require consultation with affected departments and with the resolutions' sponsors before any recommendation was made. *Convention Journal*, May 24, 1966, 26–28, 31.

The diocesan convention met but once a year and had a limited capacity for oversight. The restructured and elected diocesan council, by contrast, met monthly and enjoyed many opportunities to initiate and terminate diocesan projects. Its members were expected to serve as channels of communication to districts and parishes on what was being done in their name. The council thus served as the legislative arm of the diocese between conventions (modeling the role performed by the national council of the Episcopal Church on behalf of the General Convention), further enhancing the relationship between the diocese and the new districts.[17] The commission on structure also proposed to replace the existing district system (where districts radiated out from Pittsburgh in a random fashion) with homogeneous geographic districts composed of parishes that shared common interests: "The problem of district organization besets other dioceses. There seems to be a trend towards decentralizing program activities to districts with a representative designated by the Bishop, frequently called a 'dean' who devotes part or most of his time to district work, both pastoral and program activity. In some cases, there is considerable decentralization of Diocesan programs and budget allocations to the districts. The Commission on Structure lacked evidence on whether this plan works well enough to be worth the cost."[18]

Parish reaction to the enhanced authority of the diocesan council varied considerably. In 1976, the vestry of Calvary Church passed a resolution demanding that the council refrain from soliciting individual members of the diocese for contributions for special projects until it had obtained the permission of parish vestries. While the council might be more democratically representative than in the past, members of Calvary's vestry clearly objected to any attempt to bypass their connection with their congregation.[19] Participation in the new district system was also far from uniform. At a 1980 meeting of district leaders, the chair of District

---

17. Diocesan Council Minutes, November 11, 1975, RG4A/2.1:1, box 1DC, EDP.

18. *New Structures and Processes, Episcopal Diocese of Pittsburgh: The Final Report of the Commission on Structure* (March 1975), RG4A/2.1:2, box 2DC, EDP (quotation on 20). The parishes were themselves requested to suggest others with which they might like to be aligned, whether the motivation was geographic, economic, or political. Rev. William G. Lewis to Parish Clergy and Senior Wardens, March 24, 1975, RG4A/2.1:2, box 2DC, EDP.

19. Vestry resolution of Calvary Episcopal Church, October 25, 1976, Rev. Richard W. Davies to John A Byerly Jr., March 9, 1977, Rev. John Baiz to Rev. Richard W. Davies, March 18, 1977, RG4A/2.1:1, box 1DC, EDP.

VI (western and central Pittsburgh) described his local situation as one of "no growth and no quality of leadership and no contribution to the work of the diocese." District VI was limited by the large number of small parishes within its jurisdiction, but a larger concern of parishes in District III (Armstrong County), and District IV (Cambria, Indiana, Somerset, and Westmoreland counties) was the impact of the economic depression then ravaging their communities. A better record of participation was reported from District I (Beaver County), District II (northern Allegheny County and Butler County), District VIII (eastern Allegheny County), and District X (Fayette, Greene, and Washington counties), where a more cohesive sense of district identity prevailed. Strangely, in District V (southern Allegheny County) and District VII (eastern Pittsburgh), which contained some of the largest and wealthiest parishes in the diocese, poor attendance at district meetings continued. Perhaps the desire to maintain parish autonomy counted for more than it did elsewhere.[20]

The shift toward democratic accountability was accompanied by a growing interest in adult Christian formation, perhaps the first time in the history of the diocese that it enjoyed a profile as high as that of juvenile Christian education. To assist in lay discernment of Christian vocation, the diocese established the Training Program for Ministry (TPM), which initially offered classes at Trinity Cathedral and later in parishes across the diocese. Its course offerings—taught by both clergy and lay experts—included biblical studies, church history, liturgy, spiritual formation, and practical skills in such parochial ministries as lay reader, treasurer, and altar guild.[21]

TPM offered basic education for the active lay Christian. The Episcopal Church's decision to restore the permanent diaconate represented a much more sustained effort to break from the hierarchical model of priest over layman that had prevailed until that date. For much of the Episcopal Church's existence, the diaconate had been viewed as a transitional state prior to ordination to the full priesthood. By the early 1960s, there was a greater willingness to view the diaconate as a spiritual calling with its own peculiar charism. In 1962, the standing committee

20. District Commission Officers Minutes, December 8, 1980, RG4A/2.1:1, box 1DC, EDP.

21. Minutes of the Board of Directors, Training Program for Ministry, April 8, 1972, Rev. Everett I. Campbell, "Training Program for Ministry in the Diocese of Pittsburgh," October 1, 1977, RG4A/2.1:2, box 2DC, EDP.

approved the ordination of Jack Dolan as a perpetual deacon, even while it expressed disapproval of the principle of the perpetual diaconate. The following year, it approved two more perpetual deacons, an indication, perhaps, that the concept was winning wider approval.[22]

In 1976, the Pittsburgh's commission on ministry sponsored a conference on the nonstipendiary diaconate. Perpetual deacons should be people of faith, Bishop Appleyard told those in attendance, but they also needed to be people of maturity "seasoned in experience and the understanding of life." They should be people of integrity, with a healthy network of personal relationships, and humble enough to have a genuine concern for the people whom they were called to serve. In Connecticut, the bishop admitted, he had witnessed the worst of the perpetual diaconate, for every perpetual deacon there had subsequently changed his mind and sought priestly ordination. In Florida, by contrast, a focus on recruiting more mature candidates had produced a body of deacons who had strengthened the common life of their diocese.[23]

For some of Pittsburgh's church leaders, the perpetual deacon was set to play a special role on the new missionary frontier: the inner-city church. "The local church occupies atypical space, both physical and social, and appears to be one of the last community anchors where dependency is institutionalized in an atypical way," declared a 1977 report prepared by two clergy from Calvary Church. "With complete theologically sound bases, the local church sees people as a whole and imparts this notion by its emphasis that to be helped is to be a helper ... This stands in direct contradiction to the secular systems of dependence where one is basically a receiver of services or goods without necessarily a return." While laypeople were frequently involved in urban ministry, the report concluded, they rarely had a theology of mission or institutional recognition for the work that they did perform. The report suggested that suitable candidates be identified through a process of interviews and the development of a "contract," first with the prospective deacon's sponsoring parish and ultimately with the diocese.[24] One of the first new vocational deacons

---

22. Standing Committee Minutes, September 16, 1962, October 21, 1963, RG4A/1.8, box 10DRB, EDP.

23. Bp. Appleyard, "Remarks Made at a Conference on the Non-stipendiary Diaconate, Sponsored by the Commission on Ministry of the Episcopal Diocese of Pittsburgh," May 14, 1976, RG4A/2.1:2, box 2DC, EDP.

24. Rev. John Baiz and Rev. Beryl Choi, "A Proposal for a Lay Diaconate," February 14, 1977, RG4A/2.1:2, box 2DC, EDP.

was Ernest Figenbaum, a Westinghouse engineer whose youthful sense of call to ordained ministry had been blocked by financial circumstances. Figenbaum, who saw his role to be that of equipping the laity for ministry, was sponsored by St. Martin's, Monroeville. "I feel the emphasis on the diaconate as a separate order is justified to show this model to all Christ's people," he explained, "the model being one of servanthood—serving God in Christ."[25]

Such lay enthusiasm was not necessarily reproduced in the clergy order, many of whose members had emerged from the 1960s with a highly developed sense of alienation from church structure and ecclesiastical authority. "I have become increasingly frustrated in the role of parish priest," wrote social activist David Else. "I really enjoyed and found meaning in the pastoral ministry. I feel the Sacraments are vital to the Life of Man, and count it a fantastic privilege to administer them. And yet I found so much of the deep spiritual life, that should be within the Institutional Church, outside rather than within. I found more love of man and God, for example, expressed at Alcoholics Anonymous meetings or during a peace protest or at an NAACP banquet ... I find the priesthood, as viewed by the people, not as a servanthood but servility."[26]

Laypeople were not always impressed with such laments, especially when the clergyman in question considered himself to be on a higher spiritual plane. "I am appalled that a priest, one who counsels, one trained in pastoral matters and a psychologist to boot suggests the clergy are better able to deal with certain questions because they devote their whole lives to being Christians," fumed laywoman Portia Johnson to the archdeacon of the diocese. "I am not only appalled, I am angry. I have spent my whole life trying to be an effective Christian and I don't get paid for it." Johnson recommended that any programs be structured so as to "reverse the trend of authoritarian priests."[27]

Low clergy morale was a reality, however, and diocesan leaders did everything in their power to reverse it. With Bishop Pardue's encouragement, Pittsburgh clergyman Don Gross created a pastoral internship in 1965 that brought together clergy resident in the diocese for less than

25. *Trinity*, March 1983.

26. *Church and Community: Christian Social Relations Bulletin*, October 1970, RG4A/2.3:1, box 6DC, EDP.

27. Portia Johnson to Archdeacon Lewis, November 10, 1975, RG4A/2.1:2, box 2DC, EDP.

two years to discuss personal, psychological, and pastoral problems. A unique diocesan program when it was created, it reflected Gross's belief that effective ministry depended upon working in a pastoral setting and then reviewing that experience in a group setting (a theme that would be embraced by the founders of Trinity Episcopal School for Ministry a decade later).[28] Bishop Appleyard built upon Gross's program, appointing a committee to advise him on parochial assignments and encouraging parishes to require an annual physical and grant their clergy paid time off for study.[29] During the early 1970s, diocesan leaders implemented various workshops, clergy days, and other activities that emphasized clergy vocations. The keynote address for the first clergy conference in 1971 came from Walter Righter, former rector of All Saints, Aliquippa. Now pastor of a New Hampshire parish, Righter shared insights on the ways in which a declining parish could sustain its mission.[30]

The following year, the clergy conference heard a rather different presentation from New York clergyman Robert Terwilliger of the Trinity Institute. Terwilliger explored how clergy might respond to such contemporary phenomena as the Jesus Movement. "People have got to have immediate experiences," he told his audience. "One should himself be a participant of the experience of God before one can transmit it to another. We have to be able to say what Christ 'feels like.' We need the context." Terwilliger also expressed his concern that many Episcopal clergy were moving from a sense of vocation to one of profession (or worse, of business practitioner). "We're trying to find [our] way out of a spiritual problem with a materialistic model," he concluded. "We have to speak to the reality of something we can give our life for. We can't be concerned with status."[31]

Terwilliger's references to clergy status anxiety were very much to the point. Upholding certain employment standards for their profession

28. *Church News*, March 1965.

29. *Convention Journal*, May 12, 1970, 37.

30. Minutes of the 1971 Clergy Conference Planning Committee, January 6, 1971, RG4A/2.1:3, box 12DC, EDP. Righter was president of the Nashua Council of Churches, a delegate to two General Conventions, and the author of two articles in the *Episcopalian* on his parish's efforts to address change and make use of the trial liturgy. "1971 Clergy Conference Leaders," RG4A/2.1:3, box 12DC, EDP.

31. Minutes of the 1972 Clergy Conference Planning Committee, February 1, 1972, RG4A/2.1:3, box 12DC, EDP.

had become the most pressing concern of most Pittsburgh clergy during this period. The 1974 clergy conference presented attendees with a number of professional ethical dilemmas and explored how they might handle them: sample scenarios included an assistant palming money from the collection; a rector receiving a gift from an inactive member of the parish as an inducement to remove obstacles to a church wedding for his already twice-married daughter; a priest making use of the donated sermons of a former priest with only minor changes and without attribution; and a new rector whose predecessor wished to continue to attend services at the parish church.[32]

In 1975, the Pittsburgh Clergy Association developed its own standards of professional ethics. "I serve as professional employee," they read, "under contract, within a unit of the Church, for which I receive a specified salary and allowances from any ministrations required in the execution of the contract." The clergy association's code included a pledge of care and conscientiousness in administration, teaching, preaching, and liturgy; a commitment to weekly private study and eighty hours a year devoted to a continuing education program; and a willingness to tithe to the church and "responsible charitable agencies."[33] Many clergy were less enthused by the notion of regular clergy evaluation, but Deacon Beryl Choi—soon to be one of Pittsburgh's first woman priests—urged her colleagues to see the process as a means of identifying strengths and weaknesses. "It is not something about which we need to be defensive and negative," she reassured them, "but something positive which we can and should welcome as an enriching of our ministry and therefore of benefit to God's church and people."[34]

Clergy assessment would be only a minor innovation compared with the dramatic change in the composition of the clergy order that would take place in 1977, namely the ordination of women to the priesthood. Gender issues had been under discussion in Pittsburgh since Bishop Whitehead had encouraged parishes to allow women to serve on their vestries. The diocesan convention of 1958 approved a memorial by Benedict Williams,

32. Rev. Alex Seabrook to Bp. Appleyard, June 11, 1975, RG4A/2.1:3, box 12DC, EDP. See therein the enclosed sample cases 6, 11, 13, and 18.

33. Standards of Professional Ethics of Members of the Episcopal Clergy Association of the Diocese of Pittsburgh, n.d. (1975), RG4A/2.1:3, box 12DC, EDP.

34. Newsletter of the Episcopal Clergy Association of the Diocese of Pittsburgh, March 1976, RG4A/2.1:3, box 12DC, EDP.

rector of St. Stephen's, Sewickley, calling for an amendment to the constitution of the national church that would alter references to "Laymen" to "Laypersons."[35] In 1966, this position was reaffirmed, with one delegate even suggesting that the diocese elect a female delegate to the 1967 General Convention in an attempt to shame that body into seating her.[36]

While the convention did not follow through on this proposal, it did pass a resolution in 1971 opposing discrimination against women and encouraging their acceptance as equals in all aspects of parish life.[37] Many female (and some male) Episcopalians viewed this response as inadequate. The refusal of the all-male vestry of Christ Church, Brownsville, to allow women to serve only added fuel to the fire.[38] Other incidents—though less overtly discriminatory—only confirmed them in their view that a climate of sexual inequality prevailed in Pittsburgh. Helen Seager of Church of the Ascension, Pittsburgh, criticized the failure of the diocesan newspaper to accord married women serving on diocesan committees "the dignity of their own identity." What, she fulminated, did her husband's name have to do with her service to the diocese?[39] Equally galling was the continued refusal of Trinity Cathedral to employ women and girls in its choir, on the grounds that the men and boys' choir was an institution that did not lend itself to women vocalists; that the choir director might have difficulty adapting female voices to liturgical chants and offertory anthems; and (perhaps most infuriating of all) that the attendance of women at evening rehearsals would pose an added security problem.[40]

Churchwomen continued to make advances during the early 1970s. In February 1971, a parishioner of Christ Church, New Brighton, became the first female lay reader in the Diocese of Pittsburgh.[41] In 1975, however, a diocesan women's task force reported that, while the diocese had an overall gender balance of 60 percent women and 40 percent men, parish ministries were not staffed in the same proportion. More than four-fifths

    35. *Convention Journal*, May 13, 1958, 19.
    36. *Convention Journal*, May 24, 1966, 29, 35.
    37. *Convention Journal*, May 7–8, 1971, 31–32.
    38. Standing Committee Minutes, January 20, 1970, RG4A/1.8, box 10DRB, EDP.
    39. *Church and Community: Christian Social Relations Bulletin*, January 1972, RG4A/2.3:1, box 6DC, EDP.
    40. Memorandum from A. Sieber Holinger to Vy. Rev. A. Dixon Rollitt, October 16, 1973, RG3/1.2, box 2T, EDP.
    41. *Church News*, February 1971.

of parishes had all-female altar guilds, and two-thirds of parishes reported that their complement of Sunday school teachers was disproportionately female. By contrast, all the parishes surveyed had a male senior warden, only one reported a female junior warden, and just 11 percent of lay readers were female. Men, the task force concluded, dominated most tasks of public participation, while women tended to serve in behind-the-scenes roles. It recommended that the church cease to view the role of women with a "joking attitude" and take steps to extricate them from their traditional roles.[42] One rector, at least, took considerable offence at such a characterization, complaining that the advocates of gender equality behaved as if nothing good had ever been done prior to their involvement: "Any position or activity is open to any member of the parish who desires to participate and/or is qualified to handle a particular job. All are so announced. I will not have a token anything, be it black, white, green or pink, male, female or tirtum quid ... Before we at Christ Church are accused of being sexist oriented, and we do have our MCPs, I would remind you that it was the delegates of this congregation who introduced the resolution at Diocesan Convention enabling women to sit on the vestry."[43]

Identifying a common diocesan position on the ordination of women to the diaconate and priesthood was by no means as easy as bringing women into lay ministry. A 1972 resolution in support of female ordination failed by 31 votes to 21 among the clergy and 92 votes to 74 among the laity, its sponsor Helen Seager alleging that its opponents would do anything to defeat it.[44] Four months later, however, the standing committee accepted two women, Catherine Baur and Beryl Choi, as postulants for Holy Orders (the diaconate).[45] The diocesan convention met the following year in a greatly changed atmosphere. Despite a hostile resolution that noted the negative effects of female ordination on the Church of Sweden and cited the results of a survey of an unnamed middle-sized

42. *Church News*, March 1975. Only twenty-nine parishes responded to the task force survey.

43. Rev. Thomas E. Clemans Jr., to Portia Johnson, November 3, 1975, RG4A/2.1:2, box 2DC, EDP.

44. *Convention Journal*, May 5–6, 1972, 20, 42.

45. *Church News*, June 1972; Standing Committee Minutes, September 18, 1972, RG4A/1.8, box 10DRB, EDP. In 1967, the diocesan convention rejected a resolution that called for the amendment of national canon 50 (on the ordering of deaconesses) to declare that the Episcopal Church "does not have, nor does it intend to have, an Ordained Ministry of Women." *Convention Journal*, May 9, 1967, 23, 29.

parish in the diocese showing 63 percent of the congregation opposed, a narrow majority of delegates (130–124) rejected a call to urge the General Convention not to address the issue.[46] The standing committee endorsed Beryl Choi's request for ordination to the diaconate in September 1973, though two clergy members—Don Gross and Richard Davies—raised objections to the ordination not on the score of its validity but its regularity, in the light of the prevailing Prayer Book rubrics.[47]

As the prospect of female ordination to the priesthood loomed, two female deacons, Beryl Choi and Emily Gardiner Neal, the devotional writer, debated the issue in the pages of the diocesan newspaper. Choi argued that women enjoyed access to the same spiritual gifts as men and that the priesthood should be understood as representative of humanity in general. Neal responded that eligibility for the priesthood was dependent neither on intellect nor spirituality, but on gender. "A qualified woman," Neal insisted, "can most certainly fulfill [a ministerial role] if she is content with ordination to the diaconate which is scripturally sound." A woman deacon could duly represent all those who were in Christ, but the priest was called upon to represent Christ and had, of necessity, to be male. Jesus had deliberately chosen a male apostolate despite his "extraordinarily liberal and liberating attitude towards women in his own time." The Savior of the World could not be limited to the culture of his day: "To those women who feel called by the Holy Spirit to the priesthood, I would suggest that the Holy Spirit was given to a group—the embryo Church—as well as to individuals, therefore the mandate of the Spirit must be clear to the Church as a whole, not only to a few individuals in it. Nevertheless, to those women who feel a genuine vocation, I feel not only sympathy but a very real empathy. I was equally certain that God was calling me to another way of life. I found that I was mistaken, and had confused the leading of the Spirit with my own desire."[48]

Anglo Catholics in the diocese shared Neal's misgivings. Earl Daugherty, the rector of Church of the Ascension, Pittsburgh, argued that Choi's argument made sense only if applied to all the sacraments, not simply ordination. "If physical differences are not determinant to [the Sacrament of marriage]," he concluded with uncanny prescience, "then

---

46. *Pre-Convention Journal*, May 4–5, 1973, 45–46; *Convention Journal*, May 4–5, 1973, 23–25.

47. Standing Committee Minutes, September 10, 1973, RG4A/1.8, box 10DRB, EDP.

48. *Church News*, September 1973.

any two people could qualify. And the gay liberationists could justly appeal for the right to be married by the rites of the Church." Theirs was not the prevailing view, however. Peggy Grant of Church of the Nativity, Crafton, arguably spoke for the majority when she voiced the opinion that since the New Covenant embodied a radical respect for women, they should be permitted to develop their spiritual gifts to the fullest extent. "As I see it," she concluded, "traditions didn't work then and they won't work now. It really is as simple as that if we want it to be."[49]

The slow pace (for some) at which the Episcopal Church approached the entry of women into Holy Orders combined with the election of the new presiding bishop (John Allin) personally opposed to female ordination led many progressives to wonder if recent gains were about to be overset. Consequently, on July 29, 1974, three retired bishops conducted irregular ordinations of eleven women at a church in Philadelphia. A small group from Pittsburgh attended the ceremony, among them Richard Gressle, an assistant priest at Calvary Church, who also participated in the laying on of hands. Back in Pittsburgh, he wrote to Bishop Appleyard admitting his "offense":

> I must confess to you that this is not the first time that I have broken laws, and I tend to do this law breaking selectively. Indeed, I have probably been disobedient to civil authority often. Each time that I can remember preparing for these acts of disobedience, I can remember an intense feeling of anxiety and fear which goes along with such acts. But I think that what made the difference at this ordination was the fact that I felt completely at peace during the entire affair. I felt no excitement, no anxiety, and indeed I felt that the interface of my spiritual life and my public life were almost at one.[50]

---

49. *Church and Community: Christian Social Relations Bulletin*, September 1973, RG4A/2.3:1, box 6DC, EDP.

50. Rev. Richard L. Gressle to Bp. Appleyard, July 30, 1974, RG4A/2.1:2, box 2DC, EDP. Beryl Choi was equally euphoric: "We are all changed by this act in Philadelphia. Priesthood for women in our Church is no longer an academic issue, or something that exists only thousands of miles away in Hong Kong ... Whatever the legalities or illegalities are, those of us who participated in that service will thank God as long as we live. If we never see it again, just once we have seen the Church as she really is and could and should be, united, reconciled, unhindered by the hypocrisies and barriers of inequality and injustice." *Church News*, September 1974.

Bishop Appleyard was not pleased at this outcome. A staunch supporter of female ordination, he nevertheless maintained that the Philadelphia ordinations were unconstitutional, uncanonical, and irregular. Because their actions had been both divisive and destructive of the discipline of the church, he was uncharacteristically blunt in his opinion that the offending bishops should be severely disciplined. Although he never forbade any of his flock to attend the ceremony, he made it clear that they had gone without his blessing.[51] Four months later, when Gressle proposed that one of the Philadelphia Eleven preach at a votive Eucharist on behalf of the women of the diocese, Appleyard responded that the homily must be delivered by a woman from Pittsburgh. "I [still] continue to support the ordination of women to the priesthood and episcopacy," he told Gressle. "I do so financially, prayerfully and with every ounce of my being."[52] Portia Johnson of Church of the Redeemer, Pittsburgh, had her doubts. In April 1975, she wrote a stinging indictment of the failure of the diocese to pay for Beryl Choi and Catherine Baur Bickerton—the diocese's first two women deacons—to attend a three-day workshop for women seeking work in the Episcopal Church.[53]

Supporters of female ordination had only contempt for opponents engaging in what they regarded as purely legalistic arguments. Just as racial integration implied an acceptance of the sacramental ministry of a black priest to white laymen, they argued, so belief in female equality necessitated the admission of women to Holy Orders.[54] In 1975, when the Episcopal Diocese of Oklahoma appealed to the rubrics of the Book of Common Prayer as justification for opposing the ordination of women,

51. *Church News*, September 1974. "This is the first meeting of the House of Bishops I did not look forward to with great anticipation," Appleyard commented of the emergency meeting that followed the Philadelphia ordinations.

52. Rev. Richard L. Gressle to Bp. Appleyard, November 11, 1974, Appleyard to Gressle, December 9, 1974, RG4A/2.1:2, box 2DC, EDP.

53. "The Episcopal Church should help develop women's skills, especially at a time when they are emerging as representative persons of the Church." Portia Johnson to Bp. Appleyard, April 28, 1975, RG4A/2.1:2, box 2DC, EDP.

54. The essential connection between black integration and female ordination was underlined at a meeting of the task force on the ministry of women in March 1975, which discussed a proposed votive Eucharist on behalf of women's ministry. According to Portia Johnson, "Cecil Marshall saw no difference between offering such a votive Eucharist [in the knowledge that some would not receive the Sacrament in protest] and the Eucharist celebrated by him when people refused Communion from his black hands." Portia Johnson to Bp. Appleyard, March 24, 1975, RG4A/2.1:2, box 2DP, EDP.

Helen Seager commented satirically that a literalist approach would seem to imply that women could never be barred from receiving Communion and that only adult males needed to be baptized before receiving Communion: "I have seen a button which says 'ordain women or stop baptizing us!' Oklahoma seems to have made its choice ... It has been my experience that when the cause is justice, opponents of justice usually can be counted on to hang themselves, especially if given an unencumbered expression of their views. If Oklahoma wants to go this route, let them!! We can only gain when our opposition is this outrageous."[55]

While a majority of members of Pittsburgh's standing committee favored female ordination, there was no such majority for making the process mandatory throughout the church. In 1975, the standing committee refused to support the proposal of the Diocese of Ohio that bishops and standing committees refuse consent to the election of any bishop opposed to the ordination of women to the priesthood and episcopate.[56] That same year, Earl Daugherty of Church of the Ascension hosted a meeting of the opponents of female ordination in the diocese.[57] From this meeting emerged the Coalition for Apostolic Ministry, an Anglo Catholic pressure group whose steering committee included three priests: James Dix, Don Gross, and Charles Martin. The Coalition urged its denomination not to embrace any innovation calculated to "divide the Episcopal Church and separate us from the One, Holy, Catholic and Apostolic Church."[58]

The Coalition made every effort to publicize its views. Deacon Emily Neal even appeared on a local television show to make the case against

55. Helen Seager to Beryl Choi, John Baiz, and Robert Appleyard, n.d. (October 1975), Bp. Appleyard to Seager, October 31, 1975, Rev. John Baiz to Seager, November 4, 1975, RG4A/2.1:2, box 2DC, EDP. Appleyard merely assured Seager that he had no intention of following the example of the Diocese of Oklahoma, while Baiz informed her that she had misread the rubrics, as the sections she cited were italicized and the male pronoun was consequently to be understood generically.

56. Standing Committee Minutes, June 10, 1975, RG4A/1.8, box 10DRB, EDP. At the diocesan convention, delegates rejected a resolution obligating members of the standing committee to accept otherwise qualified women deacons for the priesthood if the 1976 General Convention approved women's ordination. The sponsor called it an infringement of the rights of bishops, rectors, and vestries. *Pre-Convention Journal*, May 9–10, 1975, 34; *Convention Journal*, November 8, 1975, 24.

57. Portia Johnson to Jack Harris, October 17, 1975, RG4A/2.1:2, box 2DC, EDP. Johnson acknowledged the right to hold the meeting but criticized the decision, not least because Beryl Choi was on staff at Ascension.

58. "A Call to Integrity," n.d., RG4A/2.1:2, box 2DC, EDP.

female ordination, and pressure was also exerted on Pittsburgh's deputies to the pending General Convention. "Mention was made," the minutes of a November 1975 meeting of the Coalition reported, "of the way in which we strive to state our beliefs—graceful rather than graceless. Hence, our teaching is vital. Sales technique is to boost your product, not just knock the competition. We need a positive statement, with ample opportunity to ask questions. We are not just against women priests as much as we are for *Apostolic* Ministry."[59]

Bishop Appleyard viewed the escalating tensions with trepidation as the 1976 General Convention loomed: "Every delegate at the General Convention will have his or her vision of what the Church's future course should be, and all positions may be defended by scripture. But I am confident that the Holy Spirit is at work in the Church, and not our will but God's will must be done. What wounds me most deeply is that partisans on both sides of the issue now invoke the Holy Spirit as if they had a secret channel to the Almighty. Such rhetoric is blasphemous, and an affront to the intelligence of dedicated men and women."[60] In Minneapolis, the General Convention overwhelmingly approved the new ministerial order. The Coalition for Apostolic Ministry was no more successful at the diocesan level. When Father Don Gross questioned the constitutionality of the General Convention's decision, his fellow standing committee members declared that they could not "morally refuse" to approve qualified candidates and authorized the ordination to the priesthood of Catherine Bickerton and Beryl Choi.[61]

Though he did not share their convictions, Bishop Appleyard did his best to conciliate Anglo Catholics within his diocese. After the Port St. Lucie meeting of the House of Bishops, which authorized a conscience clause for opponents of female ordination, he assured them of his commitment to it. "I don't consider [Anglo Catholics] dissidents at all," he declared. "I consider them faithful Christians who have a right to say that just as much as I have a right to give my opinion. As far as any schismatic movement in the Diocese, I do not feel that there is one."[62] For the most part, Appleyard was correct. Organized resistance did not translate into

59. Coalition for Apostolic Ministry–Pittsburgh Minutes, November 20, 1975, RG4A/2.1:2, box 2DC, EDP.
60. *Church News*, Fall 1976.
61. Standing Committee Minutes, October 18, 1976, RG4A/1.8, box 10DRB, EDP.
62. *Church News*, November 1977.

a substantial number of departures from the denomination. However, just as Pittsburgh had produced a leading member of the Reformed Episcopal Church in the 1870s, so it produced one of the early bishops of the Continuing Church movement in the 1970s. In January 1978, David Doren, rector of St. Paul's, Mt. Lebanon, was consecrated bishop of the Diocese of Mid-Atlantic States of the Anglican Church of North America. Doren, who had close ties to the Anglican Church of Korea, attracted controversy for bringing to his ordination a letter of endorsement from Bishop Mark Pae of Taejon, which the latter subsequently repudiated. With extreme reluctance, Appleyard found it necessary to suspend Doren from the ministry after the latter had organized a congregation and led worship services in the diocese.[63]

Those dissidents who rejected Doren's path formed a branch of the Evangelical and Catholic Mission (ECM), headed by Don Gross and Keith Ackerman, rector of St. Mary's, Charleroi. They took the view that female ordination was invalid on constitutional and theological grounds and argued that any change in the nature of the clergy order required the consent of the wider church. The proponents of female ordination responded by forming a chapter of Episcopalians United, headed by John Baiz of Calvary Church, to uphold the will of the church, as expressed by General Convention.[64] In 1978, Baiz demanded that candidates for the standing committee declare their position on the issue so that future female postulancies would not be put at risk as a result of any change in standing committee membership, as had occurred in the Diocese of Chicago.[65]

Members of ECM sometimes complained that Episcopalians United exerted undue influence over diocesan institutions. "As distasteful as ECM may be to some in this Diocese," observed Charles Martin, rector of St. Mark's, Johnstown, "we are not an assortment of malcontents. Rather we are providing an outlet and forum for Episcopalians to be

---

63. Bess, *Divided We Stand,* 112–17; Standing Committee Minutes, January 16, 1978, RG4A/1.8, box 10DRB, EDP; *Church News,* May 1978. Doren had formerly been a canon of St. Mark's Cathedral in Minneapolis, Minnesota, where he had written the nationally distributed St. Mark's Series of church school lessons. See the profile in *Church News,* February 1956.

64. *Trinity,* February 1980.

65. *Convention Journal,* October 20–21, 1978, 19.

heard and ministered to—*within* the Episcopal Church."⁶⁶ Parishioners from Calvary, Church of the Redeemer, and St. Andrew's, Pittsburgh, by contrast, submitted a resolution to the 1980 diocesan convention warning against attempts by conservatives on the standing committee to block eligible female candidates. "If the doctrine of conscience as a 'shield' can be converted into a 'sword' and undermine the will of the Church," they warned, "then the door is open for any one in a policy-making position to oppose any Church law (rather than uphold it which is their duty) merely by invoking one's personal conscience. This is anarchy."⁶⁷

THE RISE OF THE NEO-EVANGELICALS, 1966–1979

The 1970s proved pivotal in the life of the Diocese of Pittsburgh, since this marked the time during which the first manifestations of the national renewal movement began to become apparent. A distinguishing mark of this movement was its commitment to parachurch ministries (organized by churchmen, but not subject to the direction of church leaders at the national or diocesan level). In Pittsburgh, these included the Pittsburgh Pastoral Institute, the Pittsburgh Experiment, and the Anglican Fellowship of Prayer (which was national in scope but had particular ties to Pittsburgh through Bishop Pardue and Helen Shoemaker). As early as 1966, Austin Pardue personally testified to their importance. "It is encouraging to see how many new and expanded ministries have developed within the Diocese," he commented. "They are not Diocesan initiatives and for them the Diocese has no financial responsibility ... Yet, they are fostered by our clergy and lay people and by individual parishes and missions of zeal and vision."⁶⁸

The parachurch strategy reflected a concern on the part of some Episcopalians that the doctrinal integrity of national church institutions was fatally compromised. The debate over women's ordination was but a minor aspect of a wider conflict over the authority of Scripture and the nature of the church that had been simmering for over twenty years.

---

66. Rev. Charles P. Martin to Rev. Richard M. Barnes, May 16, 1980, Barnes to Martin, May 22, 1980, RG4A/2.1:2, box 2DC, EDP. Barnes denied that Episcopalians United had exerted any pressure, and insisted that *Trinity* gave fair and equal treatment to all organizations—as the February issue had made clear—and any failure to report the conference should be attributed to lost documentation.

67. *Trinity*, May 1980.

68. *Convention Journal*, May 24, 1966, 38.

In 1962, Bishop Pardue assumed the chairmanship of the so-called Committee of Nine of the House of Bishops, which sought to "solve disagreements that now exist within our Divine Democracy."[69] Many of these disagreements revolved around the controversial writings of such men as James Pike, who became bishop of California in 1958. During his eight years as bishop, Pike drew national attention with his challenges to such classical Christian doctrines as Original Sin, the Virgin Birth, the Trinity, and the Resurrection. His *Time for Christian Candor*, published in 1964, exposed the fault lines in the Episcopal Church's efforts to reconcile Christian theology with modernity. His support for birth control and civil rights and premature recognition of a woman as an ordained deacon in 1965 further identified him as an impetuous proponent of progressive causes. In October 1964, Pike visited Pittsburgh, where he was hospitably received. "He is like a kid with a new outboard motor," Bishop Pardue commented at the time. "You don't know which direction he is going to take next."[70]

Pardue's lightheartedness was by no means shared by all. "These great intellectuals in attempting to play God have only become more confused themselves," declared Dave Griffith, the man behind employee prayer circles at the Homestead works, "and are nullifying their own ministry because they cannot bring men to a Christ they do not know themselves."[71] At the 1965 diocesan convention, Charleroi delegate John Patrick requested that Bishop Pike be declared persona non grata in the Diocese of Pittsburgh (something that could be implemented only by the bishop of the diocese). On the substantive issue of Pike's theological views, however, many delegates proved reluctant to censure what they considered "opinion," even if arguably heretical—a perspective that would be reproduced at Pike's trial for heresy a year later—and the resolution was summarily defeated.[72]

Liberal clergy tended to dismiss the Pike affair as merely an expression of closet racism by southern bishops who objected to Pike's stands on civil rights. "Anyone who can lose his faith because of some remark of Bishop Pike," John Baiz of Calvary remarked sardonically, "obviously

69. *Convention Journal*, May 8, 1962, 19.
70. *Church News*, November 1964.
71. *Church News*, December 1965.
72. *Convention Journal*, May 11, 1965, 16, 22. On Pike's trial, see Stringfellow and Towne, *Bishop Pike Affair*.

doesn't have too much to begin with, and may need great pastoral care and a good deal of Christian education."[73] In 1966, resolutions proposed by the vestry of St. Andrew's, Pittsburgh, sought a more open debate on such issues as God's role in human suffering, the assured damnation of those who did not believe, and whether to permit remarriage after divorce. Bill Harding, a lay member of Church of the Advent, Jeanette, described the resolutions as contrary to church teaching and recommended that "some priest should go back to seminary and learn something."[74] For many Episcopalians, the prevailing fear was that a marriage of open intellectual inquiry and increasingly militant social activism fundamentally altered the mission of the church. "What now gives our ecclesiastical elite the authority to pose as experts in politics?" demanded Don Gross in 1970. "Do they believe that their brand of politics is the Word of God, and that others who make different political judgments are hypocritical sinners?"[75]

Illustrative of these tensions was the diocesan debate that took place after Bishop Appleyard appointed a committee in 1970 to explore the moral, spiritual, legal, and medical issues involved in legalized abortion.[76] The following year, the committee sponsored a resolution asserting the right of a woman to a medically safe abortion in the cases of rape, incest, or to preserve life and health for physical, mental, or spiritual reasons, or when a child was badly deformed. Physicians on the committee argued hat such a resolution would merely uphold current medical practice, and John Baiz of Calvary went a step further in arguing that the convention "should not push our Christian convictions on others." Several of his clerical colleagues vigorously disagreed. Don Gross maintained that the resolution would promote a culture of abortion on demand, while Richard Davies inquired how "handicap" was to be defined, given his experiences with retarded children in Brentwood. Convention delegates supported

---

73. *Church and Community: Christian Social Relations Bulletin*, December 1967, RG4A/2.3:1, box 6DC, EDP.

74. *Convention Journal*, May 24, 1966, 28–29, 32–34. The resolutions were all referred to committee and not voted upon, so the perspective of the diocese as a whole is unknown.

75. *Church and Community: Christian Social Relations Bulletin*, September 1970, RG4A/2.3:1, box 6DC, EDP.

76. *Convention Journal*, May 12, 1970, 72.

Baiz, however, and passed the resolution, the clergy narrowly (37–36) and the laity more convincingly (121–74).[77]

In 1972, a more sweeping resolution calling for the repeal of all abortion laws was presented to convention delegates, prompting Don Gross to comment that the 1971 resolution had clearly not gone far enough to satisfy its sponsors. To the astonishment of some of those present, Janet Shaw from St. David's, Peters Township, insisted that an unwanted child suffered from the same defects as a handicapped child. For Shaw, "the voices of the past can not help us today [and] the Church has got to move and re-examine the problems of the world today, including population." Another Pittsburgh cleric, Everett Campbell (who himself suffered from a physical handicap) protested that true value inhered in *being*, not in worth. This time, the resolution went down to defeat in both the clergy (10–46) and the lay (78–89) orders, but the 1971 resolution remained the official stance of the diocese.[78]

The 1973 *Roe v. Wade* Supreme Court decision rendered much of this discussion moot. In 1977, however, many Pittsburghers were shocked by a resolution supporting the Religious Coalition for Abortion Rights (RCAR) backed by Beryl Choi and Rodgers Wood, rector of St. Philip's, Moon Township, who spoke of the agony and guilt associated with both abortion and the lack of access to it. The narrow 116–96 victory came only after an amendment was adopted stating that the church did not condone abortion but opposed efforts to legislate against it and despite the comment of David St. Clair, rector of Christ Church, Greensburg, that the resolution was a "thinly-veiled disguise" for abortion on demand.[79] This RCAR resolution provoked an outburst at the 1978 diocesan convention from Alexander MacDonell, rector of St. Stephen's, Wilkinsburg, who had learned that the bishop had denied the RCAR the right to feature the name of the diocese on its letterhead. How could Appleyard contravene the will of convention, he demanded? "Who determines the policy of/for the Diocese? The Convention or the Bishop?" Bishop Appleyard was unmoved, explaining that the prohibition of which MacDonell complained applied to all groups associated with the diocese except

77. *Convention Journal*, May 7–8, 1971, 16, 32.
78. *Convention Journal*, May 5–6, 1972, 18, 40.
79. *Convention Journal*, November 11–12, 1977, 19–20.

Christian Associates of Southwestern Pennsylvania (the local ecumenical association).[80]

Pro-life advocates fought back, introducing a resolution in 1979 that urged the diocese to establish a committee to formulate a program of education on pro-life issues. In a hint of the new reliance on international precedents, its sponsors cited the commitments made by the 1958 Lambeth Conference to the sanctity and value of life. One of the most eloquent defenders of the resolution was lay deputy Nancy Chalfant, who declared, recalling her own experience of raising a handicapped daughter, that no parent in her situation would endorse abortion. After a substitute resolution entitled "Right to Choice" had been narrowly beaten back (115–119), the original resolution was then passed by the clergy (40–32) and the lay delegates (83–79). Scarcely had it been adopted than Alexander McDonell was on his feet to declare that the resolution was "deeply offensive," contrary to the mind of the General Convention, and that he would do nothing to implement it.[81]

This early introduction to one of the most profound cleavages of the culture wars provided a ready forum for those Pittsburghers associated with the nascent Neo-Evangelical party. As with the wider church, classical Evangelicalism, though not necessarily Low Church practices, had largely been superseded by the beginning of the twentieth century. What arose in the late 1960s in various parts of the church described itself as Evangelicalism, as it claimed lineal descent from its nineteenth-century forebears, but it was a very different ecclesiastical animal. Neo-Evangelicals shied away from a focus on purely experiential religion in favor of a more rigorous intellectualism (which helps explain why Sam Shoemaker, though associated with the movement, was not truly one with them). Many Neo-Evangelicals were also more inclined to stress their Anglican identity than had been the case a century before, a consequence, perhaps, of their virtual eclipse after 1900. Though, as we shall see, this self-identification would not always be so prominent over the next forty years, it nevertheless did provide a marker as the renewal movement took fire. Where Neo-Evangelicals were at one with their forebears—and ran counter to the prevailing Episcopal culture—was in their belief in the necessity of a conversion experience, or "second birth," for the mature

80. *Convention Journal*, October 20–21, 1978, 21.

81. *Pre-Convention Journal*, November 2–3, 1979, 54; *Convention Journal*, November 2–3, 1979, 21.

Christian. Such experiences were not required to be dramatic, however. Peter Moore describes his own "quiet" personal conversion as "reading the Bible and listening to Billy Graham on the radio and just absorbing the fact that Christ was real," but it was not until he was in college that he discovered one "could still believe the Bible and be an Episcopalian or an Anglican."[82]

The Evangelical revival in the United States owed much to the development of transatlantic relationships with Evangelicals in the Church of England. Oddly enough, English Evangelicalism had been experiencing a dry spell during the 1940s, and one of the sparks to its renaissance had been the revivals led by Billy Graham during the early 1950s. One of the products of these revivals was none other than John Guest, who would later be an influential voice in American Neo-Evangelicalism in the United States, particularly southwestern Pennsylvania.[83] Perhaps the most profound influence, however, was the English theologian John Stott, whose tours of American universities' student communities were well received. Stott departed from the historic Anglican emphasis on the Creeds and the Prayer Book, emphasizing the vesting of ultimate authority in Scripture. In contrast with much postwar theological debate, which stressed the role of early Christian communities in the construction of the Gospel narratives, Stott laid stress on the revelatory and inspirational qualities of the New Testament.[84]

With the encouragement of Stott, two American clergymen, Peter Moore and Philip Edgcumbe Hughes, organized an American branch of the Evangelical Fellowship in the Anglican Communion in the early 1960s. In response to the Keele Conference of 1967, which helped elevate the status of Evangelicals within the Church of England, the American branch was renamed the Fellowship of Witness in 1968 and based at St. Stephen's Church in Sewickley, Pennsylvania, whose rector, John Guest, was a born-again English Evangelical. The Fellowship sought to offer Neo-Evangelicalism to the wider church as a model for conversion and renewal,[85] with Philip Hughes maintaining that the church should be a

82. Moore interview.

83. On the impact of Graham's crusades, see Manwaring, *From Controversy to Coexistence*, 87–95.

84. Stott, "Jesus Christ." For a profile of Stott, see Steer, *Church on Fire*, 268–76.

85. A 1991 interview with Pr. Bill Lovell of the Fellowship of Witness, a group organized to bring biblical renewal to Episcopal theology and piety. Lovell was at the time the

missionary church, since "genuine authority [is found in] the energy of evangelical witness throughout the whole world," and indicting the bureaucratic structures and centralizing tendencies within the church as a threat to the autonomy of independent mission societies and newspapers. "One of the greatest threats to the Church's spirituality today," Hughes concluded, "is the pursuit of over-organization as a means to the achievement of unity."[86]

While Peter Moore, by virtue of his service at North Versailles in the early 1960s, represents one of Pittsburgh's earliest Neo-Evangelical clergy, it is to John Guest that we must turn for the most revealing account of the rise of Pittsburgh's Neo-Evangelical movement. Born into a working-class family in Oxford, England, Guest was converted at a 1954 Billy Graham rally. Of his reluctant response to the altar call, he says: "I thought, nobody is going to move, this is American hard sell, and when nobody moves we'll be so relieved that if he offers any other way of making an expression of that faith we'll do it." In his newly converted state, Guest experienced a call to ministry, studied at Clifton College in Bristol, and served in slum parishes in Bristol and Liverpool, where he learned how to interact with and evangelize young people, most notably through the medium of music. "On every street corner there was a band," he says. "I thought, 'If I'm going to reach kids I've got to play the guitar.'" By the mid-1960s, the American bug had bitten. Initially sponsored by the Scripture Union as a student minister, Guest moved to Pittsburgh in 1968 to become part of the Pittsburgh Experiment.[87]

Guest did not remain long with the Pittsburgh Experiment, however. As Michael Sider-Rose remarks, his "long hair, rock band and incessant talk about the 'Jesus Revolution' likely did not fit the mold of an organization focused on the business community."[88] Instead he plunged into student ministry, touring the region's colleges and universities with his rock-and-roll band and pressing ahead with his plans for a dedicated student ministry, the Coalition for Christian Outreach. "Our purpose," he explained in 1971, "is to mobilize the Christian forces to come on as

---

rector of Christ Church in South Hamilton, Massachusetts. See http://members.aol.com/rlongman1/EFAC.html (accessed February 29, 2008). The link appears to be dead. On the Keele Conference, see Manwaring, *From Controversy to Co-existence*, 174–90.

86. Hughes, "Credibility of the Church," 151, 157.
87. Guest interview.
88. Sider-Rose, *Taking the Gospel to the Point*, 39.

strong as other forces attracting the young today. There is so much talk about revolution these days, and it's labeled radical talk. What we're trying to do is revolutionary, too, but it's much more radical than changing existing society by violence."[89] At the same time, Guest took on a part-time position as youth minister at St. Stephen's, Sewickley. Despite its status as, in Guest's words, a "traditional, middle-of-the-road, soft liberal" parish and Guest's unconventional style, his preaching won the approval of children and adults alike.[90]

To the astonishment of many, including himself, the search committee and vestry of St. Stephen's, Sewickley, invited Guest to become their rector in 1971, with a contract that allowed him two weeks off a year for rock festivals. Guest found a number of Neo-Evangelical clergy in the diocese, most of them having been shaped by the ministry of Sam Shoemaker. William Bradbury and Dixon Rollit, in particular, showed some sympathy with the idea of the new birth in Christ. In time, Guest attracted kindred spirits to Sewickley, most notably John Howe and John Yates. Together, Guest and Howe began to transform St. Stephen's, Sewickley, into a national center for Evangelical renewal, achieving significant gains in membership in the process. Both men were key players in the Fellowship of Witness and in November 1972, the parish hosted a conference that included addresses by John Rodgers of Virginia Theological Seminary on "Evangelical Responsibility in the World Today" and John Stott on "The Christian and His Mind."[91]

The centrality of the "converted" Christian to the Neo-Evangelical worldview had implications for relationships with Anglicans in other parts of the world, where belief in the necessity of a conversion experience was widespread, most notably in Africa. A reorientation of the understanding of mission—with its colonial implications of First World material obligations to backward peoples—had been under way within the Anglican Communion since the early 1960s. At the 1963 Anglican Congress in

---

89. *Church News*, April 1971. On the Coalition for Christian Outreach, see ibid., 41–43.

90. Guest interview.

91. *Church News*, October 1972. "As the F.O.W. leadership considered its future, there was a sense of mounting enthusiasm for plans to rebuild the evangelistic mission of the church on biblical foundations. Charismatics and Anglo Catholics (some Romans included) joined in the discussions with the issues of churchmanship temporarily left aside and the question of God's Grace occupying center stage." *Church News*, December 1972.

Toronto in 1963, Anglicans from across the world sought formally to define the ties that bound the churches of the developed world to those of the developing world. The key theme of the congress—Mutual Responsibility and Interdependence in the Body of Christ (MRI)—was formulated by Stephen Bayne, the executive officer of the Anglican Communion and former Episcopal bishop of Olympia. Bayne proposed to replace notions of "giving" and "receiving" churches with a new stress on mutuality, under which dioceses in the poorer parts of the world would develop formal ties with their counterparts in the developed world and work together to define what assistance would best further the mission of the church.[92]

Mutuality in mission was a theme that the Diocese of Pittsburgh would pursue enthusiastically over the next forty years. Bishop Pardue described the Toronto congress as the commencement of a process by which the Anglican Communion might "begin to act as one Church and not as 18 separate and individual churches."[93] In 1964, St. Andrew's, New Kensington, held a workshop to help develop a greater awareness of that parish's obligation to mission.[94] The following year, the Diocese of Pittsburgh became the first American diocese to request an MRI project, earning it Bishop Bayne's fervent appreciation. The beneficiary was St. Michael's Theological College in Seoul, Korea, and diocesan leaders undertook to obtain a contribution of at least $1 from every communicant member of the diocese.[95]

It was the relationship with Africa that was to have the most long-term significance, however. Initially, this owed much to the close personal friendship that developed between Austin Pardue and Festo Kivengere, a Ugandan Anglican studying at Pittsburgh Theological Seminary. A missionary to Tanganyika in the 1940s and 1950s, Kivengere had served as interpreter for Billy Graham during an evangelistic crusade in 1960.[96] Pardue arranged for financial assistance to allow Kivengere's family to join him in Pittsburgh and agreed to ordain him as a deacon before his return to Uganda so that he could immediately be sent out into the field.[97] The

92. On Bayne's role at the Anglican Congress, see Booty, *American Apostle*, 112–19.
93. *Church News*, November 1963.
94. *Church News*, October 1964.
95. *Church News*, March 1965; *Convention Journal*, May 11, 1965, 26.
96. Coomes, *Festo Kivengere*, 119–211.
97. Rt. Rev. Leslie W. Brown to Bp. Pardue, November 17, 1964, Pardue to Brown, November 23, 1964, Festo Kivengere to Bp. Pardue, December 11, 1964, Kivengere to Bp.

relationship between Pardue and Kivengere would mark the beginning of a strong connection between the Diocese of Pittsburgh and the continent of Africa, only enhanced by Richard Martin's missionary work in Tanzania. In 1968, Martin's supervising bishop, John Sepuku, preached at Sewickley and visited Martin's former project in Pittsburgh's Hill district.[98]

The rise of the renewal movement and Pittsburgh's African connection would come together in dramatic fashion in 1973. At that year's diocesan convention, Bishop Appleyard offered a broad endorsement of the new national phenomenon of renewal. Renewal, he explained, "is our acknowledging that we are all evangelists, in the broadest and dearest sense of the word. We are all evangelists because we have all accepted Jesus Christ as our Lord and Savior. Everything else in our lives must be subordinated to this extraordinarily beautiful and simple fact. It is the cornerstone of our faith and of our lives."[99] Convention delegates responded with a request that the diocesan council establish a mission strategy, fund professional leadership, and encourage every parish and mission to sponsor a program of evangelism.[100]

Such a positive response led John Guest to emphasize to Bishop Appleyard the value of inviting Festo Kivengere, now bishop of Kigezi, to conduct a nine-day preaching mission in Pittsburgh. The diocesan evangelism commission—with Donald Wilson serving as its full-time executive secretary—made extensive preparations for the mission, including weekly prayer groups in parish homes, men's prayer breakfasts, and the promotion of personal commitments to pray for specific individuals and bring them to a revival meeting. A twenty-four-hour prayer vigil was also instituted for the entire period of the mission.[101] Over 7,000 people attended revival meetings that extended from Sewickley to Johnstown.

Pardue, January 2, 1966, Rt. Rev. K. N. Shalita to Bp. Pardue, March 1, 1966, Pardue to Shalita, March 9, 1966, Shalita to Pardue, April 21, 1966, RG2/20.1, box 10BP, EDP.

98. *Church News*, October 1968.

99. *Convention Journal*, May 4–5, 1973, 43. It is important not to overstate the nature of Appleyard's commitment to renewal, as he did not necessarily concede every position adopted by the Neo-Evangelicals. He also warned against replacing the "holy indignation of the sixties" with "a brand of religion that would substitute personal salvation for a love and concern for the disadvantaged among us" (48).

100. *Pre-Convention Journal*, May 4–5, 1973, 57; *Convention Journal*, May 4–5, 1973, 31–32.

101. Rt. Rev. Festo Kivengere to Rev. John Baiz, January 30, 1973, Bishop Festo Mission pamphlet, RG2/20.1, box 10BP, EDP; *Church News*, June 1973, September 1973.

The appeal of the mission to the young was particularly evident, from the 1,600-strong crowd at Geneva College, the 900 students at Church of the Ascension, Pittsburgh, for College Night, and the 800 who attended the Youth Rally in Monroeville. For the organizers, the one real disappointment was that while many attendees remained after the meetings for prayer and instruction, fewer than 200 sought further spiritual counseling in the months that followed.[102]

The Kivengere mission may have stoked Neo-Evangelical fires, but it was also the occasion for a revealing theological clash with more catholic-minded members of the diocese. The occasion was an expression of concern by Lynn Edwards, rector of Good Shepherd, Hazelwood, that the prayer counselors for the mission be theologically informed Episcopalians. Critical of the Evangelical tendency to downplay the significance of infant baptism in favor of the act of adult conversion—an implicit denial of the catholic element in Anglicanism—Edwards also urged that the final rally conclude with a Eucharist and not simply an altar call.

To this John Howe promptly responded that his understanding of the English Reformers was that they had focused on calling the baptized to conversion. Infant baptism, he insisted, merely replaced circumcision and was no more or less effective in bringing about the conversion of the whole person. "Our churches," Howe concluded, with exaggerated hyperbole, "are 'filled' with baptized, confirmed, committee-serving, Sunday School-teaching, bill-paying, loyal Episcopalians who have never been reborn of the Spirit. And it usually isn't their fault. How will they be converted unless we preach conversion? And why would we ever preach conversion if we shared Lynn Edwards' opinion that they don't need it?"[103]

Such sentiments proclaimed an Evangelical vision that sometimes stood outside even the conservative Anglican mainstream. Emily Neal charged Howe with being a "reformed Protestant minister, who has totally rejected Sacramental principles," while Lynn Edwards also took umbrage at the suggestion that he saw no role for personal conversion. Many people, Edwards conceded, had "never met the God who gave them spiritual birth when they were infants," yet Howe's vision of the English

---

102. *Church News*, December 1973.

103. *Church and Community: Christian Social Relations Bulletin*, September 1973, October 1973 (quotation), RG4A/2.3:1, box 6DC, EDP.

Reformation ignored the fact that the language of baptismal regeneration had survived three revisions of the American Book of Common Prayer.[104]

The combined effect of such developments was further to strengthen ties between American Neo-Evangelicals and their counterparts elsewhere in the Anglican Communion. In 1975, Pittsburgh Episcopalians welcomed a visit by David Pytches, missionary bishop of Chile, Bolivia, and Peru, who recounted the dramatic growth taking place among South American Anglicans.[105] Two years later, a visit to Chile by Robert Woodroofe, rector of St. Luke's, Bloomfield, prompted the establishment of a companion relationship with the now-separate Diocese of Chile.[106] Finally, in 1978, Colin Bazley, missionary bishop of Chile, followed Bishop Pytches to southwestern Pennsylvania. An English native, Bazley had first gone to Chile in 1962 under the auspices of the South American Missionary Society. His role, he explained, was the evangelization of lapsed Roman Catholics and—in the spirit of MRI—he assured Pittsburgh Episcopalians that he did not desire a one-sided financial arrangement.[107] One of John Guest's protégés, John Hervey, became the first Pittsburgher to subscribe to the MRI principle when he and his wife, Debbie, agreed to be prepared by the South American Missionary Society to serve as missionaries in Chile.[108]

Missions—foreign and domestic—were one part of the Neo-Evangelical program; reform of the seminary system was another. Neo-Evangelicals would have agreed with Don Gross that at the root of the shifting theological perspective of the Episcopal Church was an inadequate grounding in Christian tradition. "Our ecclesiastical establishment," wrote Gross in 1977, "is dominated by theological liberals run rampant, weak in conviction, out of touch with the cutting edge that comes from our holy God. Without losing the positive values of liberalism, our urgent need is for a spiritual renaissance ... Renewal will come when liberalism is once more wedded to what is evangelical, what is charismatic, and what is catholic. Then our balance and integrity can be restored."[109]

104. *Church and Community: Christian Social Relations Bulletin*, November 1973, RG4A/2.3:1, box 6DC, EDP.

105. *Convention Journal*, May 9–10, 1975, 20.

106. *Convention Journal*, October 20–21, 1978, 20; *Church News*, February 1979.

107. *Church News*, June 1979.

108. *Trinity*, February 1990. Hervey underwent a conversion at a Young Life camp and after graduation became office manager for the Fellowship of Witness.

109. *Church News*, Summer 1977. Gross noted that the conservative reaction had had

Members of the Fellowship of Witness believed that a better balance needed to be struck in seminary preparation between academic instruction—in which Neo-Evangelicals passionately believed—and education in the basic skills of evangelism necessary for a Christian, especially one involved in ministry, to witness to the world. Such training, while popular in nondenominational Evangelical seminaries like Fuller, had mo track record within American Anglicanism, and the prospects for instituting it within the existing seminary system appeared remote. Since church renewal relied upon active and engaged clergy, Neo-Evangelicals became increasing preoccupied with how to provide a suitable curriculum and the faculty with which to implement it.

It fell to John Guest, who, through the rectorship of St. Stephen's, Sewickley, enjoyed access to a number of wealthy Episcopalians in the diocese, to take the first step. In 1974, after securing financial pledges from these individuals to back a new Episcopal theological institute, Guest visited Bishop Appleyard and laid out a vision for a "school for ministry" to prepare future clergy for the church. When the bishop asked him why he was proposing a "school" and not a seminary, Guest was blunt: "Seminary is not a good place to train ministers. Seminarians need, in order to go out and exercise ministry, some experience in the ministry that enlarges their own vision. It's downright hopeless to train ministers in seminary because the model is academic, not ministry-oriented. They talk 'ministry,' but basically, it's a grind to get through three years and come out with a divinity degree."[110] No enthusiast for the project, Appleyard nevertheless sent Guest to see the newly elected presiding bishop, John Allin.[111] Allin was equally dubious, doubting whether, in the days of falling rolls, a new seminary would attract enough students to be self-supporting. Allin further suggested that the money instead be devoted to endowing a chair in evangelism at an established seminary. When Guest remained firm in his resolve, the presiding bishop conceded that ultimately he must respond to whatever he and others in the Fellowship of Witness felt to be God's

---

equally unpleasant repercussions, including "a tendency to idolize the 1928 Prayer Book; distortions of the truth in inflammatory publications; and a frequent failure to distinguish between hysteria and the genuine gifts of the Spirit."

110. Leighton, *Lift High the Cross*, 8.

111. "[Bishop Appleyard] wasn't always thrilled with [Trinity Episcopal School for Ministry]," says Peter Moore, "and he did occasionally say things to others that got back to us that were of a negative nature." Moore interview.

call. After failing to obtain the buildings of the Philadelphia Divinity School—which had just closed—the Fellowship of Witness resolved to seek a location in the Pittsburgh area, which seemed to them to offer innumerable opportunities for practical ministry. It would prove a fateful decision.[112]

In September 1975, the board of Trinity Episcopal School for Ministry (TESM) brought Alfred Stanway, the Australian-born former bishop of Central Tanganyika, to Sewickley to become dean-president of the new institution. The following year, temporary facilities were leased at Robert Morris College in Moon Township. Stanway invited supporters of the new seminary to make a commitment to start small while aiming high; to follow God's direction in all things; to let money follow ministry; and to choose fellow workers through prayer:

> Half the problem is that we think we know what we ought to do. We've got it all quite clear-cut, and we want the Lord to work it just according to our plan. We want Him to do this, and then this, and then this, and then this, and then we'll call that "blessed." That isn't the way it works out at all. You're in business when you say to the Lord, "We don't know what we ought to do. We lift our eyes to Thee." And then, when God gives you guidance, it's meant to be followed. In fact, you can't go to Him for guidance unless you're prepared to be obedient to the guidance you receive. So ask with assurance, expecting the next thing next, committing your hearts and minds to do whatever He shows to be His will.[113]

From the start, TESM emphasized that God's people—the clergy as well as the laity—were to be shaped by the Bible (with more than one-third of the coursework focused on study of the Old and New Testaments). Students were also urged to develop personal spiritual disciplines, and practical fieldwork was undertaken in around twenty-five parishes—with the approval of Bishop Appleyard—exposing students to a variety of theological opinions, some of which ran counter to the primary focus of the seminary. In 1978, the seminary acquired a Presbyterian church building and a former A&P store in the run-down steel town of Ambridge, six miles north of Sewickley, that would thereafter be its home. For the first

---

112. Leighton, *Lift High the Cross*, 3–4, 6–11. The report in the *Church News* also stressed the tie-in to local Pittsburgh ministries, which would give the seminarians real field experience. *Church News*, November 1975.

113. Leighton, *Lift High the Cross*, 26–38 (quotation on 28–29).

time since the nineteenth century, an expressly countercultural seminary had been established under Episcopal auspices.[114]

TESM's establishment took place in the context of a broader diocesan debate about the idea of renewal and the need for church growth. The diocesan department of evangelism, headed by George Stockhowe, rector of St. Martin's, Monroeville, hired Donald Wilson—a former businessman studying for Holy Orders—as the department's executive secretary.[115] Diocesan officials attended a conference sponsored by the Institute for American Church Growth and brought back details of the Pasadena Christian Growth Program to share at the 1977 clergy conference, and evangelism experts such as John Savage conducted workshops for both clergy and laity.[116]

In 1978, the Diocese of Pittsburgh hosted the National Episcopal Renewal Conference at Trinity Cathedral. Sponsors of this event—which sought to make successful techniques for evangelism, discipling, and Christian leadership more widely known—included the Anglican Fellowship of Prayer and the Fellowship of Witness. More than 10 percent of the 1,372 attendees hailed from the Diocese of Pittsburgh (thirty-one parishes were represented) and most had nothing but praise for what they heard. The rector of St. Andrew's, New Kensington, called it "the beginning of a whole new outlook for [my] parish," while one parishioner of Church of the Redeemer, Pittsburgh, declared that her "parish would be transformed."[117]

In some parochial settings the focus on mission was unquestionably well received. After the rector and several parishioners of St. George's, Jefferson Boro, attended a church growth seminar, the congregation instituted a program of home visiting and organized a men's fellowship and two prayer groups. In October 1978, John Guest led a preaching mission at St. George's, which helped produce the first adult discussion group in the

---

114. Ibid., 56–70.

115. *Convention Journal*, May 9–10, 1975, 23.

116. Diocesan Council Minutes, February 1, 1977, RG4A/2.1:1, box 1DC, EDP. "The Gospel message goes beyond sharing a personal experience of Jesus Christ or extolling the witness of the Episcopal Church—no matter how much we love the Church," declared the report on Wilson's workshop. "The seminar attempts to equip the Christian with a clear statement of the Good News of Jesus Christ to be shared in such a loving way that the other person might respond by faith in him alone for salvation." *Trinity*, May 1980.

117. *Church News*, October 1978, November 1978 (quotations).

parish's history. An observer from Trinity Episcopal School for Ministry declared that St. George's, with its emphasis on personal witness, prayer, fellowship, evangelism, and male discipling, was a model that other congregations would do well to follow, and its rector remarked that the most exciting aspect of renewal had been the number of people who had come to know Christ in a personal way for the first time.[118] A similar program of parish renewal was launched at Church of the Ascension, Pittsburgh, with the approval of its rector, William Bradbury.[119] Other parishes were clearly less enthusiastic about the process. In 1976, John Guest failed in a bid to allow parishes to deduct the cost of missionary work outside the parish before calculating their parochial assessments. Guest argued that such a move would encourage parishes to do mission work that the diocese either would not or could not do, but his critics clearly suspected him of trying to undercut diocesan programs.[120]

Evangelicals soon had a wider objective, namely, securing a suitable successor to Robert Appleyard. Already suffering from increasingly poor health (he underwent treatment for cancer the following year), the bishop conceded in 1979 that he had become frustrated with his inability to achieve a greater level of reconciliation within the diocese. "Some would say," he told that year's diocesan convention, "that the 1970s have been the winter of our discontent . . . and perhaps they are right. Our Church has mirrored the discontents and even the emptiness of an era. Growth has not been impressive. Many Church schools are a hollow echo of what they once were. Attendance at worship and faithfulness to the sacraments has sagged." He requested the convention to begin preparations for the election of a successor.[121]

The new bishop would face a transformed cultural context. Abroad, the Third World provinces of the Anglican Communion, now graced with a contingent of native-born bishops, had begun to assert themselves in the counsels of the worldwide church. At home, southwestern Pennsylvania had now entered its most severe period of economic decline since the Great Depression. As industrial plants closed and unemployment mount-

118. Diocesan Department of Evangelism Minutes, October 24, 1979, RG4A/2.1:2, box 2DC, EDP.
119. Fairfield/Rodgers interview.
120. *Convention Journal*, October 22–23, 1976, 19.
121. *Convention Journal*, November 2–3, 1979, 29 (quotation); *Trinity*, November 1979, June 1980.

ed, it was to religious leaders that many would turn for assistance. From the general threat to human existence posed by the nuclear arms race to the population explosion, the energy crisis, and environmental pollution, the diocesan search committee warned of the need for church-based solutions. The committee also highlighted the fragility of the local economy, especially in small towns with a single employer. Young people were fleeing to areas with more economic opportunities, the committee pointed out, leaving their parents to impose an ever-increasing burden on local social services.[122]

Though the economic crisis was significant, the committee also warned that the prevailing spiritual malaise was potentially even more deadly. "There is an obvious and widely felt spiritual hunger in the people of the world," its members concluded. "Old idols are dying or dead. Neither capitalistic materialism nor atheistic materialism can fill the void that is felt. Cults (Jim Jones) and the electronic church and the values of Madison Avenue make promises they cannot fulfill. The meaning of guilt and the reality of forgiveness are largely lost in contemporary society." This spiritual aimlessness was very evident in Pittsburgh during the late 1970s (critics pointed to the fact that there had been only one church plant between 1961 and 1980 as evidence of that). Clergy frequently worked alone and lacked the support systems to carry them through periods of spiritual loneliness. How then, committee members asked, could a new bishop harness the cultural diversity of the diocese better to serve the cause of mission?[123]

One member of the search committee was none other than John Guest. He had worked with the Pittsburgh Experiment to transform the civic culture of Pittsburgh and established TESM to transform the seminary culture of the Episcopal Church; now he looked to the Diocese of Pittsburgh to provide a model for national diocesan renewal. "Just like you could take a City and make it an example," he says today, "you could take

---

122. Search Committee for a Bishop Coadjutor, Initial Draft: Agenda for the 1980s, April 15, 1980, RG2/7.1, box 10BP, EDP.

123. Ibid. Despite the structural reorganization, many laypeople were unconvinced that service on districts and committees translated into positive action. The real problem, says Pittsburgh priest Lynn Edwards today, is that many people are vague about what a district is supposed to do. As a result, "you don't really have good attendance because people don't know why they're going." Edwards interview.

a Diocese and make it an example."[124] Critical to any such transformation would be a sympathetic bishop, and Guest had a candidate in mind: Alden Hathaway, rector of St. Christopher's Church in Springfield, Virginia.

A native of Missouri, Hathaway had been educated at Cornell University, served in the U.S. Navy (like Austin Pardue), and then studied at Episcopal Theological School in Massachusetts (now EDS). Ordained in the Diocese of Ohio in 1962, he moved to Christ Church, Cranbrook, in Michigan in 1965. In this suburban parish, he espoused a comparatively liberal attitude to the social questions of the day and joined his parishioners in seeking to address the problems of inner-city Detroit. In 1971, Hathaway accepted a call to St. Christopher's, a military parish deeply divided by the Vietnam War. He rapidly rose to positions of leadership, serving on the standing committee and the commission on ministry of the Diocese of Virginia, and was a member of the board of the Metropolitan Ecumenical Training Center in Washington, DC.[125]

As the renewal movement blossomed, the previously liberal Hathaway underwent a dramatic personal conversion, a process that worried him enough to later seek the reassurance of John Stott that he was not becoming a fundamentalist. In 1975, he attended the conference at which TESM was established. The following year, he joined the board of the Fellowship of Witness and served as its president from 1979 to 1981.[126] Hathaway espoused a theological synthesis that transcended both the subdued traditionalism that had characterized the great mass of the Episcopal Church prior to the 1960s and the modernizing tendencies that had subsequently taken hold among its elected leadership.

"[A] living faith," Hathaway declared in 1980,

> is not fed by a given set of externals alone: the old hymns, the old worship, the old ceremonies. But rather it is fed by the living Lord Jesus Christ who is behind and over and in them all, and without whom, they are all empty ... The Old Prayer Book is gone, a new one that seems to many confusing, jarring, unpredictable in its place. The ministry is a center of controversy—women's ordination, lay ministry versus ordained ... But these things were always only the outward shells of the inner life of our church which has

---

124. Guest interview.

125. Alden Moinet Hathaway, Curriculum Vita, n.d., RG2/7.1, box 10BP, EDP; *Trinity*, June 1997.

126. *Trinity*, June 1997; Leighton, *Lift High the Cross*, 103.

always been that living truth that God loves us and has given his life that in personal relationship to the risen Jesus we have eternal life.[127]

For Guest, Hathaway represented the ideal Evangelical candidate, whose sixties radicalism would serve as a cover to those less well acquainted with his more recent history. "The idea," he says, "was to have three or four [liberal candidates] … but only one conservative," a strategy that, he claims, had been a favored liberal device in the past.[128] Unfortunately for Guest, the youthful enthusiasm of one of his protégés nearly undid his strategy. While Hathaway was the only Evangelical among the five official nominees, Christopher Leighton (a member of TESM's first graduating class) insisted on putting the name of John Rodgers, dean of Trinity Episcopal School for Ministry, in nomination from the floor.[129]

Some delegates, already suspicious of TESM, viewed this as an attempt to circumvent the careful screening process that the official candidates had undergone, and Rodgers was subjected to an hour of questioning in closed session. George Werner, dean of Trinity Cathedral, went so far as to tell Rodgers that if he were elected, he (Werner) would leave the diocese.[130] The early ballots showed Rodgers with a plurality, but clearly incapable of securing a majority, and he withdrew his name. Liberals seethed as they watched Guest strategizing with his supporters (according to Guest, one even threatened him with physical violence) but proved unable to prevent a switch of votes to Hathaway, who was then elected.[131] "It is an overwhelming call," the bishop-elect told his former parishioners at St. Christopher's in January 1981. "I am truly humbled by it. I feel I have neither the capabilities nor the experience for such a position. But I am persuaded this is God's call."[132]

---

127. *Crossroads*, November 16, 1980, RG2/7.1, box 10BP, EDP.

128. Guest interview.

129. *Convention Journal*, December 6, 1980, 23–27.

130. Ibid.; Fairfield/Rodgers interview.

131. Guest interview. John Guest and John Rodgers both insist that their success in electing Hathaway depended upon the support of clergy who were not Evangelicals and deny any suggestion of a fixed election. For a liberal view, which argues that pressure was exerted on lay delegates to vote for Hathaway, see Little, "Historical Notes," 4–5.

132. *Crossroads*, January 1981, RG2/7.1, box 10BP, EDP.

BUILDING UP THE BODY OF CHRIST, 1980–1987

"I suppose there is no diocese that so well represents the broad theological spectrum that characterizes the classical Anglican heritage as Pittsburgh," mused Alden Hathaway in 1982. "All of the positions are expressed with strength, with conviction, with passionate zeal, and with political clout, as you have come to know in the very colorful push and pull of diocesan life over the past several years."[133] Such passionate zeal would soon be in evidence as the Diocese of Pittsburgh staked out its new position as a leading champion of the renewal movement. At the dawn of the twentieth century, Episcopal leaders in southwestern Pennsylvania had embraced the institutional church and the ministries that it produced. At the close of the century, they were far more inclined to repudiate institutionalism. This shift owed much to the work of Trinity Episcopal School for Ministry. Only two years later, Bishop Hathaway predicted that his diocese would be composed entirely of TESM graduates within ten years, noting that a similar situation prevailed in the Diocese of Virginia—most of whose clergy trained at Virginia Theological Seminary in Alexandria—and in the Diocese of Massachusetts—dominated by graduates of Episcopal Divinity School in Cambridge.[134] While the bishop's prediction proved not entirely accurate, it remained the case that by the mid-1990s, Pittsburgh's clerical order would be dominated by a vocal Evangelical group, committed to biblical orthodoxy, evangelism, and church planting.

From his installation onwards, Hathaway signaled to both clergy and people that he was not prepared to continue with strategies derived from the 1960s. "I came to Pittsburgh," he reflected on the eve of his retirement in 1997,

> at a time when the idea was that if people of good will organized themselves, and had access to resources, they could change society and reform it. The idea was right. The church began to see its mandate to carry its faith into the social arena. In the Appleyard years, the diocese began to apply this philosophy to the hard issues and organize itself into a form of corporate structure. It all was right, and generated energy and enthusiasm. But in the 80s it became rather inward looking. Each committee had its own vision, its own

---

133. *Convention Journal*, November 13, 1982, 33.

134. Bp. Hathaway, Notes from Clergy Day, February 7, 1984, RG2/7.1, box 10BP, EDP.

idea of what it wanted to do, and they were in competition with one another for money and attention.[135]

Such a perspective was not universally accepted. Pittsburgh layman Charles Little, for example, has argued that Hathaway's approach reflected the feelings of a man who "did not like the diocesan structure, simply because he did not understand it," and Little also blamed the demise of the Christian social relations department and the diocesan peace commission on Hathaway's "conservative agenda."[136] From the conservative camp, John Rodgers offers a different critique of Hathaway's leadership style. "Alden," he says, "had been converted out of an extremely liberal stance, so his tendency was 'Well, we must have somebody from every point of view on every committee,' which meant that nobody could ever decide anything."[137] Hathaway nevertheless broke with the Appleyard legacy in his determination to avoid the secular political posturing of his earlier clerical career. "I feel that the Church has been too political in recent years," he observed in 1981. "Rather than working together seeking God's guidance it seems to me that we have been overemphasizing resolutions, parliamentary resolutions, parliamentary procedures, majority votes, and who wins and who loses. It has been my experience that the power of the Spirit manifests itself in reconciliation and common mission."[138]

Hathaway might desire to eschew politics, but the 1980s would soon present contentious issues with decided political overtones. The first test came with the economic downturn of the early 1980s. The diocese had actively participated in hunger ministries since 1976, when it joined a coalition of church and community groups seeking to address the issue, and the diocesan council endorsed the proposal for an Allegheny County food bank to supply such institutions as the Jubilee Kitchen, in which a number of Episcopalians directly participated.[139] An early Episcopal initiative came in Homestead (a community with the largest proportion of elderly residents in Allegheny County) in 1979, when St. Matthew's Church organized a food cooperative, which the rector described as both

---

135. *Trinity*, June 1997.

136. Little, "Historical Notes," 5.

137. Fairfield/Rodgers interview.

138. *Trinity*, February 1981.

139. "A Proposal: The Pittsburgh Allegheny County Food Salvage Bank," n.d. (1980), Diocesan Council Minutes, RG4A/2.1:1, box 1DC, EDP.

a means of community outreach and a way to promote interaction among the elderly. For a membership fee of $5 and a pledge to work for the cooperative one day per week, members could purchase food at only 5 percent above wholesale cost.[140]

As the recession hit home, even clergy in the culturally conservative Beaver Valley met to discuss—and pray about—the unemployment situation and the problems associated with it; by the fall of 1982, every parish in the area was operating its own food bank.[141] The network of hunger ministries quickly spread to other parts of the diocese, including rural areas like Jeannette and Kittanning. Suburban participation was equally noteworthy, extending from the monthly collection of canned goods at Christ Church, North Hills, to Calvary Church's weekly drive for food and paper products for the East End Cooperative Mission and the special ministry of St. Martin's Church, Monroeville, which provided monthly grocery money to needy families out of its operating budget.[142] In 1984, delegates from parishes in District III (Armstrong County) complained that a costly diocesan convention dinner sent entirely the wrong message about concern for the welfare of the poor.[143]

Hunger ministries represented what Dean Werner of Trinity Cathedral bitterly described as "a kind of street-corner MASH unit." Werner frequently attacked what he saw as an enduring failure of leadership on the part of the region's business elite and sought to bring together civic, labor, and business leaders to address such problems. "We've got to show the disenfranchised that their pain is our pain too," Werner insisted, "and they have more to gain from working within the system than by destroying it."[144] More theologically conservative clergy than Werner displayed a similar degree of initiative. In Charleroi, Keith Ackerman, rector of St. Mary's Church and a former laborer at U.S. Steel's Duquesne Works, helped broker a 1984 agreement with Combustion Engineering, under which members of the United Steel Workers accepted wage cuts and changes in the seniority system in exchange for job security and

---

140. *Trinity*, May 1981.

141. Diocesan Council—District I Minutes, March 20, October 16, 1982, RG4A/2.1:1, box 1DC, EDP.

142. *Trinity*, March 1983.

143. Diocesan Council—District III Minutes, April 10, 1984, RG4A/2.1:1, box 1DC, EDP.

144. *Trinity*, June 1984.

increased company investment in the local foundry.[145] One year later, David Kinsey, rector of St. Thomas, Canonsburg, spearheaded his local ministerial association's efforts to resolve conflict between McGraw-Edison and local trade unionists. The association not only invited the company to send a negotiating team to Canonsburg, but also requested that neutral observers be present. It even organized a prayer chain to provide hourly intercessory prayer while negotiations were in progress.[146]

Such successes, though commendable, proved more the exception than the rule. In many communities, no inducement was sufficient to prevent plant closings, and Episcopal congregations increasingly instituted programs that offered job skills. St. Matthew's, Homestead, which served many residents of the Mon Valley, operated a job bank and provided job retraining.[147] St. Stephen's, Sewickley, meanwhile, launched an initiative on behalf of the white-collar unemployed known as the Christy House ministry, which provided free weekly training seminars and one-on-one counseling. The parish hosted Help Offer People Employment, which matched the skills of the unemployed with job opportunities in Sewickley, Coraopolis, Moon Township, and the Beaver Valley.[148] A 1983 district meeting was also treated to a presentation from Employment Anonymous, an offshoot of the Pittsburgh Experiment, which provided programs to help open up new avenues for the unemployed through a strengthening of their relationship with Jesus Christ.[149]

One of the most singular employment initiatives was the New Vineyards Project. Struck by the availability of work in his North Carolina hometown, the rector of St. Paul's Episcopal Church in Cary sought to develop a connection between his community and those of blighted industrial areas like Pittsburgh. Local churches interviewed prospective candidates and transmitted their details to St. Paul's; if a suitable open-

---

145. *Trinity*, November 1984. The union initially rejected the offer, but after Ackerman met with supportive workers and community representatives, it was agreed that a court injunction should be sought to force a secret ballot. After union members voted 266-193 in favor of the deal, Combustion Engineering agreed to invest an additional $3 million.

146. *Trinity*, March 1985.

147. *Trinity*, May 1983.

148. Diocesan Council—District I Minutes, June 19, 1982, RG4A/2.1:1, box 1DC, EDP; *Trinity*, March 1984.

149. Diocesan Council—District X Minutes, February 21, 1983, RG4A/2.1:1, box 1DC, EDP.

ing was found, the parish then made arrangements for applicants to travel to Cary and helped accommodate them. If they were successful, St. Paul's then provided assistance with their integration into the local community. Parishes in Aliquippa, Mt. Lebanon, North Hills, Penn Hills, Sewickley, and Johnstown all participated, and 74 of the 116 applicants subsequently found jobs in the South. In 1986, the program was extended to Washington, DC, where St. Peter's Church in Arlington, Virginia, was the facilitating parish.[150]

Some parishes also sought to put underused buildings to better use. On the North Side, John Dowker, rector of Emmanuel Church—with assistance from the congregations of St. David's, Bethel Park, and St. Stephen's, Sewickley—inspired his parish to convert a nearby house into low-rent apartments for local residents. By such means, he hoped to begin to break the cycle of poverty and establish a multiracial congregation. The parish also operated a thrift store on its premises. "We must meet the physical needs," Dowker explained, "because people have to see the love of Christ manifested in concrete, physical ways. They can't begin to comprehend that God's love is real until they see that."[151] In the declining neighborhood of Hazelwood—from which most denominations had withdrawn—Church of the Good Shepherd struggled on, with the assistance of a $10,000 grant from the diocese, operating a thrift shop and allowing local community groups to use its buildings. Bishop Hathaway frequently commended Good Shepherd's rector, Lynn Edwards, and his congregation and urged other parishes to donate household items for the thrift shop.[152] Community service was also in the minds of the vestry of St. Thomas, Canonsburg, when it voted to convert its eleven-room rectory into a residence for the families of out-of-town patients in local hospitals. The vestry had considered razing the property, but decided that this would not be the best exercise of Christian stewardship.[153]

Another significant ministry was Christian-based counseling. In 1981, Ted Wood, a priest at St. David's Church in Peters Township, joined forces with psychologist Joseph Gigandet to form Christian Counseling Ministries, which integrated biblical teaching with psychology. "We see

150. *Trinity*, March 1984, September 1986.
151. *Trinity*, April 1983.
152. Edwards interview; Standing Committee Minutes, May 20, 1985, RG4A/1.8, box 10DRB, EDP.
153. *Trinity*, April 1985.

ultimate health and wholeness in terms of one's relationship to Jesus Christ," Wood explained. "At the same time, we are well aware that emotional and psychological problems may be a stumbling block to that relationship."[154] A similar ministry was offered by the Samaritan Counseling Center of Beaver Valley, which maintained a team of physicians, therapists, and ministers to treat stress-related mental health problems. Where Christian Counseling Ministries charged fees based on the client's ability to pay, the Samaritan Counseling Center allowed those unable to afford the $40-per-hour fees to work off their debt in time devoted to local churches or other service organizations.[155]

Counseling was not the sole medical service that local Episcopalians sought to provide. Alcoholism (a social concern that had, at one time, preoccupied Sam Shoemaker) was making ever-increasing inroads in southwestern Pennsylvania.[156] Under the leadership of two priests, George Story (a recovering alcoholic) and David Else, and laywoman Nancy Bateman of Calvary, a diocesan committee on alcohol and drug abuse had been formed during the late 1970s.[157] The group's dominant figure was Else, who participated in a 1981 WQED series on teenage drug and alcohol abuse in Allegheny County.[158] Else accused many of his clerical colleagues of underestimating the extent of the problem, particularly among young people (at least 10 percent of the population was estimated to suffer from alcoholism).[159] He recommended that diocesan clergy be trained in the problems of alcoholism, noting that the Diocese of Oklahoma had a pre-ordination requirement of fifty-three hours at an institute for chemical abuse, compared with the two hours required in Pittsburgh. Else's attempts to institute such a course at Trinity Episcopal School for Ministry

---

154. *Trinity*, April 1981.

155. Diocesan Council—District I Minutes, September 18, 1982, RG4A/2.1:1, box 1DC, EDP.

156. Michael Sider-Rose notes that the first project adopted by the Pittsburgh Leadership Foundation in the late 1970s dealt with chemical dependency. See *Taking the Gospel to the Point*, 72.

157. Diocesan Committee on Alcohol and Drug Abuse Minutes, October 25, 1983, RG4A/2.1:2, box 2DC, EDP. A group of Episcopalians also helped form Parents of Teenage Drug Abuse (POTADA).

158. Diocesan Committee on Alcohol and Drug Abuse Minutes, August 31, 1981, May 25, 1982, RG4A/2.1:2, box 2DC, EDP.

159. *Pre-Convention Journal*, November 8, 1980, 54.

initially received little encouragement, with some administrators arguing that a parish-based program would be a better use of resources.[160]

Else had no objection to designing a suitable parish program. In 1982, he presented a program on interventions for members of District I parishes and TESM seminarians at St. Stephen's, Sewickley.[161] Later that year, a seminarian who had undertaken a ten-week pastoral internship at the Gateway Rehabilitation Center, headquartered in Aliquippa, offered to help set up a program for clergy, a move that paved the way for a 1983 clergy day devoted to the subject of alcoholism. Diocesan priests listened to presentations from a family therapist at Gateway Rehab on the problems faced by the families of alcoholics and from David Else on the need for clergy to have a pastoral understanding of alcoholism.[162] By 1987, Else had developed a model parish program organized around three-person core teams that shaped a parish policy—grounded in theology—on alcoholism and interventions. Five parishes participated in the program: St. Thomas, Oakmont; Christ Church, Greensburg; St. Paul's, Mt. Lebanon; St. Thomas, Gibsonia; and Trinity, Washington.[163] Another parish that adopted a proactive approach to alcoholism was St. Paul's, Kittanning, which converted a building in Ford City into a halfway house for men recovering from drug and alcohol addiction.[164]

Care for the body was necessarily complemented in Alden Hathaway's mind with care for the soul. Shortly after his arrival in Pittsburgh, the bishop commended Richard Lovelace's *Dynamics of Spiritual Life* (a popular text among Evangelicals) to his congregations. "There is much solid wisdom here for understanding the various renewal moments going on in the churches today," he explained, "and practical guidelines for the balanced stewardship of this renewed life and enthusiasm for the things of God."[165] Four years later, his passion for evangelizing the unchurched

160. Diocesan Committee on Alcohol and Drug Abuse Minutes, April 22, 1985, RG4A/2.1:2, box 2DC, EDP.

161. Diocesan Committee on Alcohol and Drug Abuse Minutes, May 25, 1982, RG4A/2.1:2, box 2DC, EDP.

162. Diocesan Committee on Alcohol and Drug Abuse Minutes, December 10, 1981, September 27, 1982, May 23, 1983, RG4A/2.1:2, box 2DC, EDP.

163. Diocesan Committee on Alcohol and Drug Abuse Minutes, April 14, May 19, 1987, RG4A/2.1:2, box 2DC, EDP.

164. Diocesan Committee on Alcohol and Drug Abuse Minutes, September 2, 1986, RG4A/2.1:2, box 2DC, EDP; *Trinity*, May 1987.

165. *Trinity*, September 1981. See Lovelace, *Dynamics of Spiritual Life*.

was undimmed. "Our church need for the last decade and a half of the twentieth century is evangelical," he declared. "By this I do not mean fundamentalist or anti-intellectual; or partisan; or spiritual elitist. But rather I mean, forthright leadership emphasizing that great stream at the heart of our Anglican tradition that puts foremost the apostolic faith and is willing and able to defend its truth in the midst of the challenges of secular thought. A leadership that elevates Holy Scripture as the reliable source of God's mind and will for the ways of persons and societies."[166]

The earliest precedents for congregational growth came from the charismatic movement within the Episcopal Church. In 1981, Dennis Bennett (author of the charismatic *Nine O'Clock in the Morning*) and his wife, Rita, led a conference on "The Healing of the Whole Person" at St. Stephen's, McKeesport, while George Stockhowe, rector of St. Martin's, Monroeville, made that parish a center of charismatic worship in the early 1980s.[167] Meanwhile, the department of evangelism constantly insisted that congregational growth must be the norm rather than the exception. Small groups of committed people, its members suggested, could achieve a great deal with a simple commitment to weekly prayer and Bible study. "Our job," Donald Wilson explained in 1982, "is to preach personal commitment to Christ, to achieve this attitude change, to give meaning to evangelism."[168] Later that year, St. James's Church in Penn Hills hosted a series of video lectures by Robert Schuller (of Crystal Cathedral fame), which stressed the need to tailor church programs to the unchurched in the local community. "I think the Christ-centeredness of the Schuller process is 'right-on,'" commented the rector of St. Stephen's, Wilkinsburg, "and the practicability and applicability of what Schuller is offering is perhaps its strongest point."[169]

Hathaway's commitment to evangelism had first to surmount certain administrative hurdles, for the 1975 reorganization of the diocese had not led to dramatically higher levels of lay participation. "During the five months that I have been Convenor [of District VII]," complained Pittsburgh clergyman Robert Baur in 1983, "the clergy have been

166. *Trinity*, September 1985.
167. *Trinity*, October 1981; Malley interview.
168. Diocesan Council—District VI Minutes, February 8, 1982, RG4A/2.1:1, box 1DC, EDP. Bishop Hathaway also commended the value of Cursillo to the laity for giving them the opportunity to have a significant encounter with God. *Trinity*, May 1982.
169. *Trinity*, June 1982.

conspicuous by their absence, and some deputies we never see at District meetings."[170] The bishop was also keen to reduce diocesan expenditures for restoring parish buildings so that the money might be released for other ministries. "Local people," he insisted, "should take care of local needs."[171]

All parishes, even those in areas of high unemployment, were called to self-sufficiency. The leadership of St. Matthew's, Homestead, which had adopted the slogan "It costs $0.90 per week to be an Episcopalian at St. Matthew's," argued that many of its new members could not afford to support the parish materially. While the standing committee did agree to treat existing loans to the parish as grants, it insisted that St. Matthew's cultivate a companion relationship with a wealthy parish before any reduction in the parish's assessment was made. The committee also forgave the outstanding assessment of St. Alban's, Murrysville, but only on the condition that its vestry make visitations to dropout families and bring in a professor from TESM to address the parish's spiritual problems.[172]

In 1983, the Diocese of Pittsburgh adopted a program designed to unite parishes behind a common set of mission objectives. The brainchild of Presiding Bishop John Allin, the program was dubbed SWEEP (Service, Worship, Evangelism, Education, and Pastoral Care). "What SWEEP has done for me," Bishop Hathaway told the diocesan convention, "is to provide that integrated picture [of diocesan and parish programs] into which all the parts fit and make sense. With this picture in mind, I believe we can order our priorities and set our goals and become effective and productive unto mission." Explicitly linking SWEEP with the legacy of Samuel Shoemaker and the Pittsburgh Experiment, Hathaway complained that Episcopalians had largely surrendered the work of evangelism to members of other denominations. "What can we do," demanded the bishop, "to

---

170. Diocesan Council—District VII Minutes, January 21, 1982, Rev. Robert Baur to Clergy and Lay Deputies of District VII, April 29, 1983, RG4A/2.1:1, box 1DC, EDP.

171. Diocesan Council Minutes, May 3, 1983, RG4A/2.1:1, box 1DC, EDP.

172. Standing Committee Minutes, February 24, 1986, RG4A/1.8, box 10DRB, EDP. Only a year before, the standing committee expressed concern that the attempt by St. Matthew's to pay its 1984 assessment by selling a community directory was a "one shot" solution, when what was needed was more effective budgeting and planned use of parish resources. Standing Committee Minutes, May 20, 1985, RG4A/1.8, box 10DRB, EDP.

build a mighty revival of the gospel faith, and though the mills have grown cold, to set on fire the hearts of the people that live in their shadow?"[173]

Hathaway's publicly expressed desire to double the size of the diocese over ten years necessitated a fundamental reassessment of how the diocese undertook mission. Parishes, declared the bishop, had to view new plants as partners in the process of forming disciples, not as competitors, and should allow for the establishment of new plants in their plans for development.[174] In Butler County, missioners established Church of the Resurrection in Cranberry Township, even as TESM seminarian Joe Vitunic and his wife, Cindy, transformed the children's club that they had established in Ambridge into a prayer fellowship. After six months in the Vitunic living room, the congregation moved to the American Legion Hall and was officially recognized in 1985 as Church of the Savior. The same year, St. Mary's, Charleroi, established a mission chapel in Bentleyville, an exceptional case of an Anglo Catholic plant in an Evangelical diocese.[175]

In McKeesport, Kevin Higgins of St. Stephen's Church launched a Bible study for the unemployed at a local Burger King. A year later, with around fifty members and under the designation Church of the Redeemer Fellowship, the community moved to donated worship space, the same year that missioners from All Saints, Aliquippa, organized Prince of Peace mission in Hopewell.[176] Such missions depended upon a mobilized body of laypeople willing to share their faith with unchurched members of their community by discussing their life *before* knowing the power of God; their experience of coming to know the love of Christ; and the difference that this had made in their lives. The senior warden of Prince of Peace testified

---

173. Standing Committee Minutes, April 5, 1983, RG4A/1.8, box 10DRB, EDP; *Convention Journal*, November 4–5, 1983, 19–20; *Trinity*, December 1983–January 1984 (quotation).

174. Bp. Hathaway, Notes from Clergy Day, February 7, 1984, RG2/7.1, box 10BP, EDP.

175. Leighton, *Lift High the Cross*, 99–102. In 1986, Church of the Savior moved into the seminary chapel at TESM. St. Elizabeth Mission closed in 1992 and Church of the Resurrection in 2004.

176. *Trinity*, April 1989. Archdeacon David Jones called Church of the Redeemer Fellowship "a powerful example of what happens when evangelism and loving service ministry are intentionally combined." *Trinity*, April 1987. The congregation was closed in 1997.

that he had been brought into the church thanks to the efforts of a group of laypeople who had made weekly visits to local neighborhoods.[177]

The concern that existing congregations might end up in conflict over fruitful mission fields was borne out in 1987 when two churches with very different mission styles—St. Stephen's, Sewickley, and Christ Church, North Hills—sought to plant new congregations in a rapidly growing area of northern Allegheny County. Bishop Hathaway advised them to do so "in the spirit of mutual concern and support for expanding the sphere of influence of the kingdom of God by reaching out to the unchurched population, both present and future."[178] Rodgers Wood, rector of Christ Church, described his congregation's experience as a time of testing. Although it was obliged to give up thirty dedicated parishioners and the associate rector, however, Christ Church continued to grow. "Clearly, in the Kingdom," Wood concluded, "one minus one equals two—two healthy, vibrant parish churches, each with its own style, to offer ministry to this growing community."[179] While the Christ Church plant—St. Brendan's, Franklin Park—exemplified the moderation of its parent congregation, the St. Stephen's plant—Orchard Hill, Wexford—would ultimately become an independent congregation and leave the diocese in 1992.

It was no accident that a majority of the missioners at the new plants had been schooled at TESM and that many of the more innovative parish ministries owed much to the efforts of clergy and laity trained at the seminary. Their relationship with those in the diocese who were *not* Neo-Evangelicals, however, was frequently cool. The latter resented the fact that candidates for ordination from other dioceses later chose to be ordained for Pittsburgh. The secretary of the board of examining chaplains recalled one particularly revealing 1982 episode: "This entire discussion opened a floodgate of words and emotions concerning Trinity Episcopal School for Ministry. A number of strong feelings were articulated by a number of Board members: 'I have a hard time even calling that place a seminary.' 'They claim to be in the stream of Anglicanism—they aren't.' 'We shouldn't

---

177. Diocesan Council—District X Minutes, September 21, 1987, RG4A/2.1:1, box 1DC, EDP.

178. Standing Committee Minutes, April 20, 1987, RG4A/1.8, box 10DRB, EDP. For an account of door-to-door visiting by members of St. Brendan's mission, see *Trinity*, November 1987.

179. *Trinity*, April 1989.

send anyone there; how did the Bishop's original policy change?' There was a good deal of self-righteous indignation filling the room."[180]

Les Fairfield, a professor at TESM who served on both the board of examining chaplains and the commission on ministry, maintains that resistance to accepting Evangelicals into the ordination process declined in the course of the 1980s, but this was not the seminary's only problem. Operating on a shoestring, TESM faced a six-year battle for academic accreditation from the Association of Theological Schools, a necessary step in acquiring outside recognition. John Rodgers admits that some of the accreditors had difficulty understanding the otherworldly character of the seminary, accepting the unanimous rejection by the faculty of the idea of academic tenure only after speaking with every professor individually. In June 1985, TESM surmounted all obstacles to become the eleventh accredited Episcopal seminary in the United States. This move was all the more necessary since many Episcopal bishops had serious reservations about sending their ordinands to Ambridge. "We were conscious at the level of first principles," John Rodgers testifies, "[that] we differed from the direction the Episcopal Church was taking." Such episcopal reservations were somewhat alleviated by the appearance of the presiding bishop at TESM's graduation ceremonies in 1983.[181]

While the rewards of ministry were potentially heightened in such an intensified atmosphere, the risk of clergy burnout was also greatly increased. Bishop Hathaway emphasized that pastoral care began with attention to the physical and mental health of his clergy and their families. "When the rectory family breaks down, or breaks up," he warned in 1983, "the hurt spreads with ripple effect throughout the parish; destabilizing marriages within the body, disturbing the harmonious fellowship and impairing its capacity for mission."[182] He encouraged priests and congregations to establish mutually supportive relationships and also urged the clergy to form cluster groups and make themselves mutually accountable to one another. They should, he said, commit themselves to Jesus Christ

---

180. Board of Examining Chaplains Minutes, March 3, 1982, RG4A/2.1:2, box 2DC, EDP.

181. Fairfield/Rodgers interview (quotation); Leighton, *Lift High the Cross*, 75-79.

182. *Convention Journal*, November 4-5, 1983, 25.

and to Holy Scripture "as first authority for proclamation, teaching and applying in light of its Catholic heritage and tradition."[183]

Low clerical morale, of course, could be the result of extremely practical concerns. In 1984, the wife of the rector of Christ Church, North Hills, testified that the burden on clergy spouses and families was heavy, with "days off" frequently sacrificed for parish needs. "I do know I would not change my life or my husband's life work," she concluded. "Together we shared the joys and pains of ministry, his to the church and to me, mine to the family and him."[184] One practical effort to deepen the bonds between clergy spouses was undertaken by Greg Malley, a professional chef and a member of St. Martin's, Monroeville. Working with the bishop's wife, Malley offered clergy spouses a series of weekly cooking lessons, gatherings that also afforded them an opportunity for the sharing of personal concerns. At the conclusion of the series, the bishop and his wife hosted a dinner for the clergy and their spouses, at which the latter prepared dishes that they had recently been taught to make.[185]

Alden Hathaway did not neglect the practical side of clerical life. He urged the standing committee to focus on the needs of part-time clergy, many of whom worked for less than the clerical minimum or even nothing at all.[186] In 1986, the bishop instructed his parishes to require an annual physical for their clergy and report the results to the diocese. Hathaway also urged them to give their clergy vacation time and meet one-third of the cost of their continuing education. "[For] the sake of the individual minister's own personal and professional well-being," the bishop declared, "there should be no one in the congregation that excels him or her in passionate enthusiasm for growth in the Gospel."[187]

Passionate enthusiasm could be channeled in unusual directions. Though generally critical of mixing religion and politics, Bishop Hathaway was willing to make an exception in the matter of military preparedness,

---

183. Bp. Hathaway, Notes from Clergy Day, February 7, 1984, RG2/7.1, box 10BP, EDP. Hathaway also took a strong stand on clergy divorce: when the divorce was with a "repented spirit," the priest might remain, but if remarriage were involved he or she would be obliged to move out of the diocese, and if there were no repented spirit then removal and temporary suspension from Holy Orders would follow.

184. *Trinity*, November 1984.

185. Malley interview.

186. Standing Committee Minutes, October 15, 1984, RG4A/1.8, box 10DRB, EDP.

187. *Trinity*, April 1986.

most specifically the quest for nuclear arms reduction. As the buildup of American nuclear weaponry continued during the early 1980s, the burgeoning peace movement pressed for a change of policy. "If this planet is to survive we must stop thinking of ourselves as citizens of individual nations," warned David Shaw of St. Thomas Church, Canonsburg, in 1981, "but instead as citizens of the world. If we are to save ourselves we must oppose militaristic actions, such as the deadly arms race, which takes food out of the mouths of the hungry."[188] That same year, the diocesan convention passed a resolution calling on the diocese to press Congress and President Ronald Reagan to initiate nuclear arms limitation talks.[189]

Bishop Hathaway had little fault to find with such sentiments. "There can be no concession," he told the diocesan convention of 1982, "to the weaponry that precludes the only justification for war at all, the hope for a better future."[190] Disarmament advocates took heart from such remarks. With Hathaway's support, the world order committee encouraged the preparation of a joint statement on disarmament from the judicatories of Christian Associates, promoted use of the publication *Countdown to Disaster* as a Lenten study, and introduced a regular "Think Peace" column into the diocesan newspaper. Titles like "Drunk on War" and "Global Terminal Illness" soon graced its pages, winning some to the cause but disquieting others.[191]

Representatives of District II (northern Allegheny County and Butler County) proved particularly receptive to the disarmament message, describing the play by a member of the world order commission entitled *Hagwine and Geneva or War and Peace* as "well-written" and commending it to parish discussion groups. While they supported Bishop Hathaway's statement opposing the nuclear arms race, they felt that it could have been "stronger and more specific."[192] In District VI (the central and western parts of the City of Pittsburgh), by contrast, many representatives felt

---

188. *Trinity*, May 1981.

189. *Convention Journal*, November 7, 1981, 17.

190. *Convention Journal*, November 13, 1982, 30.

191. Rev. Robert W. Woodroofe to William T. Green, February 24, 1982, RG4A/2.1:1, box 1DC, EDP; *Trinity*, June 1982, September 1982.

192. Diocesan Council—District II Minutes, April 19, September 20, 1982, RG4A/2.1:1, box 1DC, EDP. Butler County was the site of a 1982 nuclear freeze referendum, explained by one Episcopalian as an attempt to weigh the cost of spending on nuclear arms against the cost of health care expenditure. *Trinity*, November 1982.

that an exaggerated commitment to disarmament gave too much credit to the willingness of the Russians to reduce their stockpiles and failed to acknowledge that the Russians might be emboldened by unilateral moves on the part of the United States. Disarmament was a complex issue, they concluded, and the church should be in the business of envisioning a theological framework for disarmament rather than offering critiques of specific government policies.[193]

In 1983, representatives of Physicians for Social Responsibility led workshops at St. Alban's, Murrysville, and St. Andrew's, Pittsburgh, that discussed the likely aftermath of nuclear winter.[194] These workshops sparked considerable criticism, not least from Elsa Schultz of St. Martin's, Monroeville, who lambasted what she considered the political leftism of the peace movement. "Freedom to me is more important," Schultz concluded, "than worrying about nuclear war and keeping it in people's minds to cause stress and tension."[195] Members of the world order commission, such as Terry Webb of Trinity Cathedral, retorted that there was no political bias involved: "[To] say we are aiding the cause of Communism because we follow Christ and believe that in him we experience peace with God and through that experience want peace among God's people is astounding logic! Is the pope a Communist? Is our own bishop a Communist, or any of the bishops in our own denomination, or the Catholic Church Communists? ... Are we, as Christians, committed to God or to our country first? Doesn't our loyalty to Christ transcend political and national boundaries?"[196]

A shift away from strict pacifism became clear at the 1983 diocesan convention, however, when a resolution affirming nonviolent refusal to participate in war and preparations for war was defeated by a vote of

---

193. Diocesan Council—District VI Minutes, June 14, 1982, RG4A/2.1:1, box 1DC, EDP.

194. Diocesan Council—District VIII Minutes, February 17, 1983, RG4A/2.1:1, box 1DC, EDP; *Trinity*, March 1983. The speaker at the Murrysville meeting was Dr. John Townsend, who, during the 1960s, had authored a study of the effects of a nuclear attack on Pittsburgh. The wife of the rector of St. Alban's was elected chair of the Episcopal Peace Fellowship in 1983. See *Trinity*, June 1983.

195. *Trinity*, March 1983.

196. *Trinity*, April 1983. Jessie Hay of Fox Chapel commented that the Soviet Union had yet to deal in good faith with the free world and that weakness on the part of the United States was unlikely to help the oppressed anywhere in the world. *Trinity*, June 1983.

134–76.[197] Two years later, Kate Fetterman of Church of the Redeemer, Pittsburgh, described her part in a nonviolent protest at the Westinghouse Corporation. She argued that the acceptance of nuclear weapons was "the greatest manifestation of evil that civilization has ever known." A fellow Episcopalian at St. Thomas, Oakmont, found her logic unconvincing. Since Hiroshima, he insisted, superpower wars and proxy wars had been distinguished by the nonuse of nuclear weapons. Nor was it clear that the Russians in Afghanistan felt much of that sense of "radical connectedness" to the rest of humanity that Fetterman had invoked as her justification for her act of civil disobedience.[198] It is certainly true that by the late 1980s the world peace commission was moribund, a circumstance that one liberal layman blamed on its "infiltration" by two conservatives "who eventually put it out of business," but whether that was the sole cause cannot be definitively verified.[199]

Nuclear disarmament was not the only political issue to disturb the internal peace of the diocese. The 1977 resolution on the Religious Coalition for Abortion Rights had shaken many pro-life advocates, who had previously assumed a common mind within the diocese on the abortion issue. Their anger was only heightened when Beryl Choi gave notice in the diocesan newspaper that the RCAR—for which she was a local convener—was still active.[200] "Would that the aborted were equally alive and well," Rebecca Spanos, chair of the diocesan sanctity of life task force, retorted.[201] Over the next five months (until the editor called a temporary moratorium), critics of abortion debated those who favored a more morally neutral stance. Choi insisted that the headline to her announcement ("Abortion Group Alive and Well") had horrified her and that the RCAR only opposed *government* interference in the moral decisions of individuals. Ellen Detlefsen and Charles Reynolds, both members of Calvary Church, insisted that the RCAR addressed a wide range of reproductive issues. "They oppose those who would mandate decision-making or eliminate options in the area of reproduction or human sexuality," they explained, "whether in the name of church or state." Jane Little of St.

197. *Pre-Convention Journal*, November 4–5, 1983, 25; *Convention Journal*, November 4–5, 1983, 20.
198. *Trinity*, June 1985, September 1985.
199. Little, "Historical Notes," 5.
200. *Trinity*, March 1983.
201. *Trinity*, May 1983.

Paul's, Mt. Lebanon, argued that those who supported abortion rights did so "to minister to needs as they see them." She urged her critics to provide pastoral care to those who sought abortions and not simply criticize a pro-choice stance.[202]

From the pro-life side, David Canan of All Saints, Rosedale, questioned whether Choi could offer a biblically sanctioned defense of abortion. While he accepted the sincerity of Little's views, he shuddered "at the thought of viewing an abortion clinic as a center of Christian ministry." Arlene Epting of St. Stephen's, Wilkinsburg—who worked for a crisis pregnancy agency—also took exception to the suggestion that abortion opponents had no interest in addressing social need. "The preborn child who is conceived in less than ideal conditions," she declared, "has as much right to live as the planned, ideally suited preborn child."[203] The pro-life movement only grew as the decade wore on. Ninety Pittsburgh Episcopalians, representing chapters of the National Organization of Episcopalians for Life (NOEL) from All Saints, Aliquippa; St. Stephen's, Sewickley; and TESM were present in Washington, DC, for the 1985 March for Life. The concluding comments and final prayer were delivered by John Howe, rector of Truro Episcopal Church in Virginia and a former assistant at St. Stephen's, Sewickley.[204]

In 1990, Bishop Hathaway took the unusual step of personally participating in a demonstration in defense of the sanctity of life at a women's health center in downtown Pittsburgh. "I was seeking to be obedient to and in the spirit of the teaching of the Episcopal Church," he insisted, "that all human life is sacred from the time of its conception and therefore we must take seriously our obligation to help form the consciences of people concerning this sacredness."[205] Local NOEL chapters continued to promote the principle that Christians had a responsibility to find morally acceptable choices for women with unintended pregnancies. In 1991, Robert Munday, the administrative dean of TESM, was elected national president of NOEL, further associating the organization with southwestern Pennsylvania.[206]

202. *Trinity*, September 1983.
203. *Trinity*, June 1983, October 1983.
204. *Trinity*, March 1985.
205. *Trinity*, June 1990.
206. *Trinity*, December 1990–January 1991, March 1991. In 1996, NOEL moved its national headquarters from Washington DC, to Ambridge. *Trinity*, June 1996.

Perhaps the most polarizing debate during the 1980s concerned the place of active homosexuals in the life of the church. The resolutions committee of the 1973 diocesan convention rejected a proposed resolution from the Christian social relations department calling for the creation of a task force that would develop "a new theological insight with regards to human sexuality."[207] Progressive though he generally was, Bishop Appleyard consistently declined to endorse the radical prophetic stance adopted by such of his clergy as Alex Seabrook, chairman of the Christian social relations department. In February 1977, the bishop formally protested the ordination, by Bishop Paul Moore of New York, of a woman in an active lesbian relationship. He also refused to give his blessing to the advocacy group Integrity and warned Seabrook that he would not approve his department's majority report urging acceptance of homosexuality as an alternative lifestyle.[208] He was willing to permit theological debate on the issue, however, and so in June 1977 Seabrook faced off against another forthright speaker, John Rodgers of TESM, in a "Forum on Human Sexuality" at Calvary Church, Pittsburgh.[209]

Five years were to pass—and a new bishop installed—before the issue once again came to the fore. In March 1982, however, Calvary hosted "Opportunity for Dialogue," a seminar sponsored by the Integrity Institute for Pastoral Development. The District I congregations (Beaver County) immediately communicated to Bishop Appleyard (at this point, Bishop Hathaway was still bishop coadjutor) that the seminar appeared to affirm the gay lifestyle. "Should not the force of all our Diocesan brethren be squarely behind scripturally based and similar programs that win souls for Christ, rather than justifying homosexuality?" the district chairman inquired.[210] John Neff, rector of Christ Church, New Brighton,[211] whom

207. *Pre-Convention Journal*, May 4–5, 1973, 49.

208. Standing Committee Minutes, February 28, March 21, 1977, RG4A/1.8, box 10DRB, EDP.

209. Rev. Rodgers T. Wood to "Members of Episcopal Clergy Association," June 6, 1977, RG4A/2.1:3, box 12DC, EDP.

210. Donald F. Dunbar to Bp. Appleyard, March 5, 1982, RG4A/2.1:1, box 1DC, EDP.

211. John Neff's views on the issue were made very clear in an article in which he maintained that sexual distinctions were part of God's created order and that only in the union of man and woman could there be complete wholeness. "Sexual drives and distinctions were not the result of the fallen state of man," he wrote, "but are a part of the very fabric of creation brought into being by divine ordinance. What man does with such feelings and drives, a gift of God, can be corrupted and defiled by our fallen nature."

his district sent as an observer, declared that the District I resolution had been introduced at the seminar and that it had been "read and laughed at and laid aside." A total of eight clergy were present to hear presentations on homosexuality from psychological, theological, and sociological perspectives by staff members of Integrity and speakers from a sexual minority counseling center in Pittsburgh. Neff described the session as "informative and worthwhile as a consciousness-raising exercise, but the viewpoint they were coming from is not what the Episcopal Church states as its stand on homosexuality," and the standing committee later agreed that the seminar had failed to present all points of view.[212]

Two other clergy present at the seminar took a rather different view. Beryl Choi declared that the workshop "made an appeal for compassion and the realization that homosexuals require ministry too." Lynn Edwards, from Good Shepherd, Hazelwood, argued that the workshop—which he maintained had the bishop's approval—was merely a response to the call of the 1976 General Convention to develop a ministry to homosexual members of the church. He insisted that no attempt had been made to pass over the diversity of views on the subject, although he did criticize the lack of attention to biblical perspectives. "I am thankful to God that the Anglican ethos is comprehensive," Edwards concluded. "We are not a church that is narrow and disciplinarian . . . a group of Christians was searching the mind of Christ for answers to complex problems of human living."[213]

Over the next few years, Edwards would move toward what he considered a more pastoral stance regarding Pittsburgh's gay community. On three different occasions he attempted to establish a diocesan chapter of Integrity. In 1986, he launched a special ministry to those with AIDS—the Shepherd Wellness Community—at his parish in Hazelwood, which provided biweekly dinners for up to three hundred sufferers and their families and maintained a drop-in center complete with library, laundry,

---

Trinity, June 1982. A year later, Neff was received into the Roman Catholic Church. See Standing Committee Minutes, December 19, 1983, RG4A/1.8, box 10DRB, EDP.

212. Diocesan Council—District I Minutes, April 17, 1982, RG4A/2.1:1, box 1DC, EDP; Standing Committee Minutes, April 19, 1982, RG4A/1.8, box 10DRB, EDP. The Evangelical-Catholic Mission organized a workshop at Sewickley on March 16 that presented a contemporary Christian view of homosexuality contrary to that outlined at Calvary.

213. Diocesan Council Minutes, April 13, 1982, RG4A/2.1:1, box 1DC, EDP; *Trinity*, April 1982.

and kitchen. "People with AIDS are aware of dying and they need a place where spirituality can come into play," Edwards explained in 1994. "Many feel that they have no way into the church because they perceive a uniform criticism of who they are. So they also have no way into what the church has to say about the love of God."[214]

Edwards's relationship with Hathaway was sufficiently close that the bishop even invited him to address the clergy of the diocese, many of whom were strongly opposed to homosexual practice; to his surprise, his emphasis on compassion and mercy toward those inflicted with AIDS evoked no protest. Hathaway was nevertheless at one with the majority in Pittsburgh on maintaining the classical teaching of the church on the appropriate exercise of sexuality. At the 1987 clergy day, Hathaway declared that the blessing of homosexual covenants was a doctrinal issue and that he was unwilling to bless an "unnatural" lifestyle, though he favored an individual approach when it came to formulating a pastoral response.[215]

The following month, he took a more public stand. "The bonding for which the human soul yearns," he wrote in the diocesan newspaper, "and which sexual intercourse enacts both physically and emotionally, is only secured by the social covenant of marriage. Even at the human level, for the church to teach anything less than this is to exercise a great disservice to individuals struggling to understand and to satisfy their deepest needs as human beings." Contemporary approaches to human sexuality, Hathaway concluded, were too often couched in the language of rights rather than religious duties. The church continued to have an obligation to hold to a high spiritual view of sexuality that allowed men and women to overcome their physical separation and potentially share in the gift of creation. "Sex outside of marriage," the bishop concluded, "promises more than it can deliver."[216]

Lynn Edwards disagreed, and Hathaway's openness to debate led him to feature a letter from Edwards in the diocesan newspaper. Edwards insisted that his arguments were informed by a pastoral experience of same-sex couples who had revealed the love of Christ in their relationship and gave evidence of dying to self "whether the Church would have corporately seen them or not." He invoked the injunction to the Apostle Peter

---

214. Edwards interview; *Convention Journal*, November 7–8, 1986, 32; *Trinity*, November 1994 (quotation).

215. Standing Committee Minutes, March 9, 1987, RG4A/1.8, box 10DRB, EDP.

216. *Trinity*, April 1987.

in chapter 10 of the Book of Acts that man should not call unclean what God had blessed. He also denied that the advocates of change sought a completely new values system. "Persons in loving relationships," he wrote, "that have been outside the borders of the Church's blessing boundaries are seeking the church to expand its perimeters so that the 'classic values' ... can be recognized in their expression of sexuality."[217] In the fall of 1987, Calvary Church responded to Edwards's concerns by hosting a two-day conference on pastoral responses to AIDS, the first event of its kind in Pittsburgh.[218]

Sexuality would come to have a defining importance in the 1990s, as the culture wars within the church achieved a new intensity and spilled over into the international arena. It is important to recognize, however, that ties to the so-called Global South were under construction in the Diocese of Pittsburgh well before the Lambeth Conference of 1998 (see chapter 7). Bishop Hathaway did everything he could to strengthen the relationship with the Missionary Diocese of Chile that had begun under his predecessor. In 1985, John and Debbie Hervey had begun work in a Santiago suburb, where they offered Bible studies in English and Spanish. Prayer meetings and women's and youth groups soon followed. Later, members of their congregation were trained through Evangelism Explosion to go out and distribute free booklets containing the Gospel of John and a preliminary Bible study.[219] "Chile also gave us the opportunity to see and know for ourselves that people in every part of the globe have the same basic longing for meaningful life, for God," John Hervey reported. "The gospel is not obsolete in Chile . . . Therefore missions and missionaries are not obsolete, and never will be, until Christ come again." He urged Pittsburgh Anglicans to start prayer support groups for missionaries, join missionary support teams, start a parish mission committee, or attend a discernment conference to see if they had been called to the missionary life.[220]

A spirit of mutuality remained uppermost in the Pittsburgh-Chile relationship. While several Pittsburgh parishes provided financial support to the budding Chilean church, the latter also made a donation of $500 to

---

217. *Trinity*, May 1987.
218. *Trinity*, October 1987, December 1987–January 1988.
219. *Trinity*, February 1990.
220. *Trinity*, May 1985.

send handicapped children to the diocesan youth camp (the Chileans felt a special connection to this ministry because it operated a school for the deaf in Temuco).[221] In 1986, Bishop Hathaway traveled to South America to ordain John Hervey and confirm Bruce Barrett, a member of Church of the Ascension, Pittsburgh, serving for a year as a lay minister. Impressed by the witness of the missionary diocese, Hathaway urged other parishes to follow the lead of St. George's, Waynesburg, and develop companion relationships. "The church in Pittsburgh has a long history," he declared, "a heritage and elaborate institutional structure, and the great weight of maintaining its established life. What would it be for us to cultivate this perspective of a first generation church? Would it not give us the freedom and resources to respond more effectively to the opportunities for mission and outreach before us?"[222]

The same year that Hathaway visited Chile, Bishop Colin Bazley attended Pittsburgh's diocesan convention, where he stressed the two-way nature of the partnership. In twelve years, he declared, the missionary diocese had grown from one small parish to twelve. Such growth had come through conversion, through taking seriously the mandate of the Great Commission, and through a focus on the theological education of the laity.[223] The following year, Bazley requested Pittsburgh Episcopalians to provide financial support for two native Chileans (a pharmaceutical scientist in Holy Orders and a dental surgeon) whom he wished to send to TESM for two years of study. The next year, St. Paul's, Mt. Lebanon, established a companion relationship with a Chilean parish, which involved the exchange of letters, pictures, and newsletters.[224] The mutuality of the relationship was further emphasized when the rector of La Trinidad in Las Condes made a donation of $125 to the work of the Jubilee Soup Kitchen while visiting Pittsburgh.[225] In 1994, moreover, Bishop Hathaway participated in the consecration of Chile's first native-born bishop, Abelino Apeleo.[226]

---

221. Diocesan Council Minutes, May 4, 1982, RG4A/2.1:1, box 1DC, EDP; *Trinity*, October 1981.
222. *Trinity*, February 1986, March 1986 (quotation).
223. *Trinity*, December 1986–January 1987.
224. *Trinity*, June 1987, June 1989.
225. *Trinity*, June 1990.
226. *Trinity*, September 1994.

7

The City on a Hill

Confessional Anglicanism, the Episcopal Church, and the Anglican Communion, 1988–2006

"I HAVE OFTEN BEEN in the thick of conflicts within the Episcopal Church," the bishop of Pittsburgh reflected in 2002. "I make no apologies for this. Guarding the Faith is central to a bishop's ordination vows. But others understand the meaning of the same vows and the same Faith differently. My sense is that facing the conflicts—and sometimes taking actions that force others to face them—is a surer way to [guard] against divorce than the silence and drifting apart which are alternatives."[1] With such an assertion, Robert Duncan emphasized the extent to which the confessional identity of the Diocese of Pittsburgh had been consolidated during the 1990s. Elected in 1995 (after three years as canon to the ordinary), Duncan was a devotee of Loren Mead, author of *The Once and Future Church*, who asserted that the Episcopal Church's nineteenth-century structures instituted to gather resources and redistribute them to foreign fields were obsolete in an age when mission was as much a local as an international concern.[2]

A product of the General Theological Seminary, Duncan had made his mark as a university chaplain at both the University of North Carolina and the University of Delaware. Though raised an Anglo Catholic, he had been exposed to strong Evangelical student communities committed to renewal at Chapel Hill and Newark (the first question at his Chapel Hill interview had been "Are you saved?"). While he had visited Pittsburgh on only one prior occasion, he was well aware of the tensions within the

---

1. *Trinity*, September 2002.
2. Mead, *Once and Future Church*.

diocese, being warned by no less a figure than Arthur McNulty of Calvary Church that he would be "crazy to touch [the job] with a ten-foot pole."[3]

Developing a rapport with Hathaway, based, in part, on the latter's recognition that Duncan had administrative gifts that he himself lacked, Duncan believed that Episcopalians must cease to view the bishop as the sole instigator of change and emphatically committed himself to congregation-centered renewal. He spoke "all the [liturgical] languages," he says, and had a good grasp of which clergy were best suited to which parishes.[4] "[Bishop Duncan] surrounds himself with people that will take his lead and do their jobs within that kind of framework," says Donald Bushyager, one of Pittsburgh's bivocational priests and a former member of the standing committee.[5] He also sought to promote an ever-deeper relationship between the Diocese of Pittsburgh and like-minded Anglican provinces of the Global South. In consequence of this, however, the Duncan episcopate has come increasingly to be defined by things said and done outside the diocese, and attitudes for and against the bishop and the positions for which he stands have hardened. "I think he wanted the diocese to be talking to each other and more open and sharing," observes Lynn Edwards, now chaplain for Progressive Episcopalians of Pittsburgh (see below), yet such has long since ceased to be the case.[6]

AGAINST THE TIDE, 1988–1995

With the late 1980s came a growing realization that the first flush of evangelistic enthusiasm had spent itself. While some new church plants continued to grow, others languished and died, and the commitment of established parishes to the process varied considerably. "I believe that the great challenge before us is to learn to articulate our faith in the triune God," Bishop Hathaway warned the 1988 diocesan convention, "in such a way as to challenge the consciences and spirits of the many people living round about us who deeply and sincerely believe that Christianity in particular, and religion in general, are quite outmoded and irrelevant to modern life."[7] Some were more sanguine, arguing that future growth was

3. Duncan interview.
4. Ibid.
5. Bushyager interview.
6. Edwards interview.
7. *Convention Journal*, November 4–5, 1988, 32.

likely to take the form of small mission fellowships clustered with parent congregations in the river valleys and new plants in townships with significant population growth. In practice, there would be only three new church plants during the final years of Hathaway's episcopate [8]

Following the commitment to a "Decade of Evangelism" made by the member churches of the Anglican Communion at the 1988 Lambeth Conference, several Pittsburgh congregations sought to promote evangelistic outreach. In 1990, Ambridge's Church of the Savior brought a clergyman from the Diocese of Sydney (Australia)—an Evangelical bastion—to lead a weekend mission on evangelism. The following year, St. David's, Peters Township, hosted a seminar led by a former member of All Saints, Aliquippa, on sharing one's hope in Christ from an Anglican perspective.[9] What was revealing about such activities was that many of those involved tended to minimize their Anglican roots. "We have seen some inter-diocesan family relationships strained," admitted Pittsburgh's archdeacon in 1988. "We have generated some suspicions about the purity of the Anglicanism in some of the new congregations." [10]

The pronouncements of some Pittsburgh clergy did indeed point to a distinctive theological perspective. "The Episcopal Church has long needed to break out of the fortress mentality," declared Joseph Vitunic of Church of the Savior. "People have a deep need to express their faith in ways that are culturally relevant to them . . . we don't really need pipe organs and medieval dress and archaic language and music." His colleague in Hopewell, Thaddeus Barnum of Prince of Peace, was even more cursory in acknowledging his congregation's Anglican heritage. "Because we are in Jesus Christ," he said, "we are called into fellowship with one another. This is fundamentally important . . . we are not primarily united by common membership in a denomination, a style of worship, a warm feeling of happiness with church programs."[11]

An extreme example of such a perspective was found in Wexford, where St. Stephen's, Sewickley, had planted a mission in 1987. Orchard Hill specialized in tightly choreographed Sunday services, which employed contemporary music, did not use Episcopal prayer books or hymnals, and

8. *Trinity*, October 1988.
9. *Trinity*, June 1990, February 1991.
10. *Trinity*, October 1988.
11. *Trinity*, June 1992.

focused on gift-based ministry with small groups, youth ministry, and weekly seminars on marriage and relationships. The congregation never applied for parish status and refused to vest title of its property in the board of trustees.[12] While Bishop Hathaway defended its mode of operation, he became increasingly concerned about "the absence of ecclesiastic theology and [lack of] conformity with Anglicanism."[13] Orchard Hill's success was undeniable—membership grew from one hundred to one thousand over four years—and even *Episcopal Life*, the national church paper, gave it favorable exposure in December 1991. Ironically, this positive publicity came even as parish leaders were resolving to leave their denomination over the decision of that year's General Convention to permit the ordination of active homosexuals. The Diocese of Pittsburgh responded by seeking the repayment of $50,000 in grants and loans that it had made and requiring Orchard Hill to sever formal relationships with Episcopal parishes. Bishop Hathaway, while expressing regret over the final outcome, assured them of his good wishes and presided over a ceremony of separation at Trinity Cathedral.[14]

The Orchard Hill model was frequently offered as the gold standard of successful evangelism, yet rectors of small parishes were understandably perturbed at the tendency to devalue the work of their congregations. "The current 'wisdom' is that small churches are 'ineffective' and will soon go the way of the mom and pop grocery store," remarked the rector of St. Matthew's, Homestead, in 1991. "If anything, the megachurch simply caters to the consumerism of our culture and provides little depth to people's lives." An active force in the Homestead community, St. Matthew's had fought local rezoning plans and the erection of an incinerator. "To the success-oriented churches, [our modest growth] must seem like small potatoes," he concluded. "But for those of us who have worked long and hard to be faithful to Christ, this has to be one of our best victories."[15]

The financial weakness of parishes like St. Matthew's continued to pose a threat to the overall health of the diocese, however. In 1987,

12. *Trinity*, June 1989.

13. Standing Committee Minutes, March 18, 1991, RG4A/1.8, box 10DRB, Archives of the Episcopal Diocese of Pittsburgh, Pittsburgh, Pennsylvania (hereafter referenced as EDP).

14. Standing Committee Minutes, December 15–16, 1991, RG4A/1.8, box 10DRB, EDP; *Trinity*, February 1992.

15. *Trinity*, March 1991.

a one-time debt forgiveness and rebate strategy was adopted for eight parishes, but this proved a short-term solution as expenditures on aided and new parishes grew rapidly. The following year, the diocesan convention declined to seat delegates from the defaulting parishes of Holy Cross, Pittsburgh, and St. Christopher's, Warrendale—a marked departure from previous practice. A task force was set up to review the situation in 1989 (the year that St. George's, Jefferson Boro, and St. Peter's, Pittsburgh, both closed), which recommended the establishment of a mission fund to finance parishes willing to become "mission centers" carrying out designated ministries that corresponded with the spiritual gifts of their members. The long march from maintenance to mission had begun.[16]

The spring of 1988 was also marked by an unprecedented apology to members of the diocese from their bishop. While an impressive evangelist, Alden Hathaway had proved rather less skilled in the minutiae of administration. "It is painfully apparent to me," he admitted, "that over the past few years I have lost control of my calendar and my appointments. It is driven by the needs and desires for my time of a great variety of good and worthy projects, but the result is that they control me rather than I having any intentional order and design to the stewardship of my time." Hathaway promised to restrict travel and ministry outside the diocese and to make more frequent parochial visits in order to consolidate the gains achieved during the early 1980s.[17]

Discussions among the bishop's executive staff produced the recommendation that a canon to the ordinary be appointed to carry some of the administrative load. The choice ultimately fell on Robert Duncan.[18] Duncan's appointment would prove a pivotal moment in the evolution of the Diocese of Pittsburgh.[19] He quickly took charge of the strategic planning task force that had been formed to address the dysfunction within the diocesan family stemming from theological conflict within the national

16. *Convention Journal*, November 4–5, 1988, 17; *Convention Journal*, November 9, 1991, 19–21; *Trinity*, September 1990.

17. *Trinity*, May 1988.

18. Standing Committee Minutes, April 21–22, July 26, 1991, RG4A/1.8, box 10DRB, EDP; *Trinity*, September 1991.

19. *Trinity*, May 1992. Declared Hathaway in the same convention address announcing Duncan's selection: "If we are serious about evangelism and church growth, let alone concern for the continuing life and liability of almost a majority of our existing congregations, we have got to get a different idea of the deployment of our ordained professionals and the allocation of resources, both financial and real."

church. Mary Hays—the present canon missioner of the diocese—has described the form that dysfunction assumed within the clergy order when she came to Pittsburgh in the early 1990s as Trinity Episcopal School for Ministry's first female faculty member. "There was this big circle of liberals [at one clergy day]," she recalls, "and these little circles of some of the conservatives ... All the different circles were watching me to see what I looked like, what I would do, who I was. I'm sure that when I sat with the liberals [the conservatives'] suspicions were not allayed."[20]

Canon Duncan also assumed responsibility for oversight of the new forms of parish ministry that were emerging, including cluster ministries and twinned parishes served by lay leaders and nonstipendiary clergy (this being the rule rather than the exception in other parts of the Anglican Communion). "The traditional Anglican Church with its parochial system was designed to function within an established and settled Christendom," Bishop Hathaway declared in 1993. "As this Christendom melts away we are faced with another context for mission that begs another way of being the church."[21]

Duncan made frequent visits to encourage Pittsburgh parishes to build up the ability of their community to work and witness. "We will disciple, equip and empower our membership to demonstrate corporately the relevance of Christ in the Bellevue/Avalon area," read one parish mission statement, "and personally within the web of our relationships and daily decisions."[22] At St. Thomas, Gibsonia, where parochial conflict had dissuaded members from serving on the vestry, Duncan urged the parish to adopt a parish covenant that called for respect for differing opinions, the refusal to tolerate gossip, conflict resolution according to the principles enunciated in chapter 18 of the Gospel of St. Matthew, and unanimous endorsement of vestry decisions once they had been taken.[23] Some covenantal relationships extended beyond a single parish. In September 1993, parishes in North Versailles, Greensburg, Jeanette, and Scottdale came together in the Epiphany Partnership. The Greensburg parish apart, none could afford the services of a full-time priest, so the new cooperative

20. Hays interview.
21. *Convention Journal*, November 5–6, 1993, 29.
22. *Trinity*, December 1992–January 1993.
23. *Trinity*, March 1995.

arrangement ensured that all would continue to be affirmed as centers of witness and lay ministry.[24]

Another feature of the early 1990s was the expansion of Christian formation ministries beyond the Evangelical core parishes. Christ Church, North Hills, Fox Chapel Church, and St. Peter's, Butler, all launched programs that paired confirmation and baptismal candidates with prayer partners who also helped them evaluate their progress in such areas as worship, prayer, reading the Scriptures, service, and daily life.[25] Fox Chapel Church's rector, James Dix, assisted by laywoman Linda Manuel, also pioneered the cell group movement in a Pittsburgh parish. By 1994, Fox Chapel boasted ten different cell groups, including clusters for mothers, men, singles, and bicyclists! Group members were available to each other twenty-four hours a day, providing prayer and support in life traumas. Many parishioners experienced the opportunity to pray aloud for the first time in their lives.[26] This was a subject of particular interest to Robert Duncan, who described the phenomenon as "small, self-propagating, lay-led weekday fellowships for Bible Study, prayer, pastoral care and outreach."[27] In 1995, Duncan visited Holy Trinity, Brompton, in London—home parish of Evangelical theologian John Stott—and praised its commitments to prayer, an accessible liturgy, cell groups, youth ministry, and church planting.[28]

Such formation ministries were frequently viewed as the basis for further evangelism. Roberta Kenney, a candidate for ordination from St. Thomas, Gibsonia, declared that the implications of the Great Commission were frequently daunting but that she had benefited from the realization that conversion was effected by the Holy Spirit, not the witness of any individual. "No great powers of persuasion are needed in my conversations [with coworkers]," she added. "I talk about what Christ means in my life, how my life is governed by looking for God's will."[29] In contrast with Austin Pardue's reputed ambivalence toward transdenominational initiatives, Alden Hathaway welcomed the prospect of a 1993 Billy Graham

24. *Trinity*, September 1993.
25. *Trinity*, October 1989.
26. *Trinity*, April–May 1994.
27. *Trinity*, March 1994.
28. *Trinity*, March 1995.
29. *Trinity*, March 1992.

crusade in Pittsburgh and encouraged local Episcopalians to participate. "To miss out on the crusade," he declared, "would be like hearing that Christopher Columbus was about to land in the new world and failing to go down to the beach to be a part of it."[30] Chairing the crusade committee was Fred Fetterolf, a lay member of St. Stephen's, Sewickley. "When I became a Christian," Fetterolf testified, "I vowed to take my faith into the marketplace. I felt that in our mixed society a Christian should be visible ... I was always sensitive to the fact that not everyone in [the Aluminum Company of America] shared my beliefs, and I respected that."[31]

Episcopal evangelistic efforts also saw a temporary upturn in the mid-1990s. In October 1990, the Episcopal Church Missionary Committee moved its headquarters to Ambridge, where it could work in company with Trinity Episcopal School for Ministry and the South American Missionary Society (SAMS), both of them bodies with extensive missionary experience.[32] To secure the presence of any national church body in southwestern Pennsylvania—hardly an environment friendly to the national church—was a coup of which Hathaway sought to take full advantage. He became fascinated with the work of the Christian Missionary Alliance, which had developed a successful model for urban congregational reproduction in Lima, Peru, during the 1970s. After SAMS began to apply the Lima model in Honduras, Hathaway encouraged the notion that a "North American Missionary Society" might one day bring the concept to bear within the borders of the United States.[33] One member of the SAMS team that traveled to Honduras in May 1992 declared that the mission would "provide us with lessons we will need if the Decade of Evangelism is to be the preparation for serious world evangelization in the next century."[34]

Bishop Hathaway's hopes were also boosted by the announcement of the East Tennessee Initiative (ETI) in 1993. Sponsored by the Diocese of East Tennessee, the Initiative was launched at a symposium in St. Louis, Missouri, that sought both to assess the reasons for Anglicanism's decline in North America and to encourage Episcopalians to communicate their

30. *Trinity*, March 1993.
31. *Trinity*, April–May 1993.
32. *Trinity*, December 1990–January 1991.
33. *Trinity*, December 1992–January 1993.
34. *Trinity*, December 1991–January 1992.

faith to the wider world.[35] Twenty-five Pittsburghers, including Canon Duncan, attended the symposium. "We are starting to ask," Duncan later commented, "What is the mission of the church? Where is that mission chiefly carried out? What structures and resources will best serve that mission? The first set of questions seems to require a national political convention and centralized program to make answer. The second set of questions leads us to an emphasis on strong, particularized local congregations with regional resources in support."[36] ETI's director, John Shuler, later spoke at St. Martin's, Monroeville. The church was too much in love with being Episcopalian, Shuler concluded, and too little interested in leading men and women to a transformed life in Jesus Christ.[37] Six months later, he announced the formation of the North American Missionary Society "to plant Great Commission churches within the Episcopal tradition in alliance with other congregations and organizations which share the vision."[38]

By no means did all forms of ministry inspired by an Evangelical witness conform to the classic model of evangelism and conversion. One of Robert Duncan's most significant early experiences as canon to the ordinary was his first visit to St. Stephen's, Wilkinsburg, where he was struck by the extensive school facilities built at a time when the community boasted a large Episcopal population. As the demographics of Wilkinsburg shifted toward a minority population, so the congregation of St. Stephen's dwindled, yet the buildings remained. If they could be refashioned to serve the new population, then the parish had a future. "That was the character of [St. Stephen's]," Duncan declares today, "and if it did today what it was good at before, that was what God had created it to do."[39] The congregation responded positively to Duncan's suggestion and established a program for at-risk youth, with a combination of individual mentoring, group Bible study, and other activities that took the children away from the neighborhoods in which they lived. As a parish spokesman put it: "Our small mentoring program may not solve any of the ills of

---

35. *Trinity*, June 1993.
36. *Trinity*, September 1993.
37. *Trinity*, February 1994.
38. *Trinity*, June 1994.
39. Duncan interview.

society, but it will help 12 children know that they are unique and special in their own way."[40]

Ministries of healing that incorporated witness also proved of incomparable value. Perhaps the most radical example was provided by Shepherd's Heart Fellowship, which was established in Pittsburgh's Oakland district in 1993 as a laboratory mission to the homeless. Led by TESM graduates Mike and Tina Wurschmidt, who already had experience of homeless ministry, its members went out on Friday evenings after worship to minister to those living under the highways by offering them food and medical care. Eventually they graduated to a building of their own even as they continued to reach out to a community with which many Episcopalians were still imperfectly acquainted.[41]

Shepherd's Heart was unconventional but Evangelical. Equally unconventional but far from Evangelical was the renewal experiment undertaken at Grace Church, Mt. Washington. In December 1992, the rector-elect, Arnold Klukas, discussed with the vestry what could be done to save their marginal parish from closure. Klukas proposed a return to the Anglo Catholic vision of Grace's former rector, Robert Coster, by making the Book of Common Prayer Book's Rite One liturgy the principal form of worship (an unusual innovation for this generally Low Church diocese) and offering a Solemn Eucharist on a weekly basis. Klukas defended the use of historic Anglican social and religious customs to reach out to the local community, suggesting that on the Sunday after Ascension the parish's children could "Beat the Bounds" of the parish and invite local families to the church for cakes and ale, while on the Feast of Corpus Christi they would move in procession from the church to the heights of Mt. Washington to bless the city. Over the next two years, he transformed Grace into a place for spiritual direction and retreats and encouraged the formation of traditional Anglo Catholic fraternities, such as the Guild of All Souls (which provided proper vestments to needy parishes for Requiem Masses) and the Confraternity of the Blessed Sacrament. Klukas was also active in ecumenical dialogue, helping establish chapters of the Society of St. Augustine and St. Gregory (Anglican–Roman Catholic),

---

40. *Trinity*, April–May 1994.
41. *Trinity*, March 1996.

St. Alban and St. Sergius (Anglican-Orthodox), and Luther and Cranmer (Anglican-Lutheran).[42]

Such ties to the ecumenical movement were only part of a process that had been under way in Pittsburgh since the early 1980s. The dialogues first promoted by Bishop Mann and Bishop Pardue were extended during the 1980s to include the Roman Catholic Church. In 1981, the local Catholic priest attended the installation of John van Siclen as rector of Church of the Advent, Brookline. From this initial contact developed a pattern of clerical socializing and pulpit exchange that led van Siclen to promote prayers for the Catholic Diocese of Pittsburgh and Pope John Paul II within his congregation, a far cry from the suspicious manner in which Austin Pardue had once treated Episcopal relations with Rome.[43] Van Siclen later formed part of a group of clergy that met with Roman Catholic representatives to discuss their denominations' varying perspectives on such issues as ordination and ecclesiastical authority. Lynn Edwards, another participant, pointed out that the two denominations shared a common understanding of the organic nature of the Visible Church and the vital role played by the Eucharist in the church's relationship with the Divine.[44]

The closeness of the Episcopal-Catholic relationship in Pittsburgh was underlined by Alden Hathaway's personal friendship with Pittsburgh's Catholic bishop, Donald Wuerl. Both served on the board of Christian Associates, where they were united in the belief that discussion of doctrinal differences was an essential part of any ecumenical exchange and that it should take place between bishops and other judicatory heads, as well as professional theologians. "By rooting [the discussion] in the context of the local working experience," Hathaway pointed out, "the understanding and the respect of the church's beliefs would be increased and thereby the appreciation for the theological strengths of the various communions."[45] In 1988, Hathaway and Wuerl took the first steps that ultimately led to the establishment of the Christian Leaders Fellowship.[46]

---

42. *Trinity*, March 1993.
43. *Trinity*, February 1982.
44. *Trinity*, November 1982.
45. *Trinity*, October 1991.
46. *Trinity*, April–May 1997.

For the Episcopal Diocese of Pittsburgh, ecumenical discussions would also lead to a local concordat with the Southwestern Synod of the Evangelical Lutheran Church in America in 1989 (seven years before the concordat between the national churches), and Bishop Donald McCoid of the Southwestern Synod concelebrated with Hathaway at the diocesan convention. "[We are] not members of two different denominations," Hathaway told convention delegates, "but dear brothers and sisters in Christ bound by a common mandate to proclaim the Gospel to an unbelieving and broken world."[47] It is important to note here, however, that those who participated in the local dialogue were much more conservative than the average Episcopalian or Lutheran in the pew.[48]

By no means was every ecumenical initiative promoted from above. Pittsburgh Episcopalians made a direct contribution to grassroots ecumenism. An attendee at the 1990 Procession of Witness for Christian Unity in Brookline remarked upon the participation of Lutherans, Methodists, Presbyterians, and Catholics. "I have lived in Brookline for most of my life," he remarked "and, for the first time I shared a Christian experience with neighbors I have known for 30 years."[49] Church leaders from different denominations jointly sponsored a "Servant School" to help laypeople develop skills in ministry.[50] St. Peter's, Uniontown, shared a vacation Bible school with a Lutheran church of the same name (the Episcopalians provided the space and the Lutherans supplied the teachers), while Emmanuel Church on the North Side had a similar arrangement with local Methodist congregations.[51] Another Lutheran-Episcopal initiative was the cooperative weekly Bible study jointly sponsored by their respective congregations in Charleroi.[52] Perhaps most innovative of all was LARC (Lutheran, Anglican, and Roman Catholic), a coalition of three Brackenridge churches, which offered a youth ministry for some sixty local children from all three traditions.[53]

---

47. *Convention Journal*, November 9–10, 1989, 17–19, 30 (quotation).
48. Fairfield/Rodgers interview.
49. *Trinity*, May 1990.
50. *Trinity*, February 1991.
51. *Trinity*, October 1991, May–June 1995.
52. *Trinity*, May–June 1995.
53. *Trinity*, December 1994–January 1995.

Youth ministry would be a centerpiece of Canon Duncan's agenda. Starting in the early 1970s, a generation of diocesan youth leaders had been formed through Happening, a Cursillo-like ministry for high school students. "What I learned was to trust the Lord completely," declared Amy Fish, a participant in a 1980 Happening. "I had never taken that one step and put all my weight upon it, but I did. I was scared to death to give the talk [to forty people], but once I got up there and said the first few words, I was at ease, just like I wasn't scared."[54] Bishop Hathaway, however, remained concerned that provision for college ministry showed up poorly by comparison. In 1982, a new plan for student ministry in Pittsburgh was proposed that would allow the three parishes in Pittsburgh's Oakland and Squirrel Hill districts—St. Peter's, Church of the Ascension, and Church of the Redeemer—to minister to the student populations at the University of Pittsburgh and Carnegie Mellon University.[55]

The new campus ministry, though involving multiple models of ministry, was intended to be "a Christ-centered ministry in the Anglican tradition, rather than an evangelistic or sacrament-based approach." St. Peter's was invited to focus on international students, while Ascension's Canterbury Fellowship provided a biblically based approach that included Bible study, retreats, and worship. Church of the Redeemer, meanwhile, employed a more sacrament-based model. It also established a chaplaincy at Carnegie Mellon, which had previously lacked such an institution.[56] In 1987, Hathaway invited the diocesan youth department to lead the clergy retreat and brought in Reid Carpenter of the Pittsburgh Leadership Foundation to speak on the special problems of contemporary youth.[57] Concern for college ministry persisted into the 1990s. Diocesan leaders encouraged parishes based in college towns to work with the diocese jointly to fund a canon missioner to oversee such work.[58] In 1995, Trinity, Washington, organized a student fellowship on the campus of Washington and Jefferson College as part of its plan for parish renewal.[59]

54. *Trinity*, January 1981.

55. "Proposal for an East End Cooperative Campus Ministry for 1983," February 12, 1982, Diocesan Council Minutes, RG4A/2.1:1, box 1DC, EDP.

56. Ibid.

57. *Trinity*, September 1987.

58. *Trinity*, June 1990.

59. *Trinity*, October 1995.

Hathaway's successor proved equally committed to youth programs. "If it hadn't been for [the parish church where I grew up]," Duncan attests today, "I think I would not only have emotionally died but I would have physically died."[60] On the eve of his consecration as bishop of Pittsburgh, Duncan invited one hundred high school students to share in his vigil.[61] It was Duncan who in 1994 obtained grants for vacation Bible schools in six parishes and who worked with Charles Rosemeyer—a Presbyterian minister who believed that many children's programs were good at drawing children in and deepening their faith, but few were effective at fostering discipleship—to develop age-specific parish youth programs across the diocese.[62] In 1997, some discussion even took place as to the feasibility of establishing an Episcopal day school in eastern Pittsburgh, but interest in the project proved too low for the diocese to consider pursuing it.[63]

At the diocesan level, a new status quo might be emerging, yet the early 1990s also marked a period at which the Episcopal Church had begun to adopt a course very different from dioceses like Pittsburgh. Just returned from attending the 1988 Lambeth Conference, Alden Hathaway warned that year's diocesan convention of the threat posed to the spiritual authority of the church by the election of Barbara Harris as suffragan bishop of Massachusetts, the first woman to hold such an office. Given that the Anglican Communion was far from united on the question of women bishops and that the episcopate had been recognized as one of the bases of Anglican unity from the Chicago-Lambeth Quadrilateral onward, Hathaway foresaw trouble ahead.[64] The standing committee, meeting a few weeks later, expressed a similar concern and refused to approve Harris's election, but Hathaway nevertheless gave his episcopal consent, arguing that the ministry of women was a matter of discipline and order rather than of doctrine. The mission of evangelism, he added, had, until recently, been impaired by the exclusion of women. While disagreeing

---

60. Duncan interview.

61. *Trinity*, June 1996. "The significance of the night allowed many to renew a deep commitment to Christ," declared Brian Wallace of Church of the Ascension, "while it forced others to deal with tough personal issues. The new bishop set a precedent of love and commitment that will long be remembered by these kids as they become adult members of the diocese."

62. *Trinity*, September 1994, April–May 1995.

63. *Trinity*, December 1997–January 1998.

64. *Convention Journal*, November 4–5, 1988, 29–36.

with many of Harris's ideas, Hathaway insisted that her consecration could be contained within the limits of Anglican diversity.[65] He did later concede, however, that Harris's installation had been "at the same time, an occasion of great joy to many within our church and great sorrow to many others; a sign of the unity of our ministry made complete and a sign of that unity shattered."[66]

Within the diocese, Episcopalians were similarly conflicted as to the long-term implications of Anglicanism's first female bishop. Lise Hildebrandt, a woman priest from Pittsburgh, attended the service of consecration and was deeply moved by the experience: "Listening to the Scriptures and the preacher, seeing Bishop Harris and the presence of the multitudes, hearing the music which lifted up and wove together the traditional English, the contemporary, the Black heritages, feeling the incredible powerful presence of the Spirit," she wrote, "I have no doubt that God has indeed led our church to this new step in history, and has indeed found a bishop in Barbara Harris."[67] Conservatives pointed out that the standing committee—which included two women—had *unanimously* withheld consent and that it was not simply Harris's gender but her theology that was at issue. In another sign of diocesan divisions, ten clergy and eight laymen from southwestern Pennsylvania attended the inaugural meeting of the Episcopal Synod of America, organized in 1989 to uphold the integrity of the catholic position regarding an all-male presbyterate.[68]

Rejection of episcopal consents by Pittsburgh's standing committee was becoming increasingly common. In December 1990, it refused to consent to any candidate without viewing the biographical material and position papers distributed at the nominating convention. "Since an elected Bishop is consecrated for the entire church," its members explained, "and since the consent of the Standing Committee is not to be considered as a pro-forma exercise, but as the working of the will of the Holy Spirit throughout the entire church, the committee is establishing this procedure in order to have a more accurate view of persons for whom they are being asked to consent to be consecrated Bishops in our church."[69] For

65. Standing Committee Minutes, November 21, 1988, January 16, 1989, RG4A/1.8, box 10DRB, EDP.
66. *Trinity*, March 1989.
67. *Trinity*, May 1989.
68. *Trinity*, June 1989, September 1989.
69. Standing Committee Minutes, December 9, 1990, RG4A/1.8, box 10DRB, EDP.

conservatives, the necessity of such scrutiny was only confirmed by the controversial pronouncements of such figures as Bishop John Spong of Newark, who made an appearance on the television program *Pittsburgh Talking* in 1989.[70] Two years later, Alden Hathaway took his Newark counterpart to task: "Bishop Spong dismisses the biblical doctrines of the Incarnation, Trinity, Fall and Atonement as being irrelevant to the thought patterns of the contemporary world view. Perhaps he is right about that modern creation, but the problem is with *our* generation, *not* with the Bible... There is a battle for the Bible going on in the church and in the culture. Though he is wrong about the authority of Holy Scripture, we are indebted to Bishop Spong for identifying the fundamental issue among us, this 'mother of controversy.'"[71]

The 1990s witnessed a series of confrontations over episcopal elections, in which the question of ecclesiastical authority was always at issue. In 1992, the standing committee initially approved the election of Jane Dixon as suffragan bishop of Washington; three members were absent, however, and the standing committee requested further information. A month later it refused consent, with two of its members apparently changing their votes.[72] While two Anglo Catholic bishops—Jack Iker and Keith Ackerman (a former priest of the diocese)—were approved in 1992 and 1994, with only one dissenting vote, an ominous trend was noted in 1993 when James Jelinek, the bishop-elect of Minnesota, was reported to have presided over a parish in San Francisco that had blessing ceremonies for same-sex unions. The standing committee refused consent and Bishop Hathaway joined them in their action, stating that Jelinek's expressed intention to ignore the decisions of the General Convention "breaks the covenant we have as bishops together, and greatly impairs the unity and the authority of the church."[73] Three more women bishops—Catherine Roskam, Geralyn Wolf, and Carolyn Irish—were the subjects of refused consents in 1995 and 1996, giving some the impression that the refusals represented a lingering hostility to the principle of a woman bishop.

70. Standing Committee Minutes, April 24, 1989, RG4A/1.8, box 10DRB, EDP. Hathaway told the standing committee that he preferred to use the media to present issues of faith and belief rather than indulge in a "media-styled debate."

71. *Trinity*, March 1991.

72. Standing Committee Minutes, August 4, September 28, 1992, RG4A/1.8, box 10DRB, EDP.

73. *Trinity*, October 1993, November 1993 (quotation).

In the case of Wolf, at least, standing committee members made it clear that their disapproval was "based solely on her stance on the issue of ordination of practicing homosexuals."[74] A line in the sand had been drawn.

Homosexuality was no new controversy for Episcopalians, but it had gained fresh traction during the early 1990s as progressives sought to shift the stance of the church toward an acceptance of homosexual relationships as a valid expression of Christian sexuality. Pittsburgh Episcopalians had established St. Aelred House to care for AIDS sufferers in 1989, and Bishop Hathaway had paid several visits to the facility, but matters of sex education and clerical discipline were a different issue.[75] A bitter debate at the 1988 diocesan convention concluded with passage of a resolution that questioned the "objectivity and theological soundness" of a national study guide on sexuality and called for a greater emphasis on chastity and fidelity.[76] The standing committee also rejected a candidate for ordination because it was unconvinced that he would commit to the 1979 General Convention position on sexual standards for the clergy (though it released him as a candidate in good standing to seek ordination elsewhere).[77] It was also forced to wrestle with the issue of a noncanonically resident priest serving in a Pittsburgh parish who was known to be living in an active homosexual relationship, though this was ultimately resolved privately.[78]

It was events beyond southwestern Pennsylvania, however, that were increasingly to shape how diocesan leaders understood their role within the Episcopal Church and the Anglican Communion as a whole. In 1990, the standing committee had bitterly opposed the ordination of an active homosexual by Bishop Spong, accusing its Newark counterpart of precipitate action in defiance both of Scripture and the prevailing mind of the General Convention. Although that candidate was later forced to resign, it was clear that in Newark, at least, this was only the beginning.[79] William Frey, former bishop of Colorado and president of TESM,

---

74. Standing Committee Minutes, November 2, 1995, November 20, 1995 (quotation), January 29, 1996, RG4A/1.8, box 10DRB, EDP.

75. *Trinity*, February 1989.

76. *Convention Journal*, November 4–5, 1988, 25–26.

77. Standing Committee Minutes, October 21, 1991, RG4A/1.8, box 10DRB, EDP.

78. Standing Committee Minutes, November 21, December 19, 1994, RG4A/1.8, box 10DRB, EDP.

79. Standing Committee Minutes, January 15, 1990, RG4A/1.8, box 10DRB, EDP; *Trinity*, March 1990.

warned that every Episcopalian had a stake in the debate over sexuality and that there was a difference between what was legally permissible and what the church should sanction: "In short, there is a wide difference between what a society—or a Church—can tolerate in terms of individual behavior and what that same society or Church must support as desirable. Such an understanding seems to me profoundly biblical. Jesus did not condemn the woman taken in adultery, but did advise her to go and sin no more."[80] When a presentment was brought against Spong's assistant bishop, former Pittsburgh priest Walter Righter, for ordaining another active homosexual, it was inevitable that Alden Hathaway should be one of the ten bishops who endorsed it. Hathaway later explained that he desired to clarify the process by which church order and accountability were maintained. "In the crucial area of human sexual relations," he argued, "it is intolerable that the witness of the church be ambiguous, confusing or deceptive. Whatever the short-term gain in tolerance and justice, the long term consequences will be loss of moral authority."[81]

Even before the presentment was introduced, many Pittsburgh Episcopalians had been expressing frustration with the state of the church. Typical was a 1993 article by James Simons, rector of St. Michael's Church, Ligonier, which appeared in the newsletter *Anglican Opinion*. Simons poured scorn on the failure of the Episcopal Church to play an active role in mission work since the centralization of its operations in the early 1920s. Although he emphasized the inability of the national church to send missionaries abroad, Simons also argued that the national assessment *inhibited* the active parochial ministry of his parish, which included the provision of health insurance for two hundred children ineligible for government programs and an education program for the unemployed. "The ministry of 815 Second Avenue [the church headquarters] may be viable," he concluded, "but who knows? Communication is weak at best and what we do receive are liturgies that portray Columbus as an evil oppressor and educational materials that teach that a gay life-style should be honored. We seldom get to hear about the work of overseas missionaries. I have never seen a report that shows a correlation between what we send to New York and how lives are being changed."[82]

80. *Trinity*, June 1991.

81. Standing Committee Minutes, February 20, 1995, RG4A/1.8, box 10DRB, EDP; *Trinity*, February 1996 (quotation).

82. Simons's article, entitled "Parish-Eye View of Ministry and Structure," was reprinted in *Trinity*, September 1993.

If monies consigned to 815 were likely to be "wasted," what attitude ought the faithful Christian to adopt in relation to the national assessment? Pittsburgh Episcopalians first addressed this issue in 1991, when Mark Lawrence, rector of St. Stephen's, McKeesport, presented to diocesan convention delegates what came to be known as the Werner-Simons resolution. This required the diocesan treasurer to tell parishes what proportion of their assessment went to the national church and, if so requested, to redirect it to the support of either the Diocese of Chile, the Presiding Bishop's Fund for World Relief, or the United Thank Offering. Lawrence took the opportunity to criticize the House of Bishops for failing to censure those statements of some of its more colorful members that impaired the unity of the church. A majority of delegates apparently agreed with him, for the resolution passed by 133 votes to 77.[83]

A significant minority of Pittsburgh Episcopalians did not share Simons's views. The vestry of Christ Church, North Hills, expressed sorrow at the decision to permit withholding and the vestry of Calvary Church followed suit, calling it a poor example of Christian stewardship that punished church programs rather than leaders.[84] In 1992, sixteen of the sixty-four parishes took advantage of the new provision, diverting almost $100,000 from the national church, two-thirds of this amount going to the Diocese of Chile. Certain parishes, such as St. Stephen's, Sewickley, and St. Martin's, Monroeville, gave their entire offering to the Diocese of Chile, while others split their money between multiple beneficiaries in an effort to propitiate their entire parish family. The loss due to withholding (which also occurred in three Texas dioceses) was enough to concern national church leaders, who feared it might herald a trend.[85]

The divisions within the diocese were becoming evident at all levels of church life. In 1989, the standing committee adopted a rule giving its president the right to veto any statement about its actions that other members might wish to issue.[86] Later that year, the bishop asked the standing committee to "establish guidelines for unity, cooperation and respect in view of the controversial issues that exist in the diocese that will keep the diocese in a position to start new congregations and be credible in that

83. *Convention Journal*, November 9, 1991, 28–30.

84. Standing Committee Minutes, December 15–16, 1991, RG4A/1.8, box 10DRB, EDP; *Trinity*, February 1992.

85. *Trinity*, April 1992.

86. Standing Committee Minutes, January 16, 1989, RG4A/1.8, box 10DRB, EDP.

effort."[87] A founding member of the Irenaeus Fellowship, which brought together members of the House of Bishops concerned about the theological drift of the Episcopal Church, Hathaway made no secret of where he stood. After bitter exchanges at the 1991 General Convention revealed the degree of dysfunction within the body politic, he became more active in seeking change. "Unless the bishops honestly and directly face the root issues that divide us, as they divide the church," he opined in March 1992, "no amount of process management or interpersonal management can establish working relationships that will provide the pastoral leadership our church desperately needs."[88]

Pittsburgh progressives agreed with Hathaway about the degree of polarization, but felt that conservatives had an obligation to recognize that majority opinion within the Episcopal Church was against them. Through open letters and public forums, they sought to rally those who shared their convictions.[89] In November 1992, Presiding Bishop Edmond Browning visited the diocese, where he called for all Episcopalians to remain in charitable fellowship even as they wrestled with divisive issues. He nevertheless conceded the extent of the crisis that faced the church. "I know that there are people," he declared in his homily at Calvary, "who feel that unlike Jacob, who found a desolate place and discovered it was holy, we have taken a holy place and made it desolate."[90]

While the 1994 General Convention—which Robert Duncan described as focused less on sexuality and more on mission than those of 1985, 1988, and 1991—elected Dean George Werner of Trinity Cathedral as vice president of the House of Deputies, the diocese remained seriously divided.[91] Nor were conservatives entirely united. At Stephen's, Sewickley, from which John Guest had retired as rector in 1990 to focus on nationwide crusades, a minority began to object to what they saw as a lessening focus on "assertive, direct evangelism of unbelievers." Eventually they organized a new church in 1995, to which they then invited Guest to return. Although St. Stephen's signed a covenant to remain in Christian fellowship with those who formed what became Christ Church, Grove Farm,

---

87. Standing Committee Minutes, September 18, 1989, RG4A/1.8, box 10DRB, EDP.
88. *Trinity*, March 1991, March 1992 (quotation).
89. *Trinity*, May 1992, September 1992.
90. *Trinity*, November 1992.
91. *Trinity*, October 1994.

the affair had unhappy echoes of Orchard Hill.⁹² At his final diocesan convention, Bishop Hathaway reflected sadly on recent clergy departures from his diocese to other Anglican bodies in the area:

> We will live side by side with the new churches. We will allow them to define themselves in their separation. We will, however, hold them to the same accountability that we do ourselves; obedient to the great commission to go to the unchurched rather than to prey upon the discontent of other flocks of the fold of Christ . . . In a generation or two, these groups will come home again I pray, and our children, perhaps our grandchildren, will enjoy a wonderful American Pan-Anglicanism in full communion with the other provinces of our distinguished world church, to the glory of our Lord who prayed that we all might be one.⁹³

Hathaway's retirement proved the occasion for yet more controversy within the diocese, as the slate of candidates initially presented for bishop coadjutor did not include Robert Duncan (according to Duncan, the national church had sought to discourage local candidates in episcopal elections). When the nominating committee decided that he had not made the final cut, many people in the diocese—including some theological opponents—pressed to be allowed to put his name in nomination. Duncan instructed them to proceed with the nominating process and if they were still unsatisfied, he would accept nomination from the floor. The day before the election he signed the papers.⁹⁴ Though one candidate was a former Pittsburgher, Duncan carried the clergy order on the second ballot and was elected on the third with 61 of 102 clerical votes and 100 of 169 lay votes. "There was an incredible spectrum of people who came together for this election," declared one clergy delegate, "from conservative Episcopalians to social action-oriented people—because Bob encourages you to do the very best job of proclaiming the Gospel you can, in the particular place you find yourself."⁹⁵

92. Guest interview; *Trinity*, September 1995 (quotation); Standing Committee Minutes, November 2, 1995, RG4A/1.8, box 10DRB, EDP. Former diocesan evangelist Donald Wilson later joined the new congregation. Standing Committee Minutes, July 15, 1996, RG4A/1.8, box 10DRB, EDP.

93. *Convention Journal*, November 1995, 39–40.

94. Duncan interview.

95. Standing Committee Minutes, November 2, 1995, RG4A/1.8, box 10DRB, EDP; *Convention Journal*, December 2, 1995, 33–35; *Trinity*, December 1995–January 1996 (quotations).

BUILDING GLOBAL PARTNERSHIPS, 1996-2000

"[This] election," the newly elected bishop of Pittsburgh mused in February 1996, "was not so much about me as about us. One of the roots of this election is surely the great commitment to mission that we have built together in these last few years. Together we have accepted the truth that God has called us (as individuals and congregations) to be missionaries where we are, and we have become convinced that the mission field is all around us."[96] The missionary focus would be underpinned by a more comprehensive structure than had been the case under Alden Hathaway, given Duncan's administrative gifts. Among his early initiatives were a call for further simplification of diocesan bureaucracy, the scheduling of monthly meetings with clergy in their districts, and redoubled encouragement for lay leaders. What was required, the new bishop insisted, was "a more fluid, less static structure. We need to build structures that can respond quickly when that's needed." Parish life needed to be distinguished by dynamic worship, unbounded prayer, personal knowledge of Jesus, costly love, apostolic engagement, and sacrificial outreach. Duncan also called for a continued focus on partnerships between parishes, with missionaries and foreign dioceses, and on such evangelistic initiatives as Cursillo and the Alpha Course.[97] To promote this vision, Duncan selected Mary Hays—then a professor at TESM—as canon missioner of the diocese in 1998. Her task was to assist parishes with developing the latent abilities of their members in order that they might become "fruitful."[98]

Although Duncan continued to support the work of the North American Missionary Society, by 1996 its founder, John Shuler, had frankly declared that the Decade of Evangelism had been a failure. Only one hundred new churches had been established in United States, when a goal of one thousand had been set by the 1991 General Convention. What was needed, insisted Shuler, was a passion and desire for growth, something that required an emphasis on people rather than buildings.[99] The North American Missionary Society did lend its assistance to such Pittsburgh initiatives as Incarnation Fellowship in Robinson Township. An "equip-

---

96. *Trinity*, February 1996.

97. *Trinity*, December 1996-January 1997 (quotation); *Convention Journal*, November 7-8, 1997, 29-33.

98. Hays interview.

99. *Trinity*, June 1996.

ping ministry," Incarnation sought to establish a "chain of servanthood" based on cell groups of from five to twelve members who met for a weekly Eucharist and committed themselves to evangelizing the unchurched.[100] A similar initiative—the Western Pennsylvania Missionary Society—was launched by Neal Brown, rector of St. Martin's, Monroeville, and three of his parish families who felt called to preach the Gospel to the unchurched of Penn Hills. Brown received diocesan funding to erect an Episcopal ministry center to serve families who had recently moved into the area.[101]

Elsewhere, a number of innovative evangelistic techniques were introduced. A missionary tool employed by parishioners at Christ Church, Brownsville, was the "Jesus Video"—a presentation on the life of Christ—which they distributed to their neighbors.[102] A new focus on the young and unchurched brought St. Philip's Church, Moon Township, back from near extinction, as membership jumped from sixty to two hundred in just two years. Parishioners participated in a "6 in '96" prayer ministry, during which they prayed for six unchurched friends for one minute each day. "These evangelism relationships are like plants," declared the rector of St. Philip's. "They need a little water every day. If they don't get watered, they'll die."[103] In January 1996, Church of the Ascension became the first Pittsburgh parish to sponsor an Alpha Course, a program that introduced the unchurched to the basics of the Christian faith. Parishes in Sewickley, Monroeville, and Murrysville announced plans to follow suit, while the diocese, together with the local Catholic, Lutheran, and Presbyterian judicatories, sponsored an Alpha Training Course.[104] In 2000, St. Paul's Church, Kittanning, hosted the first Faith Alive weekend in several years. "Faith Alive has been a tool to bring life to faith—both individually and corporately—to people and congregations across the land," declared Bishop Duncan. "I commend the movement enthusiastically."[105]

Study groups also experienced something of a renaissance. Within a year, the number of prayer groups at St. Michael's Church, Ligonier, increased from one to three. "A small group takes you from a casual social

100. *Trinity*, February 1996.
101. *Trinity*, October 1998.
102. *Trinity*, February 1996.
103. *Trinity*, November 1996.
104. *Trinity*, December 1996–January 1997.
105. *Trinity*, December 2000–January 2001.

relationship to a more intimate relationship," reported one participant.[106] At St. Stephen's Church, McKeesport, the rector, Mark Lawrence, reported spectacular growth in his largely blue-collar parish thanks to a more Bible-oriented approach that included two discussion groups.[107] The rector of Church of the Ascension, Doug McGlynn, also promoted home fellowship groups. By 1997, the parish included twenty such groups, four of them student fellowships and the rest located in communities stretching from Morningside to Monroeville. "The home group allows [my wife and me] to feel more a part of the body of Christ," declared a physician at North Side Christian Health Center.[108]

Accompanying such missionary initiatives was the development of a system of parish partnerships, which, it was hoped, would resolve some of the structural problems of the small marginal parish. Participating parishes had to be located within fifty minutes of each other to permit joint staff meetings and pulpit exchanges; the struggling parish was required to reach self-sufficiency within six years; and the stronger parish pledged to continue to respect the weaker parish's identity. Five such arrangements existed by 1998: St. Paul's, Mt. Lebanon, and Grace, Mt. Washington; Fox Chapel Church and St. Paul's, Kittanning; St. Stephen's, Sewickley, and St. Philip's, Moon Township; Christ Church, North Hills, and All Saints, Brighton Heights; and St. Michael's, Ligonier, and St. Francis, Somerset.[109]

An increasingly popular alternative to parish partnerships was Canon Nine Ministry, a program originally developed for remote rural settings like Alaska to free small congregations from reliance on the clergy placement system. This national canon permitted the "setting apart" of men and women as locally ordained priests and deacons, bypassing the general ordination process. In Pittsburgh, responsibility for coordinating the small communities' initiative and developing ministry support teams passed to Linda Manuel, who had previously been involved with cell

---

106. *Trinity*, February 1996.

107. *Trinity*, February 1997. "If Christians do the sometimes unglamorous but faithful work, in most cases the church will grow," declared Mark Lawrence, "even in places where many people think it will not. [What is faithful work?] Faithful preaching of the Scripture, God-Centered worship that is sensitive to the needs of the people, and steady, balanced parish ministry by both priest and lay people."

108. *Trinity*, March 1997.

109. *Trinity*, May 1998.

group ministry at Fox Chapel Church.[110] In October 1997, the congregations in Aliquippa and Donora (both depressed mill towns) covenanted to become "total ministry" parishes. Canon Nine Ministry, explained David Ritter of All Saints, Aliquippa, followed logically from the baptismal covenant. "Being a Christian is a 24-hour-a-day calling," he explained. "After all, most ministry takes place at home or school or in the work place. The sacramental is just one aspect."[111]

Complementing this parochial shift was the changing character of the permanent diaconate. At Bishop Duncan's initiative, deacons came to be understood as "gatherers of human resources" who required systematic training. A deacon formation board was established and completion of accredited seminary courses was required. The composition of the diaconate, which had been heavily female in the early days, became more gender balanced as men entered the ministry, and the average age of Pittsburgh's deacons also declined. The then archdeacon, Greg Malley, took the line that every parish should have one deacon, with the larger parishes supporting two or three. He also sought to root out the older notion that deacons represented a "lesser" order of ministry. On one occasion this even brought him into conflict with the bishop, when the latter proposed that the deacons surrender their vote at diocesan convention because only priests were called to the counsels of the church. Malley eventually secured a compromise position: that deacons would refrain from casting a vote unless on a matter that their conscience required them to do so.[112]

In an era marked by intra-diocesan tension, it is well to recall that Robert Duncan was not above working with those who violently disagreed with some of his theological stands. Perhaps the most revealing example of this was the support he lent—as canon to the ordinary—to the formation of the commission on racism in 1993. The commission sought to encourage Episcopalians to undertake such tasks as mentoring, patronage of minority businesses, and working to ensure equal access to housing.[113] Bishop Duncan frequently called attention to the racial divisions in the wider community and praised the efforts of congregations to reach across

110. *Trinity*, April–May 1997.
111. *Trinity*, October 1997.
112. Malley interview.
113. *Trinity*, December 1993–January 1994.

that divide.[114] In 1998, the commission on racism organized the first diocesan Absalom Jones Day celebration at Trinity Cathedral, which was followed by seminars on inequality and injustice, racism in the workplace, and affirmative action in college admissions.[115] One commission objective was to ensure proportionate representation of racial groups at all levels of diocesan life, although a letter distributed to parishes in 2000 seeking the names of minority members with leadership potential brought the embarrassing admission from some suburban parishes that they had no minority members. Bishop Duncan went so far as to pledge to implement antiracism training in the diocese, despite having unsuccessfully opposed making it *mandatory* at the General Convention. Commission member Wanda Guthrie praised Duncan's role in encouraging minority leadership. "I'm amazed at how far we've come with the help of the bishop to fill positions in the diocese," she declared in 2000.[116]

For all this amicability, divisions in the diocese were not lessening. In 1996, hostility toward many of the programs of the national church led the rectors of St. Stephen's, Sewickley, and Church of the Ascension, Pittsburgh, to inform the diocesan council that the manner in which the diocese collected national assessments was fundamentally coercive. Since a failure to meet the *national* assessment was treated as a comprehensive default to the diocese, a parish that refused to pay the national assessment might lose out on diocesan program and development grants. Leaders of the protesting parishes proposed that the diocesan and national components be separated and parishes be allowed to pay their national assessment directly, redirecting it to appropriate outreach programs if they felt unable, in conscience, to fund the national church.[117]

So controversial was this proposal that the diocesan newspaper solicited the views of eight prominent members of the diocese, four in support and four opposed. Among the clergy, Rodgers Wood, rector of Christ Church, North Hills, squared off against James Simons, rector of St. Michael's Church, Ligonier, with the latter arguing that it would be as wrong to compel a parish to fund the national church as for a vestry to dictate what a member should give. "Leadership," Wood responded, "needs

---

114. *Trinity*, December 1996–January 1997.
115. *Trinity*, March 1998.
116. *Trinity*, October 2000.
117. *Trinity*, February 1996.

to be encouraged, not constantly attacked, as has become the fashion in our culture." Writing from the perspective of a member of the executive council of the Episcopal Church, Dean George Werner maintained that he wanted the conservative critics to indicate their concerns about specific national programs.[118]

Laymen had equally strong opinions. James McGough of Calvary Church, a member of the board of trustees, objected to the fact that the "missions" proposed by conservatives were not restricted either to programs sponsored by the Episcopal Church or to those that served constituencies in southwestern Pennsylvania. "Our national church is a great gift to us in America from the people of the Anglican Communion," he concluded. "I hope we never lose a vision of what, in turn, our national church can mean to the world." From the conservative side, Donald Bushyager, a member of the standing committee, observed that believers who, after biblically based discernment, had determined that a ministry was not in conformity with God's Word had a moral obligation not to support it. David Hennesey, senior warden of St. Stephen's, Sewickley, added that financial withholding might achieve some of the changes that the renewal movement had hitherto failed to accomplish. "As support for the national church becomes voluntary," he concluded, "its leadership will become more responsive to dioceses, parishes and, most importantly, to the individuals who give."[119]

The debate at the 1996 diocesan convention was heated, with Harold Lewis, rector of Calvary Church—a former official of the national church—expressing concern about the impact of withholding on program funding and Rodgers Wood noting satirically that if the principle of "no coercion" was a good one, should it not also be applied to diocesan assessments? For the proposal, Douglas McGlynn, rector of Church of the Ascension, reiterated that the national canons did not *require* support for the national church, while William Rodewald, a lay member of St. Stephen's, Sewickley, called voluntary withholding the "best compromise available."[120] By the spring of 1997, twenty-five parishes were redirecting their apportionment in the amount of $83,057, with the diocesan council

---

118. *Trinity*, March 1996.
119. Ibid.
120. *Convention Journal*, November 1–2, 1996, 20–21.

designating forty-one appropriate domestic and foreign missions as alternative recipients.[121]

In September 1997, Bishop Duncan met with the bishops of other Episcopal dioceses in Pennsylvania and with the rectors of the more liberal parishes—Calvary Church; St. Andrew's, Pittsburgh; and Church of the Redeemer, Pittsburgh—to discuss how Episcopal leaders might work through the issues dividing the church.[122] Diocesan tensions were embarrassingly revealed shortly after the launch of the new diocesan e-mail list in exchanges that disturbed many laymen. Bishop Duncan also declared that discussions at the 1997 clergy conference had been marked by "a fundamental theological fracture over the interpretation of Scripture." He added that while he still expected clergy to hold to the traditional standard of celibacy outside marriage and fidelity within it, and would not permit same-sex blessings, he believed that the time had come for a dialogue on human sexuality in the diocese to understand "the passion and compassion that drive the biblical and theological sources of our fundamentally separated positions." He also indicated that he would be willing to provide alternative sources of episcopal support for those parishes that disagreed with him.[123]

As preparations for the decennial meeting of the Lambeth Conference got under way in 1998, it became clear that conservatives in the United States looked to the Global South in resisting cultural and theological innovation in the United States. Evidence of their concerns was provided by Bishop Spong, who issued his notorious *Twelve Theses* early that year. After the standing committee had discussed Spong's declaration in May, Bishop Duncan issued a formal rebuttal. "The incarnation and atoning sacrifice of Jesus Christ are denied [in the *Twelve Theses*];" he declared, "the efficacy of prayer and the work of the Holy Spirit are declared null; scripture and creeds are no longer trustworthy guides … What John Spong proposes as a reformed Christianity abandons every revealed essential. It is not Christianity. It is a counterfeit."[124] For the progressives, Rodgers Wood retorted that the bishop of Newark had not abandoned Christianity

---

121. *Trinity*, March 1997.

122. Standing Committee Minutes, September 15, 1997, RG4A/1.8, box 10DRB, EDP.

123. *Trinity*, November 1997.

124. Standing Committee Minutes, May 18, 1998, RG4A/1.8, box 10DRB, EDP; *Trinity*, June 1998.

or God, but only the "propositional theology" that supported it, and that he was writing for the disaffected Christian for whom theology meant little: "The prime value of the Christian experience is to speak of God relationally and simply. We can do this because in Jesus we see everything that we need to know about God. Also in Jesus we know that God has experienced and understands the limits of humanity. That is a breathtaking idea, and sufficient. It is not necessary for us to explain the how and why. The doctrine can be safely left behind." Wood maintained that his bishop was suffering from "doctrinal certainty" and expressed the wish that he were more open to dialogue with the likes of Bishop Spong.[125]

Spong's *Theses* were the opening salvo in the struggle that would take place at Lambeth in June 1998. From the beginning, Bishop Duncan had believed that Lambeth 1998 would be "determinative in outlining matters that cannot be changed, in redefining the nature of the Communion as truly global, and in reestablishing the balance (and the means) by which autonomous national churches are sacrificially submitted to one another." The Thirteenth Conference, Duncan declared, emphasized the necessary limits on the autonomy of national churches, compared with the Twelfth Conference's (1988) acceptance of provincial freedom to disagree. The authority of the primates had increased and the possibility of intervention by the archbishop of Canterbury in the affairs of other provinces had been conceded. The overall effect had been to show that the Diocese of Pittsburgh was in "the mainstream of worldwide Anglicanism." Throughout the conference, Duncan met with African bishops trained at TESM, representatives of Pittsburgh-based agencies like SAMS and the Church Army, and prominent individuals like Stephen Noll, then academic dean at TESM.[126] As invitations for Duncan to address audiences around the world flooded into the diocese, the standing committee confronted the question of how to balance the bishop's diocesan responsibilities against his new role as "spokesman for orthodox perspectives within the larger Anglican Communion."[127]

The African connections that Bishop Duncan cultivated at the Lambeth Conference were hardly the first that the diocese had established. Episcopalians had been active in the struggle against apartheid in South

---

125. *Trinity*, September 1998.
126. Ibid.
127. Standing Committee Minutes, June 21, 1999, RG4A/1.8, box 10DRB, EDP.

Africa. In 1982, the Diocese of Pittsburgh sent a youth delegation to South Africa, where its members introduced South Africans to the concept of Happening. While some African Americans in the diocese criticized the trip, Bishop Hathaway pointed out that it had been privately funded and was intended to stand in solidarity with the antiapartheid stance of the Anglican Church of South Africa.[128] Over the next seven years, twenty-one Happenings took place in South Africa. In one instance, a girl who had planned to train as a fighter for the African National Congress was prompted by her Happening experience to reject this course and instead study theology at the University of Witwatersrand.[129] In 1983, Bishop Appleyard joined other church leaders in protesting the reopening of the South African consulate in southwestern Pennsylvania.[130]

Pittsburghers also increasingly looked to the war-torn nation of Uganda for an opportunity to further the relationship that had begun with the friendship between Austin Pardue and Festo Kivengere. As early as 1983, Bishop Hathaway had suggested the establishment of a formal link with a Ugandan diocese.[131] Hathaway was undoubtedly inspired by the report from Terry Kelshaw of TESM, who had just returned to Uganda for the first time since the fall of the Idi Amin dictatorship. Kelshaw confessed himself stunned by the structural deterioration and the lack of initiative among the native population. Kampala, he wrote, "is an open sewer, a running sore crying out to be healed. It seems there are no physicians, and if there is balm in Gilead, it has not been applied here ... The Christians I met are the pleasant surprise. They are free, joyous, ready to share the faith, and most welcoming, though it has to be said their church services are dull, terribly proper, and very dreary! But for them it has been worth coming."[132] African Anglicans also made their way to Pittsburgh for academic training. In 1985, Joel and Juliana Nafuma from the Diocese of Mbale settled in Pittsburgh, where Joel pursued a doctorate at the University of Pittsburgh and assisted at churches in New Brighton and Beaver Falls. Juliana, meanwhile, studied nutrition at the

---

128. Diocesan Council—District VII Minutes, June 17, 1982, Diocesan Council Minutes, December 7, 1982, RG4A/2.1:1, box 1DC, EDP.
129. *Trinity*, March 1989.
130. *Trinity*, January 1983.
131. *Convention Journal*, November 4–5, 1983, 29.
132. *Trinity*, November 1983.

Community College of Allegheny County, in preparation for work with young mothers in Uganda.[133]

African enthusiasm continued to impress those Pittsburghers who encountered it. While leading a revival campaign in Uganda in 1992, John Guest confessed himself inspired by the spirit of those Africans making a commitment to Christ. "I have a newfound respect," he said, "for the difficult task of pastoring people who for centuries have followed other gods. These faithful pastors are the real heroes. Our coming has encouraged them and given them a new hope that believers in America will stand with them as partners in evangelism."[134] The closeness of the relationship with Africa was enhanced by the role played by TESM both in sending faculty to East Africa and in training African Anglican clergy and bishops. At the 1992 diocesan convention, Ugandan priest Stephen Mongoma thanked the seminary for training many of his fellow countrymen and then called on the American church to "pull up [its] socks and join [the African churches]" in the work of evangelism.[135]

Particularly intimate was the relationship that developed between Prince of Peace, Hopewell, and John Rucyahana and his wife, Harriet. A Rwandan-born priest in the Ugandan Diocese of Bunyoro-Kitara, Rucyahana studied at TESM from 1988 to 1990, during which time he was an assistant at the parish. When it was learned that he would become diocesan director of missions on his return to Uganda and would, for the first time in his life, require a car, the parish committed itself to assist. Although a car would have cost about a quarter of the parish's annual budget, after fervent prayer it was discovered that the necessary funds had been raised through many small contributions. Prince of Peace subsequently committed itself to the Heifer Project International—on behalf of Bunyoro-Kitara—which provided breeding stock to farmers in Africa to help them build up dairy herds to feed their families and provide a surplus with which to trade. In 1994, Thaddeus Barnum of Prince of Peace traveled to Hoima, Uganda, to review progress on the "Mustard Seed Orphanage," which had been set up to care for AIDS orphans.[136]

133. *Trinity*, February 1985.
134. *Trinity*, October 1992.
135. Fairfield/Rodgers interview; *Convention Journal*, November 14, 1992, 24 (quotation).
136. *Trinity*, December 1990–January 1991, December 1992–January 1993, April–May 1994.

In 1997, John Rucyahana returned to his native land as bishop of Shyira in Rwanda.[137] Building on his existing relationship with Prince of Peace, Hopewell, Rucyahana encouraged Pittsburgh Episcopalians to contribute to the rebuilding of a nation ravaged by the 1994 genocide. In 1999, an eight-person team made a fourteen-day visit to Rwanda, where they were warmly welcomed by the local community and assured by Rucyahana of his desire for a partnership arrangement. The day-to-day realities were made clear to the delegation by Rwanda's Archbishop Kolini. "When I was called here," Kolini told it, "I knew I might leave a widow with orphans . . . They gave John Rucyahana one week to live in Ruhengeri."[138] At the 1999 diocesan convention, Bishop Duncan welcomed the decision to establish a program to sponsor Rwandan orphans and praised the warm response from parishes and individuals. "Pittsburgh and Rwanda are half a world apart," he commented, "but the future and the hope of both are being radically altered. The willingness to follow Jesus in the little things (when that is what He asks)—in this case taking the little ones into our arms—changes everything, not only 'over there,' but also right back here."[139]

The African connection would ultimately come back to haunt Robert Duncan. Already in 1998, he had softened the official line on Christ Church, Grove Farm, by permitting it to establish a relationship with the Diocese of Bunyoro-Kitara in order better to establish its "Anglican" credentials.[140] On January 29, 2000, the consecration of Charles Murphy, rector of All Saints Church in Pawley's Island, South Carolina, and John Rodgers, retired dean of TESM, as missionary bishops to the United States took place in St. Andrew's Cathedral in Singapore. Their consecrators were Emmanuel Kolini, archbishop of Rwanda, Moses Tay, archbishop of South East Asia, and John Rucyahana, bishop of Shyira.[141]

The following day, Bishop Duncan issued a pastoral letter in which he described the consecrations as "but another in the spiral of events of the last thirty years by which the fabric and the direction of our Episcopal Church are being tested and shaped." Acknowledging his friendship

137. *Trinity*, June 1997.
138. Standing Committee Minutes, January 25, 1999, RG4A/1.8, box 10DRB, EDP; *Trinity*, March 1999.
139. *Trinity*, February 2000.
140. *Trinity*, September 1998.
141. "Response to the Consecration of Bishop Rodgers."

with Rodgers, he nonetheless reiterated that he still opposed plans for an alternative Anglican province in North America (commenting parenthetically that while Rodgers resided in Ambridge, he [Duncan] did not anticipate that he would exercise many of his episcopal responsibilities in Pittsburgh). Although conceding the strain imposed upon the relationship between the Diocese of Pittsburgh and the Diocese of Shyira by the participation of Kolini and Rucyahana in the Singapore consecrations, Duncan insisted that the focus should remain upon the orphaned children of Rwanda, whose welfare no amount of ecclesiastical controversy should put in jeopardy.[142]

Some members of the diocese were more than a little perturbed by the escalating conflict and Pittsburgh's part in it. After the Anglican Mission in America (AMIA) was formally constituted in August 2000 to provide infrastructure for the emerging missionary parishes, Linda Shadgett, retiring president of the diocesan council, testified to this growing sense of unease: "Some of our more conservative family members (Anglican Mission in America) are ceasing their cooperation with the majority voice as represented by the more moderate positions adopted by National Convention on a number of controversial issues. Here in our own Diocese of Pittsburgh, the balance of power is the reverse of that in the national church. In recent years, we have been moving towards strong conservative positions on controversial issues."[143]

Shadgett did concede that Duncan and the Pittsburgh delegates to the General Convention reflected the majority view of the diocese, but she worried that the governing institutions of the diocese were increasingly failing to account for the minority viewpoint, noting that 30 percent of clergy and lay delegates had opposed a resolution commending Lambeth Resolution 1:10.[144] In fact, while it was true that the resolution commending the Lambeth resolutions as a "faithful summary of biblical truth and general trustworthy guidance in dealing with the critical issues of our times" had been opposed by 30 percent of those *present and voting*, many delegates did not cast a vote.[145]

---

142. Ibid.
143. *Trinity*, November 2000.
144. Ibid.
145. *Convention Journal*, November 6–7, 1998, 14, 18.

Confrontations with the national church continued. The standing committee continued to oppose the election of bishops whose pronouncements on inclusive theology departed from the position of their own diocese, including Charles Bennison of Pennsylvania, John Cronenberger of Newark, and William Persell of Chicago.[146] Bishop Duncan also implemented changes in clergy policy that some perceived as hostile. In April 1998, the commission on ministry shifted from national to local testing of clergy, officially to eliminate the problem of double testing.[147] Later that year, Duncan announced that he would personally present candidates for ordination from parishes outside Pittsburgh who wished to sponsor a candidate to TESM against the advice of their bishop.[148] Finally, in December 2000, the standing committee rejected the election of Katharine Jefferts Schori as bishop of Nevada; six years later, she would be elected presiding bishop of the Episcopal Church.[149]

In 1999, Bishop Duncan reported that the mood within the House of Bishops seemed to have improved, with less "Lambeth bashing," but also noted that the conservative bishops were discussing realignment.[150] The General Convention of 2000 thus represented the calm before the storm. While rejecting a rite of blessing for those living in same-sex unions, it endorsed support for heterosexuals in unmarried relationships, an indirect indication that both the House of Deputies and the House of Bishops were shifting away from acceptance of historic Christian teaching on marriage. "The General Convention," Bishop Duncan wrote in September 2000, "is symbolic of a people who are content to spend their focus and their energies on much less than the saving person and salvific power of Jesus Christ. We need a change of heart and a change of direction."[151] Duncan himself demonstrated his personal frustration with the national church by taking John Paul Chaney, a priest ordained by Bishop Rodgers, under his episcopal wing.[152] By the close of the year, discussion was already

---

146. Standing Committee Minutes, January 27, 1997, September 21, 1998, January 25, 1999, RG4A/1.8, box 10DRB, EDP.

147. Standing Committee Minutes, April 20, 1998, RG4A/1.8, box 10DRB, EDP.

148. Standing Committee Minutes, September 21, 1998, RG4A/1.8, box 10DRB.

149. Standing Committee Minutes, December 18, 2000, RG4A/1.8, box 10DRB, EDP.

150. Standing Committee Minutes, March 15, 1999, RG4A/1.8, box 10DRB, EDP.

151. *Trinity*, September 2000.

152. Standing Committee Minutes, September 18, 2000, RG4A/1.8, box 10DRB, EDP.

under way within the diocesan leadership about parish property and the ways in which the secular courts might respond to efforts of parishes and dioceses to leave the denomination with their property.[153]

POST-EPISCOPAL PITTSBURGH, 2001–2006

As the twenty-first century dawned, the first outlines of a formal confessing movement within the Episcopal Church could be dimly discerned. Despite the continued insistence of John Rodgers and others that the Anglican Mission in America was never intended to be anything more than a *mission*,[154] the Singapore consecrations led progressive observers to the conclusion that non-American bishops and archbishops were all too ready to assist their "neo-Puritan" allies in the United States to—in the words of one Pittsburgh progressive—"remake Anglicanism into a narrow Christianity unable to speak meaningfully to rapidly evolving Western societies, in spite of whatever appeal [the militants'] theology might have elsewhere."[155] Such a reading of the situation—made by a lay member of St. Paul's, Mt. Lebanon—is naturally one-sided, but expresses an underlying truth. Where a progressive would blame conservative conspiracies and the influence of wealthy conservative foundations, however, conservatives respond that they are pursuing a Gospel imperative.[156] That imperative, argues Robert Duncan, no longer allows the Episcopal Church to play its historic role as "the great chaplains to American society." Every agency of the church must now be reflexively countercultural. "God has put Pittsburgh at the center," the bishop reflected in March 2006, "at the

---

153. Standing Committee Minutes, December 18, 2000, RG4A/1.8, box 10DRB, EDP. "Conflicting views were asserted but the ultimate decision was that there was no way to deal with the situation of parish property concerns other than to follow the Constitution and Canons of PECUSA and the Diocesan Canons, in the hope of integrating the two to reach an equitable result."

154. Fairfield/Rodgers interview.

155. Deimel, "Saving Anglicanism," 5.

156. In 2004, Lionel Deimel accused the Washington-based Institute on Religion and Democracy of fostering divisive internal battles within the Protestant mainline: "Determined forces on the right," he wrote, "forces more secular than religious, have for years been working to undermine the social witness of mainline churches." *Pittsburgh Post-Gazette*, July 24, 2004. This was also the theme of Naughton's "Following the Money." See also Deimel, "Saving Anglicanism." Conservatives are not the only people to draw on wealthy foundations, however, and the degree of influence such bodies exert over theology and policy making is debatable.

absolute center of biblical missionary Anglicanism in North America [because] the diocese is so strong and Trinity [School for Ministry] is so strong."[157]

Duncan's approach, however, could not simply be dismissed as old-fashioned yearning after doctrinal certainty married to conservative politics and hostility to the rights of racial and sexual minorities, although that clearly was in the minds of some of his critics. As recently as 2004, a member of Church of the Redeemer voiced her concern that many people seemed to feel that participation in rallies and writing letters to legislators was somehow un-Christian. "Many times we favor charity over advocacy," she remarked, "but we tend to do charity from our bounty and miss the kinship required to do justice. Justice means a special responsibility to those in our family who are in greatest need."[158]

In speaking of his efforts to implement the maintenance-to-mission approach, Robert Duncan conceded that some might view this as an ideologically informed strategy. "In some ways," he said, "it was Reaganomics, but actually in a church it made a lot of sense."[159] It is a stretch, however, to maintain that all sense of corporate responsibility has disappeared from diocesan life. In 2002, the diocese provided a $10,000 grant to Building United of Southwestern Pennsylvania, a Pittsburgh-based nonprofit that helped members of local churches buy homes and take control of their finances. At Bishop Duncan's request, Mike Wurschmidt, founder and pastor of Shepherd's Heart, became involved in its day-to-day operations two years later.[160] In the town of Washington, Karen Stevenson, rector of Trinity Church, worked with members of the predominantly black Nazareth Baptist Church on a $94,000 Habitat for Humanity project. "It's not just completing the project that is important," Stevenson explained. "It's how we do it. It's about using it as an effective tool for discipleship."[161] In 2005, as the financial impact of the Calvary lawsuit (see below) began to bite home, the diocesan council still allocated $14,000 to the youth outreach program of St. Stephen's Church, Wilkinsburg. This support was significant not only because the ministry had exceeded the five-year

157. Duncan interview.
158. *Trinity*, April 2004.
159. Duncan interview.
160. *Trinity*, September–October 2004.
161. Ibid.

period for which it was supposed to be funded, but also because members of the vestry of St. Stephen's were party to the lawsuit.[162]

Pittsburgh's conservatives clearly had other objectives than the simple elimination of diocesan programs. From the perspective of the present canon missioner of the diocese, the commitment to church planting largely collapsed during the 1990s. Not until 2001 did a process for fostering church plants reemerge at the diocesan level. "People think if they just do the old things they're going to work because they worked before," Mary Hays remarks. "And they're not."[163] Bishop Duncan's call to "1:1:3" evangelism in 2001—inviting every member of the diocese to bring a person to Christ in the course of three years[164]—helped spur the emergence of twenty-first-century church plants more dependent on lay initiative and less reliant on the machinery of the diocese than any earlier model. These initiatives included Living Stones in Latrobe, which focused on contemporary worship and building a family of believers through personal connections, and Seeds of Hope in Bloomfield, sponsored by Shepherd's Heart (a singular case of a mission planting a mission).[165] For such congregations, cell groups were as much an end in themselves as a means to an end.

Many of the new missions were characterized by a much younger demographic than more established parishes; they were also appreciably more culturally conservative. At the special diocesan convention of 2003 (see below), a youth pastor from St. Stephen's, Sewickley, warned that few young people would see any reason to belong to the church if it dispensed with firm biblical witness.[166] Parachurch youth agencies in the diocese, such as Rock the World Youth Alliance, only reinforced such a perspective. Rock the World—which relocated from Virginia to Pittsburgh in the 1990s—was founded by an Episcopal priest and promoted leadership development, discipleship, and evangelism among students from middle school through college. It provided them with a hands-off approach to mentoring that allowed the students to develop a missionary style of their

---

162. *PEPtalk*, October 2004, January–March, 2005. *PEPtalk* is the newsletter of Progressive Episcopalians of Pittsburgh.

163. Hays interview.

164. *Trinity*, February 2001, April–May 2001.

165. *Trinity*, March–April 2005, September–October 2005.

166. *Special Convention Journal*, September 27, 2003, 30.

own. It also sought to mobilize young Christians to reach out to their unchurched counterparts with intentional cell groups.[167]

Rock the World's greatest achievement was the Josiah Project, which trained young Christians in evangelism, urban ministry, and cross-cultural missions to the Third World. Clayton Ingalls, a graduate of this program and now a priest in Tennessee, was sent to Singapore, where he shared the Gospel with the city's youth. "If I were realistic," Ingalls later commented, "I would not have done the Josiah Project, or spent a second summer in Singapore making an impact for God's Kingdom. If I were realistic, I would not have bought into Rock the World's goal to spark a youth revival on every continent. If I were realistic, I would not be a follower of Jesus. Realism is best at changing nothing and no one... God asks us to go beyond anything we have ever seen or considered."[168] Back in Pittsburgh, several of Ingalls's contemporaries pioneered Three Nails, another cell group venture. In 2005, members of Three Nails established a hotdog shop in the undercroft of Trinity Cathedral both to provide members with the means of earning a living and to offer a nonthreatening arena in which to engage the unchurched.[169] "Three Nails," says Greg Malley, former archdeacon of the diocese, "is preaching a Gospel message ... that basically touches people of this generation where they live."[170]

Ingalls's work in Singapore was but one aspect of Pittsburgh's expanding partnership with Third World Anglicanism. It was not a relationship with which every Pittsburgh Episcopalian was entirely happy. Some feared that the laudable goals of outreach to Africa were merely a cloak for the forging of trans-provincial alliances designed to subvert the authority of the elected leadership of the Episcopal Church. The part played by Archbishop Kolini and Bishop Rucyahana in the establishment of AMIA was not soon forgotten.[171] However, despite the urging of some progressive leaders that the partnership with the Diocese of Shyira be

---

167. *Trinity*, February 2001, Mid-June 2002.
168. *Trinity*, April 2004.
169. *Trinity*, March–April 2005.
170. Malley interview.
171. Bishop Rucyahana had a further black mark against him in that he had taken under his oversight a cell group church in Little Rock, Arkansas, which refused to come under Episcopal authority, a precursor of what occurred in many locations after 2003. See the account at http://www.saintandrews-lr.org/history.htm (accessed November 29, 2008).

discontinued, Bishop Duncan insisted that its continuation had been endorsed by no less an authority than the archbishop of Canterbury. A team from the diocese visited Rwanda in 2001 to observe how local communities were contributing to the spiritual rebirth. "[God] is calling the people of Rwanda," reported Sue McLain, a TESM-trained lay missionary, "to be an example to the world—an example of how He can turn hopeless situations around . . . One day, when people hear the name 'Rwanda' they will think of healing, reconciliation, hope and the Name of Jesus Christ."[172]

The year 2004 marked the expansion of ties to Uganda with the establishment of a diocesan relationship with Uganda Christian University (UCU). Formerly Bishop Tucker Theological College, UCU had hired TESM professor Stephen Noll as its vice-chancellor in 1999. In 2004, Noll reported that the university, whose student body had increased dramatically in the first five years of the twenty-first century, would be modeled on evangelical colleges like Wheaton and Gordon and would train religious, civic, and business leaders for East Africa's Great Lakes region. He invited Pittsburgh Episcopalians to fund student scholarships and capital endowment.[173] By 2004, however, the global situation had changed considerably. The Network of Anglican Communion Dioceses and Parishes—later known as the Anglican Communion Network (ACN)—had been formed (see below), and the Province of Uganda had declared itself to be in a state of impaired communion with the Episcopal Church. During the 2004 diocesan convention, Ardelle Hopson of Calvary Church spoke against the resolution to partner with UCU on the grounds that the UCU chancellor was Henry Orombi. "Archbishop Orombi," she said, "has described the Network, led by Bishop Duncan, as 'the faithful remnant of Anglicanism in America with whom (his Province) can remain in communion.' This statement both insults and marginalizes us who consider ourselves faithful Anglicans but who do not support the work of the Network . . . To establish a partnership with the University is tantamount to supporting what may well become an alternate jurisdiction within Anglicanism, and many of us cannot in all conscience support such an agenda."[174]

Unease about the direction of the diocese could be seen in meetings of the diocesan council as early as 2001, when a resolution was introduced

172. Standing Committee Minutes, August 20, 2001, RG4A/1.8, box 10DRB, EDP; *Trinity*, September 2001 (quotation).

173. *Trinity*, September–October 2004.

174. *PEPtalk*, November–December 2004.

that would have barred members of parishes that refused to pay any part of their national assessment, on the grounds of conscience, from holding national positions or offices (including that of deputy to the General Convention). The majority rejected such sanctions as punitive and simply urged parishes to pay their assessment, or, at the very least, to redirect it to Episcopal Relief and Development.[175] Nor could the conflict be contained within diocesan boundaries. In September 2002, Pittsburgh was rocked by the news that Bishop Duncan had agreed to appoint David Moyer, a priest in the Diocese of Pennsylvania long at odds with his bishop over matters of church doctrine, to be priest of Grace Church, Mt. Washington. Many conservative priests had hitherto fled hostile situations for the calmer waters of Pittsburgh. By contrast, Moyer was given canonical standing in Pittsburgh, even while he remained in residence at his Anglo Catholic parish in Rosemont, Pennsylvania, and continued to fight his bishop's efforts to depose him in the courts. At this time, Duncan also renewed his pledge to permit alternative episcopal oversight to any Pittsburgh parish that requested it.[176]

The 2002 diocesan convention proved a stormy affair, despite the convention theme of "One Church." Sexuality dominated the agenda, with Harold Lewis of Calvary Church and Peter Moore, formerly dean-president of TESM, moderating a debate on the issue. On the second day of the convention, delegates passed resolutions rejecting same-sex blessings, gender-neutral language for the Holy Trinity, and attempts to force priests and bishops to violate traditional Christian beliefs with clear majorities. After the vote, progressive delegates circled the room in a visible protest and the rector of Church of the Redeemer, Cynthia Bronson Sweigert, read the following statement: "We are in profound pain over the positions stated in this resolution and concerned about the consequences its adoption will have on the already fragile common life of this diocese. We believe this unyielding document further divides our people, rendering some of us invisible. Some priests and parishes will bear allegiance to the dictates of this document and the diocese, and some will bear allegiance to the dictates of the national church."[177]

175. *Trinity*, Mid-June 2001.

176. Duncan's daughter and son-in-law were parishioners at Good Shepherd, Rosemont. The bishop insisted that his action had the full support of the archbishop of Canterbury and the senior warden of Grace Church. *Trinity*, October 2002.

177. *Trinity*, November 2002.

Sweigert's prediction proved sadly accurate. On June 7, 2003, Canon Vicki Gene Robinson was elected bishop of the Diocese of New Hampshire. The elevation of Robinson, a divorced man living in a partnered homosexual relationship, presented an overt challenge to Lambeth Resolution 1:10, not least because of the relationship that would exist with his brother bishops after his consecration. Pleas of key figures across the Anglican Communion to the Episcopal Church to exercise restraint—not least from the new archbishop of Canterbury, Rowan Williams, then enthroned less than four months—went unheeded. The General Convention met that year in Minneapolis, Minnesota, where the decision to ordain women had been taken twenty-seven years before. It was here that Robinson's election was confirmed in the House of Bishops by a vote of 62–45 on largely sectional lines, with southern (and a number of midwestern) bishops strongly opposed and bishops from the Northeast and West voting in favor.[178]

For the Pittsburgh delegation, Minneapolis came as a shock. "It was if the two sides in the major conflict had completely made up their minds and were talking past each other," reflected Bishop Duncan, who described it as the most unyielding assembly he could remember. "There was a kind of deafness that I had never before seen."[179] Not even the fact that George Werner, dean of Trinity Cathedral, served as president of the House of Deputies offered much protection. It was, says Joan Malley, a lay deputy from Church of the Ascension, Pittsburgh, an "eye-opening experience" to be informed that they had a "controversial delegation." Ironically, Malley and her colleagues were seated directly in front of the delegation from the Diocese of Pennsylvania, whose members could be relied upon to vote the opposite way on almost every controversial resolution.[180] David Wilson, rector of St. Paul's Church, Kittanning, and a volunteer at the General

---

178. The vote by province was: Province I (New England)—6–0 in favor, with one abstention; Province II (New York and New Jersey)—7–1 in favor; Province III (Pennsylvania and Virginia)—10–3 in favor, with Pittsburgh, northwest Pennsylvania, and West Virginia opposed; Province IV (Southeast)—13–7 against; Province V (Midwest)—8–6 in favor, with one abstention; Province VI (Great Plains)—6–1 in favor, with one abstention; Province VII (Southwest)—8–4 against; Province VIII (far West)—14–2 in favor. These vote tallies do not include non-U.S. dioceses that are part of the Episcopal Church. See the figures at http://andromeda.rutgers.edu/~lcrew/2003_c045.html (accessed November 29, 2008).

179. *Trinity*, September 2003.

180. Malley interview.

Convention, watched the walkout by the twenty dissenting bishops. "As we gathered in the parish hall of a Lutheran Church," he wrote three years later, "across the street from that Convention Center in Minneapolis with many of those bishops to worship, pray and weep, I realized the Episcopal Church as we had known it for over 200 years would never be the same without true repentance and amendment of life for these and other actions."[181]

Robert Duncan returned to Pittsburgh convinced that the failure of the Episcopal Church to acknowledge the mind of the Anglican Communion as a whole had compromised its ability to remain a full part of the ecclesial structure. He believed that it was essential for those who dissented from departures from historic Anglicanism (always assuming this term could be easily defined) to disassociate themselves. To that end, a special convention met at St. Martin's, Monroeville, on September 27, 2003, to consider a set of resolutions that disassociated the Diocese of Pittsburgh from the actions of the General Convention and appealed to the primates of the Anglican Communion for assistance.

In his convention address Duncan conceded that both sides were likely to insist that it was their critics who had precipitated the looming separation, but argued that a realignment of relationships had been in process for some time. Echoing J. Gresham Machen's indictment of liberal Protestantism in the 1920s,[182] he insisted that there were now two churches and two Gospels coexisting within the Episcopal Church. "One church offers its fundamental good news in the values of conversion and discipleship," he said. "The other church offers its fundamental good news in the values of inclusion and liberation. Neither church is pure. Both claim allegiance to Jesus Christ." The presenting issue of homosexuality was but a symptom of a wider condition, a measure of how the contending parties understood the exercise of authority within ecclesiastical structures. It was time to see "what ecclesial structure, driven by which

---

181. See http://titusonenine.classicalanglican.net/?p=13199. Posted on May 30, 2006. The link appears to be dead.

182. A Presbyterian scholar at Princeton Seminary, Machen helped organize the more conservative Westminster Theological Seminary in 1929 and was a key player in the debates that split the Presbyterian Church and led to the formation of the Orthodox Presbyterian Church. His original thesis was first outlined in *Christianity and Liberalism*.

gospel, will gain our primary allegiance as individuals, as congregations, as clergy and as bishops."[183]

The ensuing debate exposed to public view many of the divisions that had plagued the diocese for more than a decade. Naturally enough, Pittsburgh's parachurch organizations offered Bishop Duncan their wholehearted support. Representatives of Trinity Episcopal School for Ministry, the South American Missionary Society, and Rock the World all echoed the sentiments of Don Bowers of the Church Army. "It is of the utmost importance that the umbrella I go out under is a *holy* umbrella," Bowers told convention delegates, "and that the authority is a *holy* authority. The hundreds of people to whom I've witnessed the Gospel do not ask if I'm an Episcopalian."[184]

Among the parish delegations, no such uniformity was to be found. The rectors of Calvary Church (Harold Lewis), Church of the Redeemer (Cynthia Sweigert), and St. Paul's Church, Mt. Lebanon (Robert Banse) made no secret of their opposition, while Moni McIntyre, rector of Holy Cross Church, reported that a ballot of her parishioners had produced sixty-one responses, most of them unfavorable to the resolutions being debated. For the laity, Sue Boulden complained that her parish of St. Thomas, Oakmont, had failed to provide a forum to give the congregation pertinent information on what was being discussed. Even a friendly delegate from St. Alban's Church, Murrysville, admitted that many in his parish viewed the resolutions as divisive.[185]

Concerns about the divisive quality of the debate were raised on several occasions during its course. The presenting issue of Bishop Robinson's election and consecration was frequently referenced as an undue eleva-

---

183. *Special Convention Journal*, September 27, 2003, 82–84. Later, in the diocesan newspaper, the bishop offered the following verdict: "As we enter the 21st century, the chief issue being debated among us as U.S. Episcopalians and Anglicans worldwide—the same chief issue as is being debated among Methodists, Presbyterians, Lutherans and Baptists—is the issue of the role and authority of Holy Scripture . . . The role and authority of Holy Scripture—whether Holy Scripture is primary in our decision-making, whether it is reliable, whether it is a sine qua non in the life of every Christian (either the renewal of scripture's historic function or its rejection)—is the great debate into which we are entering. What was so telling about the debates within our Special Convention and the preparatory regional hearings was how little we talked about sexuality and how much we talked about what we do—where we come down—when scripture's truth seems to threaten church unity." *Trinity*, October 2003.

184. *Special Convention Journal*, September 27, 2003, 31, 35, 37.

185. Ibid., 32, 34–35.

tion of sexual sin, a "side issue," in the words of Mary Roehrich of St. Andrew's Church, Highland Park. According to David Else of the Center for Spirituality in 12-Step Recovery Programs, what should be fundamental was the Great Commandment to love God and one's neighbor.[186] For the majority, however, Joan Malley of Church of the Ascension described how a fellow parishioner, a former lesbian who participated in a ministry that addressed sexual brokenness, had told her that the actions of the General Convention had essentially denied the validity of the transformation that she had undergone. Disregard for the feelings of others could cut both ways.[187]

Many progressives emphasized that formalizing division would only make matters worse. Ecclesiastical struggles had been the norm for some time now, argued Mabel Fanguy, rector of St. Thomas's Church, Canonsburg. Carol Henley, a chaplain at the Veterans' Administration, took umbrage at the suggestion that there were two Gospels. For her, she said, there could be only one: "Jesus as Lord and Savior." Neither side could claim they had no need of the other but must rather stay together for mutual correction. Harold Lewis, speaking on behalf of his parish, accused Bishop Duncan of falsely dubbing the actions of the Seventy-fourth General Convention as schismatic. He rejected any offer of alternative episcopal oversight—which he did not desire—and stressed that no diocesan convention had the authority to overrule the national constitution and canons.[188]

Lewis here touched upon the fundamental issue of authority. Progressives maintained that the actions contemplated by the convention—particularly any appeal to the primates of the Anglican Communion—were extra-constitutional. Rachel Nicholson added that her congregation in Canonsburg was in favor of the Episcopal Church staying together and that the primates had no authority over them. Geoff Hurd of St. Paul's, Mt. Lebanon, concurred with this. One resolution, he said, "asks the Primates to make decisions for which they have no authority . . . The Primates weren't even formed until 100 years after ECUSA existed."[189] Robert Banse, rector of St. Paul's, Mt. Lebanon, proposed that

---

186. Ibid., 31, 33, 34.
187. Ibid., 32.
188. Ibid., 30–31, 32, 35.
189. Ibid., 30, 31, 32.

the appeal to the primates be voted on separately from the request for the Diocese of Pittsburgh to be acknowledged as the bona fide expression of Anglicanism in North America, but this was not agreed to by the majority.[190]

Conservatives denied that the primates had no authority. Carolyn Hayes of Christ Church, Greensburg, and Linda Gearhart of Christ Church, Brownsville, both agreed that the Episcopal Church had made the initial departure by its action at the General Convention, while Caroline Beddemeyer of St. Peter's Church, Uniontown, asserted that the church that she had joined had begun to preach heresy.[191] Bradley Wilson, rector of Fox Chapel Church, directly addressed the issue of polity. "The national church in the USA is one of many such national churches left from the receding of the British Empire," he said, "[but] whose right is it to decide what the substance of the faith is? Is it this shrinking splinter of ECUSA or is it the whole Anglican Communion?"[192] It fell to Jay Geisler, rector of St. Steven's Church, McKeesport, and a former Roman Catholic priest, to enunciate the challenge posed to the Episcopal Church by the actions of the Pittsburgh convention. "Let the second Protestant reformation begin!" he told his fellow delegates.[193]

Perhaps the most controversial resolution of the six was that dealing with ownership of diocesan property. This allowed for the possibility of a parish that chose to leave the Episcopal Church being permitted to retain its physical plant. Its critics emphatically denied that the convention enjoyed the constitutional authority to make such a change. Bruce Robison, rector of St. Andrew's Church, Highland Park, urged that any such a change should be conducted under proper authority. Ann Staples, deacon-in-charge at St. Thomas Church, Northern Cambria, asked what the diocese would do when the national church withdrew funds for local programs, while Jackie Och of St. Paul's, Mt. Lebanon, pointed out that the convention's decisions would hardly be the last word in the legal arena.[194]

Conservatives defended the notion of a firewall against hostile legal claims. Susan Pollard, a member of St. Paul's, Mt. Lebanon, and also a

190. Ibid., 32.
191. Ibid., 31, 32, 33.
192. Ibid., 33.
193. Ibid., 36.
194. Ibid., 37, 38.

member of the board of trustees, argued that the resolution was neutral in that it allowed the diocese "to relinquish ownership over parish property in order to protect each parish and avoid any coercive action from either ECUSA or from the Diocese of Pittsburgh." She was joined in this sentiment by Grant LeMarquand of TESM, who insisted that the hierarchical nature of the church was through Canterbury, not New York, though he warned that eventually people might have to choose between the church and the buildings.[195]

"There were no demonstrations of victory as the ayes steadily outmatched the nays in a voice-by-voice numerical accounting of positions," the diocesan newspaper's account sadly concluded. "People who began the day united in the celebration of the Eucharist, ended it with evening prayer and the sad knowledge that things will never be the same again in the Episcopal Diocese of Pittsburgh. Or anywhere else in ECUSA."[196]

The next few months would only deepen that sense of polarization. With the support of Archbishop Rowan Williams of Canterbury, thirteen American bishops signed a memorandum of agreement to create a network of confessing dioceses and parishes. In January 2004, a conference at Christ Church, Plano, in Texas organized the Anglican Communion Network and elected Robert Duncan as its moderator. Duncan was in a bullish mood as he traveled from Plano to the consecration of Henry Orombi as the new archbishop of Uganda. "Anglicans abroad and Anglicans at home are being true to our received identity," he told members of his diocese, "as catholic, reformed and renewed Christians—and as missionaries of the transforming ministry of Jesus Christ."[197]

For the progressive minority, such news was most unwelcome. Constituting themselves Progressive Episcopalians of Pittsburgh (PEP), they challenged the 16-4 vote of the diocesan council to affiliate the diocese with ACN, which PEP called "an organization whose aim is to divide the Episcopal Church, USA, and to create a new fundamentalist church to replace it as the true representative of Anglicanism in the United States." The affiliation had been made precipitately, PEP leaders concluded, without consultation with parishes or parishioners and was contrary to national constitution and canons. Several parishes disassociated themselves

---

195. Ibid., 37, 38 (quotation), 39–40.
196. *Trinity*, October 2003.
197. See "Early History of the Network"; *Trinity*, February 2004.

from the move. Most were the "usual suspects," but they included the vestry of Christ Church, Indiana, whose members stated that they "recognize and honor the many diverse views that we hold as individuals on various subjects." The following month there were calls for the diocesan council to rescind affiliation with ACN, and a letter to that effect signed by 149 members of twenty diocesan parishes was presented.[198] One PEP officer, Christopher Wilkins, was blunt in expressing his disagreements with the diocesan leadership. "Why some leaders chose to abuse their authority over the last 20 years is still a mystery to us," he declared in April 2004. "What is not a mystery is that those abuses are as contrary to Christ's spirit in our church as are biblical literalism and theological fundamentalism—and those who commit them are likewise in need of repentance and reconciliation."[199]

Of considerable significance to the progressive cause was the fallout stemming from the parish property resolution passed at the September convention. In October 2003, Calvary Church filed suit in federal court on behalf of the Diocese of Pittsburgh. Claiming to represent the sentiments of local Episcopalians better than the existing leadership, the parish leadership sought to preclude the possibility of future resolutions of similar effect and to block the second reading in 2004 of an amendment to the diocesan constitution and canons that would allow the diocese to assert autonomy from the national church. Calvary's junior warden explicitly requested financial support from outside the diocese. "The outcome of this lawsuit will have an enormous impact upon Episcopalians across the country," he pointed out. "I would like to encourage everyone to give financial support to Calvary's efforts in bringing this suit. We simply are not in a position to do it alone."[200] Progressives explicitly invoked the now-infamous "Chapman memo," authored by the rector of St. Stephen's, Sewickley, distributed to parishes in liberal dioceses seeking alternative episcopal oversight, and leaked to the *Washington Post* on the eve of the Plano meeting. Chapman's suggestion of a "replacement" jurisdiction aligned with world Anglicanism and his concomitant suggestion that departing parishes should seek to retain their property filled progressives

---

198. *PEPtalk*, February 2004, March 2004.

199. *PEPtalk*, April 2004.

200. *PEPtalk*, February 2004. In March, St. Stephen's, Wilkinsburg, joined the lawsuit. *PEPtalk*, March 2004.

with fury, even though little of the strategy expressed in the memo was particularly novel.[201]

Progressives were equally resentful of what they viewed as efforts to manipulate the democratic process. A clutch of resolutions under consideration by the diocesan council prior to the 2004 convention included a pledge of loyalty to the Episcopal Church; a request from the diocesan coordinator for Episcopal Relief and Development (ERD) for a commitment of 0.7 percent of the budget to the Millennium Development Goals; support for women clergy; a requirement for vestry members to be "actual communicants" in their parish; a call for a "revival of true repentance and faith" in North America; and a condemnation of "violence, hatred or persecution toward LGBT [lesbian, gay, bisexual, and transgender] persons."[202]

All of this smacked of a return to the parliamentary struggles of the 1970s, and the president of the diocesan council, Battle Brown, declared "that the debate of many of these resolutions would damage friendships and relations among us, and would injure the diocese ... that many of these resolutions were not necessary to our life as a diocese or to our witness to Jesus Christ ... In fact, the debate of some of these resolutions is likely to create conflict and tear down our witness to Christ."[203] The diocesan council indicated that it would recommend indefinite postponement of all the resolutions and support only two: a second reading of the constitutional amendments and the establishment of ties with Uganda Christian University. While the possibility existed that convention delegates might take up any or all of the resolutions in question, it was obviously doubtful that they would ignore the council's recommendation.[204]

A further ecclesiastical upset came in May, when Bishop Daniel Cox of the Reformed Episcopal Church confirmed thirteen candidates at St. Michael's Church, Ligonier. Though it was done at the invitation of the rector, Jim Simons, and with the permission of Bishop Duncan, it did not pass unnoticed in the national media. Lynn Edwards, now chaplain for Progressive Episcopalians of Pittsburgh, pointed out that any confirmations must be performed by a bishop of the Episcopal Church or of a body

201. See the text of the Chapman Memorandum at http://www.episcopalchurch.org/3577_26104_ENG_HTM.htm (accessed November 29, 2008).
202. *PEPtalk*, October 2004.
203. Ibid.
204. *PEPtalk*, May–June 2004, October 2004.

in communion with it. To this, Bishop Duncan responded that ecumenical associates could be licensed to serve in any fashion that a local bishop permitted, and his chancellor ruled that anyone receiving the laying on of hands from a bishop in apostolic succession was validly confirmed.[205]

It was all a far cry from the early 1920s when a Congregationalist minister had made history at Calvary by joining in the laying on of hands for an Episcopal ordination. The difference, of course, was the challenge posed to Anglican comprehensiveness by the involvement of the Reformed Episcopal Church. Thanks to the initiatives that ACN had been carefully negotiating with the various Anglican continuing churches, the theological gap with the Reformed Episcopal Church no longer seemed as unbridgeable as had been the case a century before. Divisions were now less about denomination than about theology. TESM professor Les Fairfield recently described how he and John Rodgers jointly participated in the 1980s ordination of a Baptist minister (and TESM graduate) in Beaver Falls. Looking at the group assembled for the laying on of hands, says Fairfield, he "realized there were more Episcopalians ordaining this Baptist minister than there were Baptists . . . what this says about the apostolic succession I don't know."[206] Such a statement demonstrates how dramatically realignment has reshaped former ecclesial boundaries.

The Ligonier confirmations provided further tinder for the developing ecclesial conflagration. Walter Righter, recently returned to the diocese, had been meeting with members of St. Michael's—a parish that he had planted under Pardue—who objected to the course pursued by Jim Simons. This move was not well received by the diocesan leadership. When Bishop Duncan made a visit to Calvary in May 2004, he was unusually forthright when asked why he was "stalling" on allowing Righter to celebrate the Eucharist at Calvary while its rector was on sabbatical. He would be prepared to entertain such a request if made by Righter, he said, but Righter had "no damned business" holding secret meetings at St. Michael's.[207]

Duncan's outburst did not mean that he was oblivious of dissenters within his jurisdiction. Where congregations are united in their opposition to the present course of the diocese, sanctions have been few.

---

205. *Pittsburgh Post-Gazette*, May 11, 2004; *PEPtalk*, May–June 2004.
206. Fairfield/Rodgers interview.
207. *Pittsburgh Post-Gazette*, May 24, 2004.

Canon Mary Hays insists that she always awaits requests from parishes for her assistance before visiting them. "It's not easy for them either," she concedes, in reference to the more progressive parishes.[208] As far as the bishop is concerned, he has expressed a willingness to implement alternative pastoral oversight since it was first conceived by the House of Bishops in 2004, though at the time he admitted that it would "require a lot of generosity on the part of bishops and a lot of trust on the part of clergy and laity."[209] To date, only one parish—St. Brendan's Church, Franklin Park—has pursued this option. "Nobody joins the church to go to war," declared its rector, Katherine Munz, in February 2005. "We know who we are as Episcopalians." For over two years the parish has enjoyed the spiritual oversight of Bishop William Klusmeyer of West Virginia.[210]

In November 2004, ACN established the Anglican Relief and Development Fund (ARDF), which was planned to run parallel with the national church's Episcopal Relief and Development and the United Thank Offering. ARDF channeled its outreach contributions through Geneva Global, investing in relief projects on the basis of their risks, potential benefits, and likely outcome. Since many Global South dioceses felt obliged to decline money from organizations associated with the Episcopal Church after 2003, ARDF offered an acceptable route for conservative North American Anglicans desirous of serving them. ARDF's board of trustees was evenly split between representatives of the Global North and the Global South, arguably an embrace of the MRI concept that Stephen Bayne had championed forty years before.[211]

Progressives objected to ARDF on two counts. Some criticized Geneva Global for its association with the National Christian Foundation, whose website claimed that "the entire Bible is the inspired and inerrant word of God; the only infallible rule of faith and practice."[212] Many more objected to the tarring of Episcopal Relief and Development as somehow suspect in its work. When Thomas Finnie, rector of St. Peter's, Church, Uniontown, declared at the 2004 diocesan convention that ERD was guilty by its association with the Episcopal Church, Celinda Scott

---

208. Hays interview.
209. *PEPtalk*, April 2004.
210. *Pittsburgh Post-Gazette*, February 10, 2005 (quotation), April 12, 2005.
211. *Trinity*, November–December 2004.
212. *PEPtalk*, October 2004.

of Christ Church, Indiana, retorted that "the mind of this convention is that anything from the National Church is despicable." Bishop Duncan himself offered the Solomonic judgment that people in the diocese could give to outreach in a variety of ways. It was not his intention, he said, to prescribe how parishes and individuals should act in this matter. "There is no intent on the bishop's part to block money to ERD from parishes. Those parishes that designate ERD can continue to give."[213]

After 2004, divisions within the diocese hardened still further. That year's diocesan convention refused to reelect George Werner as a delegate to the 2006 General Convention, despite the pleas of conservatives such as Jim Simons and Scott Quinn. Werner's moderation had become more than many were willing to tolerate in the hostile climate. Longtime diocesan priest Leslie Reimer deplored the move. "It shows profound disrespect to his work," she said, "and how unwilling some people are to see beyond their own perspectives."[214] Outside the diocese, Christopher Leighton (along with Geoffrey Chapman, part of TESM's first graduating class), whose impulsive nomination of John Rodgers had almost wrecked the election of Alden Hathaway twenty years earlier, was charged with abandonment of communion in April 2005 along with five of his colleagues in the Diocese of Connecticut.[215] The following month, Father Alvin Kimel, rector of St. Mark's Church, Johnstown, and an author of the 1991 Baltimore Declaration—an early confessing Anglican statement[216]—announced his departure for the Roman Catholic Church. "I cannot in conscience represent the Episcopal Church to the world," Kimel explained, "nor can I in conscience summon sinners into its fellowship."[217]

If such defections as Kimel's could be found in a diocese as conservative as Pittsburgh, then the time remaining to establish ACN as a jurisdiction was short indeed. The regular diocesan convention of 2003 had extended the principle of national withholding adopted in 1996 to include the previously mandatory portion. Twenty-two of the parishes that subsequently chose to redirect funds left their allocation to the diocesan council, which divided the money between ACN, Third World

213. *PEPtalk*, November–December 2004.
214. Ibid.
215. *Pittsburgh Post-Gazette*, April 28, 2005.
216. See Radner and Sumner, *Reclaiming Faith*.
217. *Pittsburgh Post-Gazette*, May 21, 2005.

provinces that had refused money from the Episcopal Church, and missionary agencies like SAMS that had distanced themselves from the national church.[218] The 2004 diocesan convention approved the new partnership with Uganda Christian University and commended the existing relationship with the Province of Rwanda. It also approved the constitutional amendment first passed in 2003 that stated that where the national church's actions diverged from those of the "historic Faith and Order of the one holy catholic and apostolic church," the diocesan constitution and canons would apply. The vote was 79–14 among the clergy, with 8 abstentions, and 124–45 among the laity, with 3 abstentions.[219]

In October 2004, the Windsor Report was released. The report, generated by the commission appointed by the archbishop of Canterbury following the consecration of Bishop Robinson to consider the future of the Anglican Communion, indicted the Episcopal Church and the Canadian Diocese of New Westminster for violating the principle of Anglican interdependence.[220] Bishop Duncan encouraged his parishes to make use of the report as a study tool. "Let us together see where Anglicanism stands," he told them. "Let us see that the Episcopal Diocese of Pittsburgh is in line with this stand. Let us discover where and how the national Episcopal Church has gone off course. Let us grow in our theological, scriptural and ecclesiological understanding of how our Communion can move forward into the 21st Century."[221]

In such a heated atmosphere, the Calvary lawsuit exerted an even more debilitating drain on the resources of the diocese, so much so that Bishop Duncan even threatened to ask the diocesan convention to dissolve the relationship of Calvary and St. Stephen's, Wilkinsburg, with the diocese if they were not willing to reach a settlement. "By any reckoning," Duncan declared, "a congregation suing almost all of the elected leader-

---

218. *Trinity*, September–October 2004.
219. *Trinity*, January–February 2005.
220. *Trinity*, November–December 2004.
221. *Trinity*, January–February, 2005. Progressive Episcopalians of Pittsburgh, naturally enough, placed a rather different interpretation upon the Windsor Report. The commission, PEP argued, "did what many considered impossible, finding common ground among the churches whose roots reach back to the Church of England, and imagining structures and procedures to assure that those churches maintain real unity *without undue coercion* [my emphasis]." *PEPtalk*, October 2004.

ship of the diocese is an egregious break of the church order."[222] Each side accused the other of delaying tactics and—in the case of the defendants—withholding critical evidence, but at the close of 2005, the lawsuit was settled. Under the settlement, the competence of the diocesan leadership was affirmed, while it was agreed that property held and administered by the diocese would continue to be operated for the benefit of the whole. A resolution process was established for any parish church that might choose to disaffiliate from the diocese. The process included formal notice to every parish in the diocese, mediation among interested parties, and the right to seek court settlement of the property rights. Parishes that wished to disaffiliate from ACN (at that time, nine parishes were already so disaffiliated) were accorded a formal means for doing so. Bishop Duncan welcomed the settlement and urged both sides to recommit to preaching the good news of Jesus Christ in southwestern Pennsylvania, while Harold Lewis of Calvary declared that his parish had participated in "making history."[223]

Beyond Pennsylvania, the atmosphere grew noticeably grimmer. In February 2005, the primates met at Dromantine in Northern Ireland, at which time they toughened the language expressed in the Windsor Report and called for repentance by the Episcopal Church. The tone of their communiqué gave fresh heart to the majority in Pittsburgh, who were now assured that their position was that endorsed by the majority of the Anglican Communion, although their bishop warned that there were testing times ahead. He also brought word from the primates that all orthodox Anglican groups in the United States should work together in accordance with the Common Cause agreement negotiated in June 2004 with other Anglican bodies in North America.[224]

The outlines of a new province had begun to take on corporate reality. Further substance was given to this reality in November, when Pittsburgh hosted the Hope and a Future Conference. The conference attracted 2,300 registered attendees from the Episcopal Church and many separate Anglican entities. Seven Anglican archbishops spoke, as did ecumenical keynote speakers like Rick Warren of Saddleback Church in California. Among the speakers was Bishop Keith Ackerman of Quincy, a

222. *Trinity*, January–February 2005.

223. *Trinity*, January–February 2006; *PEPtalk*, September–October 2005 (quotation). In recent months the lawsuit has been revived.

224. *Trinity*, May–June 2005.

son of the Mon Valley and champion of Anglo Catholic orthodoxy. Hope and a Future affirmed the model of orthodox unity that the primates had sought.[225]

In the spring of 2006, tensions were coming to a head, as the General Convention prepared to meet in Columbus, Ohio, to frame a response to the Windsor Report. At stake was the Episcopal Church's continued membership in the Anglican Communion and the place of the Diocese of Pittsburgh in the life of the Episcopal Church. Bishop Duncan urged his flock to stand fast. The debate was not one peculiar to America or even to the Anglican Communion, he insisted, but to the whole of Western Christianity. Ecumenical colleagues across the theological spectrum had frequently expressed gratitude for the stand of orthodox Anglicans and prayed for their success. The challenge, moreover, was to finally break free of the state-church mindset that had handed many churches over to the prevailing culture. The shift in Christianity's center of gravity toward the Global South gave the Diocese of Pittsburgh a unique opportunity to educate fellow Anglicans in the nature of the global Anglican Communion: "Few of us want to be at the center of the battle for the soul of the Church in the West, but that is precisely where God has put the Episcopal Diocese of Pittsburgh. Given the toughest assignment on the battlefield, will we as Pittsburghers shrink back? Like our Steelers, we may be sixth-seeded in the contest, but that is the kind of position from which our God always selects those whom He intends to use for His purposes."[226]

Pittsburghers understood that they were participating in an event that might shatter the Anglican Communion that they had known all their lives, and that they were standing on the threshold of a new ecclesial reality. In just fifty years, Pittsburgh had indeed come to be known as much for God as for steel.

---

225. *Trinity*, January–February 2006.
226. *Trinity*, March–April 2006.

Conclusion

Lex Credendi, Lex Orandi

THE EIGHTEEN MONTHS BETWEEN the 2006 General Convention and the diocesan convention of 2007 were nothing if not eventful. Appeals for "alternative primatial oversight" (APO), renewal of the Calvary lawsuit against diocesan leaders, and finally a preliminary vote to disassociate the diocese from the national church represent the culmination of a process that began in 1952, when Sam Shoemaker first arrived at Calvary Church. It is all the more ironic that the most fervent protest against APO had come from Calvary. In a communication to Presiding Bishop Katharine Jefferts Schori dated February 28, 2007, Harold Lewis and Florence Atwood objected to the recent request of the primates of the Anglican Communion for the Episcopal Church to permit external oversight for conservative dioceses and parishes in the United States: "From its origin immediately following the American Revolution until this date the heart and soul of this church is that it is an American church based upon democratic self-determination, American morality and not subject to foreign domination ... Since the 1780s, our church has been predicated upon American values and American morality. The American value system and the evolving American concept of non-discrimination should govern our future as they have our past."[1]

For Calvary and the eight other parishes whose leaders oppose the oversight request[2] there remains a very real commitment to the actions

---

1. The Rev. Harold T. Lewis and Florence Atwood to the Most Rev. Katharine Jefferts Schori and Bonnie Anderson, February 28, 2007, copy in author's possession, originally viewed at http://titusonenine.classicalanglican.net/?p=18365.

2. *Pittsburgh Post-Gazette,* July 12, 2006. The other parishes were Church of the Redeemer, Squirrel Hill; Holy Cross, Homewood; All Souls, North Versailles; St. Brendan's, Franklin Park; St. Matthew's, Homestead; St. Stephen's, Wilkinsburg; St. Thomas, Canonsburg; and St. Luke's, Patton. Together they represented a church population of 2,700 out a total population of 20,263. There are, of course, likely to be a number of people in other parishes who share the sentiments expressed here.

taken by the General Convention in 2003. In the eyes of Calvary's leadership, such a move would seriously weaken the American church, internally and externally. They reject any attempt to delegate oversight, arguing that to force a parish to choose between being part of the Diocese of Pittsburgh and adhering to the conservative interpretation of the Windsor process is a false dichotomy. Appeals to autonomy, democracy, and social justice as the defining marks of the Episcopal Church to which they wish to belong, however, speak to a particular vision of Anglicanism, one not shared by many outside the United States and Canada.

Evangelicals also have their axes to grind. The acknowledged gap between "federal" and "communion" conservatives has made itself felt within the diocese, with the latter desperately seeking a solution to the present crisis that is resolved within existing structures of the Anglican Communion, even as the former have increasingly despaired that any solution proposed by Archbishop Rowan Williams or the Anglican Communion Office will offer any protection to those in other dioceses whose bishops are openly critical of the Windsor Report and subsequent primatial injunctions. For the federal conservatives, increasingly, solutions are being proposed within a framework that presumes that there is no hope to be had from a saving remnant theology. Thus Stephen Noll, vice-chancellor of Uganda Christian University and former academic dean of TESM, canonically resident within the Diocese of Pittsburgh, spoke to this sense of inevitable erosion within institutional structures in the summer of 2007:

> For the past seven years, I have been looking in with the eyes of the church in Africa ... *The time has come for full and final separation* between those in The Episcopal Church (TEC) who hold a false gospel and those who hold fast the truth revealed in Holy Scripture and the evangelical and catholic faith of the Church ... Once there were 60 Irenaeus bishops, then 40 AAC bishops, now there are 20 "Windsor Bishops" and a dozen (and counting down?) Network bishops ... Congregations have walked away from their sanctuaries and now worship in schools. It is now time for the Network bishops and dioceses to take this risk by breaking communion with false and lukewarm colleagues in TEC. Remember the fires of Oxford! ... *Network bishops must unite behind Robert Duncan, and Common Cause partners must uphold him* in his role as a "focus of unity" within the faithful remnant in North America. Let it be clear as day that our movement is directed toward true unity in the

Body of Christ and not a fragmentation by personality and preference. Let our movement be truly catholic and ecumenical.[3]

Similar sentiments were voiced at the St. Louis Congress in 1977; whether the present movement will prove any more successful is the question that even those who support the bishop of Pittsburgh in his present undertaking continue to wonder.

A great span of years separates the world of Joseph Doddridge from that of Robert Duncan. Doddridge could never have imagined "Steel City" as it was in its heyday or is now in its postindustrial setting. Nor, one suspects, can the present bishop of Pittsburgh fully comprehend—even if he understands it intellectually—the frontier setting that made Doddridge the circuit rider that he was. Yet the man who might have been Pittsburgh's first bishop (had things gone differently) and the man who may well be its last (at least within an undivided Anglican Communion) could probably join in enunciating the vision bequeathed to us by the writer of the Epistle to the Hebrews: "By faith Abraham obeyed when he was called to go out to a place that he was to receive as an inheritance. And he went out, not knowing where he was going. By faith he went to live in the land of promise, as in a foreign land, living in tents with Isaac and Jacob, heirs with him of the same promise. For he was looking forward to the city that has foundations, whose designer and builder is God."[4]

Fidelity to a vision is a constant that runs through the varieties of Anglican faith and witness manifested in Pittsburgh down the years, a principle espoused equally by Evangelical and Anglo Catholic; liberal and conservative; bishop, priest, and layperson. Yet that fidelity has come at a price, only now being redeemed in full measure, not just in Pittsburgh but throughout the United States and across the world. The focus, though, remains on Pittsburgh, the city that Sam Shoemaker made his own and that his disciples in the Pittsburgh Experiment earnestly sought to convert. The words of John Guest on the modus operandi of the Pittsburgh Experiment are pertinent here: "The vision was this: if you get kids in high school to make a commitment to Christ; follow them to the universities and college campuses and work with them there; sell them on the vision

---

3. "An Open Letter to Network Bishops."
4. *Hebrews* 11:8–10.

of coming back into Pittsburgh and, whether they're going into medicine or law or education or business, they come to influence Pittsburgh."[5]

This notion of Pittsburgh as a cultural template is an appealing one. How well does it apply to those Episcopalians who lived and died in western Pennsylvania down the years? The fatal association of American Anglicans with the Loyalist cause during the 1770s ensured that, for decades after the Revolution, the Episcopal Church would be a marginal ecclesiastical entity whose strongest cultural marker was its residual Anglophilia. From the 1830s to the 1870s, it was, as a denomination, largely concerned with internal theological battles, which culminated in the final triumph of the Anglo Catholic party over the Evangelicals (a significant difference from the Church of England, where the two parties remained broadly balanced). As we have seen, Pittsburgh was in no way distinguished from other sections of the American church in this respect.

Between 1880 and 1940, the Episcopal Church embarked upon a period of institutionalization, both at diocesan and national levels. Inspired by the national church idea taking hold on both sides of the Atlantic, Episcopal leaders recognized a unique role for Anglicanism within the American denominational context as the rallying point around which the various Protestant denominations could rediscover their "lost" apostolicity. Although the movement for greater organic Christian unity had largely foundered by the 1920s, institutionalization continued—particularly at the national level—as the church embraced new methods of social outreach that corresponded more closely with contemporary understandings of the role of the state in society. From Kingsley House to George Guthrie's term as reformist mayor, from the social service commission to the Conneaut Lake Summer Conference, the Diocese of Pittsburgh followed national trends.

Beginning in the late 1940s, the Episcopal Church entered what might be termed its postinstitutional phase, entailing less a rejection of central oversight mechanisms than an abandonment of the physical plant that had been sustained for almost a century, with hospitals and schools being the principal casualties. In its place, a group of charismatic church leaders—including several bishops—embraced a model of social transformation that endeavored to mobilize those educated white-collar Episcopalians who had joined the church immediately following the Second World War.

---

5. Guest interview.

Their campaigns, on behalf first of African Americans and subsequently of women and sexual minorities, were a new departure for the Episcopal Church. In the midst of this profound social transformation, the cohesive elements that had until then bound an otherwise diverse church together began to dissolve. By the 1970s, it had become unclear what the doctrinal foundations of American Anglicanism actually were, and divisions within the Episcopal Church became increasingly reflective of simple political cleavages in the outside world. A process of factional infighting steadily sapped the ability of the church to comprehend the diversity that, at least ostensibly, it claimed to embody. By the 1990s the stage had been set for a final confrontation that would begin in the summer of 2003.

This familiar—and oversimplified—summary of over two centuries of Episcopal history provides a scale against which to measure the Episcopal Diocese of Pittsburgh. With minor variations, it can be said that, during the first two eras, Episcopalians in southwestern Pennsylvania enjoyed an experience broadly comparable to that of the national church. In contrast with eastern Pennsylvania's atypical Evangelicalism, Pittsburgh was more in the Anglo Catholic mainstream, though by no means a part of the Biretta Belt.[6] The diocese remained weaker than many other metropolitan dioceses in industrial areas, however, by virtue of a strong Presbyterian presence that hindered Episcopal growth. While wealthy Pittsburgh Episcopalians contributed their share to civic improvement (most notably through St. Margaret's Memorial Hospital), they were not as influential as their counterparts in New York City, Philadelphia, and Chicago. Bishop Whitehead's early support for the Laymen's Missionary League might be seen as innovative, yet that movement spread quickly to other jurisdictions, and while George Hodges was a pioneer of the settlement house approach in Pittsburgh, the movement was already well advanced elsewhere. The story of Pittsburgh prior to 1944 is one that could be replicated in dioceses throughout the northeast. While Cortlandt Whitehead achieved a certain prominence in national affairs, this had more to do with his longevity (few bishops get to celebrate their fortieth anniversary, after all) than with charisma.

What set the Diocese of Pittsburgh on an entirely different course was a series of events that began with the installation of Austin Pardue as

6. The Biretta Belt is the term given to dioceses in the upper Midwest that were affected by the presence of Nashotah House. The dioceses of Fond du Lac and Milwaukee in Wisconsin and Springfield and Quincy in Illinois would all qualify.

the fourth bishop of Pittsburgh in 1944. Pardue's episcopate marked the beginning of a seismic shift in how lay Episcopalians in the diocese understood the purpose of the community of faith. Though the Society for the Promotion of Industrial Mission initially received the most sustained media attention—and appeared to be more in the spirit of the modern world—it was Pardue's commitment to an active prayer life and his recruitment of Sam Shoemaker that served as the catalysts for regional transformation. Through the Pittsburgh Experiment—even if this was not his original intention—Shoemaker helped break down the barriers that had separated Episcopalians from the wider evangelical subculture of Pittsburgh.

Michael Sider-Rose's portrait of Don James, who became executive director of the Experiment in 1960, speaks to that sense of enculturation, for James came to Episcopal ministry and the Experiment courtesy of the welcome that he initially received at Calvary Church: "An Episcopal priest, James was also a chain smoker, prone to colorful language and was even mildly irreverent... [He was] determined to use his status as a priest to connect with, rather than alienate, those outside the fold, and he directed the Experiment toward the same goal. James remembered fondly the nonjudgmental welcome he received when he first attended a small group discussion of the Experiment as an outsider, and he called on the organization to continue its concern for people like himself."[7]

Although the Diocese of Pittsburgh continued to adhere to the denominational paradigm during the 1960s and 1970s, at least insofar as its embrace of the civil rights movement, endorsement of women's ordination, and "democratization" of diocesan structures were concerned, the seeds of the movement for Evangelical renewal for which Shoemaker and James had striven were now beginning to blossom. This was already perceptible in the diocese as early as 1971, says Walter Righter. During that year's clergy conference several of the priests present turned their backs throughout his presentation. "It was obvious John Guest was building an empire... he had an agenda from Day One."[8]

Righter's views, of course, are those of one for whom SPIM led naturally to civil rights, female ordination, and ultimately to Gene Robinson's 2003 consecration. A fellow member of SPIM, Richard Davies, accepts the

---

7. Sider-Rose, *Taking the Gospel to the Point*, 25–29 (quotation on 27).

8. Righter interview.

first (he relocated from the University of the South to Virginia Theological Seminary because of the former's refusal to accept black students), and has come to accept the second. Davies, however, though his clerical training predates the Evangelical revival, respects TESM for upholding the authority of Scripture.[9] The implication that the Diocese of Pittsburgh has been corrupted by "outside" influences is no more and no less valid than to suggest that a similar process has occurred in the historically Anglo Catholic but now extremely liberal Diocese of Newark, where Righter served as assistant bishop a decade ago.

That said, the election of John Guest as rector of St. Stephen's, Sewickley, in 1971 and the election of Alden Hathaway as bishop of Pittsburgh in 1979 are key moments in the self-definition of Pittsburgh's Evangelical community. The 1970s marked the period when the diocese departed significantly from the prevailing theological tendencies within the national church and set the course that today has made it a focal point for ecclesiastical controversy. The establishment of Trinity Episcopal School for Ministry drove the Evangelical transformation of southwestern Pennsylvania's Anglican subculture, while Bishop Hathaway's episcopate established Evangelicalism as the prevailing ethos of the diocese. By the mid-1980s, Pittsburgh was distinct from most of its immediate diocesan neighbors (as well as the overwhelming majority of Episcopal dioceses across the nation). Where the historic Anglo Catholic outlook has generally been succeeded by a combination of social action witness and Broad Church theology, Pittsburgh returned to the Evangelicalism of the nineteenth century.

The Evangelical witness today embraced by the Diocese of Pittsburgh does make significant concessions to the world in which it now operates. The ordination of women to the priesthood has been accepted (despite John Guest's personal disapproval). A more obvious departure—which the establishment of TESM only strengthened—has been the much deeper relationship into which Evangelicals have entered with the wider Anglican Communion. Rarely did their nineteenth-century forebears think in terms of the bond that united them with Low Church Anglicans elsewhere in the world. Far more frequently did they seek to reach out to those of like mind in other American Protestant denominations. The steady collapse of the American Protestant mainline and the growing

---

9. Davies interview.

recognition that the domestic renewal movement has failed to transform the culture of the Episcopal Church can partly explain this shift, but it also reflects a new and more catholic ecclesiology for American Evangelicals, which the Diocese of Pittsburgh has helped to foster.

On a practical level, the Hathaway and Duncan years have witnessed numerous and innovative experiments in church planting, leadership formation, and evangelism. The enhanced role envisioned for the diocesan office during the 1960s and 1970s has been replaced by a focus on encouraging new ministries to emerge from grassroots initiatives. The small-group approach, pursued in a number of parishes and in programs such as Cursillo and Faith Alive, has kept active the vision of Sam Shoemaker. Parachurch ministries serving a variety of constituencies have found a home in Ambridge in the shadow of the seminary that produces the servant leaders whose skills they need.

Historically, Anglicans explained their theology under the liturgical formula *lex orandi, lex credendi* (The Law We Pray Is the Law We Believe). Today, the focus seems to be upon the inversion of this principle to become: The Law We Believe Is the Law We Pray. Anglicans in Pittsburgh and elsewhere are entering upon a confessional moment in which subscription to some confessional formula (as yet undetermined) will define one section of the Anglican family. Whatever ecclesiastical structure emerges to contain them, a majority of Pittsburgh's Episcopalians will ultimately subscribe to that formula, just as a majority outside Pittsburgh will not. All this seems a far cry from the heady days of the institutional church when Bishop Whitehead could happily dismiss any suggestion that the Church of England might exercise authority over its American relative, yet it is in the person of Whitehead's successor, Robert Duncan, that all the threads of Pittsburgh's Episcopal history come together.

There is no small irony in recalling the words of liberal Episcopal priest Diane Shepherd on the occasion of Duncan's election as bishop in 1995. "The church," she said, "has often shut its doors against a culture in dire spiritual need. Bob Duncan during his tenure here, has challenged the churches of this diocese to open doors and offer the Gospel to those in deepest need. The doors are opening in Pittsburgh—almost like Pentecost. I am grateful for Bob's election, and expectant as we pack away fear and get on with Jesus' call.[10] What will the fruit of this new Pentecost be? The Diocese of Pittsburgh awaits the future with both trepidation and godly hope.

---

10. *Trinity*, December 1995–January 1996.

Bibliography

ORAL HISTORY

Bushyager, Donald. Interview with author. October 24, 2006.
Davies, Richard. Interview with author. November 14, 2006.
Duncan, Robert. Interview with author. March 29, 2006.
Edwards, Lynn. Interview with author. November 17, 2006.
Fairfield, Les, and John Rodgers. Interview with author. April 6, 2006.
Guest, John. Interview with author. February 23, 2007.
Hays, Mary. Interview with author. December 1, 2006.
Malley, Greg, and Joan Malley. Interview with author. November 4, 2006.
Moore, Peter. Interview with author. November 16, 2006.
Nimick, Thomas. Interview with author. August 2, 2006.
Righter, Walter. Interview with author. July 18, 2006.

PRINTED PRIMARY SOURCES

Brunot, Rev. Sanson. Journal. Copied from manuscript in possession of Hillary Brunot, Archives of the Episcopal Diocese of Pittsburgh.
Doddridge, Rev. Joseph. *Memoirs, Letter and Papers: Establishment of the Church in Western Pennsylvania*. n.d. Archives of the Episcopal Diocese of Pittsburgh.
Harpster, John W. *Crossroads: Descriptions of Western Pennsylvania, 1720–1829*. Pittsburgh: University of Pittsburgh Press, 1938.

NEWSPAPERS AND PERIODICALS

Church News
Convention Journals of the Diocese of Pennsylvania
Convention Journals of the Diocese of Pittsburgh
Our Diocese
PEPtalk
Pittsburgh Post-Gazette
Trinity

SECONDARY SOURCES

Baldwin, Leland D. *Whiskey Rebels: The Story of a Frontier Uprising*. Pittsburgh: University of Pittsburgh Press, 1967. Orig. pub. 1939.
Bauman, John F., and Edward K. Muller. *Before Renaissance: Planning in Pittsburgh, 1889–1943*. Pittsburgh: University of Pittsburgh Press, 2006.

Bauman, John F., and Margaret Spratt. "Civic Leaders and Environmental Reform: The Pittsburgh Survey and Urban Planning." In *Pittsburgh Surveyed: Social Science and Social Reform in the Early Twentieth Century*, edited by Maurice W. Greenwald and Margo Anderson, 153–69. Pittsburgh: University of Pittsburgh Press, 1996.

Bess, Douglas. *Divided We Stand: A History of the Continuing Anglican Movement*. Riverside, CA: Tractarian, 2002.

Blatz, Perry K. "Titanic Struggles, 1873–1916." In *Keystone of Democracy: A History of Pennsylvania Workers*, edited by Howard Harris, 83–148. Harrisburg: Pennsylvania Historical and Museum Commission, 1999.

Bodnar, John. *Lives of Their Own: Blacks, Italians and Poles in Pittsburgh, 1900–1960*. Urbana: University of Illinois Press, 1982.

Bond, Edward L., and Joan R. Gundersen. "The Episcopal Church in Virginia, 1607–2007." *Virginia Magazine of History and Biography* 115:2 (2007) 162–344.

Bonner, Jeremy. "The Limits of Acceptable Behavior: The 'Arundel Affair' and the Social Gospel in Progressive Pittsburgh." Paper presented at the Pittsburgh History Roundtable, Senator John Heinz History Center, November 1, 2007.

Booty, John. *An American Apostle: The Life of Stephen Fielding Bayne, Jr*. Valley Forge, PA: Trinity, 1997.

———. *The Episcopal Church in Crisis*. Cambridge, MA: Cowley, 1988.

Bosher, Robert S. "The Pan-Anglican Congress of 1908." *Historical Magazine of the Protestant Episcopal Church* 23:2 (1954) 126–42.

Brignano, Mary. *The Story of St. Margaret's*. Pittsburgh: UPMC St. Margaret's, 1998.

Brown, Katharine L. *Hills of the Lord: Background of the Episcopal Church in Southwestern Virginia, 1738–1938*. Roanoke: Diocese of Southwestern Virginia, 1979.

Brown, Lawrence L. *The Episcopal Church in Texas*. Austin, TX: Church Historical Society, 1963.

Brown, William M. *The Church for Americans*. New York: Thomas Whittaker, 1896.

Buck, Solon J., and Elizabeth H. Buck. *The Planting of Civilization in Western Pennsylvania*. Pittsburgh: University of Pittsburgh Press, 1939.

Burr, Nelson R. *The Story of the Diocese of Connecticut: A New Branch of the Vine*. Hartford, CT: Church Missions, 1962.

Butler, Diana H. *Standing against the Whirlwind: Evangelical Episcopalians in Nineteenth Century America*. New York: Oxford University Press, 1995.

Calvin, Ross. *Barnabas in Pittsburgh: From Common Clay to Legend*. New York: Carlton, 1966.

Carden, Ron. "The Bolshevik Bishop: William Montgomery Brown's Path to Heresy, 1906–1920." *Anglican and Episcopal History* 72:2 (2003) 197–228.

Chadwick. Owen. *The Spirit of the Oxford Movement: Tractarian Essays*. Cambridge: Cambridge University Press, 1992.

Chalfant, Nancy D. *Child of Grace: A Mother's Life Changed by a Daughter's Special Needs*. Wheaton, IL: Harold Shaw, 1988.

Chorley, E. Clowes. *Men and Movements in the American Episcopal Church*. New York: Charles Scribners Sons, 1948.

Church, J. E. *Quest for the Highest: An Autobiographical Account of the East African Revival*. Exeter, UK: Paternoster, 1981.

Conkin, Paul K. *Cane Ridge: America's Pentecost*. Madison: University of Wisconsin Press, 1990.

Coomes, Anne. *Festo Kivengere: A Biography*. Eastbourne, UK: Monarch, 1990.

Cunningham, Raymond J. "James Moore Hickson and Spiritual Healing in the American Episcopal Church." *Historical Magazine of the Protestant Episcopal Church* 39:1 (1970) 3-16.

Dahlinger, Charles W. "Rev. John Taylor: The First Rector of Trinity Episcopal Church of Pittsburgh and His Commonplace Book." *Western Pennsylvania Historical Magazine* 1:1 (1918) 3-25.

Deimel, Lionel E. "Saving Anglicanism: An Historical Perspective on Decisions Facing the 75th General Convention of the Episcopal Church." May 31, 2006. No pages. Accessed November 29, 2008. Online: http://www.deimel.org/church_resources/saving.pdf.

DeMille, George E. *The Catholic Movement in the American Episcopal Church*. Philadelphia: Church Historical Society, 1950.

Doll, Peter. *Revolution, Religion and National Identity: Imperial Anglicanism in British North America, 1745-1795*. Madison, NJ: Fairleigh Dickinson University Press, 2000.

Douglas, Ian. *Fling Out the Banner! The National Church Idea and the Foreign Mission of the Episcopal Church*. New York: Church Hymnal, 1996.

———. "Whither the National Church? Reconsidering the Mission Structure of the Episcopal Church." In *A New Conversation: Essays on the Future of Theology and the Episcopal Church*, edited by Robert B. Slocum, 60-78. New York: Church, 1999.

Duffy, Mark J., ed. *The Episcopal Diocese of Massachusetts, 1784-1984: A Mission to Remember, Proclaim, and Fulfill*. Boston: Episcopal Diocese of Massachusetts, 1984.

"Early History of the Network." No pages. Accessed November 29, 2008. Online: http://www.acn-us.org/about/history.html.

Edsall, E. J. "Three Generations: A History of Calvary Church, Pittsburgh, Pennsylvania, 1855-1942." Unpublished manuscript, 1942. Archives of Calvary Episcopal Church, Pittsburgh.

Florin, John. *The Advance of Frontier Settlement in Pennsylvania, 1638-1850: A Geographic Interpretation*. Papers in Geography, no. 14, Department of Geography. University Park: Pennsylvania State University, 1977.

Fox, Arthur B. *Pittsburgh during the American Civil War, 1860-1865*. Chicora, PA: Mechling Bookbindery, 2002.

Furniss, Norman F. *The Fundamentalist Controversy, 1918-1931*. New Haven, CT: Yale University Press, 1954.

Gardner, Donald R. "The Society for the Advancement of Christianity in Pennsylvania." *Historical Magazine of the Protestant Episcopal Church* 23:3 (1954) 321-52.

Gillespie, Joanna B. "What We Taught: Christian Education in the American Episcopal Church, 1920-1980." *Anglican and Episcopal History* 56:1 (1987) 45-85.

Goodwin, Gerald J. "Anglican Reaction to the Great Awakening." *Historical Magazine of the Protestant Episcopal Church* 35:4 (1966) 343-71.

Gorrell, Donald K. *The Age of Social Responsibility: The Social Gospel in the Progressive Era, 1900-1920*. Macon, GA: Mercer University Press, 1988.

Gough, Deborah M. *Christ Church, Philadelphia: The Nation's Church in a Changing City*. Philadelphia: University of Pennsylvania Press, 1995.

Gross, Don H. *The Case for Spiritual Healing*. New York: T. Nelson, 1958.

Guelzo, Allen C. *For the Union of Evangelical Christendom: The Irony of the Reformed Episcopalians*. University Park: Pennsylvania State University Press, 1994.

———. "Ritual, Romanism and Rebellion: The Disappearance of the Evangelical Episcopalians, 1853–1873." *Anglican and Episcopal History* 62 (December 1993) 551–77.

Gundersen, Joan R. *The Anglican Ministry in Virginia, 1723–1766: A Study of a Social Class.* New York: Garland, 1989.

Harp, Gillis J. *Brahmin Prophet: Phillips Brooks and the Path of Liberal Protestantism.* New York: Rowman & Littlefield, 2003.

Harrison, Hall. *Life of the Right Reverend John Barrett Kerfoot, First Bishop of Pittsburgh.* 2 vols. New York: James Pott, 1886.

Harriss, Helen L. *Trinity and Pittsburgh: The History of Trinity Cathedral.* Pittsburgh: n.p., 1999.

Hart, Darryl .G. *Defending the Faith: J. Gresham Machen and the Crisis of Conservative Protestantism in Modern America.* Baltimore: Johns Hopkins University Press, 1994.

HMiranda K. *Anglican Communion in Crisis: How Episcopal Dissidents and Their Anglican Allies Are Reshaping Anglicanism.* Princeton, NJ: Princeton University Press, 2007.

Heineman, Kenneth J. *A Catholic New Deal: Religion and Reform in Depression Pittsburgh.* University Park: Pennsylvania State University Press, 1999.

Hinshaw, John. *Steel and Steelworkers: Race and Class Struggle in Twentieth Century Pittsburgh.* Albany: State University of New York Press, 2002.

History of Pittsburgh and Environs. 4 vols. New York: American Historical Society, 1922.

Hodges, Julia S. *George Hodges: A Biography.* New York: Century, 1926.

Hoffman, Steven J. "'A Plan of Quality': The Development of Mt. Lebanon, a 1920s Automobile Suburb." *Journal of Urban History* 18 (1992) 141–81.

Holmes, David L. "The Making of the Bishop of Pennsylvania, 1986–1827—Part I: The Nestor's Finest Hour." *Historical Magazine of the Protestant Episcopal Church* 41:3 (1972) 225–62.

———. "The Making of the Bishop of Pennsylvania, 1986–1827—Part II: The 'Triumph' of the High Churchmen." *Historical Magazine of the Protestant Episcopal Church* 42:2 (1973) 171–97.

———. "Presiding Bishop John E. Hines and the General Convention Special Program." *Anglican and Episcopal History* 61:4 (1992) 393–417.

Holt, Michael F. *Forging a Majority: The Formation of the Republican Party in Pittsburgh, 1848–1860.* New Haven, CT: Yale University Press, 1969.

Hopkins, John H., Jr. *The Life of the Late Right Reverend John Henry Hopkins, First Bishop of Vermont and Seventh Presiding Bishop, by One of His Sons.* New York: F. J. Huntington, 1873.

Hughes, Philip E. "The Credibility of the Church: Understanding the Church in an Ecumenical Age." In *Guidelines: Anglican Evangelicals Face the Future*, edited by J. I. Packer, 147–79. London: Falcon, 1967.

Huntington, William R. *The Church-Idea: An Essay toward Unity.* New York: E. P. Dutton, 1870.

Jenkins, Philip. *The Next Christendom: The Coming of Global Christianity.* New York: Oxford University Press, 2002.

Katerberg, William H. "William T. Manning: Apostolic Order and Evangelical Truth." In *Modernity and the Dilemma of North American Anglican Identities, 1880–1950*, 107–34. Montreal: McGill-Queen's University Press, 2001.

Kesselus, Kenneth. *John E. Hines, Granite on Fire.* Austin, TX: Episcopal Theological Seminary of the Southwest, 1995.

Kleinberg, S. J. *The Shadow of the Mills: Working-Class Families in Pittsburgh, 1870-1907.* Pittsburgh: University of Pittsburgh Press, 1989.

Krause, Paul. *The Battle for Homestead, 1880-1892: Politics, Culture and Steel.* Pittsburgh: University of Pittsburgh Press, 1992.

Kuhlman, Kathryn. *I Believe in Miracles.* Englewood Cliffs, NJ: Prentice-Hall, 1962.

Leggett, John M. "The 200th Anniversary of the West Church Site." September 24, 1989. Archives of the Episcopal Diocese of Pittsburgh.

Leighton, Janet. *Lift High the Cross: A History of Trinity Episcopal School for Ministry.* Wheaton, IL: Harold Shaw, 1995.

Lindsley, James E. *This Planted Vine: A Narrative History of the Episcopal Diocese of New York.* New York: Harper & Row, 1984.

Little, Charles. "Historical Notes on the Diocese of Pittsburgh, 1968-1996." Manuscript in author's possession.

London, Lawrence F., and Sarah M. Lemmon, eds. *The Episcopal Church in North Carolina, 1701-1959.* Raleigh: Episcopal Diocese of North Carolina, 1987.

Lovelace, Richard F. *Dynamics of Spiritual Life: An Evangelical Theology of Renewal.* Downers Grove, IL: InterVarsity, 1979.

Lubove, Roy. "Pittsburgh and the Uses of Social Welfare History." In *City at the Point: Essays on the Social History of Pittsburgh,* edited by Samuel P. Hays, 295-326. Pittsburgh, University of Pittsburgh Press, 1989.

Machen, J. Gresham. *Christianity and Liberalism.* New York: Macmillan, 1923.

MacMaster, Richard K., with Donald R. Jacobs. *A Gentle Wind of God: The Influence of the East Africa Revival.* Scottdale, PA: Herald, 2006.

Main, Jackson T. *The Anti-Federalists: Critics of the Constitution, 1781-1788.* New York: W. W. Norton, 1961.

Manwaring, Randle. *From Controversy to Co-existence: Evangelicals in the Church of England, 1914-1980.* New York: Cambridge University Press, 1985.

McDonald, Margaret S. *White Already to Harvest: The Episcopal Church in Arkansas, 1838-1971.* Sewanee, TN: Episcopal Diocese of Arkansas at the University Press of Sewanee, 1975.

McGrath, Alistair E. *The Renewal of Anglicanism.* Harrisburg, PA: Morehouse, 1993.

McWilliams, Wilson C. "Standing at Armageddon: Morality and Religion in Progressive Thought." In *Progressivism and the New Democracy,* edited by Sidney M. Milkis and Jerome M. Mileur, 103-25. Amherst: University of Massachusetts Press, 1999.

Mead, Loren B. *The Once and Future Church: Reinventing the Congregation for a New Mission Frontier.* Washington, DC: Alban Institute, 1991.

Meade, William, *Old Churches, Ministers and Families of Virginia.* Vol. 2. Philadelphia: J. B. Lippincott, 1878.

Melish, John H. *Franklin Spencer Spalding: Man and Bishop.* New York: Macmillan, 1917.

Mills, Frederick V. *Bishops by Ballot: An Eighteenth Century Ecclesiastical Revolution.* New York: Oxford University Press, 1978.

Moore, Paul. *Presences: A Bishop's Life in the City.* New York: Farrar, Straus & Giroux, 1997.

Moriarty, Michael. *The Liturgical Revolution: Prayer Book Revision and Associated Parishes: A Generation of Change in the Episcopal Church.* New York: Church Hymnal, 1996.

Mullin, Robert B. *Episcopal Vision/American Reality: High Church Theology and Social Thought in Evangelical America.* New Haven, CT: Yale University Press, 1986.

Naughton, Jim. "Following the Money." No pages. Accessed November 29, 2008. Online: http://www.edow.org/follow/Following_the_Money.pdf.

Neal, Emily G. *A Reporter Finds God through Spiritual Healing*. New York: Morehouse-Gorham, 1956.

Norbeck, Mark D. "False Start: The First Three Years of Episcopal Missionary Endeavor in the Philippine Islands." *Anglican and Episcopal History* 62:2 (1993) 215–36.

Northup, Lesley A. "William Reed Huntington: Fist Presbyter of the Late Nineteenth Century." *Anglican and Episcopal History* 62:2 (1993) 193–213.

O'Connor, Daniel. *Three Centuries of Mission: The United Society for the Propagation of the Gospel, 1701–2000*. New York: Continuum, 2000.

"An Open Letter to Network Bishops and Common Cause Partners regarding the Future of Anglicanism in North America." July 28, 2007. No pages. Accessed November 29, 2008. Online: http://www.stephenswitness.com/2007/07/open-letter-to-network-bishops-and.html.

Pardue, Austin. *Create and Make New*. New York: Harper & Brothers, 1952.

———. *He Lives*. New York: Morehouse-Goreham, 1946.

———. *Prayer Works*. New York: Morehouse-Goreham, 1949.

———. *The Single Eye*. New York: Morehouse-Goreham, 1957.

Petersen, William H. "The Tensions of Anglican Identity in PECUSA: An Interpretive Essay." *Historical Magazine of the Protestant Episcopal Church* 47:4 (1978) 427–52.

Phillips, Paul T. *A Kingdom on Earth: Anglo-American Social Christianity, 1880–1940*. University Park: Pennsylvania State University Press, 1996.

Prichard, Robert W. "The Place of Doctrine in the Episcopal Church." In *Reclaiming Faith: Essays on Orthodoxy in the Episcopal Church and the Baltimore Declaration*, edited by Ephraim Radner and George R. Sumner, 13–45. Grand Rapids, MI: William B. Eerdmans, 1993.

Pritchard, Linda K. "The Soul of the City: A Social History of Religion in Pittsburgh." In *City at the Point: Essays on the Social History of Pittsburgh*, edited by Samuel P. Hays, 327–60. Pittsburgh: University of Pittsburgh Press, 1989.

Radner, Ephraim, and George R. Sumner, eds. *Reclaiming Faith: Essays on Orthodoxy in the Episcopal Church and the Baltimore Declaration*. Grand Rapids, MI: William B. Eerdmans, 1993.

Radner, Ephraim, and Philip Turner. *The Fate of Communion: The Agony of Anglicanism and the Future of a Global Church*. Grand Rapids, MI: William B. Eerdmans, 2006.

Rainsford, William S. *The Story of a Varied Life: An Autobiography*. New York: Doubleday, Page, 1922.

"Reminiscences of Bishop R. Bland Mitchell: The Pre-1919 Church and the Nation-Wide Campaign Revolution." *Historical Magazine of the Protestant Episcopal Church* 30:4 (1961) 230–50.

"Response to the Consecration of Bishop Rodgers." No pages. Accessed November 29, 2008. Online: http://anglicansonline.org/archive/news/articles/2000/000130a.html.

Rhoden, Nancy L. *Revolutionary Anglicanism: The Colonial Church of England Clergy during the American Revolution*. New York: New York University Press, 1999.

Rishel, Joseph S. *Founding Families of Pittsburgh: The Evolution of a Regional Elite, 1760–1910*. Pittsburgh: University of Pittsburgh Press, 1990.

Sack, Daniel. "Reaching the 'Up and Outers': Sam Shoemaker and Modern Evangelicalism." *Anglican and Episcopal History* 69:1 (1995) 37–57.

Sanford, Agnes M. *The Healing Light*. St. Paul: MN: Macalester Park, 1949.

Schwartz, Sally. *"A Mixed Multitude:" The Struggle for Toleration in Colonial Pennsylvania.* New York: New York University Press, 1987.

Shankman, Andrew. *Crucible of American Democracy: The Struggle to Fuse Egalitarianism and Capitalism in Jeffersonian Pennsylvania.* Lawrence: University Press of Kansas, 2004.

Shattuck, Gardiner. *Episcopalians and Race: Civil War to Civil Rights.* Lexington: University Press of Kentucky, 2000.

Sherrill, Henry K. *Among Friends.* Boston: Little, Brown, 1962.

Shoemaker, Helen S. *I Stand by the Door: The Life of Sam Shoemaker.* New York: Harper & Row, 1967.

Shoemaker, Samuel M., Jr. *Children of the Second Birth: Being a Narrative of Spiritual Miracles in a City Parish.* New York: F. H. Revell, 1927.

Sider-Rose, Michael J. *Taking the Gospel to the Point: Evangelicalism and the Origins of the Pittsburgh Leadership Foundation.* Pittsburgh: Pittsburgh Leadership Foundation, 2000.

Slattery, Charles L. *Felix Reville Brunot, 1820-1898: A Civilian in the War for the Union, President of the First Board of Indian Commissioners.* New York: Longmans, Green, 1901.

Slocum, Robert B. "Romantic Religion and the Episcopal Church in Wisconsin: A Consideration of James DeKoven and Charles C. Grafton." *Anglican and Episcopal History* 65:1 (1996) 82-111.

Slosser, Bob. *Miracle at Darien.* Plainfield, NJ: Logos International, 1979.

Solheim, James E. *Diversity or Disunity? Reflections on Lambeth 1998.* New York: Church Publishing, 1999.

Spielman, Richard M. "A Neglected Source: The Episcopal Church Congress, 1874-1934." *Anglican and Episcopal History* 58:1 (989) 50-80.

Steer, Roger. *Church on Fire: The Story of Anglican Evangelicals.* London: Hodder & Stoughton, 1998.

Stott, John R. W. "Jesus Christ Our Teacher and Lord: Towards Solving the Problem of Authority." In *Guidelines: Anglican Evangelicals Face the Future,* edited by J. I. Packer, 39-66. London: Falcon, 1967.

Stringfellow, William, and Anthony Towne. *The Bishop Pike Affair: Scandals of Conscience and Heresy, Relevance and Solemnity in the Contemporary Church.* New York: Harper & Row, 1967.

Wainwright, Nicholas B. *George Croghan, Wilderness Diplomat.* Chapel Hill: University of North Carolina Press, 1959.

Walkinshaw, Lewis C. *Annals of Southwestern Pennsylvania.* 4 vols. New York: Lewis Historical, 1939.

Ward, Matthew C. *Breaking the Backcountry: The Seven Years War in Virginia and Pennsylvania, 1754-1765.* Pittsburgh: University of Pittsburgh Press, 2003.

Warren, Kenneth. *Triumphant Capitalism: Henry Clay Frick and the Industrial Transformation of America.* Pittsburgh: University of Pittsburgh Press, 1996.

Whitehead, Cortlandt. *The Capture of Fort Duquesne: An Historical Discourse before the Society of Colonial Wars in the Commonwealth of Virginia,* delivered at Christ Church, Philadelphia, November 27, 1898. Archives of the Diocese of Pittsburgh.

Woolverton, John F. *Colonial Anglicanism in North America.* Detroit: Wayne State University Press, 1984.

Zabriskie, Alexander C. *Bishop Brent: Crusader for Christian Unity.* Philadelphia: Westminster, 1948.

Zahniser, Keith A. *Steel City Gospel: Protestant Laity and Reform in Progressive Pittsburgh.* New York: Routledge, 2005.

www.ingramcontent.com/pod-product-compliance
Lightning Source LLC
Chambersburg PA
CBHW071147300426
44113CB00009B/1111